WORLD WAR II

WORLD WAR II

CHRISTOPHER CHANT

CHARTWELL
BOOKS, INC.

Published in 2008 by
CHARTWELL BOOKS, INC.
A division of BOOK SALES, INC.
114 Northfield Avenue
Edison, New Jersey 08837
USA

**Copyright © 2008 Regency
House Publishing Limited**
Niall House
24–26 Boulton Road
Stevenage, Hertfordshire
SG1 4QX, UK

For all editorial enquiries please contact
Regency House Publishing at
www.regencyhousepublishing.com

ISBN-13: 978-0-7858-2399-5
ISBN-10: 0-7858-2399-9

Printed in China

CONTENTS

CHAPTER ONE
THE FLOOD OF THE GERMAN TIDE

BELOW: The Polish artillery arm was indifferently equipped and, for the most part, comprised light horse-drawn rather than mechanically-towed medium and heavy equipment.

RIGHT: A Polish soldier, accompanied by a militiaman and a civilian, examine the wreckage of a German warplane. The German air force suffered heavier casualties, often from ground fire, than had been estimated, but proved very effective in the provision of tactical support for the grounds forces.

The Nazi party came to power in Germany in January 1933 with the intention of tearing up the Treaty of Versailles, signed in 1919 to end Germany's part in World War I and which had drastically curtailed the size of Germany's armed forces. Only thus, the Nazis under Adolf Hitler believed, would Germany be restored to its 'rightful' place as the most powerful nation in Europe, with all people of German blood living in areas outside the Reich properly incorporated into the new and larger 'Greater Germany'. The treaty had limited the German forces to a 100,000-man army with no armour, a small navy, and no air force. But under the leadership of General Hans von Seeckt, the army had been rebuilt during the 1920s as a highly trained, professional core on which a much larger force could be based as soon as conscription was once again

possible. Development of armour and warplanes proceeded under various guises, much of it at training areas which the USSR granted in exchange for

technical information, and civilian flying schools were used to build a large pool of trained pilots. In the spring of 1935 Hitler announced that Germany was

repudiating the Treaty of Versailles, that the country now had an air force, and that conscription would be introduced to bring its army up to a strength of 300,000 men.

The UK and France made no effective protest, which served to convince Hitler that these moribund nations had lost the will to act decisively. In March 1936 Hitler openly proved this by reoccupying the Rhineland, against the advice of his generals, who knew that the army was still poorly trained, lacked modern equipment, and was far smaller than that of France.

In March 1938, with the apparent approval of the bulk of its population, Austria was annexed to the Reich. Once again, the UK and France made no effort to prevent this from happening. Despite warnings, the British and French governments were determined to avoid war, preferring to give way to Hitler rather than run any risks. But in the autumn of 1938 the Führer (leader) made his first overt move against an independent state when he demanded that the Sudetenland, the western border region of Czechoslovakia, with its 3 million Germans, should be annexed to the Reich on the grounds that its

ABOVE LEFT: Seen here in the form of men crossing a stream on an improvised bridge, the Polish infantry fought with courage and determination, but were outmatched by the German combination of armour, artillery and infantry operating under an effective umbrella of support aircraft.

ABOVE: German troops examine destroyed Polish armour. The Polish armoured forces were small, lacked any modern tactical doctrine, and were only very indifferently equipped. These are Renault FT-17 light tanks – two-man French vehicles dating from the period of World War I.

LEFT: Polish troops in training before the outbreak of World War II. The bulk of the Polish army was located well forward against the Polish-German frontier and, once the German spearheads had broken through to link up in their rear areas, most formations were trapped and eventually forced to surrender.

RIGHT: Polish weapons gathered by the Germans in the aftermath of their destruction of the Polish army in September 1939.

BELOW: Captured Polish troops march off into captivity, to be used as forced labour under the harshest of conditions and with little food or clothing. Vast numbers of Poles were lost in this way between 1939 and 1945.

inhabitants were being maltreated by the native population.

Czechoslovakia was a model democracy, prosperous and socially advanced, with large and well-equipped armed forces in defences which would have proved difficult for the Germans to attack. The government prepared to resist but, as Hitler had foreseen, under pressure from the UK and France an 'honourable' solution was found to guarantee 'peace in our time': the Sudetenland, with all of the Czech frontier defences, was handed over to Germany. Hitler had removed a potentially difficult threat on his southern flank and was further convinced that he had nothing to fear from the UK and France. He completed the occupation of Czechoslovakia in March 1939, which now meant that the western democracies could no longer close their eyes to the true nature of Hitler's plans and accelerated the pace of their rearmament. But it would take many years to redress the long period of their military

retrenchment and inactivity, the German forces being now more than equal in strength to their potential opponents.

Hitler was ready to turn on Poland as his next victim. Here the Danzig 'corridor', providing Poland with access to the Baltic Sea but at the same time separating East Prussia from the rest of the Reich, presented Hitler with the excuse for intervention.

THE DEFEAT OF POLAND

Regardless of the non-aggression treaty between Poland and Germany, Adolf Hitler insisted on the provision of greater *Lebensraum* (living space) for the German people. Detailed planning of the campaign to take Poland started in April 1939, and on 23 August the signature of a Russo-German non-aggression pact freed Germany from the threat of any Soviet intervention against the German forces, and established a demarcation line for the future partition of Poland after Germany and the USSR had invaded

respectively from the west and the east.

One of Hitler's main concerns was to delay the UK's mobilization for as long as possible, particularly as the UK had once more reiterated its pledge to assist Poland should the latter be invaded. To this end, Hitler maintained a show of sham diplomacy to convince the world of his peaceful intent. He even postponed the start of the offensive and continued his diplomatic appearances to make sure that Poland's potential allies would be ill-prepared at the time of the German invasion. By the end of August Hitler could wait no longer, and on 1 September 1939 the invasion was launched, and with it World War II as the UK and France responded to Germany's refusal to withdraw by declaring war two days later.

Poland could not easily be defended as it was open to attack on three sides: from East Prussia, Pomerania and Slovakia. The Polish frontier contained a huge westward salient stretching 1,250

miles (2010km) from the Soviet-Lithuanian border to the Carpathian Mountains, excluding the defence requirements of the Danzig corridor linking the Polish port of Danzig with the rest of Poland. The French had advised the Poles to base their defence along the line of the Niemen, Bobr, Narew, Vistula and San rivers, and therefore behind a strong river barrier along a front of only 420 miles (675km). The Poles were unwilling to give up the industrial and agricultural regions to the west of this line, but could not defend 1,250 miles effectively; Marshal Edward Rydz-Smigly, Poland's commander-in-chief, exacerbated matters by deploying many of his troops in Danzig and around Poznan, although he had received accurate intelligence reports on the forces massing against him. On 1 September, this huge front was defended by only 17 divisions, three infantry brigades and six cavalry brigades. There was no adequate command structure between Rydz-Smigly and the commanders of the Pomeranian, Modlin, Poznan, Lódz, Krakow, Carpathian, Prussian and Narew Armies. There were also the Pyskor and the Wyskow Groups in reserve, the former including Poland's only tank unit, the Warsaw Armoured Brigade. The Polish air force had only 433 operational aircraft, the majority of them now obsolete and including the PZL P.7 and P.11 fighters and the PZL P.23 bomber.

Hitler's objective was the swift destruction of the Polish armed forces. Converging attacks on Warsaw would be launched from Silesia, Pomerania and East Prussia, and the German forces would execute two pincer movements, one on Warsaw and another farther to the east with the task of trapping Polish forces retreating in that direction. The German army had 13 armoured and motorized divisions in the vanguard of the offensive, and 31 infantry divisions. The forces were deployed in two main

RIGHT: German infantrymen wait in the lee of a tank for the order to move forward against their next objective.

BELOW: Though Western propaganda portrayed the German army as a armoured juggernaut, crushing beneath the treads of its tanks all that the Junkers Ju 87 Stuka dive-bombers had not already destroyed, the German Panzer arm was in reality troubled by the mix of its tanks, their modest capability, and their comparatively poor reliability. Where the Germans did have a decisive advantage, however, was in the concentration of their armour in dedicated Panzer divisions, used in full accord with carefully prepared tactical and operational doctrines.

army groups. Army Group North, commanded by Colonel-General Fedor von Bock, comprised on its left flank the 3rd Army under General Georg von Küchler, and on its right flank the 4th Army under General Günther-Hans von Kluge. Army Group North would attack from East Prussia and Pomerania, its left flank taking on the Polish forces in the corridor and then driving south toward Warsaw, while its right would attack from Pomerania and defeat any Polish troops guarding the corridor. Army Group South, commanded by Colonel-General Gerd von Rundstedt, had on its left wing the 8th Army under General Johannes Blaskowitz, on its right wing the 14th Army under General Wilhelm List, and in its centre the 10th Army under General Walther von Reichenau, its task being to attack from Silesia and Slovakia. The 8th Army would engage Polish forces in the region of Poznan-Kutno, the 10th Army would drive north-east toward Lódz and on to Warsaw, and the 14th Army would strike across the Carpathians, pinning down the Poles around Krakow and Przemysl.

Each army group was supported by an air fleet: Luftflotte 1, commanded by General Albert Kesselring, would operate

with Army Group North, and Luftflotte 4, commanded by General Alexander Löhr, would support Army Group South. The two air fleets had 897 bombers, dive-bombers and ground-attack aircraft, 210 fighters and 474 reconnaissance and transport machines.

Poland did not begin its general mobilization until 11.00 on 31 August and was thus caught with 13 of its 40 divisions still moving toward their concentration points, while a further nine were not yet mobilized when the Germans attacked. Ahead of the armies, the Luftwaffe prepared the way, its mission being to destroy the Polish air force on the ground, then to assist the German ground forces, attack military installations and communications, and terrorize the civilian population. Despite a gallant resistance, the Polish air force was effectively destroyed by the third day, although Polish pilots maintained sporadic attacks until 17 September, operating with great determination and skill. The Luftwaffe, however, reigned supreme. Its Junkers Ju 87 Stuka dive-bomber units delivered pinpoint attacks at crucial moments and locations, the German ability to co-ordinate air and ground forces representing a new feature

in warfare, giving great flexibility to fast-moving armoured and motorized formations lacking the support of traditional artillery unable to keep pace with them.

Within a week the German forces had advanced deep into Poland, their armoured units pushing on ahead of the infantry. If the German equipment was modern, so were the tactics, and generals such as Guderian, Höpner, Hoth, von Kleist and von Wietersheim quickly displayed their skill in command of the Panzer divisions. Against them, the Poles, having only one armoured brigade, could do little, and the Polish armies on the frontiers were quickly driven back by the German offensive. Rydz-Smigly ordered his forces to withdraw eastward on 6 September, but this was already too late to save the frontier armies. The German 10th Army rapidly approached Warsaw, and though its two Panzer divisions had reached the city they failed to take it on 8 September for lack of infantry support. The rest of the 10th Army reached the Vistula two days later and defeated the Lódz Army, while farther to the north, the German 4th Army reached and crossed the Vistula and began its march on Warsaw.

front. General Heinz Guderian, who had enjoyed great success earlier in the campaign in the Danzig area with XIX Panzer Corps, was instrumental in the second pincer movement. On 9 September the Panzers crossed the Narew river upstream of Lomza, reaching Brest-Litovsk on 15 September, the 3rd Panzer Division pressing ahead to make contact with leading elements of the 10th and 14th Armies approaching from the south. The 14th Army had reached Lvov in the east before wheeling north to meet General Guderian. The pincers met and snapped shut, trapping thousands with no hope of escape.

The Soviets were surprised at the speed of the German advance, and on 17 September announced that Poland and its government had now ceased to exist

LEFT: A German column on the move. Right through the war, the German army was heavily reliant on the use of draft animals, which limited the overall speed of the advance to that of the horse. The Allies were more extensively motorized and mechanized, an advantage which increased as the war progressed.

BELOW: German troops prepare to cross the German-Polish frontier, in this case against no discernible opposition.

The Pomeranian and Poznan Armies, falling back on Warsaw, met the German 8th Army, which attempted to block its retreat north of Lódz. Although virtually surrounded by Germans, the commander of the Poznan Army, General Kutrzeba, resolved to strike south against the flank of the main German advance to the east. This courageous move resulted in the Battle of the Bzura, in which the Poles succeeded in capturing bridgeheads across the Bzura river near Lowicz and driving back the German 30th Division. This crisis drew into the battle Panzer and motorized corps, and even a corps from the 4th Army in the north. These reinforcements, and the persistent Stuka attacks, forced the 170,000 Poles to surrender after a hard fight at Lowicz on 19 September.

To the south the German 14th Army had driven on and reached the San river. Meanwhile, the inner pincers were closing around Warsaw as the 3rd Army encircled the city from the east and the 8th Army from the west. At the same time, a start was made on the outer pincer movement as the 3rd Army's left-hand column struck out for Brest-Litovsk, 100 miles (160km) behind the

THE FLOOD OF THE GERMAN TIDE

Conquered Poland became the fiefdom of Hans Frank, a brutal man who was finally condemned for his crimes by the Nuremberg war trials tribunal and hanged in 1946.

and that the USSR must intervene to protect their own sphere of interest, namely the portion of Poland east of the Narew, Vistula and San rivers. The Soviet armies swarmed across the virtually undefended eastern frontier of Poland, ending any further hopes the Poles may have had of resisting. The Soviet columns rolled west on a broad front, and on 18 September occupied Vilna, meeting the Germans at Brest-Litovsk. The ruin and subjugation of Poland was nearly complete; on 18 September the Polish government fled to Romania, while Warsaw and Modlin were still holding out against the Germans. Warsaw, which was being violently bombarded daily by air and heavy artillery, surrendered on 27 September, while Modlin held out valiantly for a further day.

Thus in less than one month the nation of Poland, with its 35 million people, was eliminated from the map. The geographical area was divided into two by the Treaty of Delimitation and Friendship, signed on 28 September by Germany and the USSR. In central Poland, the demarcation line connected the Bug and Vistula rivers, and was marked by the San river in Galicia. Lithuania was incorporated into the Soviet sphere in return for German sovereignty over parts of the province of Warsaw and the whole of Lublin. Poland had lost 694,000 prisoners to Germany and 217,000 to the USSR, but 100,000 Poles had been able to make their escape to the west by way of Romania.

THE WINTER WAR

Finland, with a population of only some 4.5 million spread over 130,000sq miles (336700km²), was now the location of one of the most amazing conflicts in

history, in which Finland's tiny army was able to hold out against the might of the USSR and, at the beginning of a campaign that lasted 105 days, inflict severe casualties on the aggressor. A Russo-Finnish Non-Aggression Pact had been signed in 1934, but on 14 October 1939 the Soviet leader, Iosef Stalin, began to make various territorial demands on Finland in return for a considerable border adjustment in Karelia. Finland, wishing to retain its neutrality, offered to compromise on these demands, but the USSR would brook no interference with its plan. The Soviet forces were already prepared for the offensive, having reconnoitred the Karelian isthmus and Finland's ports, roads, industrial areas and fortifications from the air, and reached the conclusion that the Finns were hopelessly ill-equipped to defend themselves.

On 30 November, without any formal declaration of war, the Soviet land, sea and air onslaught began, with Helsinki bombed heavily right from the start. The Finns had begun calling up their reserves, but when the Soviet offensive started the commander-in-chief, Marshal Carl Gustaf von Mannerheim, had only nine divisions at his disposal. The II and III Corps were deployed in the Karelian isthmus with five divisions under Lieutenant-General Hugo Ostermann; the IV Corps was on the east shore of Lake Ladoga with two divisions under Major-General J. Woldemar Hagglund; the Central Finland Group comprised the V Corps of nine frontier battalions under Major-General Vilpo Tuompo; the Lapland Group with four independent battalions commanded by Major-General Kurt Wallenius; while two incomplete divisions (I Corps) and a cavalry brigade formed the reserve. Facing these limited Finnish forces, the Soviets had in the Karelian isthmus the 7th Army with eight divisions, a tank corps and two independent tank brigades to force the Mannerheim Line, take Viipuri, and push on to Helsinki; on the east shore of

Lake Ladoga the 8th Army with six divisions was to assist the 7th Army by drawing off the Finnish defence; farther north the 9th Army with four divisions was to launch two columns, the more southerly to make for Oulu and the more northerly for Kemi in central Finland; and in Lapland the 14th Army with two divisions was to take Petsamo and sever Finnish links with Norway.

Mannerheim knew there were good lines of communication only in the centre of Finland and that the Finns must prevent the Soviets from reaching them. He was familiar with Soviet tactics and military manuals, and was thus able to predict Soviet thinking, which was tied rigidly to set formulae. In the event, manuals were useless in the

winter conditions of Finland, where the Soviets immediately succumbed to the cruel weather, while heavy snow blocked their advance and grounded their aircraft. On the other hand, the Finns proved themselves masters of irregular warfare, striking hard in the dark or during snowstorms, or appearing without warning on skis, dressed in white, to attack and disappear; in fact, to the Soviet forces the Finns seemed to be everywhere. Many booby-trap devices were used to slow the invaders, minefields guarded all approaches, and the Finns were expert at destroying tanks with 'Molotov cocktails' – bottles filled with a mixture of crude kerosene, tar and petrol. Mannerheim's reservists mostly wore their own clothes, perhaps

with an identifying cap or belt, but no matter how indifferent they appeared by more conventional military standards, the Finnish soldiers were perfectly suited to the conditions.

The Finns were amazed as masses of heavy tanks bore down on them, but the Soviets seemed uncertain as to how they could use their matériel superiority to the greatest effect, and the tanks became trapped in the snow. The Soviet troops were inexperienced and unco-ordinated, also lacking in winter warfare training, while Stalin's purges of 1937–38 had

LEFT: A useful extemporized weapon, favoured by the Finns, was the 'Molotov cocktail', a bottle filled with petrol and other flammables that would break on hitting a tank, with the spilt contents then catching fire.

ABOVE: Soviet troops pose for the camera as they breach the Russo-Finnish border in 1944. In 1939 they had faced an altogether harder task, in appalling weather, having been severely mauled by the smaller Finnish forces.

In the winter warfare of 1939–40, better trained and better equipped Finnish troops, fighting on home ground and fully acclimatized to the harsh conditions, were able to perform far better than their Soviet opponents.

robbed them of many of their best leaders. At first the Soviet soldiers bore up well, but as the temperature continued to plummet their morale began to flag. Their weapons froze, and many thousands of them died from the cold. The Finns were better clothed and knew how to keep their weapons serviceable in such conditions; they also had the advantage of fighting in territory with which they were familiar.

The Soviets were checked on almost all fronts. They did manage to take Petsamo, in the far north, in the middle of December by overwhelming the small Finnish defence with the superior firepower of a large force based on Murmansk. In the south, however, on the Karelian isthmus, that separated Lake Ladoga from the Gulf of Finland, the Mannerheim Line comprised 90 miles (145km) of anti-tank obstacles, field

fortifications, ditches and trenches, which stopped the Soviets as they tried to break though a line of which they know virtually nothing. The fighting was almost continuous, with the Soviets constantly committing fresh divisions and constantly being beaten off. The Soviet 7th Army's 139th and 75th Divisions reached Tolvajärvi on 12 December, but here their 45,000 men, 335 pieces of artillery and 140 tanks were ambushed and annihilated by seven Finnish battalions under Major-General Paavo Talvela's group with 9,000 men and 20 pieces of artillery.

In central Finland, the column of the Soviet 9th Army was counter-attacked at Suomussalmi on its intended advance to the port of Oulu on the Gulf of Bothnia which, if successful, would have cut Finland in two. Major-General Hjalmar Siilasvuo led the Finns in this furious

battle; the Soviet 163rd Division was cut off after a Finnish attack lasting 17 days, while the Soviet 44th Division was destroyed as it also tried to retreat. Some 800 men of the 44th Division dug in and the Finns attacked them at will, at the same time capturing an assortment of their weapons.

There emerged a pattern of attack and counter-attack on all fronts, and both sides rapidly became exhausted. The Finns pushed the Soviets back toward the USSR, by which time the Soviets had lost approximately 27,500 dead. Stalin was furious, and on 12 December the League of Nations condemned the Soviet aggression in Finland. Hitler remained neutral and refused to allow Italian aid to Finland to pass through Germany. The USSR, therefore, determined to beat the Finns at all costs, committed some 45 divisions, or 40 per cent of the Soviet land forces of European USSR. Stalin also changed the senior leadership of the forces on the Finnish front, with Marshal Semyon Timoshenko assuming overall command. Timoshenko's primary task was to create a breakthrough on the Karelian front, but after failing to penetrate the Mannerheim Line, the Soviet 7th Army was shifted to the Gulf of Finland, the 13th Army taking its place with its right flank on Lake Ladoga. Timoshenko's forces totalled 24 infantry divisions with three more in reserve, backed by 20 regiments of artillery and seven armoured brigades, all supported by 450 aircraft.

Mannerheim rightly predicted the Soviets would attack east of Summa village, in the west of the Karelian isthmus, where the open fields would allow the Soviets to concentrate armour and infantry. The offensive began on 1 February 1940 in bitterly cold conditions. The Soviets had learned vital lessons since November, and were now better co-ordinated, often directed from observation balloons. They used trains of armoured sledges drawn by tanks to move infantry, and employed

The Finns withdrew in good order, counter-attacking all the while, and took up a new defensive, which, being longer than the Mannerheim Line, stretched their resources. The Finns nonetheless continued to harass the Soviet forces, the

ABOVE LEFT: A German 1.5-in (37-mm) anti-aircraft gun, in use on the coast of the Gulf of Finland. In 1939–40 the Germans did not provide much material support for the Finns as a result of their Non-Aggression Pact with the Soviets of August 1939.

ABOVE: Finnish troops prepare for a river or lake crossing.

FAR LEFT: A German and Finnish military liaison team assesses the tactical situation.

LEFT: The Finnish commander-in-chief was Marshal Carl Gustaf von Mannerheim, an ex-Tsarist officer and an expert in defensive warfare.

flamethrower tanks. Heavy artillery deluged the Finns, steadily wearing them down, and the widespread bombing of the Finnish rear areas marked the beginning of the end. The Soviets attacked in massive waves, and despite huge losses to the Finnish artillery, machine gun and rifle fire, finally began to make progress. On 6 February the final assault began when three divisions with 150 tanks attacked along a 5-mile (8-km) line with the support of 200 aircraft. On 7 February, the Soviet forces penetrated the region of Muolaa, striking at Summa. Timoshenko then shifted the weight of the offensive farther to the east, and by 11 February the Soviets had broken through the Mannerheim Line.

THE FLOOD OF THE GERMAN TIDE

RIGHT: The fight against Soviet aggression was a national effort, as represented here by Finnish women serving as auxiliaries to spot and report the numbers and course of approaching Soviet warplanes.

FAR RIGHT: The Soviets made extensive use of armoured vehicles, but suffered huge losses to mines, artillery and dedicated anti-tank teams armed with anti-tank grenades and 'Molotov cocktails'.

BELOW: To bypass the more ponderous Soviet units and formations, Finland used its excellent ski troops to cut their lines of communication, before trapping them for destruction.

Soviet losses averaging 800 men and between 10 and 20 tanks per day during 20–22 February.

On 24 February the Soviets seized Koivisto island, in the frozen Gulf of Finland, the 7th Army having been instructed to cross the ice to take Viipuri on the mainland. Soon after, the main road linking Viipuri to Helsinki was taken by the Soviets. The Finns had by this time lost 25,000 men killed and 43,000 wounded, and were physically and morally exhausted. Continued resistance seemed impossible because there was no more manpower and ammunition available. Mannerheim, therefore, felt that it was time to find a solution which would end the fighting. On 12 March 1940 the Russo-Finnish Treaty was signed, ceding 16,000sq miles (41440km²) of Finland to the USSR, leaving the Finns with a frontier which left them effectively naked to further Soviet aggression and giving the Soviets almost the whole of Karelia. But the Soviet losses had also been enormous, with something in the order of 200,000 dead and 400,000 wounded.

THE GERMAN SEIZURE OF DENMARK & NORWAY

On 14 December 1939 Vidkun Quisling, the leader of the small Norwegian fascist party, the Party of National Union, alleged that British intervention in Scandinavia was imminent. Hitler immediately ordered preliminary studies for a possible expedition to Norway, with Denmark as a possible stepping stone in the process. At this time Germany was obtaining two-thirds of its high-grade iron ore from northern Sweden via the ports of Luleå in Sweden and Narvik in Norway. If the Allies were to cut these supply lines, Germany's war-making industries would be hard hit. Various means of achieving this were considered, including the mining of the Leads, the sea corridor between the mainland and the islands off Norway's western coast, which German merchant ships used to avoid running into the British navy. Finally, it was the Russo-Finnish 'Winter War' which, in November 1939, afforded the Allies the opportunity of sending troops to Scandinavia for intervention on Finland's behalf.

On 6 February 1940 the German ship, *Altmark*, a supply vessel for the pocket battleship *Graf Spee*, was seen in Norwegian territorial waters. Believing she was carrying Allied prisoners, the British intercepted her, freeing 299 merchant seamen. This incident convinced Hitler that the Allies might act first in Scandinavia, and Lieutenant-General Nikolaus von Falkenhorst was immediately appointed to plan and lead the proposed conquest of Norway and Denmark. The operation was initially planned for 20 March, but was delayed until 9 April.

Meanwhile the Finnish surrender had brought the Allied plans for intervention on Finland's side to a halt, and they decided to lay mines, landing troops only in response to German aggression while wholly underestimating the time that would be required to deploy in strength in the main Norwegian ports before the arrival of the Germans.

The German forces comprised two formations for the invasion of Denmark and Norway: the XXI Corps with two mountain divisions and five infantry divisions for the Norwegian part, and the XXXI Corps with the 170th and

ABOVE: The Germans were able to use only modest numbers of light tanks in the Norwegian campaign.

LEFT: German troops land at a Norwegian port. The invasion of Norway required the use of nearly all of Germany's sea-lift capability, and the German navy suffered heavy losses in the process.

succumbed within 24 hours on 9 April; it was plain that the Danish government appreciated the military hopelessness of its position and it acceded to a German occupation in exchange for continued home rule. At most of the principal Norwegian ports, the assault troops landed without interference, or were delayed only slightly by brave but largely ineffectual resistance.

In Norway, the Germans landed at Kristiansand, Stavanger, Bergen, Trondheim, Narvik and Oslo. In the process, two Norwegian coastal defence vessels were blown out of the water at Narvik; at Trondheim, the heavy cruiser *Admiral Hipper* and four destroyers forced the fjord entrance; at Bergen the cruiser *Königsberg* was damaged but landed enough troops to capture the town; Rear-Admiral Oskar Kummetz's force came under heavy fire in the long Oslofjord, and the *Blücher*, the German navy's most modern heavy cruiser, was

ABOVE: The heavy cruiser, Admiral Hipper, *and four destroyers, were responsible for the delivery of the army forces to take Trondheim.*

RIGHT: The small northern Norwegian port of Narvik was central to Allied plans for the Norwegian campaign, but the small operation fought here revealed the Allies' lack of readiness for war against a skilled opponent such as Germany. Even so, the Germans lost 10 fleet destroyers in the two naval battles fought at Narvik.

198th Divisions for the Danish element. These two formations would be supported by all available warships and 41 troop transports, and in the air by the Luftwaffe with 290 bombers, 40 Stukas and 100 fighters. The element of surprise was necessary for success, yet most of the troops and their supplies had to be transported by sea. The German plan was thus based on the launch of a lightning attack on vital objectives, using fewer than 9,000 assault troops, and nowhere did an initial landing force exceed 2,000 men.

At about the same time, Allied troops destined for Scandinavia also embarked, and the British Home Fleet put to sea. The German preparations were in fact noticed, but the Norwegian government did not call for general mobilization. Thus, when the German invasion force slipped past the Home Fleet, it met no organized resistance on landing. As expected, Denmark

sunk and the pocket battleship *Lützow* was damaged and compelled to withdraw. Consequently, half the force intended for Oslo was lost, but the city was taken by airborne troops. The sea route to Oslo was temporarily blocked, so that German supplies and reinforcements could not be landed, while Stavanger and its airfield at Sola were taken by paratroops.

At Narvik, the German 3rd Mountain Division disembarked successfully from ten destroyers, but neither its equipment or supplies arrived, nor did one of two tankers intended to refuel the destroyers for their homeward journey. The destroyers thus remained in the Vestfjord, leading to Narvik, where they were discovered at dawn on 10 April by Captain B.A.W. Warburton-Lee, commanding the British 2nd Destroyer Flotilla, who had taken the initiative by sweeping into the fjord. In the resulting battle, during which Warburton-Lee was

killed, half the German destroyers were disabled or destroyed, the other half being destroyed three days later when another flotilla entered, led by the battleship *Warspite*. Some 2,600 German survivors joined the German forces on shore, and were supplied with weapons from a nearby Norwegian depot.

The assault phase left Denmark a conquered country, with German garrisons established in the major towns of Norway. The Allies had completely failed to prevent the landings, although they did achieve some success at sea. The battle-cruiser *Renown* damaged the German battle-cruiser *Gneisenau* on 9 April; a British submarine sank the light cruiser *Karlsruhe*; and the *Königsberg*, damaged at Bergen, was later sunk by British naval aircraft.

The Germans at Narvik would have been unable to withstand an immediate Allied assault, and the Allied naval

THE FLOOD OF THE GERMAN TIDE

The Germans, in the Norwegian campaign, again made successful use of their air power for tactical purposes. This is a view of a demolished Norwegian bridge, seen from the cockpit of a Heinkel He 111 twin-engined medium bomber.

commander, Admiral of the Fleet Lord Cork and Orrery, favoured such action. However, the land commander, Major-General P.J. Mackesy, disagreed, arguing that Narvik's harbour area was strongly fortified with light artillery and machine gun posts. Mackesy wished to take two unoccupied positions on the approaches to Narvik, where he could build up his forces until the snow melted and an overland advance became feasible. The deadlock between the two British commanders, however, gave the Germans the time they needed to consolidate their position and score a moral advantage by claiming that the Allies had been brought to a standstill before Narvik.

The Norwegian commander-in-chief, General Otto Ruge, had the unenviable task of trying to hold the large areas of Norway still unoccupied by the Germans and regaining what the Germans had taken. Ruge believed he could hold out

until Allied reinforcements arrived, and decided to retain as much as possible of the open country around Oslo where Allied troops, unaccustomed to mountain warfare and lacking the equipment for it, might be successful. But the Germans delivered reinforcements and equipment immediately Oslo was once again open to them, and Ruge's forces were threatened at too many points for him to concentrate more than a small proportion in any one sector. By mid-April, he could no longer hope to hold the Oslo area, and fell back to the north-west to make a stand to the south of Lillehammer in the Gudbransdalen and Osterdalen. Ruge believed that, in this region, his forces could hold the Germans long enough for the Allies to send major reinforcements, and also prevent the Germans in the south from linking up with those at Trondheim on the coast in the centre of the country.

Only at this stage did the Allies begin to appreciate that the key to the reconquest of Norway was Trondheim, the port city which was the main link between the north and south of Norway. Therefore Trondheim joined Narvik on the list of major Allied objectives. The Allies planned a frontal assault on Trondheim from the sea, and a pair of subsidiary landings at Namsos, 80 miles (130km) to the north and at Åndalsnes, 150 miles (240km) to the south. Major-General A. Carton de Wiart commanded the Namsos force, comprising the 146th Infantry Brigade and a demi-brigade of French Chasseurs Alpins, while Brigadier H. de R. Morgan led the Åndalsnes landing with the 148th Infantry Brigade. Both landings were a success, but the British chiefs-of-staff then abandoned the frontal assault on Trondheim, which would have placed the fleet at risk. Instead, the northern and southern forces decided to close in on Trondheim from Namsos and Åndalsnes, where the forces already landed would be strengthened. But the Germans had already rendered the Allied thinking obsolete by their own programme of reinforcement. The Luftwaffe had complete mastery of the air and the Allies were subjected to continual air attack, in which Namsos, in particular, afforded no protection. However, the Namsos force advanced to Verdal at the head of the fjord, some 50 miles (80km) from Trondheim, but there met a powerful German force on 21 April, and withdrew in heavy snow. Carton de Wiart recommended that his force be evacuated, and this was accomplished on 2–3 May under heavy air attack.

In response to Ruge's request for reinforcement, Morgan and his 148th Infantry Brigade had advanced from Åndalsnes to Lillehammer to link up with the exhausted Norwegians. On 24 April, Major-General B.T.C. Paget and the 15th Infantry Brigade reinforced them, with Paget assuming command. The Allies faced the Germans with determination, and there followed a series of bitter battles as the Allies were forced to fall back to Åndalsnes, from which they were evacuated on 1 May.

All the Allied forces were withdrawn from the Trondheim area, as the Inter-Allied Supreme War Council had decided on 26 April, to allow the Allied effort to concentrate on the recapture of Narvik. The Norwegians were greatly disappointed by the abandonment of central Norway, the superiority of the Germans now being perfectly obvious.

The Allies had failed in the Trondheim area, and a mixed and improvised force of 6,000 Germans was by now holding 20,000 Allied troops at bay at Narvik.

Lieutenant-General Claude Auchinleck now arrived to take command of the Allied land forces in the Narvik area, whose withdrawal from central Norway meant that the Allied strength in this area could be increased, although some British troops were deployed to check any German attempt to advance overland from Trondheim.

ABOVE: German soldiers photographed in a captured Danish fort. Realizing the futility of trying to fight Germany's surprise invasion, the Danes capitulated without resistance in exchange for a measure of continued self-government.

FAR LEFT: German troops on the Arctic circle. Northern Norway was of strategic importance to Germany for its port of Narvik, whence Swedish iron ore was shipped to Germany, and as the launch point for the offensive into the northern USSR from June 1941.

LEFT: Major-General Frederik Christian Essemann, commanding the Danish army's 2nd Jutland Division, emerges from his headquarters to surrender to the Germans on 9 April 1940.

THE FLOOD OF THE GERMAN TIDE

RIGHT: The British prime minister in April 1940 was Neville Chamberlain, seen here at the time of the 'Munich crisis' of September 1938, when Czechoslovakia was sacrificed for 'peace in our time'.

BELOW: British troops on their way back to the UK after one of the several evacuations of Allied troops from central and northern Norway in May and June 1940.

Reinforcements included Major-General Marie Émile Béthouart's 1st Chasseur (Light) Division, two battalions of the French Foreign Legion, four Polish battalions, and 3,500 Norwegians. The German commander, Lieutenant-General Eduard Dietl, had also been reinforced and, on paper at least, 13 Allied battalions faced 10 German battalions in the Narvik area. Dietl and Béthouart were both mountain warfare specialists.

At midnight on 27 May Béthouart led a force, with gunfire support from an all-British naval force, in an assault south across the Rombaksfjord, about a mile (1.6km) wide, while simultaneously, two Polish battalions attacked east on the south bank of the fjord. By 17.00, the German garrison had retreated inland and Béthouart's forces were on the outskirts of Narvik. He then stood aside to let the Norwegian 6th Division enter the town. On 7 June, the Germans found the Allies gone and the port installations demolished. The Allies had slipped quietly and secretly away in four convoys, between 4 and 8 June, a

move necessitated by the deteriorating situation in France.

The battle-cruisers *Scharnhorst* and *Gneisenau*, with the heavy cruiser *Admiral Hipper*, were in the area, however, and on 8 June a British tanker and armed trawler were sunk and the troopship *Orama* was hit. Later, the Germans spotted the British aircraft carrier *Glorious*, the fire of the *Scharnhorst* and *Gneisenau* setting her alight and also sinking the destroyer *Ardent*. Another destroyer, the *Acasta*, then launched a torpedo which severely damaged the *Scharnhorst*.

So ended the last action of the Norwegian campaign. On 10 June Ruge signed the surrender of the Norwegian army. The Germans had lost 5,636 men killed; the Norwegians had lost 1,335, the UK 1,869, and France and Poland about 530 between them. Although

Allied action had not achieved its objective in cutting the iron route, or in reconquering Denmark and Norway, the action at sea meant that the losses suffered by the German navy would ultimately result in there being too few ships available for the proposed invasion of England.

GERMANY STRIKES TO THE WEST
On 10 May 1940 the Germans forces began their largest operation to date in World War II. In one week, the Netherlands surrendered, Belgium had been largely overrun, and France was already talking of defeat. The offensive was not an operational surprise even if it did secure the element of a tactical one, the two sides being approximately equal in numbers of men and equipment. Until the beginning of 1940, the French commander-in-chief, General Maurice

Scheldt estuary and Antwerp. Gamelin hoped the Belgian army of 18 divisions would delay the Germans on the German/Belgian border in the region of Fort Eben-Emael, which was believed to be the strongest fortress in the world. The French believed the Maginot Line was strong enough a barrier on their own border with Germany, and were confident that no surprise attack could be launched through the forested hills of the Ardennes. Most of the remaining Allied field formations were deployed behind the Maginot Line in case of a breakthrough. The Allies were thus deployed with two strong flanks and a weak centre, with their armour committed to the north.

That the Germans planned to make their major attack though northern Belgium was true until the original plan was compromised and Lieutenant-

LEFT: French H-35 tanks on the move. The French had useful numbers of capable tanks, but these were deployed in 'penny packets' to support the infantry, rather than concentrated and trained as decisive battlefield formations.

BELOW: In the battle for France, the 7th Panzer Division was commanded by Erwin Rommel, seen here during a troop inspection.

Gamelin, had been broadly correct in his conception of German strategy, and his defensive measures stood a chance of success. It was reckoned that the Germans would try for a lightning victory, based on the Schlieffen Plan of 1914, with the main attack coming through Belgium. Belgium had expressed its neutrality in 1936 but, unlike the Netherlands, had co-operated to some extent with the Allies in planning the defence of its eastern frontier. Gamelin prepared alternative plans for the Allies to advance the British Expeditionary Force (BEF) of nine divisions, under General Lord Gort, and the 1st French Army Group of 22 divisions, including two light mechanized ones, under General Gaston Billotte, to either the Dyle or Escaut rivers when the German invasion began. The French 9th Army, under General André Cora, would at the same time close on the right to the Meuse river, while the mechanized 7th Army, under General Henri Giraud, moved its seven divisions, including one light mechanized and two motorized, up the coast on the left flank to secure the

THE FLOOD OF THE GERMAN TIDE

Panzergruppe 'von Kleist', containing the XIX Panzer Corps under General Heinz Guderian; XLI Panzer Corps under General Georg-Hans Reinhardt; and XIV Motorized Corps under Lieutenant-General Gustav von Wietersheim; in addition, the 5th and 7th Panzer Divisions formed the XV Panzer Corps, under General Hermann Hoth, attached to the 4th Army. The armour was to act as a battering ram to thrust through the Allied lines in the Charleville-Sedan area and quickly push to the coast.

For the offensive against Belgium and the Netherlands, Army Group B was led by Colonel-General Fedor von Bock, consisting of 29.5 divisions, including three Panzer and two motorized. After von Manstein's plan was accepted, von Bock's forces were reduced in strength, making him naturally concerned that his two remaining armies would be equal to their tasks: the 6th Army was to force and cross the Albert Canal, and the 18th army to take the Netherlands, whose army totalled eight divisions. Army Group C, commanded by Colonel-

ABOVE: German armour seen during a brief pause for rest, refuelling and rearmament, during its high-speed punch through north-eastern France.

RIGHT: The Panzer forces comprised tanks for concentrated offensive effort, motorcycle teams for tactical reconnaissance, and trucks for the delivery of all-important fuel, ammunition, and other essential supplies including food for the men.

General Erich von Manstein, the chief-of-staff of Army Group A, suggested that most of the Panzer divisions (and thus the main weight of the offensive) should drive through the centre in the area of the Ardennes and thus through the weakest part of the French defence, while the Allied armies were drawn into north-eastern France and Belgium by the advance of Army Group B. After discussion at the Oberkommando des Heeres (OKH, or army high command), von Manstein's plan was approved by Hitler. For the offensive to the west, therefore, the German forces were deployed with Army Group A, commanded by Colonel-General Gerd von Rundstedt, and comprising 45.5 divisions (including seven Panzer and three motorized), with General Günther von Kluge's 4th Army from Army Group B sweeping through the Ardennes in the centre. The armour was organized as

horrendous losses of World War I, that the fighting of a defensive campaign would result in fewer casualties, while the Germans were working to a brilliant plan, exploiting in full the capabilities of their mobile forces to provide quick breakthroughs and thus the speedy defeat of their enemies for minimum manpower and matériel losses.

On 9 May Hitler ordered his forces to cross the frontiers of the Netherlands, Belgium and Luxembourg at dawn on the following day. They achieved total surprise with their airborne attack in

LEFT: Heinz Guderian in his special command vehicle, equipped with maps, radio equipment and (bottom left) an Enigma cipher machine.

BELOW: Built of concrete and tunnelled deep into the ground, the Maginot Line was the heart of France's defence system. The Germans avoided it by the simple expedient of passing around its northern end though neutral Belgium.

General Wilhelm Ritter von Leeb, was to attack with 19 divisions from southern Germany toward the Maginot Line, so pinning the French forces in the south.

The Germans thus totalled 134 divisions, including reserves, with which to face the Allies' 130 divisions. The French had as many tanks as the Germans, but the German armour was generally superior in qualitative terms, being better organized in specific Panzer divisions, and far superior in fast-moving armoured warfare, having been designed and trained for independent operations with the Luftwaffe as support. The French were hampered in their belief, the result of their

THE FLOOD OF THE GERMAN TIDE

Belgium and the southern Netherlands, and for the first time airborne forces won a decisive victory more or less unaided, especially in their seizure of Fort Eben-Emael by a gliderborne *coup-de-main* attack. Allied troops were not brought to the alert until after the assault had begun, and by daylight on 10 May, German paratroops had captured bridges around the Hague and Rotterdam in the Netherlands, together with the main airfields. The first of von Bock's three armoured divisions advanced across the lower Maas (Meuse): the Dutch were unable to resist for long. The French 7th Army was trying to link with the Dutch army near Breda, but found the Germans already there and withdrew behind the Scheldt. The German 18th Army, under General Georg von Küchler, quickly

overran the country and on 15 May the Dutch government capitulated after a devastating bombing attack on the city of Rotterdam.

Simultaneously with the attack on the Netherlands, the Germans pierced the Belgian frontier defences, with General Walther von Reichenau's 6th Army attacking along the Meuse and the Albert Canal; airborne troops captured three of the main bridges along the canal immediately west of Maastricht. On the same day, in a brilliantly executed manoeuvre, German gliders landed on top of Fort Eben-Emael and the Belgian garrison surrendered. The Belgian army retreated to the line of the Dyle river as the Allies put their Dyle Plan into operation. The BEF advanced to the Louvain-Wavre position and the French

1st Army moved forward to Namur. One third of the French first-line armoured vehicles were now on or behind this 22-mile (35-km) line linking Wavre with Namur. But to the south, in the 95 miles (155km) between Namur and Longeron, the French had only 12 infantry divisions; more importantly, only four cavalry divisions and two cavalry brigades were in position at the time of the German arrival. The French were short of anti-tank and anti-aircraft guns, and ground defences were lacking, especially around Sedan, the junction point of the French 2nd and 9th Armies. It was on these forces that the German Blitzkrieg (lightning war) offensive fell.

The British and French forces were still advancing into Belgium as Heinz Guderian and Major-General Erwin

WORLD WAR II

Rommel (leading the 7th Panzer Division) spearheaded the armoured thrust through the Ardennes. Using the full width of the roads, the advance was rapid and no effective resistance was met on the way through Luxembourg and the Belgian part of the Ardennes. On 12 May the Panzergruppe von Kleist and the XV Panzer Corps of Lieutenant-General Hermann Hoth reached the Meuse, from which the French cavalry, after a short delaying action, retreated after blowing up the bridges.

The XV Panzer Corps was on a more northerly route, heading for Dinant, and Rommel arrived here on 12 May. The Panzergruppe von Kleist advanced toward Sedan, which fell to Guderian's XIX Panzer Corps as its defenders were hammered by Stuka and bomber attacks, while Monthermé fell to Lieutenant-General Georg-Hans Reinhardt's XLI Panzer Corps. The advance of Army Group A comprised the greatest concentration of tanks yet seen, which extended for more than 100 miles (160km) from end to end. The French were wholly bewildered by the pace and style of the German advance, which had been undertaken with great offensive spirit.

The Germans crossed the Meuse near Sedan and Monthermé, initially by infantry and motorcycle regiments, and pontoon bridges were then thrown across by the engineers for the vehicles of the Panzer regiments. The Germans had deliberately chosen to attack at the junction of the French 2nd and 9th Armies, where second-rate troops were deployed. On 14 May, the 9th Army retreated 10 miles (16km), but the retreat rapidly became a panic-stricken flight. Guderian's bridgehead was now 31 miles (50km) wide and 15 miles (25km) deep. By 16 May, the Germans were moving forward at the extraordinary rate of 40 miles (65km) per day. Guderian's XIX Panzer Corps then swept forward toward Abbeville and the southern coast of the English Channel, the tank commanders

having been instructed to keep moving for as long as they had fuel. Thus, in four days, the Panzergruppe von Kleist and the XV Panzer Corps were able to destroy eight divisions from the French 2nd and 9th Armies and had opened a breach of some 80 miles (130km) in the French front.

The French had no real reserve with which to plug this gap, but the Allies, more importantly, had not fully grasped the implications of the situation in which they now found themselves, and thus stood no chance of sending what reinforcements they had to the places where they were needed most. The available reserves (22 divisions including three armoured at the start of the campaign) were therefore deployed on a piecemeal basis, their movement toward the front being hampered by Luftwaffe attack. The Allies were often

applying their minds to a situation which was at least several hours out of date, and relations between the powers were not ideal. The British and French forces, between the North Sea and Luxembourg, were under Billotte's overall command; Billotte was not an effective co-ordinator, as a result of which communications were extremely difficult.

The Germans made very effective use of the Allied confusion to speed their advance, but then the Panzer divisions were ordered to halt. The German high command was surprised at the ease at which the Meuse had been crossed, and every day expected a French counter-attack. Hitler wanted the Panzer divisions to wait until the arrival of sufficient infantry to provide flank cover along the Aisne river; von Kleist therefore ordered Guderian to halt on the night of 15 May. Guderian protested, and

One of the mainstays of the German armoured force in the first part of World War II was the PzKpfw III medium tank. This was reliable and well-protected, but carried only modest offensive armament. The tanks pictured are those seen later in the middle part of the war, after side armour had been added to protect the upper part of the tracks, the running gear, and the junction of the hull and turret.

ABOVE: Adolf Hitler savours victory in Paris.

RIGHT: Although the British managed to extract more than 325,000 men at Dunkirk, nearly all of the heavy weapons and equipment had to be sacrificed. These are anti-aircraft guns, whose barrels have been destroyed to prevent their use by the Germans.

List, whose 12th Army included the Panzergruppe von Kleist, mediated and ordered Guderian to obey the halt command, but added that Guderian's formation could continue a 'reconnaissance in force' to the west. Guderian construed this as allowing him to send the whole of his 1st and 2nd Panzer Divisions (two-thirds of his corps) which, on 17 May, pushed a bridgehead across the Oise river at Muy. By 19 May the divisions had reached Péronne, and by nightfall on 20 May had reached Abbeville at the mouth of the Somme river. The motorized divisions were hard on Guderian's heels, assuming the defence of the sector along the Somme from Péronne to Abbeville, and providing flank protection against any attack from the south, as Guderian

after some argument the advance was resumed for a further day. On 16 May, Rommel's 7th Panzer Division forced the Franco-Belgian border, quickly advancing to surprise Le Cateau at dawn the following day, thus achieving an advance of some 31 miles (50km), during which units of the French 18th Division and 1st Armoured Division were scattered and the rear areas of the French 9th Army thrown into confusion. Next, Guderian was most surprised to receive a further order to halt. This time, von Kleist was decidedly hostile toward Guderian, who offered his resignation. General Wilhelm

turned north. Guderian had already cut the BEF's lines of communication to its bases south of the Somme, and now desired to cut its line of retreat to the sea.

Von Rundstedt's Army Group A was now able to wheel north and north-east to trap the Belgian army, the BEF and the French 1st Army being in a pocket between his own army group and von Bock's Army Group B. However, von Rundstedt's southern flank, between the mouth of the Somme and Sedan, was very weak. This was noticed by the French, but they were too preoccupied with their attempts to restore their battered centre to make any immediate response, especially as the very speed of the German advance gave them scant time to rally dispersed forces. Gamelin ordered a combined attack from north and south of the Somme to isolate the Panzer spearheads, but at this time Gamelin was replaced as commander-in-chief by General Maxime Weygand, who postponed the order while he assessed the situation. It was doubtful if the proposed attack would have succeeded, since the Luftwaffe had control of the air.

On 19 May, the second of two local counter-attacks by the incomplete French 4th Armoured Division, under Colonel Charles de Gaulle, against the left flank of the XIX Panzer Corps between Crécy and Marle on the Serre river was successful in itself, but made little difference to the campaign as a whole.

Meanwhile the Allies were losing the campaign in Flanders. Weygand visited the northern group of armies, directing the BEF and part of the French 1st Army to counter-attack towards Cambrai and Bapaume under cover of the Belgian army's retreat to the Yser river. Weygand's enthusiasm was giving the Allies the impression they were succeeding, and Gort had to explain that his troops, under great pressure from the east by Army Group B, could not break off and turn through 90° and move to the south. On 21 May Gort nevertheless had some success in a local assault on Arras.

Two British light infantry battalions, a motorcycle battalion, and 74 tanks from the 4th and 7th Royal Tank Regiments, plus 70 French tanks, caught the 7th Panzer Division unawares, making Rommel believe he had been attacked by very strong forces with hundreds of tanks. But there was no attack from the south to complement the British effort from the north. Weygand ordered one on 22 May, but communications were poor: the supreme headquarters did not even have a radio. The French 10th Army lacked the troops and ammunition to fulfil Weygand's orders, and the divisions were no longer where Weygand thought they were.

At Arras, however, the confidence of the Germans had been shaken and the high command was now convinced that the Panzer units were taking too many risks. Even so, Guderian's XIX Panzer Corps was in the process of striking north, isolating Boulogne on 22 May and Calais the next day, before pressing forward to the Aa river at Gravelines, only 10 miles (16km) from Dunkirk. Reinhardt's XLI Panzer Corps also reached the canal line from Aire to Gravelines via St. Omer, which was sparsely defended. There was then nothing between the Panzer divisions and Dunkirk, the last port of escape for the BEF, but it was at this juncture that von Rundstedt ordered von Kleist to halt his armour: Hitler wanted to preserve it for the coming offensive south of the Somme, the land around Dunkirk being thought too marshy for tanks, and Field-Marshal Hermann Göring had affirmed that his Luftwaffe could achieve the task unaided. As was his propensity, Guderian protested, but this time the order was quite definite.

As the Germans delayed, the BEF escaped from Dunkirk. With such a desperate situation in Flanders, Gort had decided that the BEF must be evacuated, and the British government, headed by Winston Churchill rather than Neville Chamberlain since 10 May, agreed. The

withdrawal into the Dunkirk perimeter began, the French XVI Corps taking over its defence from the British. Vice-Admiral Bertram Ramsey planned the operation in which 338,000 men, including 113,000 French, were taken off the beaches at Dunkirk during the nine days up to 4 June. Vessels of all types and sizes made the two-way journey across the Channel time and time again, braving Luftwaffe attacks off the coast of France. For the most part, however, the Royal Air Force was able to check the Luftwaffe and so prevent it from stopping or severely disrupting the evacuation. Allied troops were also evacuated from Boulogne, Le Havre, Cherbourg, St. Nazaire and Bordeaux. In all, some 500,000 men were rescued during the month ending 26 June. The Belgians had surrendered on 28 May, having given the British time to withdraw to Dunkirk.

The Germans had suffered 60,000 casualties and captured more than 1 million prisoners in their lightning campaign. The Belgian and the Dutch armies had been destroyed, and the French had lost the support of 12 British divisions, most of whose equipment fell into German hands after the evacuation. Having lost 30 divisions, Weygand could now look to only 66 divisions, many of which were not at full strength, for the impossible task of defending the area from Abbeville to the Maginot Line. Two British divisions were still in France, south of the Somme, and two more would be sent over later.

The Germans had been given the time to bring up the mass of their marching infantry and reorganize. On 5 June they began their southerly assault with 140 divisions. The Germans' three objectives were to advance between the Oise and the sea to the lower Seine below Paris; to advance in a south-easterly direction to defeat the French army in the Paris-Metz-Belfort triangle, and thus render useless the Maginot Line defences; and to pierce the Maginot Line in the direction of Nancy-Luneville.

RIGHT: Soldiers come ashore at a port in southern England after their evacuation from Dunkirk.

BELOW: The most pitiful victims of any war are the civilians, who are either caught up in the fighting or forced to flee ahead of it as refugees. These are French refugees photographed in May or June 1940.

Weygand deployed most of his remaining strength on the Somme-Aisne line, his troops posted in a series of strongpoints linked on the French maps but which, in fact, had large gaps between them where there was inadequate artillery cover. Both minefields and mobile reinforcements were sadly lacking. Weygand's plan to stand and fight was extremely inflexible and resulted in his troops often being by-passed or encircled by the Germans.

Army Group B attacked and crossed the Somme on 5 June, while Army Group A attacked across the Aisne, where the French resisted with some determination but to no good effect. The Panzer divisions then fanned out in a southerly direction: the XIX Panzer Corps headed south and east toward the Swiss frontier; some elements of Panzergruppe von Kleist struck out to the south-east in the direction of Dijon, Lyon and the Mediterranean coast; and other units of the Panzergruppe von Kleist turned to the south-west toward Bordeaux.

The 4th Army attacked on the extreme right flank between Amiens and the sea, the 7th Panzer Division quickly reaching the Seine at Rouen. By now, the French armies were fracturing into unco-ordinated fragments. On 14 June, Army Group C struck at the Maginot Line. The Luftwaffe supported the armoured formations, bombing defended positions before the assault.

The imminent arrival of the Germans in Paris set off a new flood of refugees, causing congestion on the roads and providing targets for the Luftwaffe. On 10 June, the French government left Paris for Tours, with Bordeaux as its ultimate destination. On 14 June, German troops entered Paris, which had been declared an open city. On 16 June, at a meeting of the French council of ministers, prime minister Paul Reynaud argued that resistance must continue, if necessary from abroad. He was supported by Brigadier-General de Gaulle (now the undersecretary of defence) but by few others, and therefore resigned. His successor was the aged Marshal Henri Pétain, a hero of World War I, who negotiated for an armistice.

The Panzer thrusts continued, and by 22 June, the day of the French armistice, which came into effect three days later, the Germans had overrun all but southern France. The 7th Panzer Division had reached Cherbourg, while the 5th Panzer Division had driven on to Brest. The XVI Panzer Corps had taken Lyon and Grenoble, and the XIX Panzer Corps had reached the Swiss frontier and turned north-east to Belfort. The Maginot Line had finally crumbled.

With France's defeat now a certainty, the Italian dictator, Benito Mussolini, declared war on France, and on 21 June 450,000 Italians attacked the French Alpine front. The 185,000 French troops deployed there successfully held off the Italians, and nowhere were they able to break through the French defences, saving south-eastern France at least from Axis occupation. The Franco-German armistice was signed at Compiègne on the same site as the 1918 armistice, when Germany was the defeated power. Hitler allowed Mussolini to occupy Corsica, Savoy and parts of Provence, while the Germans occupied northern, eastern, western and south-western France, thus gaining control over the entire Atlantic and northern coasts of Europe.

It should be noted that in September 1940, Nazi Germany, Fascist Italy and Imperial Japan signed the Tripartite Pact, which officially established the so-called Axis powers.

THE BATTLE OF BRITAIN

With the end of the fighting between French and German forces on 25 June 1940, Germany's only still-active enemy was the UK. Convinced, up to this time, that Britain would either refrain from going to war or make only a token gesture, Hitler now felt that something would have to be done about the recalcitrant British, if they continued to deny the realities of the situation or refused his 'last appeal to reason'. Up to this time no serious planning for an invasion had been undertaken, and now the army and navy were at loggerheads over the way in which an invasion should be undertaken. The army wanted a major cross-Channel effort on a broad front, but the navy was unwilling to contemplate even a narrow-front assault across the Straits of Dover, so great had been its losses in the Norwegian campaign. Whatever type of assault was finally adopted, both the army and navy agreed that the essential prerequisite was command of the air to prevent the Royal Navy from cutting the invasion fleet to pieces, and to give the assaulting forces the necessary air support against the Royal Air Force.

Now promoted to the unique rank of Reichsmarschall, Hermann Göring was certain the Luftwaffe could fulfil this task, despite its losses in the French campaign. In fact, Göring's ambitions for his air force went further still: he was convinced that the Luftwaffe on its own could destroy the Royal Air Force and dominate the skies over southern England, thus persuading the British that continued resistance was futile and that they should seek a negotiated peace. But the Luftwaffe had been designed and steadily increased as a purely tactical air force, and Göring was now grandiosely entertaining its commitment in a strategic campaign, for which it was neither equipped nor trained, against the best air force the Germans had yet to meet.

The standard German fighter throughout the first stages of World War II was the Messerschmitt Bf 109E, which was fast, agile, well-protected and moderately well-armed.

in northern France to the west of the Seine river. Between them the three air fleets had some 3,600 aircraft, of which about 2,700 were serviceable on 1 July.

Facing this formidable German strength was the RAF's Fighter Command, under the command of Air Chief-Marshal Sir Hugh Dowding: No. 10 Group, led by Air Vice-Marshal Sir Quintin Brand in the west of England; No. 11 Group, led by Air Vice-Marshal Keith Park in London and the south-east of England; No. 12 Group, led by Air Vice-Marshal Trafford Leigh-Mallory in East Anglia and the Midlands; and No. 13 Group led by Air Vice-Marshal Richard Saul in northern England and Scotland. At the beginning of July the squadrons of these four groups had an

establishment strength of some 871 single-engined fighters, of which 644 were serviceable. Although the supply of aircraft from the factories and repair units would often cause concern during the forthcoming battle, the real problem was the acute shortage of pilots, despite the fact that other RAF commands, and even the Fleet Air Arm, had been combed for suitable replacements. But although it was considerably outnumbered, Fighter Command had certain distinct advantages: firstly there was radar and its associated fighter control system, backed up by visual observers stationed around the coast of Britain. This allowed fighters to be sent up in the right numbers and at the right time to intercept the most important

ABOVE: The head of the Luftwaffe was Reichsmarschall Herman Göring (left), seen here in conversation with Werner Mölders, who was not only a superb tactician, but also a great fighter 'ace'.

RIGHT: The line of Chain Home radar stations, that eventually surrounded Britain's coast, provided adequate early warning of incoming Luftwaffe raids.

So while the planning for the invasion continued, the Luftwaffe's three main formations were to start the battle to win air superiority if not outright supremacy: these were Luftflotte 5 under Colonel-General Hans-Jürgen Stumpff from bases in Norway; Luftflotte 2 under Field-Marshal Albert Kesselring from bases in the Low Countries and north-eastern France; and Luftflotte 3 under Field-Marshal Hugo Sperrie from bases

Fourthly, there was the question of the aircraft involved. The Luftwaffe's air strength for the Battle of Britain was divided into four main types: twin-engined bombers; single-engined dive-bombers; twin-engined heavy fighters; and single-engined fighters. The British relied mainly on Supermarine Spitfire and Hawker Hurricane single-engined fighters, which were slightly inferior to the Messerschmitt Bf 109 in terms of firepower but otherwise comparable in terms of agility and performance. This last was in the process of being improved by the large-scale introduction of constant-speed propellers. And once battle had been joined, the British fighters would prove markedly superior to the other three main classes of German aircraft.

There is no way of fixing a date for the definitive beginning of the Battle of

LEFT: A British radar operator watches her display screen, ready to report any sign of German activity.

BELOW: The Germans placed great reliance on the Messerschmitt Bf 110 twin-engined heavy fighter and multi-role warplane. This had heavy armament and good range, but lacked the outright performance and agility to cope with the attacks of the RAF's Hawker Hurricane and Supermarine Spitfire single-engined fighters.

German raids. Luftwaffe intelligence had underestimated the importance of this British control system, and the Germans thus failed to devote anything like sufficient attention to the elimination of the easily visible coastal radar stations.

Secondly, the British pilots were initially fresher than their opponents, and enjoyed the advantage of operating over their own country. Return flights to base with a damaged aircraft were relatively short, and pilots forced to bale out landed on friendly territory. The Germans, on the other hand, faced the gruelling flight back to the continent with damaged machines, or had to bale out over England or the Channel. From the latter they were usually fished out by the efficient British air-sea rescue service to become prisoners-of-war.

Thirdly, the key to domination of the skies over England lay with the fighters, and here again the RAF had an advantage: by the time the German fighters reached southern England, their length of time in the combat zone was tightly limited if they were to return to base without running out of fuel.

concentrated their attacks on the bombers and tried, wherever possible, to avoid combat with the German fighters, which in themselves posed no real threat to the UK as they carried no offensive armament. This coastal phase of the battle raged through July and the first week of August, and resulted in a serious setback for the Germans. Fighter Command's losses were acceptable, but German bomber losses were relatively heavy, and the Junkers Ju 87 dive-bomber, hitherto regarded as a war-winner, was revealed to be easy prey for single-engined fighters.

Hitler appealed to the UK to come to terms on 19 July, but with the British refusal three days later the Germans began in earnest to prepare plans for the defeat of Britain.

On 1 August Hitler set the scene for the next phase of the battle by allowing attacks on the mainland of the UK from 5 August onward, the Luftwaffe taking the attack to the British forward fighter bases, coastal radar stations, and other targets in southern England. Poor weather delayed the start of the German offensive until 8 August, and the second phase in fact lasted for only 16 days. Large numbers of relatively small forces wandered into southern England, strafing airfields and ports to draw up the British fighter defences and engage them in close combat. The brunt of the defence was borne by No. 11 Group which, because of the short warning time available, was only able to send up its squadrons individually or in pairs to meet the raids as they came in. Nevertheless, the British handled the German raids successfully, albeit at the price of quickly exhausting front-line squadrons.

Dowding's genius was apparent at this time: he let his subordinates get on with their jobs, and concentrated with remarkable skill on keeping up the flow of pilots and machines to the squadrons which needed them; he also rotated new squadrons to the front at just the right moment to replace front-line units on the verge of exhaustion.

ABOVE: When operating in conditions of German air superiority, the Junkers Ju 87 Stuka dive-bomber proved very effective in destroying point targets. The Germans, however, did not have this advantage in the Battle of Britain and Stukas were savaged whenever they appeared.

RIGHT: The nerve centres of RAF Fighter Command were its control rooms, such as this one at Stanmore Park, where data on incoming raids were received, processed, and used to despatch the right squadrons to the correct locations for an interception.

Britain, but by 1 July it may fairly be said to have entered upon its first phase, with harassing attacks on British coastal shipping, ports and installations made by Luftflotten 2 and 3. The German plan was simple: by attacking these easily accessed targets with bombers, the British fighters were being drawn up into combat on terms favourable to the German fighters and decimated. Underestimating the real strength of Fighter Command, the Germans imagined the British would quickly begin to lose more aircraft than they could replace, and would thus be easy meat for the second phase of the German attack. The German plan backfired badly: the British fighters, positioned with the aid of radar,

On the two main days of this second phase, 8 and 15 August, the Germans made 1,485 and 1,786 sorties respectively, which Fighter Command was able to contain and also inflict severe losses on the Messerschmitt Bf 110 heavy fighters, as well as on the twin-engined bombers. At this time, British fighter tactics were in the process of transition from the pre-war mass formations of 12 or more aircraft toward the German tactical concept of two pairs of fighters, each covering the other, while within each pair, one pilot took the lead with the other flying as his protective wingman. This was altogether more suitable in air combat between fast fighters, as it was tactically more flexible. The more numerous, but slightly slower Hurricanes, were in general tasked with the more important role of destroying the German bombers, while the Spitfires concentrated their efforts, to hold off the German fighters. The combination of target allocation, and the nature of the German tactics, was to prove a winner in the weeks ahead. Ending on 23 August, the

ABOVE LEFT: Bombs explode on the RAF airfield at Helmswell.

ABOVE: German Dornier Do 17 twin-engined medium bombers flying over London.

LEFT: Pilots of a Supermarine Spitfire squadron enjoy a brief moment of relaxation before being scrambled on another mission.

RIGHT: The Messerschmitt Bf 109E fighter of Franz von Werra, shot down over England where he was taken prisoner. In January 1941, von Werra was sent with other German prisoners to Canada, possibly becoming the only German airman to make his escape from there, returning to Germany via the still-neutral USA.

BELOW: Pilots rush to their Hawker Hurricane fighters as their squadron is scrambled to meet a German raid.

second phase of the battle left the British in command of the skies over southern England and the Germans in some disarray as a result of their heavy losses.

The Luftwaffe now stepped up its efforts by introducing mass bomber formations into what became the third phase of the battle starting on 24 August. The idea was for 100 or more bombers, in close formation and escorted by many fighters, to beat their way through to the British fighter bases and destroy them. The fighters would deal with any British aircraft that rose to intercept, and any RAF machines that escaped would find their bases destroyed. This third phase, which lasted to 5 September, was the closest the Germans came to breaking Fighter Command, and the margin was very close indeed. Although the Germans again lost heavily, the British suffered the loss of over 450 aircraft and, more importantly, more than 230 pilots were killed or wounded. At the beginning of September, Fighter Command had very little left to throw into the fray: for the

had been multi-engine bombers. The UK had won the first strategic air battle in history, and had driven off the German threat of invasion.

THE NAVAL WAR 1939–40

While the period of inactivity along the Western Front between September 1939 and May 1940 was regarded by the newspapers as the 'Phoney War', it was not so for the men of the U-boats, the Royal Navy and the merchant navy. From the morning of 3 September 1939, when the U-boats and surface ships, already at

LEFT: Caught by the camera gun of a German fighter, a Hawker Hurricane fighter attempts to break away from combat with smoke beginning to stream from its engine.

BELOW: Even as the Battle of Britain was being fought, the naval war between British surface vessels and German U-boats continued. Here a depth charge explodes in the wake of the destroyer by which it was dropped.

first time reserves were being used more rapidly than they could be replaced. It was at this stage that the Germans made their most significant error. Throughout this period, Bomber Command had been trying to carry the war to the Germans, attacking large concentrations for the projected invasion by day, and targets in Germany by night. For the first time, on 24 August, Berlin was bombed. Hitler was so enraged that he ordered attacks on Fighter Command to cease, so that all German efforts might be devoted to the destruction of London.

Just as the destruction of Fighter Command seemed imminent, therefore, the Luftwaffe switched to the day-time bombardment of London, this fourth phase of the battle beginning on 7 September. Up to the end of the month, German bombers wrought considerable havoc on London, but Fighter Command was given some breathing time, with the result that both Nos. 11 and 12 Groups'

squadrons could then concentrate on the massed German bombers and fighters. The destruction of these was great, and the supremely successful 15 September has since been celebrated as Battle of Britain Day. Losses at this rate were too heavy for the Luftwaffe to sustain, consequently on 1 October the last phase of the battle began. Fighter-bombers ranged over southern England by day, while bombers struck at London by night, but the tide against the Luftwaffe had now definitely turned. On 12 October, Hitler cancelled his orders for the invasion of the UK and the Battle of Britain was won.

There was, of course, the Blitz on London and other industrial centres from November onwards, but the Battle of Britain was effectively over by 31 October. The British had lost 915 aircraft against the Germans' 1,733. In human terms, the Germans had fared even worse, for a large proportion of the losses

their war stations, received the signal from their high command, telling them that war with France and the UK had been declared, the shooting war began in earnest.

The British and French had planned co-operation, but it was the Royal Navy which took the lead in policy-making. Although Hitler had endorsed the international protocol banning unrestricted submarine warfare, or the sinking of merchant vessels without warning, and had given strict instructions to Commodore Karl Dönitz and his U-boat arm to obey the regulations, the Admiralty assumed the U-boats would not abide by the rules. This prediction seemed to be borne out when the liner, *Athenia*, returning to England on the first day of the war, was torpedoed by U-30 in the Western Approaches: this mistake arose from the belief, by the Germans, that it was in fact a troopship. As a result, the British initiated their full convoy system, and within a few weeks U-boats were sinking merchant ships on sight.

The U-boats had their greatest successes against warships, sinking the

ABOVE: The elderly aircraft carrier Courageous *was sunk by a torpedo fired by U-boat U-29 on 17 September 1939.*

RIGHT: A celebratory return to base for the U-47, after it had sunk the old British battleship, Royal Oak, *at Scapa Flow on 14 October 1939.*

LEFT: *The battle-cruiser* Scharnhorst, *together with her sister ship,* Gneisenau, *was one of the most important German warships of World War II.*

BELOW LEFT: *Günther Prien, the commander of the U-boat U-47 when it sank the* Royal Oak.

old aircraft carrier *Courageous* on 17 September and almost sinking the new aircraft carrier *Ark Royal*. On 14 October U-47 penetrated the waters of the Home Fleet's base at Scapa Flow in the Orkney Islands, sinking the old battleship *Royal Oak* in an undertaking whose propaganda value to the Germans considerably exceeded the naval importance of the destruction of an obsolete ship. But this episode had an important strategic effect, for it persuaded the British that the Home Fleet should abandon its main base until the defences of Scapa Flow had been further improved.

The heart of British naval strategy was the containment of the German navy in the North Sea by the laying of mine-fields in the English Channel and by the Home Fleet's control of the passage between the Orkney Islands and Norway. This policy of containment had worked admirably in World War I, and the

Admiralty hoped to repeat its success while the resources of the British Empire were mustered to build up the country's strength. Conversely, if the German fleet should ever break out into the Atlantic, its ships would disrupt the convoys bringing raw materials and munitions from Canada and the USA, thus starving the British Isles into submission. Luckily for the British, the German navy failed to exploit the temporary withdrawal of the Home Fleet in October–December 1939. Germany's two new battle-cruisers, *Scharnhorst* and *Gneisenau*, made a sortie from Wilhelmshaven on 21 November, passed north of the Shetland and Faeroe Island groups without being sighted by British patrols, and attacked the armed merchant cruiser, *Rawalpindi*, which was patrolling off Iceland. In a hopelessly unequal fight the liner lasted for exactly 14 minutes and the German ships made their escape back to Germany. But the foray had done very little to break the

the heavy cruiser *Exeter*, but the combination of three opponents was too much for the battleship, which sought refuge in the River Plate off the Uruguayan capital, Montevideo. Skilful British propaganda suggested that a capital ship and an aircraft carrier were in the area, whereas only one more cruiser was available. The captain of the *Admiral Graf Spee* was ordered by Hitler to avoid the indignity of having his ship sunk, and Captain Hans Langsdorff scuttled the ship off Montevideo.

The Battle of the River Plate did much to hearten the British and little to encourage the Germans, the *Deutschland* having managed to get back to Germany after sinking only two ships. By the end of 1939 the British had checked the first German challenge to British control of the sea for the loss of only 15 merchant ships totalling 61,000 tons.

In home waters there was a new danger, however, in the form of the magnetic mine. The Germans, unaware that the British had their own, hoped to block British ports with a mine to which

ABOVE: In the Battle of the River Plate, the German pocket battleship, Admiral Graf Spee *(background) was outmanoeuvred by British cruiser forces, including the heavy cruiser* Exeter *(left), and the light cruiser* Achilles. *The other cruiser is the* Ajax.

RIGHT: Captain Hans Langsdorff, convinced that the British had brought in additional ships, including an aircraft carrier, scuttled the Admiral Graf Spee *in the River Plate estuary before killing himself.*

British hold on the northern outlet to the North Sea and the Germans had been lucky to escape the concentration of forces which were in the vicinity.

The Germans had appreciated, even before the outbreak of war, how tight the British blockade would be, and to avoid this ensured that two pocket battleships, the *Admiral Graf Spee* and *Deutschland*, put to sea in the August before the outbreak of war. Once the Polish campaign was over, Hitler authorized attacks on British and French shipping, and soon the Admiralty was receiving reports of ships being sunk by unknown raiders all over the Atlantic. Eight hunting groups were formed, but only one of them had success, when on 13 December three cruisers caught the *Admiral Graf Spee* off the estuary of the River Plate on the eastern coast of South America. The German ship inflicted heavy damage on the largest British ship,

there was no known countermeasure. Losses were severe, including not only merchant shipping but also such important warships as the battleship *Nelson*, which was badly damaged while entering harbour. But the British soon discovered what was the appropriate solution to the problem: ships were quickly equipped with degaussing gear to neutralize the magnetism of their hulls. As the British already had a magnetic mine of their own, this first German attempt to gain a tactical advantage with what was supposedly a secret weapon was not successful.

The work of RAF Coastal Command's shore-based aircraft also played an important part in defending

shipping from U-boat attacks, especially in the waters surrounding the British Isles. But the lack of suitable aircraft in adequate numbers, and more seriously the lack of a suitable weapon, robbed Coastal Command of a significant return for its efforts. The standard pre-war bomb for the anti-submarine task was totally inadequate, and in the spring of 1940 a modified naval depth charge had to be introduced as an emergency measure. Fortunately for the British, this serious technical limitation was matched by German problems with their torpedoes, which often failed to detonate on impact.

The German invasion of Norway in April 1940 put a definite end to the Phoney War. It took the British and French navies by surprise, although the first contact was made between an Allied force, on its way to lay mines in

Norwegian waters, and the German invasion forces. Many opportunities were lost by the Royal Navy through bad planning and lack of co-ordination, and the devastating power of dive-bombers against warships came as an unpleasant shock. Nevertheless, it was the German navy which suffered more during the Norwegian campaign. At the outset, the new heavy cruiser, *Blücher*, was blown out of the water by Norwegian coastal defences, while Fleet Air Arm Blackburn Skua dive-bombers sank the smaller cruiser, *Königsberg*, at Bergen. The two Battles of Narvik accounted for half the total German destroyer strength, a catastrophic loss which crippled subsequent German naval operations. The battle-cruiser *Renown* surprised the new battle-cruisers, *Scharnhorst* and *Gneisenau*, in a snow storm off the Vestfjord, scoring a damaging hit on

FAR LEFT: The Admiral Graf Spee *and its sister ships,* Deutschland *and* Admiral Scheer, *were of a hybrid cruiser type, with diesel propulsion for a great range in the commerce-training role. They were designed with the firepower to outshoot anything that could catch them and the speed to outrun anything that could outshoot them.*

ABOVE: The Admiral Graf Spee, *burning after the ship had settled on the shallow bottom of the River Plate estuary.*

one of them before they escaped. The two German ships later scored an easy kill when they encountered the British aircraft carrier, *Glorious*, as she was evacuating RAF personnel from northern Norway, while the *Scharnhorst* was crippled by a torpedo from one of the escorting destroyers. Neither did the *Gneisenau* escape without damage, for she was torpedoed by a submarine, thereby seriously depleting the strength of the German navy by June 1940.

The crisis in France in May and June 1940 meant an immediate end to the Anglo-French intervention in Norway, and soon the ships were involved in the enormous problem of evacuating troops from France, in an undertaking that rescued 338,000 British and French troops, but at a heavy cost in ships sunk

or damaged. For a time it seemed as though Hitler might really invade the British Isles, and the Royal Navy's entire resources were devoted to what many saw as a last-ditch stand. Only afterwards was it clear that the German navy had suffered far too heavy casualties in Norway to be capable of supporting a seaborne invasion, and when the Luftwaffe failed in its attempt to destroy the RAF, the threat of invasion gradually receded. It would have eased the minds of the British defenders to have known that the strongest opponents of the proposed invasion were Hitler's naval staff.

The situation after Dunkirk was nonetheless extremely gloomy for the British. Not only were they now faced with the Italians in the Mediterranean, without the help of the French navy, a

ABOVE: A quarter of Heinkel He 60 coastal reconnaissance floatplanes is caught overflying a U-boat in this propaganda photograph. What the U-boat arm most desperately needed from the Luftwaffe throughout the war, and so seldom received, was timely long-range reconnaissance support deep in the Atlantic.

RIGHT: A British warship bombards the port of Cherbourg in northern France. Once it had been taken by the Germans in June 1940, the port made a useful base for German coastal forces operating in the English Channel.

vital element of pre-war strategy, but they also faced a hostile coast, whose ports now accommodated German surface and subsurface forces, stretching from Bordeaux to the Arctic Circle. The Royal Navy's strategic position of September 1939 had been outflanked to the north, west and south, and if the Germans had possessed a stronger navy, with more understanding of the principles of sea power, they could have forced the recalcitrant British to negotiate an armistice. The gravest consequence for the British was that the U-boats were now able to operate from the Bay of Biscay, a fact which left them more fuel once they had reached the convoy routes. As a result, a huge strain was brought to bear on the already hard-pressed escort forces.

The end of the Norwegian campaign and the defeat of France marked the beginning of what would be known as the Battle of the Atlantic, which was to rage essentially unabated for five years. It was not only the most vital maritime campaign of the entire war but also possibly the most importantly strategic of all, the Atlantic being the means by which the US and the UK were linked. Had the Atlantic lifeline been cut, the industrial might of the US could not have been brought to bear against Germany, and the essential supplies provided by Canada and the USA would have been unavailable to the British.

Fortunately, the British had taken timely steps before the war to remedy their weakness against U-boat attack The existence of the Asdic sonic underwater detection equipment was suspected by the Germans, but nothing was actually known about it until after the fall of France. A massive programme of cheap utility convoy escorts, the corvettes had been started in 1939, and the first of these was ready in April 1940. In conjunction with the timely realization of how radar could be used, these countermeasures proved to be just in time to stave off disaster.

The commander-in-chief of the German navy until January 1943, when he was succeeded by Admiral Karl Dönitz, was Grand Admiral Erich Raeder.

THE ITALIANS ARE CHECKED IN NORTH AFRICA

At the time of Italy's entry into the war in June 1940, there were some 236,000 Italian troops under the overall command of Marshal Rodolfo Graziani in North Africa. The Italian 5th Army was in western Libya, and in the east was the Italian 10th Army, under General Mario Berti, consisting of the XXI and XXII Corps with three infantry divisions, one Blackshirt division, and one native Libyan division. The Italians had 1,811 guns, 339 light

for four days as it withdrew, firing on the Italian columns which presented excellent targets. On 16 September the Italians reached and occupied Sidi Barrani, where they halted, Graziani's main concern at this stage being the construction of a metalled road and a pipeline back to the border in order to receive supplies and water.

The British expected the Italians to push straight on to Mersa Matruh, and planned to attack them when they moved. Meanwhile, the Italian positions at Sidi Barrani were bombarded by the Royal Navy and bombed by the Royal Air Force. In October the British situation in the desert was improved by the arrival of the Matilda I infantry tanks of the 7th Royal Tank Regiment. Designed specifically for the support of infantry, the Matilda I had armour proof against Italian anti-tank guns. The 2nd Royal Tank Regiment and the 3rd Hussars also arrived at this time. Wavell was now planning a short, swift raid against Sidi Barrani, and from this idea there developed an ambitious plan for a far-reaching offensive. On 28 October

ABOVE: General Sir Archibald Wavell was the British commander-in-chief in the Middle East between August 1939 and July 1941.

FAR RIGHT: Benito Mussolini, Italy's leader, was a vainglorious Fascist who was deposed in 1943. He was later restored to power over the rump of a Fascist state in northern Italy, and was killed ingloriously by partisans in 1945.

tanks and 151 first-line aircraft. The British commander-in-chief in the Middle East, General Sir Archibald Wavell, had five divisions (some 100,000 men), but of these only 36,000 men were in Egypt as the strength of two incomplete divisions: Major-General M. O'Moore Creagh's 7th Armoured Division with two brigades, and Major-General P. Neame's (from August Major General N. M. de la P. Beresford-Peirse's) Indian 4th Division with two infantry brigades and part of its artillery. The British had 225 armoured vehicles. On 8 June Lieutenant-General Richard O'Connor assumed command of all troops in the Western Desert Force, later to be renamed the XIII Corps.

The desert produced nothing for the support of armies. There were no roads, except along the coast, although there were a few recognizable tracks. Skilled

driving could overcome the difficulties of desert terrain, but good navigation was essential in a practically featureless landscape. The British forces felt more at home than the Italians, and possessed some measure of vital desert sense. The British kept the Italians off-balance with frequent raids into Cyrenaica by elements of the 7th Armoured Division. Graziani was under pressure from Mussolini, the Italian dictator, to take the offensive, but felt that his army was not ready. Thus it was only on 13 September that the 10th Army finally went over to the offensive. Two Italian columns advanced, one along the coast through Sollum, the other through the desert south of the escarpment parallel to the coastal strip, although it soon gave up this exposed route, moving through the Halfaya pass onto the coastal strip. The small British covering force fought an unhurried battle

to penetrate the Italian defences at night to avoid detection, and moonlight would be necessary if the forces were to get into formation after the move through the desert. Dumps of ammunition and supplies were placed half-way between Nibeiwa and Mersa Matruh, and all preparations were made under conditions of the greatest secrecy. The training of the troops was accomplished by way of exercises, which provided valuable experience. Only a few people knew that exercise number two on 9 December was to be the real attack.

While a force under Brigadier A.R. Selby attacked along the Maktila coast road, the British 7th Armoured Division and the Indian 4th Division struck through the gap in the Italian defences at dawn on 9 December. One battalion attacked near Nibeiwa at 05.00 to draw the attention of the Italians to this non-essential sector, while the Indian 11th Brigade, 7th Royal Tank Regiment, with 48 tanks, and the divisional artillery of the Indian 4th Division with 72 guns, slipped through to form up beyond for the attack. Surprise was complete: at 07.00 the artillery shelled the camp at Nibeiwa and the tanks approached the north-west entrance, destroying 20 unmanned Italian tanks before bursting into the camp with the infantry in their

LEFT: The Italian tank force in North Africa had a number of moderately useful medium tanks, but placed far too great a numerical and operational significance on its CV-33 light tanks, which were cheap to produce but of no real operational value.

BELOW LEFT and BELOW: The British armour was technically superior to the Italian armour it faced, but was modest in numbers, poorly supplied with spares, and operated by units which often failed to understand the real nature of armoured warfare in the context of the Western Desert.

the Italians moved against Greece, and Wavell now had to do without certain of his resources, which were transferred to help the situation there. He was therefore anxious for immediate action against Sidi Barrani. Wavell's daring plan called for the penetration of a 15-mile (25-km) gap in the defences of Sidi Barrani in the area where the rocky terrain had prevented the

Italians from building an anti-tank ditch, leaving an gap which they could not properly cover for their lack of adequate numbers of mines and anti-tank guns.

This Operation Compass entailed detailed logistical and tactical planning, in that it would be necessary for some units to cross 75 miles (120km) of open desert. The Matilda I tanks would have

10 December after it was subjected to naval bombardment. On 11 December the Indian 4th Division crushed the remaining resistance east of Sidi Barrani and the 7th Armoured Brigade cut off the 64th Catanzaro Division, caught on the move between Buqbuq and Sollum. The British, for 624 casualties, had taken 38,300 prisoners, 237 guns and 73 tanks.

Much to O'Connor's dismay, the Indian 4th Division was then transferred to Sudan and was replaced on 18 December by Major-General I.G. Mackay's Australian 6th Division. But without waiting for the arrival of the Australians, O'Connor launched his remaining force in pursuit of the disorganized Italians. On 16 December the Italians evacuated Sollum and all posts on the Libyan-Egyptian frontier, falling back to Bardia. The 7th Armoured Division and the British 16th Brigade followed up, cutting the road linking Bardia with Tobruk farther to the west. The Italian XXIII Corps, commanded by Lieutenant-General Annibale Bergonzoli, was ordered to hold Bardia with 45,000 troops. The

ABOVE: A Universal (or Bren-gun) Carrier leads a British heavy artillery tractor past a Fascist monument on one of the few roads in North Africa. The desert campaign was largely dependent on the availability of fuel for the various forces' motorized and mechanized equipment.

RIGHT: Australian soldiers take cover as a bomb detonates in the background.

wake. The Italians fought sporadically, their artillery being the most resilient, but gave up when they were unable to stop the advance of the tanks. By 10.40 it was all over: 2,000 Italians had been taken prisoner and 35 tanks were in British hands.

The 7th RTR then wheeled north with the Indian 5th Brigade to attack the fortified camp known as Tummar West, which was held by the 2nd Libyan Division. This fell at 16.00. On the following day, the Indian 4th Division cleared Tummar East following a spirited Italian resistance.

During the evening of 9 December the 7th Armoured Division reached the sea, isolating the survivors of Tummar, and cutting the road from Sidi Barrani west to Buqbuq. The Italian pocket at Maktila had also been cleared. Sidi Barrani itself fell during the evening of

exploit the breach. At dawn on 3 January the attack was launched, with 120 guns and naval and air bombardments in support. The Australian 6th Division entered the ditch and the tanks rolled across the bridge into Bardia, meeting only ineffectual resistance. The efforts of the Italian air force were destroyed, and on 4 January the Allies reached the sea, having cut the Italian garrison in two. The Italian forces surrendered to the XIII Corps, yielding 45,000 prisoners, 460 guns, 131 tanks and 700 trucks.

The next objective was Tobruk, with its deep-water port and the nearby El Adem airfield, which were to be captured intact. The defences of Tobruk had not yet been completed and extended along a perimeter of about 40 miles (65km). The Italian defence was based on the XXII Corps, consisting mainly of the 61st Sirte Division with 25,000 men. Tobruk had already been surrounded after an unopposed advance by the 7th Armoured Division. The Australian 6th Division joined it and the attack began at dawn on 21 January. The Australians broke into the perimeter south of Tobruk and the

LEFT: An Italian anti-aircraft gun in North Africa. The British were able to secure and maintain air superiority over the Western Desert until the Germans arrived in February 1941, when there developed a see-saw numerical and technical battle before the British regained almost complete air superiority later in 1942.

BELOW LEFT: The Italian air force made extensive use of aircraft such as the SIAI-Marchetti SM.82 to deliver urgently needed supplies across the Mediterranean as the British aircraft, submarines and surface warships based on Malta began to decimate the Italians' ability to convoy ships across to North Africa.

BELOW: An Italian artillery position in the Western Desert.

defences of Bardia, on an 18-mile (30-km) perimeter, were new and complete, with strongpoints located at about every 820yds (750m), an anti-tank ditch 13ft (4m) wide and 4ft (1.25m) deep, and dense barbed wire entanglements and minefields.

O'Connor had only 23 tanks left for lack of adequate spare parts. For the attack on Bardia, therefore, he decided that the infantry must cross the anti-tank ditch over a special assault bridge, clearing the mines with the aid of engineers to allow the Matilda I tanks to

Matilda I tanks then entered the breach and took the Italians by surprise. The defence made a few counter-attacks with some spirit, but the battle was over by nightfall. There was little damage to the harbour, and the seawater distillation plant remained intact. Some 25,000 Italians and their weapons were captured.

The 7th Armoured Division then advanced towards Mechili and on 24 January the 4th Armoured Brigade engaged the Italian tanks, knocking out nine while the others escaped. On the same day, the Australian 6th Division made an appearance at Derna.

The Allies had done remarkably well to advance so far. The logistic problem of maintaining the advance had been enormous, but O'Connor had wanted to keep the Italians off-balance. On 29 January the Italians evacuated Derna. O'Connor ordered the Australian 6th Division to continue its pressure in the coastal region while the 7th Armoured Division advanced towards Msus. But the Allies had only 50 cruiser tanks left, most of which needed a major overhaul. O'Connor wished to await the arrival of two regiments of the British 2nd Armoured Division, scheduled to reach him at any time, but air reconnaissance revealed signs of the Italian evacuation from Cyrenaica, which, if this was to be intercepted, required immediate action. Graziani by now had lost heart, having suffered the disappointment of seeing his tanks beaten at Mechili.

The retreating Italians used the coast road, while the Allies, cutting across from Mechili to Beda Fomm, had to cross rough desert. Creagh's advance was headed by a mechanized all-arms column, whose 50-mile (80-km) trek was making a slow advance. The armoured cars of Lieutenant-Colonel J.F.B. Combe's 11th Hussars reached Msus on 4 February. On the next day, they and the 2nd Battalion, The Rifle Brigade, arrived south of Beda Fomm, positioning themselves astride the road down which the first Italian column would come

German force Hitler had reluctantly agreed to supply in an effort to save the Italian North African 'empire'. At this time Lieutenant-General Richard O'Connor was planning an immediate advance from El Agheila to Sirte and thence to Tripoli, but General Sir Archibald Wavell was instructed that Cyrenaica must be secured with the smallest possible force so that more units could be sent to support the Greeks. Wavell envisaged no danger from the Germans before the summer, and

OPPOSITE ABOVE: Italian armour, such as this Carro Armato M.13/40, was not available in sufficient numbers for their campaign in North Africa.

OPPOSITE BELOW: Italian infantry surrender.

LEFT: Field-Marshal Jan Smuts visiting South African troops in North Africa.

BELOW: Erwin Rommel (left).

marching from Benghazi. Confused fighting raged throughout the following day, with burning tanks littering the site. The Allies were helped by the fact that the Italian tanks had arrived in small groups, making them easy targets. The British tanks had manoeuvred into good firing positions, using the lie of the land to their advantage, while the Italians were unable to co-ordinate an effective counter-attack, and another 20,000 Italians were captured.

The British finally reached El Agheila. The XIII Corps, with two under-strength divisions, had overcome the huge logistical problems of advancing 560 miles (900km) and had destroyed the nine divisions of the Italian 10th Army.

THE GERMANS ENTER THE NORTH AFRICAN FRAY

Lieutenant-General Erwin Rommel arrived in Tripoli on 12 February 1941 with the leading elements of the small

THE FLOOD OF THE GERMAN TIDE

At dawn on 24 March, the reconnaissance group of the 5th Light Division and the Italian Ariete Division attacked El Agheila. The British defenders pulled back without a fight, taking up new positions at Mersa Brega, which Rommel attacked on 31 March with the aid of some 50 Junkers Ju 87 Stuka dive-bombers. Rommel encountered some resistance but the British retreated, their columns streaming back in some disorder toward Benghazi and Mechili. Many armoured vehicles broke down and the British could not prevent a substantial body of German and Italian troops advancing north along the east coast of the Gulf of Sidra and fanning out to the north-east in the general direction of Tmimi. For days, Rommel exploited his success without informing his superiors and, in less than a fortnight, forced the British to give up most of Cyrenaica with the exception of Tobruk. In the process, the Germans also took a number of important prisoners, including O'Connor, who had been found hopelessly off course on his way by car to Tmimi.

ABOVE: German artillery in action during the Axis forces' unsuccessful siege of Tobruk from April 1941.

RIGHT: British infantrymen double past a knocked-out German tank during the see-saw fighting of the North African campaign.

deployed the 2nd Armoured Division, Indian 3rd Motorized Brigade and Australian 9th Division in Cyrenaica. Rommel found the Italians preparing for a stand at Sirte with one incomplete armoured division and four infantry divisions, mostly without artillery. As his Deutsches Afrika Korps arrived, Rommel moved elements of its 5th Light Division forward to a position some 20 miles (32km) west of El Agheila. It was his wish to attack early in May, but he was ordered to wait until the 15th Panzer Division arrived.

By the end of March, 15 Axis convoys had delivered 25,000 men, 8,500 vehicles and 26,000 tons of supplies in Tripoli, despite harassment from the Royal Navy and the Royal Air Force, and Rommel persuaded the Italians that Tripolitania, to the west of Cyrenaica in Libya, could be held with German help.

Wavell decided that Tobruk must be held: Major-General L.J. Morshead and the Australian 9th Division, plus other elements, withstood several attacks by Rommel's forces. On the night of 13–14 April the Germans cleared a way through the anti-tank ditch and the 5th Light Division's armour moved forward from the south with infantry riding on the tanks and moving up behind them. The infantry was annihilated by the Australian artillery and 250 German prisoners were taken. Rommel was furious and on 16–17 April personally directed the Ariete Division in another attempt, which was again unsuccessful. A further attack by the 5th Light Division between 30 April and 4 May, in the area of Bir el Madauar and Giaida, farther to the west, was also a failure.

Meanwhile, the 15th Panzer Division had taken Bardia on 12 April, which was unoccupied along with Forts Capuzzo and Sollum, but then found its way to Egypt blocked by forces under the command of Brigadier W.H.E. Gott. With his forces thus dispersed, Rommel was instructed to await reinforcements

before again attacking Tobruk. At the same time, the British were delivering about 100 tons of supplies into Tobruk every day. The arrival of the 15th Panzer Division concerned Wavell, but British

reinforcement arrived via the 'Tiger' convoy of fast merchant ships: on 12 May 43 Hawker Hurricane fighters and 238 tanks, made up of 135 Matilda I, 82 cruiser and 21 Mark VI light, were unloaded at Alexandria, all of this being vital to Operation Battleaxe, which Wavell was planning for the relief of Tobruk. Wavell's forces now comprised the Western Desert Force under Lieutenant-General Sir Noel Beresford-Peirse, including the Indian 4th Division, 7th Armoured Division and the 22nd Guards Brigade.

In the second half of May, Operation Brevity was launched in the area of Halfaya, Sollum, Capuzzo and Bardia, and although not a success in itself, Brevity provided useful experience. The Battleaxe plan was for an advance on a 20-mile (32-km) front between Sollum and Sidi Omar, with infantry and a brigade of infantry tanks on the right, and a brigade of cruiser tanks and support groups on the left. Wavell hoped to secure this area, defeat the Axis troops laying siege to Tobruk and, finally, perhaps to advance to the area of

ABOVE: Though fast and agile, the Crusader cruiser tank generally suffered from the same limitations as most British tanks of the period, namely armament that was inferior to that of opposing tanks.

LEFT: German armour, such as these PzKpfw III medium tanks, was reliable and adequately armed, and was generally handled with greater skill by the Germans, even in the later stages of the North African campaign.

RIGHT: Italian armour in the North African desert.

BELOW: German troops, including a paratrooper (in a coat and with a shallow-brimmed helmet), take a look at an Italian anti-aircraft gun position.

Derna and Mechili. The forces besieging Tobruk were mostly Italians, the 15th Panzer Division guarding the Libyan-Egyptian frontier and the 5th Light Division deployed on the coast between Tobruk and the frontier. The number of men, guns and tanks on each side was roughly equal. The Germans were well-supplied with anti-tank weapons, however, including about 12 3.465-in (88-mm) dual-purpose anti-aircraft and anti-tank guns, which could stop any British tank at a distance of 1,640yds (1500m), well beyond the effective range of the tanks' own guns.

Operation Battleaxe began on 15 June with the Royal Air Force bombing of the German forces. The British advanced but Rommel committed only a small part of his armour, while making excellent use of his guns to inflict major losses along the flanks of the British effort. The 7th Armoured Brigade took Capuzzo, then things began to go wrong for the British. The Indian 11th Brigade and the 22nd Guards Brigade failed to take Halfaya,

cruiser and 64 infantry tanks. Wavell was now replaced by General Sir Claude Auchinleck, who arrived on 1 July.

The date for Auchinleck's first effort, Operation Crusader, was 18 November, the objective being yet again the relief of Tobruk. Auchinleck organized his strength as the 8th Army, under the command of Lieutenant-General Sir Alan Cunningham. The British believed the key to the successful relief of Tobruk lay in the destruction of the two Panzer divisions, but Cunningham was uncertain of how best to seek and win a decisive armoured battle. By mid-November, the

LEFT: A German soldier poses for the camera with North African children.

BELOW: German troops photographed during a moment of respite.

and in the evening the 7th Armoured Brigade clashed with the 5th Light Division, in the process being trimmed to a strength of just 37 fit tanks. The next day saw rapid movement and hard fighting, during which Rommel launched two counter-attacks. Heavy fighting occurred around Halfaya, and the 7th Armoured Brigade fought a running battle with the 5th Light Division down to Sidi Omar. Rommel then struck east,

hoping to surround the Western Desert Force and thus preventing the British from uniting their forces, and crippling a good many tanks in the process. On 17 June the British called off the offensive, having by this time a mere 22 cruiser and 17 infantry tanks available to them. Wavell withdrew the British and commonwealth forces before their last line of communications was cut by Rommel, having lost 1,000 men, plus 22

8th Army of six divisions and six independent brigade groups contained the greatest concentration of armour yet achieved by the British, with 724 tanks at the front and 200 more in reserve. On the right flank was the XIII Corps (ex-Western Desert Force) under the command of Lieutenant-General A.R. Godwin-Austen, with the New Zealand Division, Indian 4th Division and 1st Army Tank Brigade. On the left flank was the XXX Corps under the command of Lieutenant-General C.W.M. Norrie, with the 7th Armoured Division with 473 tanks, the 4th Armoured Brigade Group, the South African 1st Division and the 22nd Guards Brigade Group.

Possessing an armoured strength of about 400 tanks, the Axis force comprised the Italian XX (Mobile) Corps with two divisions; the DAK with the 15th Panzer Division, 21st Panzer Division (ex-5th Light Division), Afrika Division and Italian Savona Division, together with the Italian XXI Corps with four divisions. The Afrika Division and four Italian divisions were surrounding Tobruk, with the 15th Panzer Division behind and to the east of them. One Italian division was deployed in the frontier area with the 21st Panzer Division astride and to the south of the Trigh Capuzzo.

Cunningham planned to employ the XIII Corps, consisting mostly of infantry and a tank brigade, to pin the Axis forces in the forward area, while the more mobile XXX Corps crossed the undefended frontier south of Sidi Omar, from where it would advance toward Tobruk or Bardia. The 'Crusader' attack began at dawn on 18 November in torrential rain, and the XXX Corps advanced to Gabr Saleh. However, Rommel thought that this was only a reconnaissance in force and kept his armour back at Gambut, which denied Cunningham the armoured battle in which he expected to achieve a significant victory. The 7th Armoured Division then moved forward to Sidi Rezegh, just

outside the Tobruk perimeter, and here was counter-attacked by the 21st Panzer Division. Meanwhile, the 4th Armoured Brigade Group remained at Gabr Saleh to guard the XIII Corps' right flank. Plans went ahead for the breakout, on 21 November, from Tobruk, where Major-General R.M. Scobie now commanded a British and Polish garrison centred on the 70th Division. Rommel, accordingly, rushed his armour to the Sidi Rezegh area to prevent the breakout.

So began a most confusing battle. For three days tanks, armoured cars, and infantry and artillery attempting to drive south from Tobruk, were opposed by the German and Italian forces watching the perimeter, which were in turn counter-attacked by the British 7th Armoured Brigade supporting the breakout. The German armour attacked in its turn, having rushed from Gabr Saleh. The battlefield extended for 20 miles (32km) and was often obscured by clouds of dust. Each side used tanks captured from the other.

Rommel became impatient with the slow pace of the battle, and on 24 November set off at the head of the 21st Panzer Division, with 100 tanks from the area of Bardia to reach the Mediterranean by way of Sidi Omar and a wheel 180° to the left, so striking the British in the rear. But he had no significant success and overextended his lines, the 21st Panzer Division having been strung out along the Trigh el Abd with its forward units at Sidi Suleiman. The action deteriorated into a series of sporadic bouts wherever Rommel appeared to take personal command. On 26 November the German tanks withdrew into Bardia. Meanwhile, the British reorganized, and both collected and repaired significant numbers of knocked-out tanks. On 26 November, Auchinleck replaced Cunningham as commander of the 8th Army with Lieutenant-General N.M. Ritchie, but directed the battle personally; the British forces south of Tobruk made good

progress, forcing Rommel to return his tanks back into the fray.

The Axis forces were now on the verge of exhaustion, and Rommel retreated after some confused engagements south of Tobruk; no more supplies could be delivered to him before the end of December. On 5 December Rommel withdrew his forces east of Tobruk and a general retreat began the next day, with Rommel's rearguards fighting methodical delaying actions, which XIII Corps could not simply brush aside. The British reached Benghazi on 25 December, the Germans fighting vigorously at Agedabia before withdrawing to El Agheila. The XXX Corps reduced the Axis garrisons near the Egyptian frontier, and 15,000 prisoners were taken at Bardia on 17 January 1942. For the loss of 17,700 men and sizeable numbers of armoured vehicles, the British and commonwealth forces had relieved Tobruk, gained invaluable combat experience, driven the Axis forces from Cyrenaica, and inflicted some 38,000 casualties on them.

GERMANY TAKES YUGOSLAVIA AND GREECE

The Balkan campaign was planned by Hitler as a direct result of Italy's failure to gain success against Greece, which Benito Mussolini's forces had invaded in October 1940. German troops had already entered Bulgaria, which signed the Tripartite Pact on 1 March 1941, the Greek government rightly inferring that Germany was planning an invasion, leading them to request help from the UK. On 14 February 1941 General Sir John Dill, the Chief of the Imperial General Staff, and Anthony Eden, the Foreign Secretary, flew to Cairo to assess the situation with local commanders, and a conference was held in Athens on 22 February with Greek political and military leaders. It became clear that the UK was lacking the strength both to help Greece and to ensure victory in Africa at this time. Yet the British government

Wilson, along the Aliakmon Line stretching from the mouth of the Aliakmon river, north of Mount Olympus, to the Greek-Yugoslav frontier near Flórina. Greek troops were also to be deployed to hold a weaker Metaxas Line north of Serrai in Macedonia to delay any German offensive from southern Bulgaria toward Thessaloníki. A further 13 divisions would continue to hold the Greek-Italian front in Albania between the Ionian Sea north of Sarande and Lake Okhrida via Tepelenë.

These positions left the extreme southern part of the Yugoslav-Greek border, the so-called Monastir gap, exposed to any German advance from the southern part of Yugoslavia, at the time a neutral zone, a fact that caused dispute at the conference. There were insufficient divisions to plug this gap effectively, and the conference decided to communicate with the British ambassador in Yugoslavia for an assessment of the situation and a request to the Yugoslav government for the protection of the frontier and the

LEFT: Field-Marshal Wilhelm List commanded the German 12th Army, which from starting points in western Bulgaria advanced into south-eastern/central Yugoslavia and Greece from 9 April 1941.

BELOW: German infantry in the invasion of Greece, during which time they enjoyed all the advantages derived from virtually uninterrupted air superiority.

knew full well that an offensive against the Axis forces was needed to prevent them from crushing Greece, so giving Hitler a stronger case in his attempts to persuade Turkey to join the Axis powers. There were two elements in the British commitment to the defence of Greece: first, the despatch of an expeditionary force consisting of 58,000 British, Australian and New Zealand troops, together with 100 tanks, to the Greek mainland; and second, the establishment of a combined British and Greek defensive force consisting of some seven divisions under the command of Lieutenant-General Sir Henry Maitland

ABOVE: German officers take in the sights of conquered Athens from the Acropolis.

RIGHT: German paratroops on Crete, while suffering very high casualty rates, nevertheless succeeded in taking the island.

Simovic, offered the Allies some hope. This was short-lived, for an angry Hitler was now determined to destroy Yugoslavia. So superior were the German forces that Hitler declared war on Yugoslavia and Greece simultaneously on 6 April 1941, a mere week behind his original schedule, the defeat of Yugoslavia taking just 12 days. German troops swept through the country and then into the north-eastern part of Greece before Wilson's forces had completed their defences along the Aliakmon Line.

The German forces in Yugoslavia comprised the 2nd Army in the north, and the 12th Army, together with General Ewald von Kleist's 1st Panzergruppe in the south-east. The Germans were supported in the extreme north-west by the Italian 2nd Army and in the centre by the 3rd Army of Hungary, which had signed the Tripartite Pact on 12 December 1940 as its fourth member. Possessing only obsolete weapons, the Yugoslavs were in indefensible positions themselves. On

6 April Belgrade was heavily bombed and a Blitzkrieg offensive began. The right-hand elements of the 1st Panzergruppe covered 310 miles (500km) in seven days down the valley of the Morava river to Belgrade. By 8 April its left-hand formation, the XL Panzer Corps, had taken Skopje, the next day reaching Prilep, and armoured units entered Thessaloníki on 10 April. From the north the 14th Panzer Division rushed through Zagreb, driving south toward Sarajevo, which it seized on 15 April. The morale of the Yugoslavs was very low, and the government surrendered the country on 17 April. However, many Serbs refused to admit defeat and continued to fight the Germans under the command of Colonel Draza-Dragoljub Mihailovic.

The Greek resistance was more stubborn. The Army of Macedonia took on the German XXX Corps and XVIII Mountain Corps, which entered northern Greece from southern Bulgaria on 6 April. There was severe fighting in the region of Kelkayia and Istibey.

prevention of any German movement from south-western Bulgaria. The only contingency plan available, should the Yugoslavs fail, was to hold the Olympus mountains and withdraw south-west towards Grevena to block the Monastir-Flórina valley route.

Events in fact moved with a speed that overtook the Allied planning for a defence of the Monastir gap. German pressure on Yugoslavia to become an ally proved sufficient, and Yugoslavia signed the Tripartite Pact on 25 March. Then an anti-Axis coup by a small band of Yugoslav officers, led by a former chief of the air staff, General Dusan

forced a breach between the left of the British forces and the right of the Greek armies retreating from the Albanian front. The SS Leibstandarte Adolf Hitler Brigade captured Grevena on 21 April, continuing forward to effect the capture of Ioánnina.

The situation was clearly beyond Allied redemption, and on 19 April British and Greek generals agreed that, in the best interests of both countries, the British and commonwealth expeditionary force should be evacuated from the Greek mainland. Rear-Admiral H.T. Baillie-Grohman made the arrangements for the withdrawal, and despite the fact that the Luftwaffe had control of the air and all embarkations had to be made at night, the operation was successful. Four-fifths of the British troops, more than 50,000 men, including some Greeks and Yugoslavs, were evacuated. Again, as at Dunkirk, all the heavy equipment had to be abandoned. The majority of the

LEFT: Major-General Bernard Freyberg (right), a New Zealander, was the Allied commander on Crete.

BELOW: German troops cross a river in Greece using a commandeered local boat.

German forces also approached through Yugoslavia: the 2nd Panzer Division crossed the Greek frontier at dawn on 8 April and advanced to reach Thessaloníki on the same day. The SS Leibstandarte Adolf Hitler Brigade swept into the Monastir gap, the collapse of the Yugoslavs bringing the right wing of the German 12th Army, under Field-Marshal Wilhelm List, up to the Aliakmon Line. Wilson was compelled to withdraw the expeditionary force from the coast near Mount Olympus through Kozam up to the Siatista pass and on to Lake Prespa. The left flank of this arc was weak and included several large gaps. This new position could not be held, and as the Germans pushed through the Aliakmon valley Wilson, on 16 April, ordered his forces to fall back to Thermopylai, on the instructions of the Allied commander-in-chief, Field-Marshal Alexandros Papagos. The German XVIII Mountain Corps crossed the Aliakmon Line, bypassed Mount Olympus, and reached Larissa on 18 April. At the same time the XL Corps

ABOVE: Men and vehicles of the German 12th Army on the move in Greece.

RIGHT: A German soldier brings in a captured New Zealander.

airborne assault led by Lieutenant-General Kurt Student, the man who initially developed this type of tactic. He commanded the newly created XI Fliegerkorps, which included the 7th Parachute Division with three infantry regiments. The air support needed for the operation was provided by the VIII Fliegerkorps, commanded by General Wolfram von Richthofen. The forces available for Merkur included 500 bombers and fighters, a similar number of transport aircraft, and 72 DFS 230 assault gliders. The primary objectives were the three airfields.

The defence of Crete was based on one British infantry brigade supported by numbers of Greek, Australian and New Zealand units evacuated from Greece. By the time the assault began, the Allied force numbered some 42,000 men, although was poorly co-ordinated as a

result of the island's indifferent communications, lacked cohesion, and was woefully ill-equipped. The Greek evacuees had brought some light weapons with them, but there were very few heavier supporting weapons: for example, there were only 68 anti-aircraft guns to protect an island 160 miles (260km) long, while tools and signalling equipment were also scarce. Air support for the ground forces was minimal: the RAF in the Middle East had suffered heavy losses in past months, and by 19 May, after heavy bombardment from the Germans, there were only seven operational aircraft left on the island. This inadequate defence force was entrusted to Major-General B.C. Freyberg on 30 April, giving him little time to prepare.

After the defences of the three airfields had been subjected to air attacks, the Germans began their

evacuees were taken straight to Alexandria in northern Egypt, but some went to Crete to swell the Allied garrison on that island. On 24 April 16 Greek divisions surrendered to the Germans at Thessaloníki.

Crete was strategically significant in the Mediterranean in that Suda Bay, on its north coast, was an ideal fuelling base for the Royal Navy between Malta and Alexandria, and also in the fact that the airfields at Máleme, Rétimo and Heráklion also provided a supply link with Tobruk, the focus of British resistance in the Middle East. Hitler also realized the strategic value of the island, and on 25 April ordered the planning and execution of Operation Merkur, in which Crete was to be taken by a colossal

German forces in Caneá, taking the town on 27 May.

This final push by the attackers persuaded Freyberg that Crete could not be held, and he asked for permission to order an evacuation. This involved the movement of about 20,000 men, in the form of 4,000 from Heráklion on the north coast and the rest from Sfakia beach on the southern coast. On 28 May the troops were lifted from Heráklion. It took until 2 June to complete the evacuation, by which time the cruiser *Calcutta* and the destroyers *Hereward*, *Kashmir*, *Kelly* and *Imperial* had been sunk. Some 800 troops and the ships carrying them failed to reach safety.

The fight for Crete had been bloody: the Allies lost 1,800 soldiers killed, a similar number wounded, and 12,000 taken prisoner. Royal Navy casualties amounted to 1,828 men killed and 183 wounded as well as three cruisers and six

LEFT: The workhorse of the German air transport arm was the Junkers Ju 52/3m, but this suffered very heavy losses during the German airborne invasion of Crete.

BELOW: The Greek navy's two battleships in April 1941 were the Kilkis and Limnos, ex-US Navy pre-Dreadnought ships of no real operational value. Both ships were sunk by German dive-bombers.

operation on 20 May. Paratroops of the 7th Fliegerdivision were dropped on the approaches to the airfields at Rétimo and Heráklion, and to the west of the town of Caneá. It was intended that the landings should take place where there were few defenders, but inadequate German intelligence meant that the paratroopers arrived in areas where there were Allied defenders. There was intense fighting, especially in the area of Máleme, where the Germans landed among the New Zealand 22nd Battalion. None of the three airfields was taken on the first day as planned, and the Germans were unable to back the invasion with sufficient supplies. Their problem was exacerbated by the failure of two German convoys to land troops and stores on the island on 21 and 22 May, the result of the interception of the convoys by three Allied cruisers and their accompanying destroyers, which sank ten ships before the rest of the German convoys fled in disorder without landing any men or equipment. The Royal Navy paid heavily for its successes: two cruisers, the *Fiji* and *Gloucester*, and two destroyers, the *Juno* and *Greyhound*, were

sunk by air attack, and other ships were badly damaged by wave after wave of German bombers.

By 24 May the air attacks were making it impossible for the Royal Navy to continue its patrols near Crete in daylight. Admiral Sir Andrew Cunningham, commanding the Mediterranean Fleet, could no longer guarantee the prevention of German seaborne landings. But Student was still faced with the problem of taking the airfield at Máleme. His orders were that the Gruppe 'West', commanded by Major-General Eugen Meindl, was to be concentrated to take Máleme, and that the 5th Mountain Division was to land and join the troops at Prison Valley in the Chania region: together they were to take Caneá and Suda on the western and eastern sides of the isthmus linking the Akrotiri peninsula to the rest of Crete. On 21 May, therefore, Student concentrated his forces at the perimeter of Máleme airfield, while Lieutenant-General Julius Ringel's mountain troops landed under heavy fire on the airfield itself. These troops managed to break out of Máleme and establish contact with the

THE FLOOD OF THE GERMAN TIDE

RIGHT: The British managed to evacuate most of their men as well as many Allies at the end of their defeat in Greece, but the undertaking was very costly to the Royal Navy, which lost many ships.

BELOW: Greek officers at the surrender of Greece. The Greeks fought with determination but were short of many essentials when faced by skilled opponents fielding the latest weapons.

destroyers. One aircraft carrier, three battleships, six cruisers and seven destroyers were also damaged to a greater or lesser degree. Yet for the Germans this was a Pyrrhic victory, for they had lost almost 7,000 men out of an invasion force of 22,000, with 200 aircraft destroyed. Invasion by air, on this scale, was still very much a novelty, and the results were awaited in Germany with keen interest. In the event, the scale of the losses, especially among the elite troops of the airborne arm, were so great that Hitler steadfastly refused to authorize any similar operation after this time. Thus plans for an airborne invasion of Malta were abandoned by Hitler in June 1942.

The Greek campaign had been largely a political gesture, undertaken by the British and commonwealth forces largely for political reasons, namely the desire of the British government to show that it was willing to support an ally, and so

help Turkey in its refusal of German blandishments. In overall terms, however, it had been a very costly 56 days, and the commitment to Greece had effectively prevented the British and commonwealth forces in North Africa from achieving a major strategic success.

OPERATION BARBAROSSA: THE GERMAN INVASION OF THE USSR

On 5 November 1937 Hitler revealed to his senior military commander and Joachim Ribbentrop, the foreign minister, that his long-term ambitions in Europe were the seizure of the *Lebensraum* needed for a greater German state, by force if necessary, for the requirements of the German people were paramount. In light of this decision, which involved all people of German ethnicity as well as German nationals, Hitler announced that between 1938 and 1943 both Austria and Czechoslovakia were to be taken, Poland was to be defeated and occupied and, finally, the USSR was to be invaded and conquered. Those present to hear Hitler's

WORLD WAR II

monumental plan were totally thunderstruck for, among other things, the German armed forces were completely unready for even the smallest part of this huge scheme, even allowing for the expansion that was continuing. The professional military men were also distressed by the fact that Hitler had wholly failed to take into account the probable intervention of France and the UK once the nature of Hitler's concept had become clear.

But despite their fears, Hitler's plans met with initial success, despite the intervention of France and the UK. By the end of 1940, of Hitler's targets only the USSR was left, the UK remaining steadfast in its refusal to accede to a German victory. It should be noted, however, that while the concept of *Lebensraum* was the avowed reason for the German expansion, and Germany's victories in 1939–40 were rich in resources, another less overtly stated factor in the German leader's thinking was his long-established hatred of Communism. In Hitler's mind, therefore, the defeat of the USSR would at one and the same time serve to spearhead what he believed to be the western world's inevitable crusade against the 'disease' of Communism, to lead to the destruction of the racially inferior Slavs by the superior Teutons, and to secure all of the

USSR's territory and resources for the benefit of the German people. Thus was Germany committed to the largest military undertaking of modern history, a huge and complex series of campaigns which would decide the outcome of World War II. For it was in the huge areas of the USSR's western reaches that Germany was to deploy the majority of its forces against a Soviet war machine that, after devastating military reserves in the second half of 1941 and first half of 1942, grew enormously in size and capability to the end of World War II in 1945.

Germany's approach to the war with the USSR reveals Hitler's political astuteness at its most effective. In 1939 he wished to have no distractions as he dealt with the rest of Europe, so a Russo-German Non-aggression Treaty was signed in Moscow on 23 August, confirming in its secret terms that the USSR was to invade Poland shortly after the Germans had launched their own campaign from the west, and take the eastern portion of the country. At the same time, Germany was to provide

USSR with technical assistance in return for raw materials and foodstuffs. With the possible threat to his east thus obviated, Hitler could then turn his undivided attention to the problems of France and the UK. Thus Germany was able to launch its attack to the west in April and May 1940 in the knowledge that there was no threat to its eastern borders. But throughout this time Hitler was nonetheless thinking of the great enemy that he must crush. His preoccupation with planning the defeat of the USSR was not evident during the Battle of Britain, though after the war it emerged that even if the Luftwaffe had succeeded in gaining air supremacy over the southern part of the UK, Hitler would probably not have ordered an invasion as he needed to husband his forces for the onslaught, even though this was finally delayed and weakened by the late decisions to secure Germany's southern flank by taking Yugoslavia and Greece. Yet even before the formal postponement (in fact abandonment) of the invasion of the UK, German land forces were being moved from north-

LEFT: The USSR was ruled with an iron hand by Iosef Stalin, a man in many ways as evil as Adolf Hitler, but whose ruthlessness and determination in the second half of 1941 helped to save the USSR from defeat by Germany.

BELOW: The Soviets had vast quantities of matériel in June 1941, but it was poorly maintained, badly used and, in the case of vehicles such as these T-26 light tanks, technically obsolete.

THE FLOOD OF THE GERMAN TIDE

summer and autumn before the onset of the terrible Russian winter. The plans developed all through the spring of 1941, the troops trained, and all that was necessary for the campaign was massed with the greatest secrecy along the frontier with the USSR. All was ready for the start except for one thing: the German armies knew what they had to achieve at the tactical and operational levels, but the high command was operating in something of a strategic void as it could not get Hitler to commit himself to a stop line. The German armies were thus condemned to surge forward eastward into European Russia, while the high command could only hope that the Soviets would capitulate after its major cities had been overrun. Hitler refused to entertain any consideration of the USSR's implacable determination to survive, and had fixed no final objective for his men. The nearest the Germans came to establishing a strategic goal was

ABOVE: Movement of heavy equipment by draft animals was still very much the norm in the first years of the war on the Eastern Front, and the pace of operations was determined largely by that of marching men and plodding animals.

RIGHT: Virtually the only wholly motorized or mechanized formations were the German armoured divisions, which undertook deep pincer movements to trap huge Soviet forces for destruction by the infantry moving slowly in the wake of the tanks.

west Europe across Germany and German-occupied Poland toward the new German-Soviet frontier created by the conquest of Poland. Although apparently only a minor issue at the time, the abandonment of the plan to invade the UK was, with the decision to attack the USSR, one of the two most important, and ultimately fatal, grand strategic decisions taken by Hitler, for it condemned Germany to a two-front war, something he had said he would never entertain.

Planning for Operation Barbarossa began in December 1940. Despite their shock at the audacity and sheer size of the task confronting them, German military planners worked with their accustomed professionalism to produce a variety of plans. These were examined and successively discarded, their best features worked into the definitive plan that slowly emerged. The date set for the start of the invasion was 5 May 1941, which would give the German armies a good campaigning season through the

press on to take Moscow. In the north, Field-Marshal Wilhelm Ritter von Leeb's Army Group North comprised the German 16th and 18th Armies as well as General Erich Höpner's 4th Panzergruppe (three Panzer and three infantry divisions), and was to drive through the Baltic states to take Leningrad, the spiritual home of Bolshevism. Farther north again, Finland, a co-belligerent rather than ally, was to commit its forces, under the command of Marshal von Mannerheim, to retake the Karelian isthmus and threaten Leningrad from the north, as well as driving toward Lake Onega to cut the Soviet rail communications with Murmansk in the far north. Here Colonel-General Nikolaus von Falkenhorst's Norway Army was to

LEFT: Expecting the 1941 campaign to be over before the onset of the Russian winter, the Germans were poorly equipped for winter campaigning and were forced to make use of every item of Soviet winter clothing they could seize.

BELOW: A PzKpfw III medium tank and supporting infantry in a blazing Soviet town.

the occasional mention of a vague line running from Arkhangyel'sk, on the White Sea in the north, to Astrakhan at the mouth of the Volga river on the Caspian Sea in the south. The Germans thus embarked on Barbarossa with the clear political goal of destroying the USSR and seizing its land and resources, but with a totally unclear military objective, which was to bedevil the efforts of the troops in the field.

Barbarossa was huge and bold. Three German army groups were to invade the USSR. In the south, Field-Marshal Gerd von Rundstedt's Army Group South comprised the German 6th, 11th and

17th Armies, the Romanian 3rd and 4th Armies, General Ewald von Kleist's 1st Panzergruppe (five Panzer and three infantry divisions) and two Hungarian divisions, and was to crush all the Soviet forces between the Black Sea and the Pripyet marshes. In the centre, Field-Marshal Fedor von Bock's Army Group Centre comprised the German 4th and 9th Armies together with General Heinz Guderian's 2nd Panzergruppe (five Panzer and four infantry divisions) and General Hermann Hoth's 3rd Panzergruppe (four Panzer and three infantry divisions), and was to advance on the Warsaw-Smolensk axis and then

ABOVE: The speed and distances covered in the first weeks of the German invasion of the USSR played havoc with the durability and reliability of the German armour, which was in a poor state by September 1941.

RIGHT: German troops start to cross the German-Soviet border on 22 June 1941 on a corduroy road typical of those used in the western part of European Russia at this time.

non-aggression treaty, Iosef Stalin had few illusions about Hitler's long-term plans. In the south was Marshal Semyon Budenny's South-West Front of six armies (52 infantry and 20 tank divisions) facing Army Group South. In the centre was Marshal Semyon Timoshenko's West Front of three armies (30 infantry and 8 tank divisions) facing Army Group Centre, and in the north was Colonel-General F.I. Kuznetsov's (soon Marshal Klimenti Voroshilov's) North-West Front of two armies (20 infantry and 4 tank divisions) facing Army Group North. In the far north, facing the Finns and the Germans, were three Soviet armies. The Soviets also had some 3 million men, with another million in garrisons throughout the rest of the USSR. Once the war had started, mobilization began to increase this number rapidly. The main trouble with the Soviet forces, however, was quality rather than quantity, for Stalin's purges of the mid and later 1930s had robbed the armed forces of most of their best commanders. The Soviet soldier was adequately trained in the basics and very durable, but lacked initiative and had weapons inferior to

those of the Germans. The two most notable exceptions to this last were the artillery and the new T-34 medium tank. The inferiority of Soviet weapons was most notable in the Soviet air forces, whose sole world-beater at this time was the Ilyushin Il-2 ground-attack warplane, available as yet in only small numbers, and the prototypes of a number of other advanced warplanes. The Soviet forces were massed along the frontier rather than deployed in depth, which greatly helped the German pincer tactics, the standard Soviet tactics calling for attacks after large numbers of troops had been massed, which made it all but impossible for the Soviet troops to counter the German armoured pincer movements.

With preparations on the German side almost complete, there occurred an episode typical of Hitler and which completely jeopardized Barbarossa. This was Hitler's decision that Yugoslavia and Greece would have to be subjugated before the invasion of the USSR was committed, with the result that Barbarossa forces were bled of the resources to defeat these two nations. This also meant that Barbarossa itself

drive toward Murmansk. In all, the German plan envisaged the advance of some 3 million men, of whom 250,000 had been provided by satellite countries, in 162 divisions along a 2,000-mile (3200-km) front. As usual, the major tactical scheme to be used was the now-standard pincer movement, in which the armour broke through and then closed behind the enemy's main forces, trapping them and then pressing forward, while the trapped forces were mopped up by the slower-moving infantry which, like the bulk of the artillery and logistic forces, still relied heavily on horses. Four months were considered sufficient for this huge undertaking.

The Soviets were heavily deployed along the same frontier, for despite the

resistance serving a purpose in slowing the German advance.

One of the major problems faced by the Germans was the complete disparity in the speeds of their various forces: the logistic support for the mechanized forces was very much faster than that for the infantry, the latter slowed by the plodding speed at which the huge number of horses could bring up food, ammunition and other vital supplies. The problem was partially solved by allowing the armoured forces to press on as spearheads, leaving the infantry to mop up, but the determination of the Soviet pockets further delayed the infantry, leading to dissension in the German camp as the gaps between the armour and the infantry lengthened. Convinced of the all-important factor of speed, the Panzer

LEFT: A Soviet officer briefs his men.

BELOW: Men of the 2nd SS Infantry Division Das Reich move through a burning Soviet village during the summer of 1941. Later a Panzergrenadier and finally a Panzer division, 'Das Reich' was one of 38 Waffen-SS divisions to see service in World War II, gaining a reputation for superb fighting qualities but also notoriety for its savagery and war crimes.

had to be postponed by five weeks, a delay that cut into the already short campaigning season, with disastrous results, the start of Barbarossa now being scheduled for 22 June 1941.

Prefaced by the standard artillery and air bombardments of the Soviet front-line ground and air forces, the German armies headed east at 03.00. At the tactical level surprise was total, and nowhere did the Germans encounter anything but the most limited opposition as they broke through what was in effect a cordon defence. Soviet warplanes were caught on the ground and destroyed in huge numbers by the Luftwaffe's fighters and bombers, while the modest numbers which managed to get into the air were easily destroyed by German pilots with far greater operational experience, flying qualitatively better aircraft. On the ground, most of the Soviet forces were caught completely unawares by the speed and power of the German advance and were quickly overrun or bypassed. The Soviet forces, cut off in groups of up to an army in size, were contained by the German infantry and then destroyed. Hopeless though their prospects were, most of these Soviet pockets fought with great courage and determination, their

commanders wished to press on regardless of the infantry, but the army group commanders, almost all of them infantry, artillery, cavalry and engineer officers by training, often tried to prevent this from happening. Inevitably, the marching infantry's lack of speed slowed the rate of overall advance, although it was still very rapid by the standards of the time.

Understandably, the Soviets were in total disarray. Had it not been for the extraordinary perseverance of the mass of Soviet soldiers and the implacable resolution of the Soviet dictator, Iosef Stalin, it is conceivable that the Soviet armed forces might have been dissolved. But these two factors just about held the Soviet armies together. Appalling as the losses were, Stalin was prepared to sacrifice almost any number of men to

slow the German advance, for he appreciated the overriding need to dismantle the USSR's most important industrial facilities along the Germans' axes of advance, removing them to new sites beyond the Ural mountains. It is impossible to give a succinct idea of the efforts made by the Soviet men and women, from the very young to the ancient, to save the industrial plant on which, ultimately, the survival of their nation depended. Yet most of it was saved, and that which proved impossible to remove was destroyed to prevent it from falling into enemy hands. It was a national effort which ultimately saved the USSR, with lives being sacrificed in their hundreds of thousands to accomplish this task. Faced with the possible destruction of his country and his political philosophy, Stalin displayed no element of humanity at this time: commanders were shot or replaced wholesale, and losses were deemed acceptable being the price of slowing the German advance.

Although Stalin was successful in this, the German progress was nonetheless remarkable, especially that of Army Group Centre, with its two

its one real chance of taking Moscow easily and in good time.

In the south, by 21 August, the German forces had almost reached Kiev, the main city of Ukraine. With the aid of Guderian's armour coming down from the north past the eastern side of the Pripyet marshes, Kiev was now turned into an enormous pocket. When the city finally fell on 20 September, some 665,000 Soviet troops fell with it in the pocket just to the east. While this

LEFT: The crew of a German 0.79-in (20-mm cannon) wait for a target of opportunity as German infantry push forward around it.

BELOW: A German soldier searches a Soviet prisoner.

Panzergruppen. By the middle of July the 2nd and 3rd Panzergruppen had closed the trapdoor on a huge Soviet pocket to the west of Minsk, and once the slower forces had arrived to seal it off, the armour was then able to advance once more. But the Soviet losses in this early stage of the campaign were so great as to be almost incomprehensible: at Minsk, for example, the Soviets lost around 330,000 men, 2,500 tanks and 1,500 pieces of artillery, although there is still no complete agreement as to the accuracy of these numbers. By 5 August Army Group Centre, again in the form of its two Panzergruppen, had trapped 310,000 Soviets, 3,200 tanks and 3,000 pieces of artillery at Smolensk. Army Group Centre was thus only some 200 miles (320km) west of Moscow by this time, with virtually nothing to block its advance. Although making adequate progress to its north and south, Army Groups North and South were facing problems not experienced by Army Group Centre, being opposed by high-quality Soviet forces in a vast and difficult terrain, while Army Group South was suffering from a lack of adequate armoured forces for the task in

hand. For as the German forces advanced to the east, the 2,000-mile (3200-km) front on which they had started out was gradually widening, leaving the Germans with little alternative but to thin the troops at the front so as to be able to cover it completely. At the same time, the great length of the advance made supply increasingly difficult, especially as men, machines and horses were becoming rapidly exhausted by the heat and dust of the Soviet summer, and by the very distances involved. Inevitably, the lack of depth in the German army, whose rapid expansion had emphasized the creation of 'tooth' at the expense of 'tail' elements, began to exert a major effect.

At this time Hitler stepped in, and the lack of proper strategic planning immediately became clear: the 2nd Panzergruppe and the 2nd Army were detached to aid Army Group South, while the 3rd Panzergruppe was similarly detached to aid Army Group North. Although the short-term results of this alteration in emphasis helped the two flanking armies to catch up with Army Group Centre, the long-term result was that the central force missed was happening, General Erich von Manstein's 11th Army had been making good progress down the Yuzhni Bug river toward Crimea.

In the north, Hoth's forces had also enabled Army Group North to speed its advance, and real progress was being made in the direction of Leningrad. Although much of the momentum of the early days had been lost, October found the Germans handily placed: von Leeb was able to take Leningrad under siege in October, von Bock was still pushing on from Smolensk with his infantry, and von Rundstedt reached the Don river on 15 October, posing a threat to the major industrial cities of Kharkov and Rostov. Only in the Finnish theatre was progress slower and more limited. The Finns were content just to retake the portions of Finland lost in the 'Winter War', and von Falkenhorst's army in the far north was bogged down in very difficult terrain far short of its target.

In the air, the Luftwaffe continued to dominate, having destroyed more than 4,500 first-line Soviet aircraft for the loss of less than 2,000 of its own machines. But in the rear areas the problems of the Germans were increasing: units which could have been used to good effect at the front now had to be detached to guard the lines of communication against the growing threat of Soviet partisan groups. But worst of all, the weather was beginning to break. The autumn rains had begun, turning the unmetalled Russian roads to mud and further hampering the German advance in a foretaste of the freezing winter that was still to come. The Germans were running out of time, and the delay occasioned by the Balkan excursion of April was now having its effect.

Now Hitler changed his mind once more. Moscow once again became the primary objective, and von Bock was given back the land and air forces lent to von Leeb and von Rundstedt. Army Group Centre was thus able to accelerate its progress, and between 30 September

and 7 October created yet another great Soviet pocket, this time just to the west of Vyazma, where the haul was more than 650,000 men. A little under a fortnight later, the leading elements of Army Group Centre reached Mozhaisk, only 40 miles (65km) from Moscow. On the map, the German position seemed to be good, but at the front it was rather poor, for all formations were down to less than 50 per cent strength in men and machines, and the change in the weather had caught the Germans totally unprepared. As it was expected that the campaign would be over before the arrival of winter, no preparation had been made to provide the troops with winter combat clothing. Moreover, at the beginning of November, front-line German formations had begun to detect the arrival of fresh Soviet reserves, just at the time when they themselves were approaching the limits of their endurance. At the same time, the Soviets had reorganized their command structure. Budenny had been replaced as commander-in-chief of the South-West Front by Timoshenko, whose place as head of the West Front had been taken by the greatest soldier the USSR was to produce in World War II, General Georgi Zhukov. Under Zhukov's driving force, the defences before Moscow were strengthened, and try as they might during November and December, the Germans were unable to break through, leading to desperate fighting in appalling winter conditions.

Timoshenko's arrival in the south strengthened the Soviet resistance there, and on 15 November the Germans were driven out of Rostov-na-Donu, where the Don river debouches into the Sea of Azov, in this, the first major German reverse of the Soviet campaign. The German command structure was also altered at this time: by 5 December Field-Marshal Walther von Reichenau had replaced von Rundstedt, and Field-Marshal Günther-Hans von Kluge had succeeded von Bock. By this date the

temperature had fallen far below freezing point, the only winter clothing available being that which had been stripped from the Soviet dead and prisoners; the German armies had reached the limit of their endurance, with the result that they paused, exhausted, a mere 25 miles (40km) from Moscow.

Then the Soviets struck back. Fresh troops, arriving from Siberia and thus used to the cold and equipped for it, were carefully marshalled by Zhukov and unleashed in a great counter-offensive around Moscow. The German generals called for a strategic retreat in the face of this Soviet attack, but Hitler absolutely forbade any such move. Quite extraordinarily, the Germans were able to hold their position at a moment when any withdrawal might have turned into a rout. Up to the end of the year, the great Soviet offensives around Moscow, and near Izyum in Crimea, slowly drove the Germans back, finally dashing any hopes of defeating the USSR in one devastating round. Hitler's decision to hold Moscow was typical of the German dictator, and within the context of the battle for it was a brilliant piece of insight. Unfortunately for the Germans, however, it further reinforced Hitler's high opinion of himself as a military genius, and also served to convince him of the basic correctness of holding ground regardless of the cost in men and matériel. This latter conviction was to cause the German army enormous and needless losses in the years to come in what was known to the Soviets as the 'Great Patriotic War' and to the western world as the Eastern Front of World War II.

The final results of the campaign infuriated Hitler, and he completely reshuffled his high command to make himself the actual as well as titular head of the German armed forces. Field-Marshal Walther von Brauchitsch lost his job as commander-in-chief of the army, and Hitler also took over as head both of the Oberkommando des Heeres (OKH, or army high command), with General

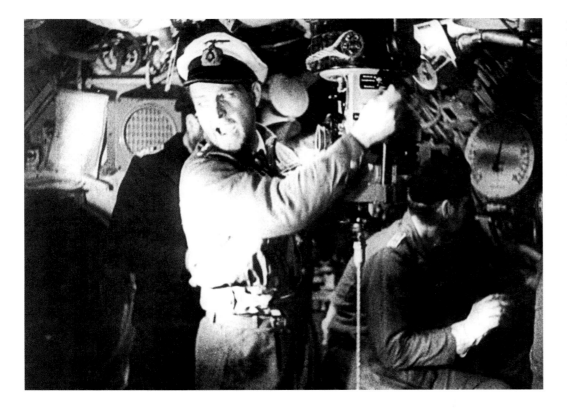

important declaration of sympathy by exchanging 50 old destroyers in exchange for a 99-year lease of British bases around the world. These destroyers were fit only for second-line duties, but made it possible for newer destroyers to be released for fleet work; many of the old 'four-stack' destroyers were still in service at the end of the war.

Coastal escorts and air patrols proved moderately successful against the U-boats, so forcing them to venture into the Western Approaches in search of targets. Here the new U-boat bases in the Bay of Biscay gave the Germans an important advantage, and the British were hard- pressed to extend cover to convoys deeper in the Atlantic. But Iceland had been occupied in July 1940 by British and Canadian troops to

LEFT: The commander of a U-boat at the periscope of his command. Despite the high percentage of losses it suffered, the U-boat arm never had any real difficulty in attracting the men to operate its boats, and morale remained high until the very end.

BELOW: U-boats left for Atlantic patrols with every nook and cranny stuffed with supplies in an effort to extend their patrol endurances. This is the 'Type IXB'-class boat U-123 taking on supplies.

Franz Halder as its chief-of-staff, and of the Oberkommando der Wehrmacht (OKW, or armed forces high command), with Field-Marshal Wilhelm Keitel as its chief-of-staff. The OKH ran the war on the Eastern Front and the OKW that on other fronts. Among other field commanders replaced were von Leeb and Höpner. Although they failed, and their failures cost them the war, the Germans had performed a prodigious feat in purely military terms. But so too had the Soviets. The Germans had lost some 800,000 men, most of them difficult to replace veterans, while the Soviets had suffered some 1.5 million men killed and somewhat more than 2 million taken prisoner, as well as millions of civilian dead. Yet in the long term, Stalin's policy proved strategically sound, in that it saved the USSR's most important war-making industries.

THE BATTLE OF THE ATLANTIC 1940–41

As the threat of a German invasion of southern England receded, the Royal Navy was able to concentrate once more on the problem of the Atlantic convoys. In September 1940, the USA made an

The worst problem for many convoy escorts was their lack of endurance. Destroyers were designed for high-speed attack, with slender hulls unsuited to North Atlantic weather, and their turbines were not economical. Many of the older destroyers were turned into long-range escorts by replacing one of the boilers with additional bunkerage, and the first of these was taken in hand in January 1941. The corvettes, which were now coming into service in large numbers from British and Canadian shipyards, had good endurance but lacked speed. This was inevitable, for the design had been framed to make the best use of available machinery, but by 1941 U-boats had taken to attacking convoys on the surface at night, and at top speed were capable of out-distancing a corvette. Another problem was that convoy work demanded a great deal of loitering to investigate a suspected underwater contact, or high-speed dashes to find stragglers before herding them back to the convoy.

The answer was the creation of a fully optimized North Atlantic escort, possessing both long endurance and moderately high speed and carrying all the weapons and sensors needed for the anti-submarine task. The answer to the need was the 'River'-class frigate, which had twice the power of the corvette and ample space for the weapons and sensors required. Unfortunately, none

ABOVE: A resource always in short supply on a U-boat was fresh water, and things that went by the board were often washing and shaving on more than an occasional basis, as revealed by these U-boat men.

RIGHT: With Malta too dangerous for use as a main fleet base in the Mediterranean, the British operated the Mediterranean Fleet from Alexandria and the smaller but still very potent Force H (illustrated) from Gibraltar.

prevent a possible German occupation, and the island provided airfields and a refuelling base which partly offset the U-boats' advantage.

Throughout 1941 the USA was benevolent in its neutrality, for President Franklin D. Roosevelt knew that US interests would not benefit from a German victory over the UK. In March 1941, the Lend-Lease Act was enacted, allowing more ships and equipment to be provided. In April the USA declared that its defence zone, in which US merchant ships were escorted by US Navy warships, would be extended to 26° West, regardless of whether they were carrying war matériel to the UK or not.

Canadian warships would similarly be allowed to escort US ships. The US Navy was already handing over its escorted ships to Anglo-Canadian escorts at a predetermined Mid-Ocean Meeting Point, but in August 1941 this so-called 'Chop Line' was moved to 22° 58' West to relieve the strain on British escorts.

While all this was happening on the convoy routes, the German navy was planning a bold stroke. The battleship *Bismarck* was ready for sea in the spring of 1941, in the hope that it would be sent into the Atlantic with the heavy cruiser *Prinz Eugen*, to attack convoys which could disrupt the whole delicate organization, even for a short time, and allow the U-boats to slaughter unescorted ships. A further aim was to effect a junction with the battle-cruisers *Scharnhorst* and *Gneisenau*, which were at Brest. The prospect of three Nazi capital ships at large in the Atlantic

LEFT: The UK was dependent on its maritime lines of communications for its food, oil and raw materials, so the loss of every merchant ship was a blow both for inward deliveries and outward exports, as well as reinforcements, weapons and supplies to its force in Africa, the Middle East and the Far East.

BELOW: The German battleship, Bismarck, is caught by the camera in the North Sea during 1941. This great ship was hunted down and sunk in May of that year in the North Atlantic.

was ready until early in 1942, but existing escorts were given as much new equipment as possible to help them fight back in the meantime. In May 1941, the first surface warning radar set went to sea in a corvette. Although the Asdic detection device was very effective in locating submerged U-boats, it had a weakness in that contact was lost during the final stages of a depth-charge attack. To remedy this, a new ahead-firing weapon had to be developed, which promised to increase the rate of 'kills'. The resulting Hedgehog was a multiple spigot mortar, firing small contact-fused bombs in a pattern, the first ship being equipped with it by the end of 1941.

All these countermeasures were needed as a matter of the greatest urgency, for 1941 was a critical year, with shipping losses increasing rapidly and ever-increasing numbers of U-boats coming into service. From a total of 755,000 tons in 1939, shipping losses rose to 3.991 million tons, or 1,000 ships, in 1940. And despite rising output from the shipyards and ever-increasing skill in anti-submarine tactics, the total rose to 1,300 ships, or 4.328 million tons, in 1941. Losses at this rate were unsustainable over the long term, and in August 1941, at the 'Atlantic Charter'

meeting, the USA agreed that its warships would henceforward be permitted to escort all merchant ships irrespective of nationality, while

appalled the British, who were therefore prepared to do anything to prevent the break-out of the *Bismarck*.

On 21 May 1941 the *Bismarck* and *Prinz Eugen* sailed from Bergen, heading for the Denmark Strait between Greenland and Iceland on their way to the Atlantic shipping routes. Their departure was reported to the Admiralty and two days later they were sighted by a pair of British cruisers patrolling in the Denmark Strait. The old British battle-cruiser *Hood*, and the new battleship, *Prince of Wales*, had been in Iceland, so they were able to intercept the German ships on the morning of the following day. The British seemed about to frustrate the German plans, but then the *Hood* blew up after firing only three salvoes, apparently as a result of a fire caused by a German shell. Although the *Prince of Wales* was only slightly damaged it was so new that half its guns were not firing, and the admiral commanding the cruisers ordered her captain to break off the action. For

ABOVE: The German light cruiser, Karlsruhe, *was sunk off Norway on 9 April 1940, while ferrying men for the landing at Kristiansand in southern Norway.*

RIGHT: The battleship King George V *was one of Britain's capital ships involved in the search for the* Bismarck *during May 1941.*

Bismarck's gunnery was wild and the German ship failed to score a hit on either ship, apart from a single medium-calibre shell which failed to detonate. Under a hail of fire the Bismarck rapidly became a flaming hulk, and her guns were silent in half an hour. The ship lay so low in the water that the British shells were having no real effect, and after another hour of gunfire the British commander, Admiral Sir John Tovey, ordered the cruiser Dorsetshire to sink the Bismarck with torpedoes. The Bismarck's career had lasted for three days, and there were but 110 survivors.

The Germans had placed too much faith in the Bismarck's ability to withstand attack. The ship should have returned to Germany after the damage suffered to its fuel tanks, caused by the Prince of Wales, and might well have eluded the Home Fleet in the poor visibility that prevailed. Instead, Lütjens opted to continue the Atlantic sortie with what amounted to major battle damage, and was later forced to make for Brest for lack of fuel. The German

FAR LEFT: Admiral Karl Dönitz began World War II as the commodore commanding the U-boat arm, and ended it as a grand admiral as commander-in-chief of the German navy, and second and final leader of the Third Reich in succession to Adolf Hitler.

ABOVE: Fairey Swordfish torpedo bombers on the flight deck of the British aircraft carrier Victorious. *The ship was commissioned in May 1941, serving with distinction until well beyond the end of World War II.*

two days the whereabouts of the German ships was unknown, but eventually massive air and sea searches located the Bismarck, the Prinz Eugen having already been detached to Brest. The aircraft carrier Ark Royal was able to launch a torpedo-bomber strike, and two torpedoes damaged the battleship's

steering gear; by nightfall on 26 May Vice-Admiral Günther Lütjens knew that his ship was doomed.

On the following morning the Home Fleet battleships Rodney and King George V approached the Bismarck and opened fire at the modest range of 16,000 yards (14630m). This time the

navy had often been accused of tactical timidity, but on this occasion it showed a degree of foolhardiness that is difficult to understand.

With the destruction of the *Bismarck*, the German navy virtually abandoned all idea of using its surface fleet aggressively. Certainly it was never the same threat to the Atlantic convoys again, Hitler admitting as much early the following year when he ordered the *Scharnhorst*, *Gneisenau* and *Prinz Eugen* back to Germany. The *Bismarck*'s sister ship, the *Tirpitz*, was completed late in 1941, but also spent a largely inactive career in Norwegian waters, content to tie down British ships by the mere threat of its presence rather than by making any determined attack.

By the end of 1941 the Battle of the Atlantic had become nothing more than a grim struggle of attrition. The entry of the USA into the war was only a matter of time, but Admiral Karl Dönitz tried to keep his U-boats from precipitating hostilities. Between September and December 1941 a series of incidents, including the torpedoing of three American destroyers off Iceland, strained relations to breaking point, but still the spirit of isolationism was strong enough to keep the USA from declaring war on Germany. In December 1941 the impasse was finally resolved by the Japanese attack on Pearl Harbor, followed by Hitler's monumentally foolish and unnecessary declaration of war on the USA. The American entry into the war marked the end of the first phase of the Battle of the Atlantic, though in fact its grimmest part was yet to come.

ABOVE: One of the Royal Navy's most impressive warships, the updated battle-cruiser Hood *was fast and powerfully armed, but succumbed to the plunging long-range fire of the* Bismarck *on 24 May 1941.*

RIGHT: The Bismarck *in action against the* Hood. *The German long-range gunnery was, as always, excellent in terms of accuracy and rate of fire.*

CHAPTER TWO

THE ALLIES FIGHT BACK
East Africa & the Middle East

In addition to Libya, the Italian empire in Africa included Eritrea, Italian Somaliland and Abyssinia (Ethiopia). In the last, under the command of the Italian viceroy, the Duke of Aosta, were 250,000 troops, of whom 90,000 were metropolitan Italians. But these forces had only 24 medium and 39 light tanks, and the Italian air force's component in this theatre was only 34 Fiat CR.42 biplane fighters, which were outclassed by the Royal Air Force's Gloster Gladiator biplane and Hawker Hurricane monoplane fighters. The Italians were also short of artillery, ammunition, fuel and basic foodstuffs.

General Sir Archibald Wavell, the British commander in the Middle East, considered the Italian forces to be a threat to the British in Kenya to the

south and in Sudan to the west, the Italians having taken Kassala, Gallabat and Kurmak in Sudan, and the Moyale salient in Kenya in July 1940. Wavell also believed the Italians could be defeated by an internal revolution of Abyssinian patriots, with the help of Allied forces, and that the deposed Emperor Haile Selassie might be restored to his throne. Major Orde Wingate, in Khartoum, in his capacity as commander of Haile Selassie's forces and the emperor's military adviser, had been entrusted with the task of organizing, as irregular forces, the thousands of Abyssinian refugees in Kenya and Sudan.

Meanwhile, the British and commonwealth forces in Kenya and Sudan were adopting an aggressive defensive posture, although the Indian

5th Division failed to retake Gallabat in Sudan during November 1940.

Wavell organized the forces available to him into two commands, excluding those of Wingate. An expeditionary force comprising the Indian 4th and 5th Divisions was to attack from Sudan toward Eritrea under the command of Lieutenant-General William Platt, while Lieutenant-General Alan Cunningham's force in Kenya comprised the 11th and 12th African Divisions, plus the South African 1st Division. The Duke of Aosta appreciated that his forces faced a triple British and commonwealth attack, disposing his forces accordingly: Lieutenant-General Luigi Frusci defended Eritrea with three colonial divisions and three brigades; Lieutenant-General Guglielmo Nasi was to stop Wingate with four colonial brigades; and Major-General Carlo de Simone had the task of defending southern Abyssinia

ABOVE: Bersaglieri (fast-marching light infantry) of the Italian army in North Africa.

LEFT: Italian soldiers bid farewell to their families before embarking for the sea voyage to East Africa before Italy entered the war in June 1940 and, as it turned out, a wholly uncertain future.

of hard fighting, the Italians withdrew yet again, this time to the formidable Keren escarpment, where they re-formed on 1 February. Here, the Italians made a vigorous stand, and the 1st Battle of Keren was an Italian victory. Platt then mounted a full-scale offensive, backed by bomber and ground-attack aircraft in the 2nd Battle of Keren. Although the Italians employed their reserve divisions, Keren fell on 27 March and the British were able to reach Asmara, in Eritrea, on 1 April, before pushing on to Massawa on the southern coast of the Red Sea by 8 April.

Cunningham, meanwhile, launched Operation Canvas, which achieved its objective, the port of Kismayu in Italian Somaliland, on 14 February. The next obstacle was the Juba river, and here Cunningham found a weak spot in de Simone's defences, pushing his forces across in two places as de Simone's forces began to disintegrate. On 22 February Jelib was cleared and the southern door to Abyssinia was open. Cunningham's forces drove on, reaching Mogadishu, the capital of Italian Somaliland, on 25 February, and entering Addis Ababa on

ABOVE: Italian and native troops in East Africa.

RIGHT: An Indian soldier belonging to a camel patrol in East Africa.

and Italian Somaliland with ten colonial brigades. In addition, each general had a variable number of irregular native forces, and two Italian formations, the Savoia and Africa Divisions, which were held in general reserve.

On 18 January the Italians abandoned their forward positions at Kassala and Gallabat, and fell back to Agordat and Barentu in Eritrea, and to Chilga in Abyssinia. Platt committed his offensive from Sudan on 19 January 1941. The German defeat at Sidi Barrani had demoralized the Italians, and the Indian forces were able to make some headway. The Italians retreated from the Sudanese-Abyssinian frontier, where they considered the ground too flat to resist a British mechanized attack. Platt advanced quickly, reaching the Italian positions on 25 January. After five days

6 April after a triumphant drive. Cunningham continued north to meet Platt, on his way down from Asmara.

Wingate's Gideon Force came east from Khartoum, making for Jebel Belaia, its supply train including 15,000 camels. Haile Selassie accompanied Wingate, and many local chiefs joined their emperor as they marched. The Italians thought the Gideon Force was larger than it was, and withdrew to Burye and Debra Markos on the road to Addis Ababa. The Gideon Force advanced to Burye, where a force of 7,000 under Colonel Natale fell to Wingate's 450. Supported by the Royal Air Force, Wingate's raids combined audacity, endurance and deception. Now demoralized, the Italians withdrew, losing another 2,000 men in the process, to Debra Markos, where Nasi was in

ABOVE LEFT: Italian and native troops welcome a party of German volunteers in East Africa during 1940.

ABOVE: Italian troops in Abyssinia, the kingdom they captured in 1935–36 in the face of almost universal condemnation but no practical opposition.

LEFT: Indian troops in Eritrea.

ABOVE: Abyssinian soldiers were notable for their courage and endurance.

ABOVE RIGHT: Mk VI light tanks, such as these, were useful in the particular conditions prevalent in East Africa.

RIGHT: Indian soldiers in a Universal (or Bren-gun) Carrier.

command. Wingate continued his well-planned raids, and Abyssinian deserters joined the Gideon Force at the rate of over 100 per day. On 1 April the Italians withdrew up the valley of the Blue Nile to join other forces at Dessie.

Italian rule in Abyssinia had now collapsed. The Duke of Aosta left Addis Ababa to Haile Selassie and sought refuge in the Amba Alagi heights. Platt and Cunningham arrived in the foothills and, caught between these forces, Aosta had little chance as his forces were also short of water and ammunition and subject to heavy air bombardment. He surrendered with 7,000 men on 16 May. Longer resistance was put up by Nasi, who eventually surrendered in the Gondar area on 27 November.

Other British forces had crossed from Aden on 16 March to retake Berbera, the capital of British Somaliland, which had earlier been taken by the Italians. These forces cleared the Italians out of British Somaliland before linking with Cunningham's forces.

At the end of March 1941 the pro-British regent of Iraq was toppled by the Axis-supported prime minister, Rashid Ali, backed by an army mutiny. British-Iraqi relations deteriorated rapidly and when the British sent elements of the Indian 10th Division to Iraq, Rashid Ali decided to challenge the British, choosing to attack the RAF training school at Habbaniyah, on the Euphrates river west of Baghdad, and Iraqi troops moved to positions overlooking the airfield on 29 April. The British were worried as they had important oil interests in the area, and feared that the rebels might sever the oil pipeline between the Kirkuk oilfields and Haifa on the coast of Palestine. On 30 April the Iraqis demanded the end of flying operations from Habbaniyah and that the British personnel should be restricted to the base. The RAF commander, Air Vice-Marshal Smart, replied that any interference with flying would be regarded as an act of war.

As the diplomats sought a solution, Iraqi forces laid siege to Habbaniyah. Smart prepared defences round the 7-mile (11-km) perimeter with 1,000 RAF personnel, 1,200 locally raised levies and as many of the 9,000 civilians on the station as were willing to help. Three hundred men from the Indian brigade at Basra were flown in, and eight Vickers Wellington twin-engined bombers arrived from Egypt. The British ambassador demanded the withdrawal of the Iraqi troops, and Smart was ordered to attack his besiegers when Rashid Ali refused to comply.

Before dawn on 2 May all 33 available aircraft, plus the eight Wellingtons, took off to pound the Iraqi positions. The Iraqis replied with artillery fire but were unable to hit Habbaniyah's power station or water tower. Some 200 sorties were flown on this first day of overt hostilities, and the British maintained the pressure until 5 May. On 6 May a foot patrol found that the Iraqis had abandoned their positions, and it was soon established that they had withdrawn in two directions: to the east, they had blocked the road to Baghdad at Fallujah at the point it crossed the Euphrates; and to the west they had deployed at Ramadi, where the Rutbah road passed between the Salt Lakes and the Euphrates.

The British sent in the hastily assembled Habforce, drawn from the 1st Cavalry Division in Palestine. This force crossed into Iraq on 13 May, moved east across the desert in very high temperatures, where they found the approach to Habbaniyah flooded by the Euphrates. It was additionally harassed by German aircraft flying in Iraqi

colours. The Germans now found themselves obliged to airlift supplies to Iraq as the Axis powers had to help Rashid Ali in order to maintain Arab goodwill. Not until 23 May, however, did Hitler order a military mission to Baghdad, but by then he was too late: as the RAF bombed targets throughout

TOP: Bristol Blenheim Mk IV bombers, though obsolete by that time, remained useful in the North African and Middle Eastern theatres of war.

ABOVE: Halifax bombers proved useful in the bombing of German garrisons in the Dodecanese islands.

THE ALLIES FIGHT BACK

The French fleet's main base in North Africa was Mers-el-Kébir, near Oran in Algeria, and it were here that the fast battleships, Dunkerque *and* Strasbourg, *armed with 13-in (330-mm) guns, were based after the fall of France.*

Iraq, political opinion was beginning to swing away from Rashid Ali. Colonel Ouvry Roberts, commanding the British and commonwealth land forces, seized the Fallujah bridge on 19 May, thus opening the road to Baghdad for Habforce. Rashid Ali fled to Persia, and on 3 May the pro-British regent returned to Baghdad.

Farther to the west, suspecting that Hitler might also have designs on Lebanon and Syria, which was still held by the Vichy French, the British decided to act first. An expeditionary force, led by Lieutenant-General Sir Henry Maitland Wilson, and comprising the Australian 7th Division, British 1st Cavalry Division, Indian 5th Brigade Group and the Free French Legentilhomme Brigade, entered Syria on 8 June. This force had no tanks and few armoured cars, while General Henri Dentz, the Vichy French commander in Syria, had two divisions.

The Australians crossed the frontier from Palestine in two thrusts: one up the road from Acre to Beirut and the other up the Litani valley toward Rayak. Further inland, on the desert flank, the Indian 5th Brigade advanced ahead of the Free French toward Damascus. The Vichy French put up spirited resistance, being extremely bitter that the Free French brigade should have been used against them. The Syrian campaign lasted for five weeks. Vichy French resistance meant that the British had to send reinforcements, and two brigades of the British 6th Division were diverted to Syria from the Nile delta. Damascus fell to the Allies on 21 June. After Operation Battleaxe in the Western Desert, aircraft were sent to Syria, promptly neutralizing the Vichy French air force which had been harassing the Allied advance.

On 23 June, Wilson called for an all-out offensive against Dentz, using four forces. The Australian division was to continue its northerly thrust up the coast toward Beirut, and would now have the support of the Royal Navy; the British

6th Division would cross the mountains from Damascus to threaten Beirut from the east; Habforce from Iraq was to advance on Palmyra and Horns, and Major-General W. J. Slim's Indian 10th Division was to advance from Basra, up the lines of the Euphrates and the railway connecting Baghdad and Aleppo into northern Syria.

The 6th Division's advance from Damascus made little progress in terrain ideally suited to defence and against stout resistance. Habforce was gallantly resisted by a small Foreign Legion garrison at Palmyra, which did not capitulate until 13 July. The Indian 10th Division was hampered by logistical difficulties, but made progress to take Deir-ez-Zor on the Euphrates and then, on 3 July, Tel Kotchek. Next, it advanced towards Aleppo. On the coast, the Australians broke through Dentz's main defensive position on the Damur river covering Beirut, but it took five days of fierce fighting with the support of 60 field guns ashore and five cruisers and eight destroyers off the coast, in addition to heavy air bombardment. Dentz was not reinforced, and lost 6,500 men, most of his aircraft, a destroyer and a submarine. He requested an armistice on 11 July and the surrender agreement was signed at Acre on 14 July. All Frenchmen were given the chance of joining de Gaulle and the Free French, but out of 38,000 only 5,700 did so.

Syria and Lebanon settled down to an uneasy peace under British military occupation and Free French political control, now that the UK's northern flank in the Middle East was secure against German infiltration.

NAVAL WAR IN THE MEDITERRANEAN

The defeat of France in June 1940 completely altered the naval balance of power in the Mediterranean, for the Royal Navy now had to operate in this sea without French support. It was outnumbered by Italy's navy, whose North African colonies provided air

bases south of the main British supply route through the central Mediterranean to complement those to their north in Italy, Sicily and Sardinia. The British were determined to hold the Suez Canal and to prevent the Axis powers from reaching the Middle Eastern oilfields: the common strategic weakness of both Italy and Germany was their lack of oil.

Fear that Mussolini and Hitler would be unable to resist the temptation to seize the remnants of the French navy, much of which had steamed to North African ports at the time of the French armistice in June 1940, led the British to take drastic action. When the French rejected a British ultimatum to put their ships out of all possible reach of the Axis powers, the British, on 3 July 1940, attempted to destroy the French ships in their harbour at Mers-el-Kébir in Algeria. The price to pay was French enmity, but at least the Italian navy now had no chance of suddenly doubling its strength.

It had been decided, right from the start of hostilities with Italy, that despite its proximity to Italian air bases and its lack of defences, the island of Malta was indispensable to the Royal Navy if the central Mediterranean was to be controlled. Malta possessed airfields and a large dockyard, which meant that it could act as a forward base for naval and aerial attack forces operating against the Italian convoy route linking Italy and its

ABOVE LEFT: The commander-in-chief of the Mediterranean Fleet through much of its most important service in World War II was Admiral Sir Andrew Cunningham.

ABOVE: The main base of the Italian navy at Taranto, in southern Italy, was the location of an epoch-making British victory, when carrierborne aircraft attacked the battleships and cruisers in the harbour on 11 November 1940.

LEFT: The Italian heavy cruiser, Pola, under British air attack. With her two sisters, the Pola was blasted by the fire of British battleships in the Battle of Cape Matapan on 28 March 1941.

commander in the shape of Admiral Sir Andrew Cunningham. Their first shock came at the Battle of Calabria on 9 July 1940, when Cunningham's flagship, the battleship *Warspite*, pursued the Italian flagship to within sight of the Italian coast, scoring a hit at great range, while only 11 days later the Australian cruiser, *Sydney*, sank the Italian cruiser, *Bartolomeo Colleoni*, in a running fight

off Crete. It soon became evident that the Royal Navy had established a moral ascendancy over the Regia Navale, and that it more than offset the latter's numerical superiority.

Cunningham was not happy with limited success, however, and a lethal blow was planned against the Italian fleet. On the night of 11 November 1940 the aircraft carrier *Illustrious* launched a

ABOVE: The Italian battleship Littorio *rests on the bottom of Taranto harbour, her deck awash, after the British carrierborne air attack on 11 November 1940.*

RIGHT: The Italian heavy cruiser, Zara, *nameship of a four-strong class, was one of the three such ships sunk in the Battle of Cape Matapan.*

North African possessions and forces. Malta could never have supported a main fleet because of its proximity to Italian airfields, so the British established two heavy forces at opposite ends of the Mediterranean: these were Force H at Gibraltar and the Mediterranean Fleet at Alexandria.

Mussolini referred to the Mediterranean as 'our sea' and the 'Italian lake', but his naval commanders now found themselves opposed by a supremely gifted British naval

strike of 21 Fairey Swordfish biplane torpedo-bombers against the main Italian base at Taranto. Within two hours, two battleships had been badly damaged and a third sunk outright for the loss of just two aircraft. This was the first seaborne air attack against a defended base, and was studied with great interest by the Japanese.

British land forces from Egypt were also doing well against the Italian forces in North Africa, but in January 1941 the Germans came to the aid of their Axis partners. The highly capable X Fliegerkorps, a specialized anti-shipping attack formation, was sent to Sicily to deal with the British aircraft carrier and other warships which were causing the Italian navy so many problems. On 10 January *Illustrious* was very badly hit and only just managed to crawl into Malta. As soon as another carrier arrived, Cunningham returned to the offensive, and in March 1941 the *Formidable*'s torpedo-bombers scored a hit on the new battleship *Vittorio Veneto*. During the

night of 28–29 March, Cunningham's three battleships pressed on, hoping to find the Italian ship. Instead, they ran into two heavy cruisers, which had been sent back to look for a sister ship earlier damaged by a torpedo. The resulting Battle of Cape Matapan was an Italian disaster, for the cruisers had no idea they were facing three radar-equipped battleships armed with 15-in (381-mm) guns. Within minutes the *Fiume* and *Zara* were blazing wrecks, and shortly after the *Pola* too was also sinking, after being hit by torpedoes from destroyers. The Battle of Cape Matapan ranks as one of the decisive sea battles of the war, not because of its rather limited results but because it determined the future attitude of the Italian high command. Cunningham was furious at not having intercepted and sunk the *Vittorio Veneto*, but had to withdraw during the following morning to avoid air attacks. But the full significance of the battle did not become

ABOVE: The British battleship Valiant *was badly damaged, mined and sunk by Italian frogmen in Alexandria harbour during December 1941. She had, in fact, only sunk a few feet to the bottom of the harbour and her decks remained clear. Although immobilized, she was able to give the impression of full battle-readiness. She was raised and repaired in South Africa before being returned to the Mediterranean to support the landings in Sicily and at Salerno in 1943, before sailing for the Far East.*

LEFT: The British aircraft carrier Eagle *was a stalwart of Mediterranean and African operations until 11 August 1942 when, covering the Malta-bound convoy of Operation Pedestal, the ship was struck by four torpedoes from the U-73 and sunk to the south of Cape Salinas.*

ABOVE: The British aircraft carrier Indomitable, *under air attack near Malta. Operations in the narrows of the Mediterranean exposed major ships to intense air attack, but were vital to the continued existence of Malta as a major thorn in the side of the convoys struggling to nourish the German and Italian forces in North Africa.*

ABOVE RIGHT: The Ark Royal *was struck by a single U-81 torpedo on 13 November 1940, sinking the next day.*

RIGHT: Supported by a pair of destroyers, the crippled tanker Ohio, *carrying vital fuel, limps into Malta's Grand Harbour on 15 August 1942, after which she broke into two from the damage she had sustained. There were insufficient yard facilities to repair the tanker, so the two halves were used for storage, and later as barracks for Yugoslav troops.*

clear until the following May during the evacuation of Crete, when the British suffered heavy casualties but were left unmolested by the Italian fleet. Later still, even after the battleship *Barham* and carrier *Ark Royal* had been torpedoed at sea, and the battleships *Queen Elizabeth* and *Valiant* crippled by the attacks of 'human torpedoes' in Alexandria, the Italian surface fleet, mindful of Matapan, remained firmly on the defensive.

The position of Malta was always precarious and the British had to ensure that the island was always kept supplied with aircraft, ammunition, fuel and all manner of other supplies. In July 1941, a special fast convoy was run to Malta, and in September the carriers *Ark Royal* and *Furious* ferried fighters. More submarines were also sent to operate from the island, and between June and September nearly 300,000 tons of scarce German and Italian shipping was sunk by the forces based on Malta. The German naval staff

in Rome described the situation as 'catastrophic', for the Italian troops in North Africa were being harried by the Empire forces in Egypt and were also running short of essential supplies. When the Germans were forced to send

the Deutsches Afrika Korps, under Lieutenant-General Erwin Rommel, to help the Italians, this may have been militarily necessary, but as far as naval matters were concerned it merely exacerbated the supply problem. The

LEFT: An Italian submarine at sea. The submarine arm was one of the more effective elements of the Italian navy, and fought with courage as well as skill.

BELOW: The Italian battleship Roma *was to have been surrendered to the Allies at Malta as part of the Italian armistice agreement of September 1943, but was sunk by the detonations of two German radio-controlled 'Fritz-X' glide bombs on 9 September while en route to Malta.*

only other assistance the Germans could offer was a modest number of U-boats, which more than justified their presence by sinking the *Ark Royal* and *Barham*.

The reverses suffered by the Royal Navy left Malta very vulnerable, especially after December 1941 when the light forces based at Malta ran into a minefield and lost one cruiser and one destroyer, with two more cruisers damaged. The only ships capable of running the gauntlet of constant air attack were submarines, and even they had to submerge in the harbour during daylight. Some daring trips were made by fast but capacious minelayers, like the *Manxman*, but the cost was high and supplies were only the barest minimum needed to keep the island's defences effective. Eventually, after the USA had entered the war and a combined amphibious landing in North Africa had

An Allied convoy at sea with strong naval escort.

been proposed, the decision was taken to lift the siege. Some idea of the problem can be gathered from the size of the operation, which involved 14 fast merchant ships escorted by two battleships, three carriers, seven cruisers and 20 destroyers. Operation Pedestal was the largest convoy battle of the war. Fought on 10–13 August 1942, it cost nine merchant ships, one aircraft carrier and two cruisers. But the five ships which limped into Malta's Grand Harbour, including the tanker *Ohio*, carried sufficient supplies to save Malta's civilian population from starvation.

The improving state of affairs in North Africa, marked by the British victory in the 2nd Battle of El Alamein, was compounded by the Allied invasion of French North-West Africa in November 1942. With Axis forces cleared out of North Africa during May 1943, the shipping route between Gibraltar and Alexandria could be reopened, and Allied forces soon regained the initiative. In July 1943, the Allies landed in Sicily, and only two months later the same forces were landed on the Italian mainland. The conquest of Italy was to prove more difficult than anticipated, but from the naval point of view, once the Allies had gained a foothold in Italy, the most important obstacle had been overcome. The Mediterranean was now firmly under

Allied control, theirs to use not only as a base for the support of operations in southern Europe but also as a shorter and altogether more convenient supply route to the Far East.

The last act of the naval war in the Mediterranean was unexpectedly dramatic. The night before the landings at Salerno on 9 September 1943, an armistice came into force between the Allies and the Italians. The landings went ahead as planned, however, for the Germans clearly had no intention of surrendering. By the terms of the armistice the Italians had to deliver the three modern battleships, *Roma*, *Vittorio Veneto* and *Italia* (ex-*Littorio*) from La Spezia for internment at Malta, but on 9 September they were attacked by German aircraft carrying radio-controlled bombs. The *Roma* was hit, caught fire, and blew up, leaving the other two battleships to meet the *Valiant* and *Warspite* on the morning of the next day and steam into Malta.

THE AGONY OF STALINGRAD

The first two months of 1942 were truly agonizing for the exhausted German soldiers on the Eastern Front. The cold was extreme, and there was only inadequate winter clothing available. The running of vehicles was almost impossible, and oil froze solid unless engines were kept running the whole time. The Soviets, however, whom the Germans imagined to be as near to the limit of their endurance as themselves, had sprung the great strategic surprise of General Georgi Zhukov's counter-offensive around Moscow on 6 December 1941. Denied Hitler's permission to make strategic withdrawals to more easily defended positions, the German generals had to stand and fight during December. Divisions and corps were deployed in 'hedgehogs' providing all-round defence, and in many cases were cut off. Slowly, the Soviets drove the Germans back over the ground they had taken in November 1941. The trials, hardships and losses

sacrifices of the Soviet people, throughout the summer of the preceding year, were vindicated as new weapons and equipment began to pour in an ever-increasing torrent from the factories uprooted from European Russia and re-established to the east of the Urals. Then the spring thaw saw the return of the mud which had checked the German advance in the preceding autumn; it now also hampered the Soviet offensive in March until the warmer weather dried out the ground. As there were few metalled roads in the USSR, the autumn and spring mud periods marked the beginnings and ends of campaigns throughout the Great Patriotic War, as it had in previous wars.

March, April and May 1942 were marked by a slackening of the pace of operations as each side paused to rest, regroup and rebuild its forces after the intensely harsh winter campaign. But

LEFT: By the second half of 1942, Soviet weapons and tactics had improved out of all recognition, compared with those of June 1941, and emphasized the importance of tightly concentrated attacks by armour and infantry with powerful artillery and air support.

BELOW: German infantry on the move. The man on the right is carrying the mount for a machine gun to be used in the sustained fire role.

each side suffered in the notably severe winter of 1941–42 are almost impossible to imagine, but gradually the Soviets won back much of the land lost at the end of the German offensive: in the north, the great salient between Lakes Ladoga and Ilmen, with its head at Tikhvin, was taken by the Volkhov Front; the Kalinin, West and South-West Fronts took back great areas between Staraya Russa and Kharkov in the centre of the theatre; the South-West Front also drove a large salient into the German lines across the Donets river at Izyum; finally, in the far south, the Caucasus Front retook the Kerch peninsula in Crimea and was renamed the Crimean Front as a reward.

The Germans were unable to halt the remorseless advance of the Soviet forces, which made effective use of the increasing amount of matériel aid sent by the USA and UK by means of the Arctic convoys to Murmansk and Arkhangyel'sk, and who also appeared to possess an inexhaustible supply of fresh troops from Siberia. At the same time, the farsightedness of Iosef Stalin and the

THE ALLIES FIGHT BACK

Soviet troops in the Krasny Oktyabr factory in the northern part of Stalingrad. The fighting here see-sawed back and forth with heavy losses on each side, but throughout this period tanks were driven straight off the production line into combat.

even as front-line troops welcomed this interval, the planning staffs were busy preparing their next moves. First off the mark were the Germans, with many of their losses of the last few months replaced by the arrival of fresh German troops and some 51 divisions from Hungary, Italy, Romania, and even a volunteer division from Spain. In a preliminary offensive between 8 May and 27 June, the Germans managed to straighten their line by crushing the salients won by the Soviet winter offensive. The most important of these was the great Izyum salient, crushed by Field-Marshal Fedor von Bock's Army Group South on 17–29 May. By the end of June, the Germans felt themselves ready to launch their major summer effort of 1942.

This Blau (Blue) campaign once again reveals how the basic competence of German military planning had been destroyed by the vagaries of Hitler's strategic 'genius'. As conceived, Blau was to secure for Germany the important oilfields near Maykop in the northern Caucasus: Army Group South was reorganized into two smaller army groups, with the 1st Panzerarmee (ex-1st Panzergruppe) and 17th Army of Field-Marshal Wilhelm List's Army Group A to advance south-east and then south-west to take the fields, and the 4th Panzerarmee and 6th Army of Colonel-General Maximilian von Weichs's Army Group B to drive from the area of Kursk and Kharkov on the upper part of the Donets river to secure the line of the great eastward bend of the Don river and

so secure the left flank of Army Group A. Then Hitler's greedy eyes spotted Stalingrad, a major industrial city on a westward bend of the Volga river, and just beyond the objective of Army Group B. The plan was now changed, and Stalingrad became a primary objective in itself. At the same time, Army Group A was given extra objectives in the form of the Black Sea coast as far south as Batum near the border with Turkey, and all the Soviet oilfields in the Caucasus as far south as Baku on the Caspian Sea. From a realistic campaign with one major objective and a strategic covering campaign, Hitler had altered the concept to overextend the capabilities of Army Group A, while denying it the cover which should have been provided by Army Group B. The original plan had been possible but dangerous, as a Soviet offensive from Stalingrad down the Don toward Rostov-na-Donu could have cut off Army Group A. But the revised plan amounted to virtual suicide as Hitler's lack of a clear strategic goal, and the consequent dispersal of the German effort, was yet again to lead to disaster.

The main effort by Army Group South, as the German forces in this area were still designated, had meanwhile started punctually on 28 June with the drive to the Don. Voronezh fell to the 4th Panzerarmee on 6 July, and von Bock's forces seemed well on the way to fulfilling Hitler's original intentions. Then early in July came the reshuffle of Army Group South into Army Group A (7 July) and Army Group B (9 July), with Bock commanding the latter until the arrival of von Weichs on 13 July, the day on which Hitler finally decided to alter the original plan.

At first all progressed satisfactorily. Army Group B continued to make steady progress in clearing the bend of the Don, with Colonel-General Friedrich Paulus's 6th Army of 18 divisions moving smoothly down the Donets corridor between the Don and Donets rivers to take all but the eastern end of the Don

Group B had been slowing down, and Hitler now decided to switch the 4th Panzerarmee back to Army Group B. Now under the personal command of Hitler, Army Group A now began to struggle in its forward advance some 1,250 miles (2000km) distant in East Prussia. The 11th Army had been transferred north to reinforce the siege of Leningrad, and when List and Colonel-General Franz Halder, the OKH chief-of-staff, protested, they were both removed. Army Group A inched forward, eventually reaching points just 70 miles (110km) from the Caspian Sea. Despite being almost completely cut off from reinforcements and supplies, the North Caucasus and Trans-Caucasus Fronts fought with the utmost determination, yielding ground as slowly as they could.

LEFT: German prisoners march into a captivity from which only a small percentage ever returned.

BELOW: Soviet artillerymen fire their gun over open sights against a short-range target.

bend by 22 July. Colonel-General Hermann Hoth's 4th Panzerarmee was now detached from Army Group B to bolster Army Group A, which had been making only slow progress toward the line of the lower Don against determined Soviet opposition: Rostov-na-Donu, almost at the mouth of the river, had fallen only on 23 July. Coming into the line on List's left flank, the 4th Panzerarmee helped to speed the advance across the Don and south into the Caucasus, and also gave the Germans another axis of advance toward Stalingrad from the south-west.

In Crimea, meanwhile, Colonel-General Erich von Manstein's 11th Army had achieved a major success when, on 2 July, the great port bastion of Sevastopol had fallen, costing the Soviets another 100,000 men. As the Kerch peninsula had been cleared once more in the middle of May, this left Crimea wholly in German hands, which delighted Hitler so much that he promoted von Manstein to field-marshal.

By 1 August, the 1st and 4th Panzerarmee of Army Group A had made significant progress into the Caucasus. Further north, however, Army

ABOVE: German troops in action. The fighting in Stalingrad was as bitter as any in World War II, being agonizing for both sides.

RIGHT: A Soviet nurse attends to a wounded soldier.

Farther north, reinforced by the 4th Panzerarmee and benefiting from stronger air support, Army Group B finally reached the Volga on 23 August. It now readied itself for the attack on Stalingrad, whose defence was in the hands of the Stalingrad Front, established on 12 July under the command of General A.I. Eremenko. The Soviets were determined that Stalingrad should not fall, and supplies and men were rushed into the area, while the armament factories in the city stepped up their efforts further still.

The scene was now set for one of the climactic battles of the war. The slow progress of Army Group A meant that the southern Caucasian oilfields were now out of Germany's reach, making Blau's major objective Stalingrad, a city of 500,000 inhabitants stretching for some 18.5 miles (30km) along the western bank of the Volga river. More than 255 of the USSR's vehicles had been built here, as well as tanks, guns and other weapons, so the city was important to both sides.

The assault on Stalingrad was undertaken from the north-west by the 6th Army and from the south-west by the 4th Panzerarmee, both of which had reached Stalingrad's outer defence perimeter by 17 August. Defending Stalingrad were the 66th, 4th Tank, 62nd, 1st Tank, 64th, 51st and 57th Armies, each about the equivalent of a German corps in strength. The 6th Army, with only one Panzer division, with which Blau had begun, now had two, and it was one of these, the XIV Panzer Corps, which made the main breakthrough of the outer Soviet defences on 22 August. On the next day, the corps reached the Volga just to the north of Stalingrad, between Yerzovka and Rynok. By the end of the month the rest of the 6th Army and the 4th Panzerarmee had broken through the outer defences and had closed up to the middle Soviet line, already breached by XIV Panzer Corps. The fighting, although already intense, now grew even fiercer as the Germans prepared to move into the city itself.

Strangely enough, the 6th Army failed to make serious attempts to throw a bridgehead across the Volga to the north of the city. This would have been a costly and precarious undertaking as the river is wide and fast-flowing, but if successful would have cut off the city from reinforcements from the north and east, and also prevented the movement of Soviet river traffic bringing in more troops and weapons. But here the earlier diversion of the 4th Panzerarmee to Army Group A made its effect felt. The relatively slow progress made by the 6th Army on its own had given the Soviets just enough time to strengthen their defences on the east bank to make any assault crossing virtually impossible.

By the end of August, Stalingrad had been virtually cut off on three sides, with the Soviets holding a perimeter some 30 miles (50km) long and 18.5 miles (30km) wide. The Germans were now well placed to pursue their offensive by any one of several means, the least costly of which would have been a slow

and methodical siege, after a river crossing, to invade the city from the east. Instead, they chose a frontal assault. Given the Soviet determination to hold on at all costs, the result was inevitable: Stalingrad became a 'meatgrinder' battle, with an apparently inexhaustible number of men available to become casualties.

The Germans continued to pound slowly forward during the first part of September, and by 12 September had reduced the Soviet perimeter to just 30 miles (50km) as they reached the out- skirts of the city. It was now that the bloodiest part of the battle began. The XIV and XXIV Panzer Corps of the 6th Army and the XLVIII Panzer Corps of the 4th Panzerarmee had played their most important roles in reaching and isolating Stalingrad. It was now basically an infantry responsibility to reduce the final defences. The intensity and bitterness of the fierce fighting which now characterized the rest of the Battle of Stalingrad was rivalled by those of a few other battles of World War II, but nothing equalled the horror of Stalingrad. Street by street and house by house, the Germans pushed forward

against fanatical resistance, taking and inflicting great casualties The main weapons of this phase of the battle were infantry such as grenades, bayonets and sub-machine guns, supported by light artillery. Areas changed hands frequently, but the general trend was still a slow German progress.

By 13 October, Stalingrad had been finally cut off on the west bank of the Volga when XLVIII Panzer Corps broke through the residential area in the south to reach the west bank of the Volga at Yelshanka. The most important part of the city, the industrial area in the north, remained in Soviet hands, however, which the 62nd Army was determined as ever to hold. With his infantry exhausted, Paulus was forced to change tactics; frontal assaults were now called off in favour of methodical artillery and air bombardment in an effort to flatten the factory complex area and its defenders at the northern end of the city. This change suited the Soviets more than the Germans, however, for the rubble caused by the bombardment provided excellent cover for the defence and made progress for the attackers almost impossible.

LEFT: German infantry in Stalingrad during the autumn of 1942. With their defeat at Stalingrad early in 1943, the Germans had effectively lost the war on the Eastern Front, and with it their chance of winning World War II.

BELOW LEFT: A Soviet mortar team among the ruins of Stalingrad, where the fighting was undertaken on a street-by-street, building-by-building basis.

BELOW: A German tank rumbles through shattered Stalingrad. As the Soviets cut off the German 6th Army, supplies of essentials such as vehicle fuel, food, medicine, etc., were being steadily exhausted as the Luftwaffe failed to deliver on its promise to deliver all necessary supplies by air.

Street fighting in Stalingrad: the German perspective (above) and that of the Soviets (right).

furthering this exhaustion, with the winter freeze coming again as a ghastly shock. The date 18 November marked the climax of the German summer offensive of 1942, neither of whose major objectives had been accomplished.

The dramatic plummet of the temperature to freezing conditions was something for which the Soviets had been waiting, for they knew it would shift the tactical balance in their favour and had therefore been planning a winter counter-offensive. The success of this showed clearly, had the Germans been prepared to admit the fact, that the Soviet military had matured enormously during the past 18 months, most particularly at the upper levels, where planning and logistical efforts had not always been undertaken with a degree of proficiency and professionalism.

Stalingrad lay at the head of a shallow salient into the Soviet lines, with the first-rate 6th Army and 4th Panzerarmee in the city. To concentrate

these German forces at the decisive point, however, the Germans had been forced to entrust the defence of the salient's shoulders on satellite armies of uncertain abilities: these were the Romanian 3rd Army to the north-west and the Romanian 4th Army to the south. Responsible for planning the Soviet counterstroke, General Georgi Zhukov recognized that this was the Axis's weak point. At 07.30 on 19 November, the South-West and Don Fronts, commanded by General N.F. Vatutin and General K.K. Rokossovsky respectively, crashed forward from the line of the Don through the Romanian 3rd Army. A day later, the forces of the Stalingrad Front to the south of the beleaguered city also launched a major offensive, this time against the Romanian 4th Army. Three days later the spearheads of the two Soviet offensives met at Sovetskiy, 30 miles (50km) to the rear of Paulus's desperate troops in Stalingrad. Army Group B only just managed to extricate

The struggle continued unabated, and by 18 November the German 295th Infantry Division had reached the Volga in a couple of places, and had even managed to secure a bridgehead on the island opposite the celebrated Tractor and Krasny Oktyabr factories, from which tanks were driven straight out into combat as soon as they came off the assembly lines. Just as at Moscow 12 months earlier, the Germans were now exhausted but were still clawing forward slowly, while as in the year before the autumn rains played their part in

itself to the south-west, but five Romanian divisions had been cut off just to the west of Kletskaya and surrendered on 23 November. The 6th Army and part of the 4th Panzerarmee were cut off in Stalingrad, the besiegers having now become the besieged.

Although precarious, the German position was still salvageable: the sensible thing would have been for Paulus to have broken out to the south-west to rejoin the rest of Army Group A before the Soviets were able to consolidate in his rear. This was the course urged on the German commander by his immediate superior, von Weichs. But Hitler's interference was yet again to cost Germany dear: so involved was Hitler in the whole Stalingrad operation that he had decided to assume personal command, directing Paulus by radio and bypassing von Weichs. Still sure of the need to take Stalingrad and of the benefits of never pulling back, Hitler ordered Paulus to stand fast. Although initially unsure, Hitler had been persuaded to come down on the side of a stand at Stalingrad by

the promises of Reichsmarschall Hermann Göring. His Luftwaffe, Göring assured Hitler, could supply the 400 tons of supplies needed by the German forces trapped at Stalingrad by means of a simple airlift. So Hitler ordered Paulus to hold 'Fortress Stalingrad' and await relief by Army Group Don, hastily formed from the 11th Army and other available units under the command of von Manstein, in whose capabilities Hitler had great confidence.

Operation Wintergewitter (Winter Storm) was not only intended to effect the relief of the 6th Army but also to kick-start a resumed offensive. Armeegruppe Hoth, east of the Don, was to advance from the area of Kotelnikovo against the Stalingrad Front and meet the 6th Army striking south-west from Stalingrad. Armeeabteilung Hollidt, the half of Army Group Don on the west bank of the river, was meanwhile to press forward against the Don Front to keep this latter from interfering with the advance of Armeegruppe Hoth. After the relief of the 6th Army, all three

components of von Manstein's force were to fall on the Don and South-West Fronts and restore the line as it was before 19 November.

Wintergewitter began on 12 December, making good progress for two days. But too much time had elapsed while Army Group Don was being formed, and the Soviets were able to halt the offensive with the forces they had rushed into the area since their own offensive, principally the 2nd Guards Army and the VII Tank Corps. By 23 December the LVII Panzer Corps, the main strike force of the Armeegruppe Hoth, had been halted only 30 miles (50km) from Stalingrad. Paulus was ordered by von Manstein to break out toward the LVII Panzer Corps, but refused to do so after consulting Hitler. The 6th Army's last chance had just passed, and Army Group Don was itself now in great peril. On 24 December the Soviets launched yet another offensive, this time by the South-West and Stalingrad Fronts against von Manstein's overextended and tired forces. Harried by superior forces, von Manstein was pushed

LEFT: The fighting in Stalingrad raged under a pall of smoke, ash and dust hanging in the air.

BELOW: A German sniper at Stalingrad.

THE ALLIES FIGHT BACK

ABOVE: Soviet infantry move forward across snow-covered terrain.

ABOVE RIGHT: The Soviet defence within Stalingrad was co-ordinated by Lieutenant-General V.I. Chuikov (here flanked by other officers), the commander of the 62nd Army.

RIGHT: Looking increasingly gaunt and exhausted as the weather worsens and their food supplies dwindle, German soldiers prepare for action at Stalingrad.

back toward Rostov-na-Donu, east of which he only just managed to hold open a corridor for Army Group A to escape from the Caucasus. The need for Army Group A to retreat had been made clear by the westward advance of the Stalingrad Front in December, and was hastened by the Trans-Caucasus Front's offensive of 1 January 1943. Only the 1st Panzerarmee managed to slip past Rostov-na-Donu to reach comparative safety, the rest of Army Group A falling back into the Taman peninsula opposite the Crimea.

The plight of the 6th Army in Stalingrad was now desperate. The Luftwaffe was able to fly in nothing like the quantities of food, fuel, ammunition and medicine required, and the winter cold was taking a heavy toll of the fit as well as the wounded. The reduction of the German pocket was in the capable hands of Rokossovsky and his Don Front, which now deployed seven armies against Paulus's formations, at first thought by the Soviets to number only a few divisions. In fact some 200,000 men were trapped in the city. Rokossovsky called upon Paulus to surrender on 8 January, launching a major offensive two days later when his demand was refused. Hitler also refused to countenance a surrender and the Soviet offensive slowly crushed the German pocket from the west. On 14 January the Germans lost their major airfield, Pitomnik, and on 25 January their only other airfield, Gumrak. The 6th Army was now totally

FAR LEFT: The stolid endurance of the Soviet soldier is evident on the face of this man.

LEFT: By the end of 1942 the qualitative superiority of the armour with which the Germans had begun their invasion of the USSR had disappeared, and Soviet industry was now able to turn out larger numbers of tanks at least equal, and in some case superior, to anything the Germans could field in significant numbers.

cut off and collapsing fast. Hitler clutched at straws: no German field-marshal had ever surrendered, so Paulus was elevated to this rank. But all this was in vain, and by the end of January all of the 6th Army, apart from the XI Corps in the industrial area of the city, had surrendered. The XI Corps finally surrendered on 2 February, and the German agony in Stalingrad was over. Some 100,000 men had died in the Don Front's offensive, and another 93,000 had been taken prisoner.

The summer campaign had cost Germany much more than lives and equipment, although these in themselves had been bad enough. But of greater significance was the fact that the Soviets had proved themselves capable of fighting the Germans on their own terms and beating them. The quality of Soviet leadership and general military capability had risen sharply since the previous year, while the German ability to wage war had considerably declined. With a few exceptions, the satellite forces deployed by Hitler had proved mediocre, and the burden of stemming the regular Soviet

offensives was now to fall ever more heavily on the German armies. It was to prove a hopeless task.

The Soviets were not yet through with their winter offensive. On 12 January 1943, the Bryansk, Voronezh, South-West and South Fronts (the last being the renamed Stalingrad Front) flooded forward from the general line of the Don, between Orel in the north and Rostov-na-Donu in the south. Army

Group B and Army Group Don, soon to be renamed Army Group South, resisted stubbornly but were driven steadily back by the remorseless Soviet pressure. By 2 February, when the second stage of the offensive began, the Soviet armies had reached a line from Taganrog in the south, up the Mius, Donets and Oskol rivers, to Livy in the north. During 2–20 February, the Soviets again swept forward, their most

ABOVE: A Soviet mortar team in the window of a ruined building.

ABOVE RIGHT: The commander of the German 6th Army, Field-Marshal Friedrich Paulus, walks with the aid of a stick to surrender his command on 31 January 1943.

RIGHT: Soviet troops fighting in conditions typical of urban warfare.

important conquest being Kharkov. There then occurred one of the most remarkable pieces of tactical genius seen in the war. Although outnumbered by seven to one, von Manstein restored his position in the south, retaking Kharkov on 14 March. In an offensive between 18 February and 20 March, when the spring thaw put an end to operations, von Manstein had used his forces brilliantly, switching his armour from place to place with consummate skill and determination to throw the Soviets back to the line of the Donets. But

strong air support. The Deutsches Afrika Korps came through the desert 20 miles (32km) south of the Via Balbia, the Italian XX (Mobile) Corps through the centre, and an extemporized group under Colonel Werner Marcks along the Via Balbia itself. The British forward troops fell back as planned, the 200th Guards Brigade being swept along in front of the Germans, who reached Agedabia on 22 January. Rommel had advanced 55 miles (90km) in 48 hours and now ordered his forces to move through Agedabia and turn east in the direction of Saunnu to prevent the 1st Armoured Division's withdrawal to Msus, its supply base. However, the 1st Armoured Division escaped largely as the result of the excellence of the British artillery support. A running battle developed on 23 January, and two days later the DAK struck north, its two Panzer divisions advancing abreast, to capture Msus airfield. Rommel then

LEFT: The most celebrated commander of the British 8th Army was General B.L. (soon Sir Bernard) Montgomery, who became a field-marshal later in the war and received a peerage after it.

BELOW: A British infantryman with a Bren light machine gun in typical North African terrain at El Alamein.

despite this having secured von Manstein's place among the great leaders of all time, the fact remains that the Soviet winter offensive had pushed the Germans back still farther.

BRITISH VICTORY AT EL ALAMEIN

In January 1942, Lieutenant-General A.R. Godwin-Austen's XIII Corps was at the gateway to Tripolitania, exactly where Lieutenant-General Richard O'Connor's XIII Corps had been the year before. In 1942, however, more than seven Axis divisions had escaped back into Tripolitania. General Sir Claude Auchinleck was anxious to pursue them, but could not do so until Benghazi had been made operational as a supply base.

The British deployed the 200th Guards Brigade (the renumbered 22nd Guards Brigade) at Mersa Brega, just to the east of El Agheila, with the 1st Armoured Division's Support Group. The rest of the 1st Armoured Division was at Antelat and the Indian 4th Division in the Benghazi area. Three British defensive positions were planned: the frontier area, using the Axis defences between Sidi Omar and Halfaya; Mersa Matruh; and the El Alamein bottleneck between the Mediterranean and the northern edge of the great Qattara depression. The offensive against Rommel was to continue on 15 February, with Tripoli the objective.

But Rommel struck first. At dawn on 21 January, and recently boosted by the arrival of 54 German tanks with their crews and fuel, the German commander launched three columns to the east with

THE ALLIES FIGHT BACK

Corps by Lieutenant-General W.H.E. Gott. Auchinleck maintained that a further British offensive would not be possible until June, and that it was Rommel's intention to forestall British preparations by taking Tobruk.

The Gazala line was a series of defensive boxes, each held by one infantry brigade group and surrounded by a perimeter of barbed wire and mines. Each brigade group had its own artillery, engineer and logistic units. The armour was held in reserve, with the XXX Corps responsible for manoeuvring it. Lieutenant-General C.W.M. Norrie and XXX Corps were also responsible for the security of the southern half of the front, from the Trigh Capuzzo to the Trigh el Abd. The 1st Free French Brigade occupied Bir Hacheim, with the Indian 3rd Motorized Brigade extending from Bir Hacheim to the south-east. The 1st and 7th Armoured Divisions were now 9 miles (14.5km) south of 'Knightsbridge', with a crossroads of tracks leading to Sidi Muftah, Gazala and Bir Hacheim. The Indian 29th Brigade was at Bir el Gubi.

ABOVE: A hallmark of Erwin Rommel's command style was his belief that he and his staff should be as far forward with the fighting men as possible. Here Rommel's headquarters' convoy passes armoured vehicles as it moves toward the front.

RIGHT: One of the British 8th Army's most glaring limitations disappeared with the arrival of large numbers of thoroughly reliable, well-protected and adequately armed US tanks, in this instance, M4 Sherman medium tanks.

moved north-west across country to Coefi, on the coast, to surprise and cut off Benghazi. At the same time, a German feint was directed at Mechili and it was not until Axis mobile formations approached Benghazi, from the south, that Lieutenant-General N.M. Ritchie finally agreed to evacuate Benghazi, although this had been previously requested by Godwin-Austen. The Indian 4th Division at Benghazi managed to escape encirclement but only at a high cost.

On 3 February Rommel reached the Gulf of Bomba and was now 375 miles (600km) from his base in flagrant disobedience of his orders, which had ordained only limited operations. Meanwhile, the 8th Army retreated to a line between Gazala to Bir Hacheim; Godwin-Austen resigned and was replaced as commander of the XIII

part of the operation into the great wheeling movement of the DAK to the south of Bir Hacheim. On 27 May each side experienced some success but also some defeat. Crüwell's frontal attacks were not totally successful and Rommel's force was severely mauled in its clashes with 1st and 7th Armoured Divisions. By the end of the day, the XXX Corps was able to counter-attack and the Panzerarmee Afrika became trapped in the minefields. Bir Hacheim held out and drove off the Italian Ariete Division. On 28 May, Rommel directed the mass of his armour against Got-el-Oualeb, which was held by the left flank of the British 50th Division, and took 3,000 prisoners. The capture of this allowed Rommel to make a gap through the minefields and concentrate his armour in the 'Cauldron', to the west of Knightsbridge, where a

LEFT: One of the key weapons in the German arsenal was the 3.465-in (88-mm) gun. Though conceived as an anti-aircraft weapon, and very successful in this role, its high muzzle velocity made it an excellent anti-tank gun, with the range to hit and destroy Allied armour at ranges well beyond the capabilities of the tanks' own main guns.

BELOW: The start of the 2nd Battle of El Alamein was marked by a huge nocturnal bombardment by British and commonwealth artillery.

Gott's XIII Corps was deployed along the northern sector, with the South African 1st Division blocking the Via Balbia opposite Gazala, and the 50th Division blocking the track running parallel to the coast road farther to the south. Gott was also responsible for the static positions in the rear, including Tobruk, the whole front having been screened by a system of armoured car patrols. A few days before Rommel attacked Auchinleck, expecting it to come in the centre, Auchinleck advised Ritchie to place his two armoured divisions near El Adem, but Ritchie did not do this as he was concerned that the Germans would fall on his desert flank.

Rommel's forces were divided into two. Under Lieutenant-General Ludwig Crüwell were the Italian XXI and X Corps, which would engage the 8th Army, preventing it from manoeuvring. Rommel would head his Panzerarmee Afrika, comprising the Italian XX Corps and the DAK. Ritchie had some 994 tanks and 190 aircraft, while Rommel had 560 tanks and 497 aircraft.

On 26 May Crüwell began his frontal assault while Rommel launched his own

ABOVE: The predecessor of the M4 Sherman was another medium tank, the M3, known in various forms as the Grant and Lee. This introduced the hull and dynamic system retained for the Sherman, but had an obsolescent armament pattern, having a 3-in (75-mm) gun in a sponson on the right of the turret, with only a limited traverse arc, and a 37-mm gun in the turret which was capable of all-round traverse.

RIGHT: An Axis shell detonates close to a British truck.

The 8th Army then withdrew to the frontier, losing contact with Tobruk, where the South African 2nd Division was surrounded. Rommel launched his assault on Tobruk at dawn on 20 June after heavy air bombardment. A breach was made in the outer defences, and by nightfall the garrison had surrendered. The Axis forces took 33,000 prisoners and captured a great quantity of vehicles and supplies.

This great victory at Gazala illustrates Rommel's tactical genius, and Hitler promoted him to field-marshal. Rommel now kept up his advance and quickly regrouped his forces. The DAK was despatched toward the Libyan-Egyptian frontier with the Italian mobile corps, and here the British held only a delaying position. Ritchie ordered the XIII Corps to delay the Axis armour while the rest of the 8th Army, reinforced by two fresh

divisions, prepared to give battle at Mersa Matruh. At this stage Auchinleck decided to take personal command of the 8th Army. The Germans advanced and the British withdrew to El Alamein, where they were reinforced by the Australian 9th and Indian 4th Divisions.

The El Alamein line was a 40-mile (65-km) gap between the Mediterranean and the Qattara depression, being a salt marsh below sea level where outflanking was impossible. The XXX Corps was deployed in the northern sector with the XIII Corps in the south, below the Ruweisat ridge.

Rommel's advance to El Alamein was so rapid that on 1 July he had only 6,400 men, 41 tanks and 71 guns. Nevertheless, he ordered an immediate attack, which failed. Rommel had overstretched himself, and now had to regroup his forces, withdrawing his

battle of attrition was waged until 9 June. The Cauldron, too, was a defeat for the British, who fought hard but were unable to drive back the 15th Panzer and the 90th Light Divisions, their attacks of 5 and 6 June being repulsed with heavy losses. The Germans took 4,000 prisoners and the British lost many tanks. The French fought a gallant but isolated battle at Bir Hacheim until 11 June, when Ritchie ordered them to withdraw.

Ritchie's forward defences as far south as the northern perimeter of the Cauldron were still intact, held by South African 1st and British 50th Divisions. Ritchie still had 330 serviceable tanks and estimated that one more armoured battle might exhaust the Axis forces. But Rommel quickly seized the opportunity to cut off the South African division and the right flank of the British division, setting off quickly before Norrie could counter-attack. In a fierce battle near Knightsbridge on 12–13 June, Rommel defeated Ritchie's armour, leaving him only 50 cruiser and 20 infantry tanks.

German units behind a static front line of Italian divisions, dug in behind wire and mines. A see-saw battle then developed on the El Alamein line, with neither side achieving any significant headway.

After the fighting in this 1st Battle of El Alamein had died down, major changes in the British command structure were made. General Sir Harold Alexander replaced Auchinleck as commander-in-chief, and Lieutenant-General Bernard Montgomery took command of the 8th Army. Montgomery arrived on 13 August, immediately launching himself into what he saw as his three main tasks: restoration of the 8th Army's confidence; defeat of Rommel's planned offensive; and the launch of Operation Lightfoot, which would drive Rommel from Egypt. Montgomery brought in two new corps commanders with him in the persons of Lieutenant-Generals B.G. Horrocks and Sir Oliver Leese, now entrusted with the XIII and XXX Corps respectively. Montgomery altered troop deployments, and

LEFT: A cheap way to fit a larger-calibre gun into an armoured chassis, incapable of accepting a larger turret, was to replace the turret with a fixed barbette carrying a limited-traverse gun of the calibre desired, so creating a self-propelled gun. These Italian self-propelled guns of the Semovente 40 series are armed with 2.95-in (75-mm) guns, while the Carro Armato M13-series tanks, from which they were derived, carried a 47-mm gun.

BELOW LEFT: A British tank passes the wreckage of a German PzKpfw III medium tank.

BELOW: An armoured car of a New Zealand unit escorts Axis prisoners to the rear after the 2nd Battle of El Alamein.

Commonwealth infantry accept the surrender of the crew of a German tank, possibly immobilized by lack of fuel.

requested and received reinforcements for the XXX Corps, where the Australian 9th, South African 1st and Indian 5th Divisions were deployed in the northern sector. In the area of the XIII Corps, Montgomery sent the newly-arrived 44th Division to reinforce the positions on the Alam el Halfa ridge. The New Zealand Division was deployed between the Ruweisat and Alam el Halfa ridges, and the remainder of the front was covered by the 7th Armoured Division. Montgomery ordered that all the defences were to be strengthened and that no withdrawal was to be considered.

Rommel was now ill. He knew British supplies were flowing in and he planned to attack on 30–31 August, with all his mobile formations passing by night through the thinly-held British front south of the Alam Nayil ridge and advancing 30 miles (50km) through

mined country to deploy south of the Alam el Halfa ridge. They would then drive to the north, reach the Alexandria road and cut off the 8th Army. Rommel had at his disposal 200 battleworthy German tanks and 240 Italian medium tanks in poor condition.

The 8th Army had somewhat more than 700 tanks, of which 164 were M3 Grant vehicles from the USA, and now fielded the powerful 17-pdr anti-tank gun. The British knew Rommel was coming and his diversionary attacks against the sector of the XXX Corps did not deceive Montgomery. Rommel's initial advance in the Battle of Alam el Halfa on 30 August was hampered by minefields, and next day he changed his objective to a frontal assault by the armour of the 22nd Armoured Brigade south of Alam el Halfa. A furious battle ensued, and the DAK's attack was

repulsed. British bomber and ground-attack sorties were continuous, and the night of 1–2 September was the worst the DAK had ever experienced; Rommel decided to withdraw the next day. Montgomery was tempted to counter-attack, but not wishing to take risks did not press this home.

The British and commonwealth victory in the Battle of Alam el Halfa was a psychological turning point. Rommel was promised all kinds of reinforcements by Hitler, but it was the British who were now receiving supplies in abundance, including US M4 Sherman medium tanks and many 4.13-in (105-mm) guns.

The Axis forces dug in and laid 500,000 mines in two major fields, producing a honeycomb effect. Five infantry divisions faced the British, with battalions guarding sectors approximately 1 mile (1.6km) wide by 2 to 3 miles (3 to 4.5km) deep. The armour of the Ariete and 21st Panzer Divisions guarded the southern sector, while the 15th Panzer and Littorio Divisions held the north; held in reserve, the 90th Light and the Trieste Divisions were deployed along the coastal road. With Rommel now on sick leave, General Georg Stumme was in command.

On the other side of the front, troop training and rehearsals had persuaded Montgomery to revise the original Lightfoot plan. He now aimed to contain the Axis armour while the infantry divisions were destroyed. The definitive plan had three phases: the break-in by both corps, the dogfight, and the break-out. Montgomery ensured he had an adequate reserve, and when he had committed this where necessary, formed another reserve from a quiet sector. He had also formed an armoured rival to the DAK in the form of Lieutenant-General H. Lumsden's X Corps.

Montgomery planned to attack Rommel's northern sector, while successfully convincing the Axis forces that the attack would be on the southern defences. The 8th Army had 1,229 tanks and was superior in all equipment, as suggested by the fact that the Axis forces had only 496 tanks.

At 21.40 on 23 October, the 8th Army's attack was launched, taking the Axis forces by total tactical surprise. Under cover of a huge artillery barrage, sappers led the advance and cleared the mines. The armour came next with infantry following. The XIII Corps launched its diversionary attack, pinning down the 21st Panzer and Ariete divisions in the south. In the north, the XXX Corps made two inroads into the minefields, with the Australian 9th Division on the right and the New Zealand Division on the left. While neither reached its planned objective, their action began the crumbling away of the Axis infantry, as envisaged by Montgomery. German armoured counter-attacks were beaten off and the Axis commanders were forced to commit all their reserves. Montgomery urged his forces to carry on with their attacks, and the battle became one of firepower. Rommel, by now returned, came off the worse. Montgomery created a new strike force for the break-out stage, Operation Supercharge, which was to be spearheaded by the New Zealand Division. Meanwhile, the Australian 9th Division was doing well in the north, having cut the coastal road. Air attacks, causing major disruption in the rear of the Axis forces, heralded the beginning of Supercharge, characterized by fighting of great ferocity on 2–4 November. The New Zealand Division, reinforced by two British infantry brigades, fought hard to force a breach for the X Corps to pass through, losing many tanks in the process.

By now the Axis forces had been totally outnumbered, and even to force a stalemate was no longer possible. They had only 187 tanks left, 155 of which were Italian and incapable of withstanding the fire of the Shermans. Rommel prepared to disengage on

3 November, even though Hitler had issued a typical no-retreat order. Under cover of a skilful rearguard action, Rommel managed to extricate many of his surviving troops, but had to leave behind a great deal of equipment which the British took in addition to 30,000 prisoners. The Allies lost 13,560 men and 500 tanks.

Rommel began his long retreat to Tunis, followed steadfastly by the 8th Army and without even making a stand at Halfaya or El Agheila, so precarious was his position.

THE MEDITERRANEAN AIR WAR

At the time of its entry into World War II in June 1940, Italy had a comparatively large air force, the Regia Aeronautica, whose reserves of properly trained men and adequate aircraft were in short supply, especially in the fighter arm; in overall terms it was short of modern combat aircraft. The majority of fighters were Fiat CR.32 and CR.42 biplanes, which were nonetheless appreciated by most Italian pilots for their manoeuvrability. The few monoplane fighters available had been designed to meet a similar outmoded concept of air war, with speed, rate of climb, armament, and defensive features, such as pilot protection and self-sealing fuel tanks, sacrificed to the demands of manoeuvrability. The best elements of the Regia Aeronautica were undoubtedly its bomber squadrons, which were equipped with the Savoia-Marchetti SM.79 three-engined monoplane. This could be used for conventional bombing or torpedo attack, in which the Italians were very skilled.

The pilot rushes toward a Hawker Sea Hurricane of the Fleet Air Arm, currently in land service in places such as Malta. Although conceived as a pure fighter and used as such in the Battles of France and Britain, the Hurricane matured as an excellent fighter-bomber, with underwing armament after it had become obsolete as a pure fighter.

The shortest route to and from India, the Far East and Australasia lay through the Suez Canal, making this an area of paramount importance to the British war effort. But without control of the Mediterranean, control of the Suez Canal was of little practical use. The key to the Mediterranean was the island of Malta, lying at about midpoint between Gibraltar and the Suez Canal and, unfortunately for the British, a mere 60 miles (100km) south of the island of Sicily, which accommodated several Italian airbases. Almost immediately after their declaration of war, the Italians began air raids from these bases attacking Malta.

Pre-war British plans had assumed that, because of its location close to Italy and far from sources of reinforcement, Malta could not be held, so little thought had been given to practical measures for its retention. Yet the first Italian raids were beaten off with some losses, and the island's defence seemed to be becoming more feasible. Its fighter defence was initially vested in the three survivors of four Gloster Sea Gladiators in reserve on the island, and these severely mauled the Italians until reinforcements, in the form of some Hawker Hurricanes, arrived at the end of June and the beginning of August. With the arrival of these aircraft, the Italian attacks gradually became ineffectual in strategic terms. The British realized that the island was indeed defensible, and were determined to hold on to it. There was to be very serious air

ABOVE: Generally outnumbered and flying warplanes of inferior quality, the Italian air force nevertheless fought courageously.

RIGHT: Impressed with the success of their biplane fighters in the Spanish Civil War of 1936–39, many Italian pilots wanted to retain them and, when forced to switch to monoplanes offering higher performance, demanded the retention of an open cockpit and an armament of 0.5-in (12.7-mm) machine guns, so that agility would not be compromised. These fighters, such as the Fiat G.50 and Macchi C.200, were in every respect inferior to their Allied counterparts.

The British, on the other hand, had only a few aircraft in North Africa and Malta, most of which were obsolete. But although reserves were small, the Royal Air Force had a distinct advantage in the quality of its aircrew and ground organization. The mainstay of the British fighter arm in the Mediterranean was the Gloster Gladiator biplane, comparable in performance with the CR.42. Apart from a moderate number of obsolete bomber types, the British also possessed some fairly modern Bristol Blenheim monoplane light bombers. In the early stages of the campaign, therefore, the quality of the aircraft used by each side meant that the type of air warfare likely to be fought would be that which might have taken place over northern Europe in the mid-1930s. At the outset of the war with Italy, the British had some 300 aircraft in the Mediterranean and African theatres, and the Italians some 480, excluding those in metropolitan Italy.

fighting, but Malta was to survive Italian and German attacks, eventually taking the offensive against the Axis airfields and shipping, and as such playing a major part in the final Allied success in North Africa.

It was during December 1940 that the island's first proper offensive air strength arrived, in the form of a squadron of Vickers Wellington twin-engined medium bombers. From then on the offensive strength of the island grew rapidly.

In North Africa, meanwhile, the Royal Air Force was playing an important part in the rout of the Italian advance towards Cairo. Reinforced by aircraft flown in across the southern Sahara from the Gold Coast, the RAF had shown itself to be superior in all important respects to the Regia Aeronautica. Yet the early successes in Malta and North Africa were to have unfortunate repercussions. With the Axis cause humiliated by the reverses suffered by the Italians, Hitler decided he must bolster the efforts of his southern ally, and in December 1940 the first elements

LEFT: For a time in July 1940, the air defence of Malta rested with a small number of Gloster Sea Gladiator biplanes, out of a total of 18 deposited on the island earlier in the year as spares for the carrier Glorious. *Flown by Royal Air Force and Fleet Air Arm pilots, these were the strength of the so-called Hal Far Fighter Flight.*

BELOW LEFT: A German warplane much used for patrols and anti-ship attacks in the Mediterranean theatre was the Messerschmitt Bf 110C twin-engined multi-role warplane.

BELOW: Macchi C.200 fighters of the Italian air force patrol above an Axis merchant ship in the Mediterranean.

of the X Fliegerkorps reached Sicily, the German formation's bombers soon to be put into action against Malta.

In January 1941, German aircraft seriously damaged the carrier *Illustrious*, lying in Malta while temporary repairs were being carried out. With a target of this importance on the island, the Germans and Italians, naturally enough, stepped up their attacks very considerably for a period of one week in the middle of

January. Furious battles raged over the island, but the defence held, and *Illustrious* was able to depart for proper repairs on 23 January. This miniature Blitz, however, was a portent of what was still to come.

During the same period, the aircraft of Air Chief-Marshal Sir Arthur Longmore's Middle East air forces were operating with considerable success against the Italians in Greece, providing the Greeks with much-needed tactical air support. Although no British land forces were involved at first, Longmore was finding the strain of the Greek campaign increasingly severe, yet was being ordered to supply ever larger numbers of his aircraft to this theatre. Longmore's difficulties were further increased when the Germans invaded Greece in April 1941. The British forces put up a gallant but hopeless defence, and the RAF units in the area were able to do little more than slow the Germans down, at a great cost to themselves. If the obsolescence of the biplane had not been fully clear before the Greek campaign, it was amply demonstrated by the success of the Luftwaffe's modern bombers and fighters, and the biplane was now rapidly to disappear from the RAF's front-line inventory.

ABOVE: In 1941 and 1942 Malta's Grand Harbour at Valetta, on the north-eastern coast, was one of the most heavily attacked places in the world. Here the crew of a 40-mm Bofors anti-aircraft gun await the inevitability of yet another raid.

ABOVE RIGHT: Shipping and facilities in Malta's Grand Harbour come under Axis air attack.

RIGHT: The British sea and air strengths, based on Malta, played havoc with the Axis lines of maritime communication across the Mediterranean, especially with aircraft such as the Martin Baltimore (seen here taking off) and its predecessor, the Martin Maryland.

fighter ace, Hans-Joachim Marseille. In a short and spectacular career, Marseille shot down 158 Allied aircraft before his own death, which resulted not from combat but from an engine problem.

Nevertheless, the RAF gradually improved its overall performance throughout the period, pioneering the widespread use of fighter-bombers operating in close support of the land forces. The Western Desert was an ideal place for such developments, which were to play an extremely important part in the Italian and North-West European campaigns later in the war. Large numbers of modern aircraft gradually found their way out to North Africa, and by the autumn of 1942 the Allies had secured almost total air supremacy over Libya. In the closing stages of the war,

LEFT: The best anti-ship warplane used by the Italians was the SIAI-Marchetti SM.79 Sparviero. This three-engined warplane had been conceived as a conventional bomber but also proved itself an excellent anti-ship warplane with two air-launched torpedoes.

BELOW: A member of a Supermarine Spitfire fighter's ground crew chalks up the 1,000th Axis warplane downed by the air component of Malta's defences.

Coming at the same time as Rommel's first offensive in North Africa, the Greek campaign proved too much for the already overextended RAF units in the area, and meant that the British could hold neither Greece nor Cyrenaica. Longmore had been succeeded by Air-Marshal Arthur Tedder, who decided to cut his losses and provide no air defence for the island of Crete, which fell to German airborne assault in May 1941. Tedder was now free to concentrate on his prime areas, Malta and North Africa. By the middle of July, British successes in East Africa, Iraq and Syria had further reduced Tedder's worries, leaving only the two prime areas in which most combat aircraft could now be concentrated. This concentration was essential since, by now, elements of the Luftwaffe had arrived in North Africa.

For the rest of 1941 and 1942, the fortunes of the air war in North Africa closely reflected the pattern set by ground operations, the prevailing side generally enjoying a fair measure of air superiority. Although the Germans rarely deployed a great number of aircraft in this theatre, their performance in the air was of a very high quality, epitomized in the great

THE ALLIES FIGHT BACK

with the Allies gradually crushing the Axis forces into Tunisia from the east and the west, their air superiority was total, and played a vital role in checking the last German offensives in the area. By May 1943, once the Axis forces in Tunisia had capitulated and brought the North African war to an end, the Desert Air Force was a powerful tactical formation, possibly the most highly-trained and experienced force of its kind in the world.

During this period, Malta had suffered tremendous punishment, but had in turn played a significant part in the reversal of Axis fortunes in North Africa. Between June and October 1941, for example, Malta-based aircraft had sunk 115,000 tons of Axis shipping taking supplies to North Africa, action which seriously affected Rommel's efforts. Hitler decided, in October 1941, that the problem of Malta must be solved by drastic measures. Field-Marshal Albert Kesselring was recalled from the Eastern Front to take command of air operations against the island, and the II Fliegerkorps joined the X Fliegerkorps at Italian bases

ABOVE: Germany's most versatile warplane of World War II, and a rival to the British de Havilland Mosquito in this respect, was the magnificent Junkers Ju 88 twin-engined machine. This is a Ju 88A-14 bomber, used in the anti-ship role in the Mediterranean theatre during 1942.

RIGHT: An Allied transport burns after being struck by a bomb in the Mediterranean.

for the operation, which was launched on 22 December 1941. First the airfields and then the towns came under attack. The pattern and nature of the defence followed that which had been set by London a year before, and both the civilians and troops behaved with great gallantry and fortitude. Despite the strength of the German and Italian offensive, the islanders never faltered, despite being frequently close to breaking point. The first stage of Kesselring's offensive lasted up to June 1942. By this time Malta was on the verge of starvation and its aircraft almost out of fuel and ammunition. Convoys bringing in supplies of all kinds had suffered very heavily, but sufficient supplies arrived in June to revitalize the defence and cause Kesselring to call a temporary halt. In July, the German offensive was begun again, but after a last desperate effort in October this too was overcome by the island's fighters. Meanwhile, Allied shipping based on Malta had been striking at the Axis convoys to North Africa, action which finally starved Rommel of almost all essential supplies.

By the beginning of 1943, therefore, Malta was firmly in control of the central Mediterranean, and the fate of the Axis forces in North Africa was now sealed.

THE AXIS FORCES ARE ELIMINATED FROM NORTH AFRICA

Operation Torch was the Allied plan to land US and, to a lesser extent, British forces in the French territories of Morocco and Algeria, then quickly to build them into a potent 1st Army which would advance east to take Tunisia and link with the westward advance of the 8th Army. The Allies faced a problem of where to land, however, and this was complicated by the threat of U-boats in the Atlantic and Mediterranean, the range of Axis aircraft, and possible French opposition. Although there were no Axis forces in French North Africa, the proximity of Tunis to Sicily made it likely that the Germans and Italians would attempt to counter Allied landings there.

Operation Torch was the first large-scale amphibious operation to be launched over such long distances and the first Anglo-American combined operation. There were three landings: the Western Task Force, which landed at Casablanca, and was wholly American

ABOVE: For much of the time that Malta was under Axis siege, single-engined fighters could be delivered only by recourse to an expedient, namely take-off from an aircraft carrier operating at the fighters' extreme range from the island. Here a Supermarine Spitfire land-based fighter, carrying a large external tank, is brought up to the flightdeck of the US carrier Wasp, *before taking off and heading toward Malta.*

LEFT: Here, captured German aircraft, including Messerschmitt Bf 110 and Junkers Ju 52/3m machines, are seen in North Africa.

THE ALLIES FIGHT BACK

US troops prepare for their November 1942 landings in French North Africa.

under Major-General George S. Patton, and which was conveyed from the USA in US ships; the Centre Task Force which landed at Oran, with US ground troops led by Major-General Lloyd R. Fredendall, coming from the UK in British ships; and the Eastern Task Force which landed near Algiers and was predominantly British under Lieutenant-General K.A.N. Anderson, leading the Allied 1st Army. Anderson's forces were to secure Tunis, being under the nominal command of an American officer, Major-General Charles W. Ryder, whom, it was hoped, would be less likely to excite French hostility.

Lieutenant-General Dwight D. Eisenhower was now Allied commander-in-chief, and it was envisaged that his forces would meet up with General Sir Bernard Montgomery's 8th Army to expel the last Axis forces remaining in North Africa.

The landings took place before dawn on 8 November 1942, but not without some opposition from the Vichy French. Their naval installations and ships at Mers-el-Kébir and Oran fired on the Allies, and there was fierce fighting at Oran itself. Admiral Jean-François Darlan, commander-in-chief of the Vichy French forces, called for a ceasefire throughout French North Africa on 10 November, which saved Casablanca from Allied assault. The Allies had landed safely, however, and the race for Tunis was on. Anderson immediately organized his 1st Army's eastward advance. Between Algiers and Tunis were 400 miles (650km) of mountainous,

inhospitable terrain, consequently his forces went by sea to Bône, then overland to approach Tunis. By now, however, Hitler had decided to establish a bridgehead around Tunis and Bizerta: German and Italian troops, originally intended as reinforcements for Rommel, arrived in growing numbers, with the Luftwaffe taking over important airfields in Tunisia. By the end of November there were 15,000 Axis combat troops and more than 50 tanks in Tunis, organized into the XC Corps under General Walther Nehring. Nehring ordered General Georges Edmond Lucien Barré, the Vichy French commander in Tunisia, to clear the way for the Germans toward Algeria, but Barré refused to co-operate. In mid-November, pro-Allied French ground troops formed a thin defensive line to keep the Germans at bay as the 1st Army advanced.

Anderson's forces, in the form of the 78th Division and a detachment of the 6th Armoured Division, made good progress, coming into contact with German battle groups probing westward on 17 November. On 18 November the 36th Brigade beat off a German attack at Djebel Abiod. The British attacked toward Tunis, together with a few US units known as Blade Force, but were repulsed. The Germans carried out round-the-clock bombing. Anderson's lines of communication were weak, and a depot system was lacking. However, Anderson had established contact with Barré and the French. Anderson tried for another month, with US reinforcements, to crack the German defences, but torrential rain made movement difficult. On 24 December, Eisenhower abandoned the immediate attempt to capture Tunis and Bizerta. A stalemate ensued, the Allies having lost the race for Tunis.

Meanwhile, Montgomery had advanced 1,500 miles (2400km) miles from Egypt to Tunisia in two months, after his victory at El Alamein. On 23 November Field-Marshal Erwin Rommel withdrew into Mersa Brega.

LEFT: US troops wade ashore in French North-West Africa during Operation Torch in November 1942. Vichy French resistance was only sporadic.

BELOW: US carrierborne warplanes, such as the Douglas SBD Dauntless, provided the landed troops with air support.

Montgomery decided to attack on 15 December, planning to pin Rommel in a frontal assault with two divisions, while the New Zealand Division carried out a 200-mile (320-km) outflanking march through the desert to block Rommel's withdrawal down the coastal road. Rommel's air reconnaissance spotted Lieutenant-General Sir Bernard Freyberg's New Zealanders approaching, and when they reached the coastal road, on the night of 15 December, the New Zealanders found that all Rommel's forces, except the rearguards, had already passed through. Rommel was ordered to delay the 8th Army for at least two months before falling back to the Mareth Line, just over the Tunisian frontier, but his 21st Panzer Division was sent on ahead to Tunisia.

Tunisia's coastal plain contains the ports of Sousse, Sfax and Gabès, and there are two mountain ranges, the Eastern and Western Dorsales. French forces under Lieutenant-General

THE ALLIES FIGHT BACK

Men load 3-in (75-mm) ammunition for the main gun of an M4 Sherman medium tank before it is landed over the beach in French North-West Africa.

Alphonse Juin occupied the passes in the Eastern Dorsale as far south as the Gulf of Gabès. As they arrived, the Anglo-American troops were held in reserve along the Western Dorsale or in the plain between the two. The command system was complicated by the French refusal to take orders from the British, and Eisenhower assumed tactical control of the front. There was no dominant personality to lead the Allies: Anderson's 1st Army was in northern Tunisia and Fredendall's US II Corps was at Tébessa, with Major-General J.E. Welvet's French Constantine Division forward at the Faid pass and at Gafsa.

Operation Satin, devised by American planners, called for an advance of the US II Corps from Tébessa. The 1st Infantry and 1st Armored Divisions, with the Constantine Division, would push through to Sfax or Gabès, cutting the Axis lines of communications between

Tripoli and Tunis. The plan was vetoed, however, the 1st Armored Division deemed to be too inexperienced.

The Axis powers now had some 47,000 Germans and 18,000 Italians formed into the 5th Panzerarmee under Colonel-General Jürgen von Arnim, and comprised the 10th Panzer Division, 334th Division, Broich Division and 501st Tiger Tank Battalion. The Italians formed the XXX Corps, while the Luftwaffe had control of the air.

Operation Eilbote (Express Messenger) was launched to roll up Allied positions in the Eastern Dorsale from north to south. On 18 January 1943 a diversionary attack was made by the 10th Panzer Division against the British 6th Armoured Division at Bou Arada, but was stopped by British artillery, mines and the mud. Major-General Friedrich Weber's 334th Division struck farther south along the Eastern Dorsale,

cutting off and destroying the French garrisons. An effective, but late counter-attack by Brigadier-General Paul Robinett's Combat Command B, of the US II Corps, put an end to Eilbote, but with the Fondouk pass and 4,000 prisoners fallen to the Germans.

On 30 January the 21st Panzer Division, with approximately 150 tanks and strong air support, attacked the Faid pass and 1,000 French surrendered. Fredendall misjudged the situation and did not send enough help. All the passes were now in German possession, although their attempts to take Maknassy failed. Farther to the east, on 23 January, Rommel slipped out of Tripoli and began to withdraw to the Mareth Line, consisting of old French fortifications on the Libyan-Tunisian frontier, which Rommel considered antiquated and now untenable. Meanwhile, Montgomery took Tripoli.

The Germans now planned to attack the Allied front by a north-westerly thrust from Faid to Fondouk, with the 10th Panzer Division attacking from Faid to Sidi Bou Zid while the 21st Panzer Division made a southerly detour to approach the US positions from Maknassy. The Americans were unaware of the scale of the German operation, which was launched on 14 February. The 10th Panzer Division occupied Sidi Bou Zid and Combat Command C bravely counter-attacked the next day, with the result that the Germans destroyed two tank, two artillery and two infantry battalions of the US II Corps in three days.

Anderson now realized this was a major offensive and ordered prompt withdrawal of all forces to the Western Dorsale. He sent units of the British 6th Armoured Division and 1st Guards Brigade to hold the passes of the Western Dorsale, including those at Sbiba and Kasserine. The German armour pursued the Allied retreat, taking Sbeitla on 17 February. Rommel then ordered the Deutsches Afrika Korps assault group to seize the Kasserine pass, through which he would then advance to Le Kef. The 21st Panzer Division was to break through Sbiba pass and also make for Le Kef, but the pass was heavily defended and the 21st Panzer Division was repulsed. The 10th Panzer Division moved up to the Kasserine pass, which was held by the US 26th Infantry Division and the 19th Combat Engineer Regiment. After being thrown back, the Panzers eventually forced their way through. The 10th Panzer Division struck out toward Thala and was repulsed by the British 6th Armoured Division and the artillery of the US 9th Division. As a result the Germans withdrew from the Kasserine pass, the Allies reoccupying it on 24 February, closing up on the Axis positions on the Eastern Dorsale.

There was now considerable tension and mistrust in the Allied command, with low morale and complacency also

apparent, especially in the US II Corps. This changed after 15 February, however, when General Sir Harold Alexander, as Eisenhower's deputy, set up his 18th Army Group headquarters to exercise tactical control over the land battle. Like Montgomery, Alexander insisted on training, discipline and no thoughts of withdrawal. There were problems, too, on the Axis side. Von Arnim thought the Kasserine pass should be the final objective of a

TOP: A German self-propelled anti-aircraft gun in the dock area of Tunis as the Axis tries to strengthen its last toehold in Africa.

ABOVE: Part of a typical German mixed armour and infantry unit.

LEFT: Increasingly overwhelmed by the Allies' numerical and matériel superiority, the Germans in particular fought with their accustomed skill as the Axis steadily lost ground in Tunisia.

British troops on the Mareth Line, the defence built by the French before the war to deter any Italian forays into French North Africa. Rather than fight their way through the Mareth Line, the British opted for a deep outflanking movement through the Matmata Hills to the south, forcing the Axis troops to fall back from the Mareth Line.

counter-attack, while Rommel was convinced that a thrust from Tébessa to the coastal city of Bône would cut the Allied line of communication. Von Arnim was a difficult man to deal with, but on 23 February Rommel became commander of the new Army Group Afrika. General Giovanni Messe was now commander of the German-Italian 1st Army, including the DAK, whose task it was to defend the Mareth Line.

Montgomery was now preparing to attack Rommel's main position southeast of Gabès and had pushed his advanced forces almost to the Mareth

Line. But Rommel attacked first. On 6 March he threw the 10th, 15th and 21st Panzer Divisions against positions defended at Medenine by nearly 500 anti-tank guns, repulsing them with heavy losses. Rommel then returned to Germany on sick leave, handing over command of the Army Group Afrika to von Arnim, reinforced by the Hermann Göring Panzer Division, Manteuffel Division and 999th Division.

On 6 March Alexander placed Lieutenant-General Patton at the head of the US II Corps, which was a change for the better. Alexander's formula for

success was to feint with one fist and hit with the other. He saw two stages to defeating the Axis: passing the 8th Army through the Mareth Line and the Gabès gap to unite his two armies; and tightening a land, sea and air noose around the Axis forces, to weaken them by blockade so that they would be unable to withstand the final blow. Alexander regrouped the forces into national units.

The Long Range Desert Group confirmed that there was a way around the Mareth Line for the 8th Army, through the desert west of the Matmata hills, and that the route back to the sea was through a narrow defile, the Tebaga gap. Lieutenant-General Sir Oliver Leese's XXX Corps was to breach the Mareth Line in the coastal area, while the New Zealand Corps would make for the Tebaga gap, with Montgomery keeping the X Corps and the 1st and 7th Armoured Divisions in reserve. The results of this Operation Pugilist were disappointing. The XXX Corps advanced in heavy rain and reached Wadi Zigzaou, where it was intercepted by the 15th Panzer Division. The XXX Corps became bogged down in the mud and proceeded no farther. Freyberg's New Zealanders seized the entrance to the Tebaga gap on the night of 21–22 March, but next morning found the 21st Panzer Division blocking the way forward. Montgomery now sent the X Corps and the 1st Armoured Division to Tebaga, which arrived on 26 March and immediately attacked. The Desert Air Force ably supported the Allied drive, which was highly successful, stunning the Axis forces. But the breakthrough at El Hamma was too late to prevent Messe from regrouping his forces along the Wadi Akarit, where he was obliged to defend only the 8-mile (13-km) line between the Gulf of Gabès and the lake of Chott el Fedjadj.

Patton's II Corps had meanwhile taken Gafsa on 17 March, it being Patton's task to support Montgomery by drawing off the Axis forces. On 28

although von Arnim had been left without proper communications, sufficient petrol, or replacements of armour and artillery. By now he had 16 exhausted divisions with which to hold 135 miles (220km) of front. Alexander's plan, Operation Vulcan, gave the 1st Army the task of capturing Tunis, while the US II Corps, now led by Lieutenant-General Omar N. Bradley, was to capture Bizerta, the 8th Army to draw off the Axis reserves. It took until 7 May for the Allies to succeed in taking Tunis and Bizerta, and the Axis forces now had their backs to the sea. They received no further supplies, for Hitler was now starting to focus on the possible defence of Sicily, a likely candidate for the Allies' next strategic movement. Even so, each Allied attack was vigorously fought off. Montgomery and his 8th Army attacked Messe at Enfidaville twice but failed to break through.

Alexander's *coup de grâce* was Operation Strike on 6 May, when the British 4th and Indian 4th Divisions attacked side-by-side on a 3,000-yard (2745-m) front astride the road linking Medjez and Tunis, supported by 650

ABOVE LEFT: Truck transport was of vital importance to the Allies in the closing stages of the North African campaign as the front line moved steadily farther from the ports from which supplies could be unloaded.

ABOVE: Men of the British 8th Army and US II Corps of the Allied 1st Army link up in Tunisia.

LEFT: German troops moving toward the front.

March he attacked vigorously along the road from Gafsa toward Gabès, repulsing the 10th Panzer Division at El Guettar. Montgomery's forces attacked the Wadi Akarit on 6 April. Three divisions of the 8th Army, supported by 450 guns, tore a gaping hole in the Axis position, but when the X Corps' tanks entered the battle, von Arnim's forces retreated. The 8th Army passed through the Gabès gap and the two Allied armies finally linked.

The Allied build-up had been continual. Now they lacked for nothing, having control of numerous airfields. Nevertheless, the Germans and Italians fought hard to hold Tunis and Bizerta. Hitler would not sanction evacuation,

RIGHT: A U-boat comes under Allied air attack. Long-range land-based aircraft and carrierborne warplanes played an increasingly important and successful part in the campaign against the U-boat during 1942 and 1943.

RIGHT: A U-boat comes under Allied air attack. Long-range land-based aircraft and carrierborne warplanes played an increasingly important and successful part in the campaign against the U-boat during 1942 and 1943.

BELOW: A US poster encourages men to enlist in the US Navy.

guns and tactical aircraft. When the defences were breached, the 6th and 7th Armoured Divisions rushed through at speed heading for Tunis. Von Arnim knew they were coming, but they were short of everything necessary to meet the attack. But the way to Tunis was open at last, Tunis and Bizerta had been captured, and it was truly the end of the line for the Axis forces in Africa, who surrendered on 13 May. Some 130,000 Germans and 118,000 Italians were taken into Allied hands.

THE WAR AGAINST THE U-BOAT, JANUARY 1942–MAY 1943

Any hope that the USA's December 1941 entry into World War II would lighten the burden on the British and Canadian navies was misplaced. Admiral Karl Dönitz had already planned to move many of his U-boats across the North Atlantic to dislocate shipping along the USA's eastern seaboard, and five days after Pearl Harbor he launched Operation Paukenschlag (Drum Roll). This succeeded beyond all expectation, for the US Navy was caught with virtually no means of protecting its shipping. The U-boats called this the 'second happy time', for merchant ships were unescorted, uncoded radio messages gave constant positions, and all navigation lights were still lit. The US Navy had pinned its hopes on offensive patrolling by destroyers rather than on convoys, therefore its considerable efforts were largely wasted. The U-boats gleefully noted the regularity with which destroyers passed at high speed, and surfaced as soon as the patrol had gone,

secure in the knowledge that they could continue to sink shipping for a few hours without interruption. The US Navy was woefully short of anti-submarine aircraft, and the US Army Air Forces' available aircrews were not adequately trained for this particular task, problems which were reflected in a massive rise in shipping losses. Between 1 January and 31 March some 60 tankers were sunk in the Caribbean alone, and losses along the whole of the east coast exceeded a million tons during the same period.

The short-term answer was for the British to transfer 24 anti-submarine trawlers, fitted with Asdic, and ten 'Flower'-class corvettes to the US Navy. Even private aircraft were pressed into service, flying patrols along the coast in an effort to scare off the U-boats. In April a convoy system was initiated, but did not become universal until June. Significantly, the U-boats then returned to their main hunting-ground in the mid-Atlantic, where they were out of reach of shore-based aircraft.

were now available to set up offensive support groups to carry the fight to the U-boats. A solution was also found for the problem of the 'black gap', the area in the middle of the Atlantic out of range of shore-based aircraft and in which the U-boats scored their greatest successes. Four-engined Consolidated B-24 Liberator bombers, with extra fuel tanks, had helped to narrow the gap, and the definitive solution was found in the decision to take aircraft to sea with the convoys. The first escort carrier, a merchant ship fitted with a small wooden flight deck, had been tried in the autumn of 1941, and although it was soon sunk, this was only after it had been appreciated how effective were the capabilities so offered. Orders were placed for more such merchant ship conversions to be followed by purpose-built vessels, and these latter started to enter the water from US yards in

LEFT: The threat of Allied air attack led the Germans to construct huge pens of thick reinforced concrete to provide safety for U-boats between patrols.

BELOW: The Allies' ability to locate and attack U-boats was much enhanced by the combination of better tactics, improved technical equipment, and larger numbers of specialized escort and anti-submarine warships. This is the ex-Admiralty yacht Enchantress, a notable feature of which is the lattice mast supporting the HF/DF ('Huff-Duff') radio direction-finding equipment. This allowed the position of a broadcasting U-boat to be fixed with considerable accuracy.

Another heavy burden on the Allied escort forces resulted from the Allied decision to supply weapons and equipment to the USSR, following the Germans' Barbarossa invasion. Losses were heavy as the convoy routes to Murmansk and Arkhangyel'sk passed close to the German airfields, U-boat bases, and surface warship anchorages in central and northern Norway. The most unfortunate convoy of all was PQ-17, which in July 1942 had 23 out of 37 ships sunk, resulting in the loss of 99,000 tons of cargo, 3,350 vehicles, 430 tanks and 210 aircraft in just one convoy action. The PQ-17 disaster resulted from a premature report that the battleship *Tirpitz* had put out to sea: the battleship did not make contact, but the convoy was deliberately scattered, so that the battleship's guns would not have a concentrated target, and the ships were then picked off singly by U-boats and warplanes.

By the autumn of 1942, however, British and US production was starting to have an effect, as enough new escorts

ABOVE: Another Allied success was the Liberty ship, a simple yet efficient mercantile design that could be built quickly from prefabricated sections to offset the loss of other vessels to the U-boats.

RIGHT: The bridge crew of a U-boat scans the horizon for evidence of a convoy to attack or a warplane to be avoided.

ever-larger numbers. With the support groups, the escort or 'jeep' carriers showed that the time had come to turn to the offensive. Events in the Atlantic were now moving toward a climax, for U-boat completions were also moving toward a peak.

It remained to be seen if Dönitz would realize his ambition of sinking merchant ships faster than they could be built. At this moment, the Allied leaders made what seems in retrospect to have been a rash move. Goaded by demands from Stalin for a second front but daunted by the obvious problems of landing in Europe, the Americans settled for the Operation Torch amphibious landing in North Africa at the end of 1942. While there were advantages to be gained by clearing Axis forces out of North Africa, particularly the elimination of the airbases which menaced the supply-route to Malta, the main motive behind the North African project was political, in that it was to placate Stalin and get US troops into the land war against the Germans. A major problem

for Torch, however, was that the great convoys bringing US troops and their weapons and equipment straight across the Atlantic would need massive

protection against U-boats. To achieve this, the new escort carriers and support groups were removed from the Atlantic for the duration of Torch.

Dönitz could not realistically be expected to forego such an opportunity, and although his U-boats failed to stop the Torch convoys from reaching North Africa, they were quick to exploit the reduced strength of Atlantic escort forces. As a result, the losses of Allied merchant ships rose to 619,000 tons in October and to 729,000 tons in November. They fell again in December because of the severe weather, but at the end of that month Allied shipping losses for 1942 totalled 7.79 million tonnes. U-boat construction was slower than Dönitz had hoped, but there were nonetheless 312 boats in service at this time, as compared with 91 at the end of 1941.

As 1943 began, the Allied leadership appreciated that the decisive moment of the war had arrived. If the U-boats continued to sink ships at the rate evident in the later part of 1942, the UK would be forced out of the war: the advocates of an increased strategic

bomber effort from the UK could not ignore the fact that continued oil tanker losses would soon cripple current efforts, and success in a secondary theatre, such as North Africa, was equally pointless if communications across the Atlantic were cut. Thus it is all the more remarkable that there was a running squabble in the UK between the Air Ministry and the Admiralty, in which the Bomber Command lobby was far too successful in blocking the transfer of four-engined bombers to Coastal Command for the anti-submarine role. Even after January 1943, when the Casablanca Conference issued a directive to the Allied bomber chiefs to give top priority to defeating the U-boats, the response was the bombing of U-boat construction yards. Not until the end of the war did these raids destroy a single U-boat, although they did delay production and caused ancillary

damage; but they also led to the loss of many bombers, which could have been put to better use over the Atlantic.

Meanwhile, the convoys were suffering appalling losses in a series of battles as ferocious as any yet seen. In the first two months of 1943 atrocious weather hampered the U-boats as much as it did the convoys, but in March a great four-day battle took place between 17 U-boats and a convoy, in which 13 ships, totalling some 60,000 tons, were lost. Single fast and slow convoys, bound for Halifax on the eastern side of Canada, were then attacked by 40 U-boats, the German attack being so fierce that the escort commanders decided to combine the two convoys to strengthen the escort. Before the U-boats' grip could be loosened by the arrival of shore-based aircraft, they had sunk 141,000 tons of shipping. The British and Americans were close to

despair, for no matter what technical wizardry their scientists could produce, and no matter how many ships were being built, the U-boats were winning. In the first three weeks of March more than 500,000 tons of shipping were sent to the bottom of the sea; it appeared that the convoy system had at last failed.

This was a truly black moment for the Allies, but then the virtual coincidence of three factors finally turned the tide. Firstly, the escorts and more importantly the escort carriers diverted for Torch became available once more in the Western Approaches, and by delaying the departure of two large convoys to the USSR, the Admiralty was able to form five support groups, the US Navy also introducing the first of its new escort carrier groups. Secondly, 'Ultra' information, garnered by cryptanalysis of intercepted German signals allowed the routing of convoys

ABOVE LEFT: An interim step in the introduction of aircraft to tackle mid-ocean attacks was the CAM-ship. This was a merchantman adapted with a catapult to launch a single Hawker Hurricane fighter. Once it had tackled the enemy, the Hurricane had to ditch in the sea, whence the pilot hoped he would be rescued.

ABOVE: Survivors of the disastrous PQ-17 convoy through Arctic waters to a northern Soviet port. Ordered to scatter, in the belief that a German surface force was about to descend upon it, the convoy became easy prey for German aircraft and U-boats.

THE ALLIES FIGHT BACK

One of the definitive answers to the U-boat threat was the availability of greater numbers of genuinely long-ranged aircraft such as the Consolidated Liberator. This was large enough to carry considerable fuel as well as radar and a sizeable weapons load.

away from the known positions of U-boat 'wolf packs'. And thirdly, the Atlantic Convoy Conference in March led to an immediate pooling of Allied escort resources, which made for more efficient deployment of ships. Another, but less obvious factor, was German inferiority in the technical race. Not until January 1943 did the Germans realize that the Allies were using centimetric-wavelength radar equipment, and a suitable search receiver could not be produced in time to affect the issue of the Allies' growing capability in finding and successfully attacking surfaced U-boats.

Shipping losses suddenly became fewer toward the end of March, and in April dropped by 50 per cent. Six U-boats had been sunk in January, 19 in February, 15 in March and 15 in April, but in May the figure soared to 41. The Allies were now being more selective in their offensive measures, with aircraft and ship patrols concentrated where the U-boats were most likely to be found, notably the Bay of Biscay. The U-boats were saving time by crossing the bay on the surface at high speed, and the Allies appreciated that if the boats could be forced to make most of this passage

under the water, it would cut their time on patrol in the middle of the Atlantic. When Ultra revealed that U-boats were refuelling at prearranged points in mid-Atlantic from 'milch-cow' U-boats, these underwater tankers were made top priority targets for the support groups. The Allied shipbuilding and aircraft-production programmes were now getting into their strides, and ships and aircraft for the anti-submarine task were being delivered in significantly larger numbers and with a markedly improved package of weapons and sensors.

The tactics used by escorts and aircraft were improving all the time, and new weapons were being introduced to exploit the ideas put forward by scientists and servicemen. The leading British anti-submarine expert, Commander Frederick J. Walker, introduced the creeping attack, using one escort to track a U-boat from a distance while using radio to direct another to move slowly into attack position: the unsuspecting U-boat was unable to hear the slow propeller revolutions of the attacking ship, and also believed that escorts dared not drop depth charges while moving slowly, for fear that the detonations would blow off the sterns of their own vessels. When Walker found that U-boats were diving deeper than ever before he asked for a 1-ton depth charge, the USA responding with the Fido homing torpedo, designed to home onto the noise of a diving U-boat's propellers.

The introduction of escort carriers meant new tactics, too, for these could be vulnerable to torpedo attack.

A most important adjunct to radar and Asdic was 'Huff-Duff' (high-frequency direction-finding), which made it possible for ships to pinpoint the position of a U-boat transmitting a sighting report back to base, as demanded by Dönitz. Although the Germans picked up information about Huff-Duff from monitored messages, their scientists were sceptical about the possibility of producing a high-precision

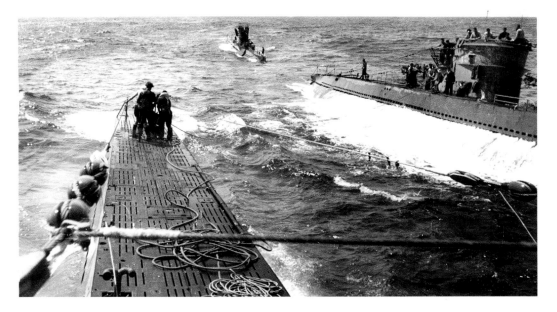

set small enough to go into a warship, and the rash of unexplained losses was therefore attributed to a new type of Allied radar. Even when a photograph of a destroyer fitted with a Huff-Duff mast was taken by agents at Algeciras in Spain, near Gibraltar, the German censor deleted the mast before the photograph could be circulated.

By this time the German navy had effectively abandoned all notions that its surface vessels could be committed in any useful way to the Battle of the Atlantic. In February 1942, the battle-cruisers *Scharnhorst* and *Gneisenau*, and the heavy cruiser *Prinz Eugen*, made as brilliant dash eastward along the English Channel from Brest toward German ports in broad daylight. But however much this exploit may have annoyed the British, it availed the Germans nothing, for the removal of the three ships from Brest meant that a surface intervention from north-western France could now be discounted. Apart from her role in forcing the PQ-17 convoy to scatter, the *Tirpitz* did nothing; for Hitler, the last straw as far as the German surface forces were concerned, was the Battle of the Barents Sea on 31 December 1942. The

heavy cruisers *Lützow* and *Admiral Hipper*, supported by six destroyers, sortied to attack the JW-51B convoy bound for the USSR, but the eight

destroyers of the escort fought them off using a brilliant mixture of bluff and tactics. Hitler was so enraged by this display of ineptitude that he threatened to lay up the entire surface fleet. This provoked the resignation of Grand Admiral Erich Raeder, commander-in-chief of the navy, to be replaced by Dönitz. Although Dönitz did little to implement Hitler's threats, the change meant that the Kriegsmarine was now completely committed to winning the U-boat war. The last surface action involving a major surface warship of the German navy occurred in the Battle of the North Cape on 26 December 1943, when the battle-cruiser *Scharnhorst*, together with five destroyers, tried to intercept the JW-55B convoy, which was being escorted by 14 destroyers, covered by a force of three cruisers, and covered at a greater distance by the battleship *Duke of York*, one cruiser, and four destroyers. The *Scharnhorst* was separated from the destroyers, which had

LEFT: A rendezvous between a 'milch cow' supply submarine and a U-boat, the object being to refuel operational U-boats in mid-ocean, thereby extending the length of their patrols.

BELOW: Iceland was an important gathering point for westward bound transatlantic convoys.

The Germans failed to appreciate the value of a long-range force of strategic heavy bombers until it was almost too late, and then squandered invaluable time and resources on efforts to solve a technically difficult problem, namely the Heinkel He 177, with four engines geared to drive two propellers. For lack of anything else, therefore, the Luftwaffe had to soldier on with improved versions of the twin-engined medium bombers with which it had begun the war.

been ordered to fan out and search for targets, and was then trapped by the heavier British units before sinking under a welter of gunfire.

Despite propaganda assertions to the contrary, the U-boat arm was compelled to concede defeat in May 1943. The U-boat remained a potent threat to the end, but after May the issue was no longer in doubt. German ingenuity produced many brilliant innovations, but the shortage of materials, dislocation of industry, and continuing remorseless pressure by the Soviet forces on the Eastern Front, made matters steadily worse as each month went by. When the surrender came in May 1945, new and deadlier U-boats were in existence, but only in tiny numbers, and even these had been delayed while scarce resources were wasted on more exciting projects.

THE BOMBER OFFENSIVE 1940–42

With the exception of the German bombings of Warsaw at the climax of the Polish campaign in September 1939, and of Rotterdam in May 1940, the use of large-scale bombing had at first been deliberately avoided by both sides. Each feared that large numbers of civilian dead would spur retaliation and, according to the theories of strategic air warfare prevalent in the 1930s, would inevitably lead to the total destruction of cities. During most of 1939 and the first half of 1940, therefore, the British, French and Germans studiously avoided any possibility of attacks on major targets where there were civilians in the area. Only military targets were attacked, and only then using utmost caution. But the razing of Warsaw had demonstrated what could

actually be achieved with mass bombing, and the lesson was repeated in May 1940 with the destruction, perhaps accidentally, of the old quarter of Rotterdam by German bombers.

Targets attacked during the French campaign and opening phases of the Battle of Britain had usually been military, with little thought given to retaliation. Apart from attacks on oil installations and naval bases, for example, Bomber Command usually confined itself to raids in which propaganda leaflets were dropped. But then the Germans bombed London after some aircraft had strayed off course, and Prime Minister Winston Churchill called for retaliation against Berlin during August. From this time on, the scale of air operations of a supposedly strategic nature was gradually stepped up, principally by the British, it being the only means they had of striking at the Germans. The first raids of September and October were mere pinpricks, with only about 100 tons of bombs dropped on each sortie. So inaccurate was the navigation of most crews that very few of the bombs landed anywhere near their targets. Daylight raids had been attempted, but the losses had been so heavy that Bomber Command decided to switch to a policy of night bombing of large targets to minimize casualties.

Both the British and Germans employed what were really medium bombers, although they had been designated as heavy bombers at the time of their introduction. All these were twin-engined aircraft: on the German side the celebrated Heinkel He 111 and Dornier Do 17, with the Junkers Ju 88 joining them in 1939; and on the British side the Handley Page Hampden, Armstrong Whitworth Whitley and Vickers Armstrong Wellington. Germany had been developing a true strategic bomber in the mid-1930s, but at the death of the chief protagonist of the four-engined bomber concept, Lieutenant-General Walther Wever, the idea was dropped.

two were the Avro Lancaster, a four-engined development of the unsuccessful Manchester twin-engined bomber, and the Handley Page Halifax. Not very successful, but the first British four-engined bomber of World War II to enter service was the Short Stirling. This last type developed many of the techniques present in the Lancaster and Halifax, but had only a short operational career as a front-line machine before being relegated to training duties and service with the airborne forces.

While these bombers were under development, Bomber Command had been trying its best with night raids against targets in Germany. After the Coventry raid, the two main targets became the German oil industry and civilian centres of population. Attacks

LEFT: RAF ground crew load belts of 0.303-in (7.7-mm) ammunition into the twin-gun rear turret of a Vickers Wellington twin-engined medium bomber.

BELOW: The Vickers Wellington was by far the best of the British twin-engined medium bombers, and developed into a very capable maritime patrol warplane later on in its career.

This was to prove a grave disadvantage for the Germans during the war, for they had to use medium bombers, designed for the tactical role, for tasks that often required a strategic bombing capability. Subsequent efforts to design a true heavy bomber produced the Heinkel He 177, an odd machine, with four engines driving two propellers. The type was rushed into production too quickly and never proved really successful because of intractable engine problems. It should be noted, however, that the mass use of tactical bombers at short range did give the Germans some strategic capability, as the Blitz on London at the end of 1940 and the beginning of 1941 demonstrated. The high point of the German strategic effort with manned bombers against the UK, however, may be considered to be the raid on Coventry on 14 November 1940, which proved to be a considerable shock to the British.

The British had given little thought in the 1930s to four-engined heavy bombers, but when they did, three types, two of which were excellent machines, emerged in the early war years. The best

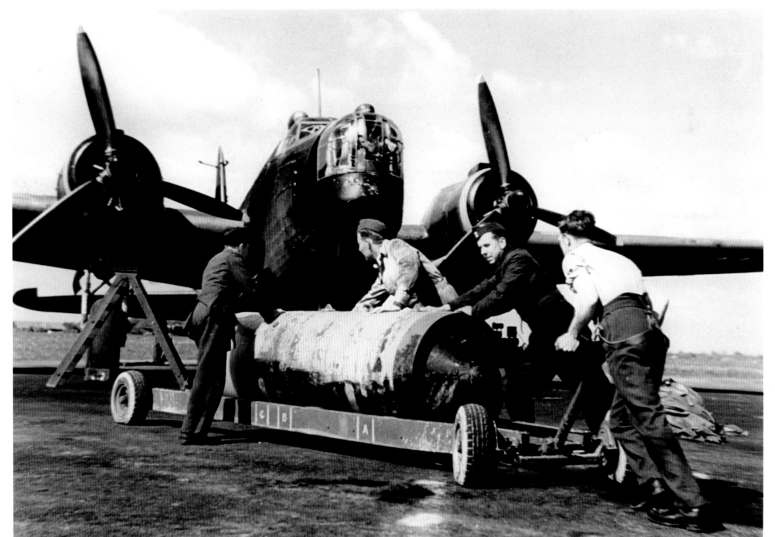

ABOVE: Bomb bursts from a British daylight raid in June 1941. When escorted by fighters, light and medium bombers were still able to operate by day, but by this time the steadily growing heavy bomber force was operating only at night.

ABOVE RIGHT: Ground crew load bundles of leaflets into an Armstrong Whitworth Whitley twin-engined bomber. This was the standard 'weapons load' of British bombers, despatched to 'attack' Germany in the autumn and winter of 1939–40, for it was feared that real bombing would spur German retaliation.

on the latter, the British hoped, would sap Germany's will to fight the war, at the same time disrupting the lives of the workforce on which the war industries depended. But if a workable concept was there, the weapons with which to implement it were not. Apart from the bombers, with their inaccurate navigation and indifferent bomb sights, the bombs themselves all too frequently failed. An assessment of the German bombing of London showed that about 10 per cent were duds, and that 60 per cent of bombs fell in open areas where their effect was minimal. There seems no reason to suppose that British bombs were any better.

At first, the inaccuracy of bombing was not suspected by the British, but from November 1940 photographs of raids began to reveal an alarming

inaccuracy. Combined with Bomber Command's desire to strike at larger targets, this meant that from May 1941 British bombers began to attack the residential parts of German cities with incendiaries. Some high-explosive bombs were also dropped, so that the civilian population would keep its head down until the fires started by the incendiaries had a chance to get properly going. But the problem was still inaccuracy. A partial solution was found in the pathfinder force: drawn from the best crews in Bomber Command, they were to use their superior navigational and piloting skills to go ahead of the main force and mark the target with special flares. Following up, the bomber force would then not have to concentrate on pinpoint navigation over the target, but could instead devote its energies to dropping its bombs as close to the markers as possible. With the

introduction of this method, Bomber Command's results began to show some steady improvement.

At the same time, Air Chief-Marshal Sir Arthur Harris was appointed to the leadership of Bomber Command, and it is with Harris that the British strategic bombing effort is most closely associated. Harris inherited a force of some 500 twin-engined bombers, and immediately set all his considerable energies to building up his force to maximum strength, hastening the introduction of the four-engined types and improving the combat efficiency of his crews. The second half of 1941 may properly be considered a preparatory period, and it was only in the spring of 1942 that Harris began to secure important victories with night bombers, the most significant being the first raid by 1,000 bombers on Köln during the night of 31 May. To launch this raid, Harris had had to take crews

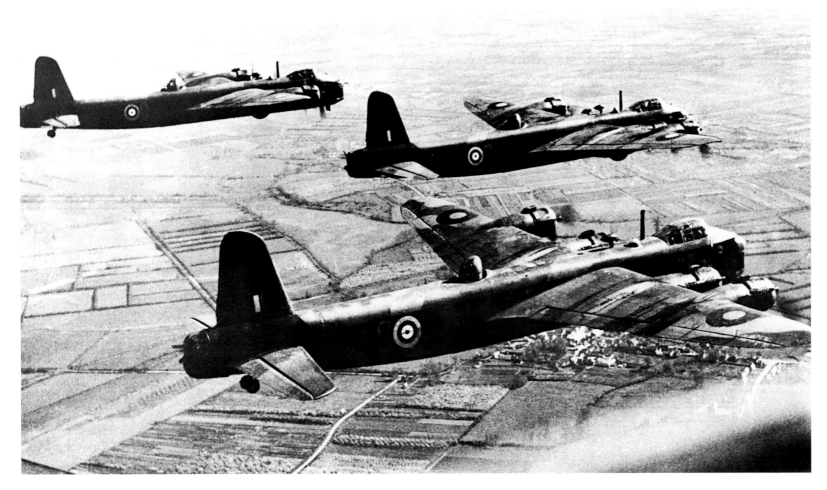

LEFT: The RAF's first four-engined heavy bomber of World War II was the Short Stirling. This was not a great success as the span, and therefore the area, of its wings had been restricted to allow the bomber to use current hangars.

BELOW: Fires rage in the docklands area of London in the aftermath of a German Blitz in 1940. The German attacks on London, though achieving little, were one of the factors that persuaded the British government to place greater emphasis on the bombing of German cities.

and aircraft from training units all over the country, but although the raid's significance in purely military terms was small, its importance in raising the morale of the British civilian population was considerable, putting Bomber Command's efforts well and truly on the map.

Harris benefited from good relations with Churchill, and so was able to cut through the RAF chain of command to deal directly with the prime minister, giving Bomber Command a certain autonomy within the RAF. An example of the relationship at work was Harris's steadfast unwillingness to give Coastal Command the relatively few four-engined machines it so desperately needed, these being Consolidated B-24 and Boeing B-17 aircraft from the USA. Churchill backed Harris in the latter's claims that the only thing that mattered was the bombing of Germany. Harris entirely overlooked or ignored the fact that even a few four-engined aircraft,

that would hardly be missed by Bomber Command, could have turned the scales in the Battle of the Atlantic, so ensuring the continued supply of fuel and raw

materials on which his bombers' effort was built. To Harris's credit, however, it should be pointed out that he worked very closely with the Ministry of

ABOVE: This photograph, of a boy with his soapbox cart, encapsulates the British sangfroid and 'business as usual' attitude prevalent during the London Blitz.

ABOVE RIGHT: Bombs explode in the docks.

RIGHT: A Heinkel He 111 twin-engined medium bomber of the Luftwaffe flying over London.

Economic Warfare in selecting targets. Even if these were not always destroyed, at least Bomber Command was attacking the right places, which had not always been the case.

While Bomber Command was gradually stepping up the quality and quantity of its raids late in 1942, the US Army's 8th Air Force was arriving in Britain to take its share of the bomber offensive. Flying B-17s and B-24s, the Americans thought that the greater

LEFT: The devastation caused after a shot-down bomber fell in the Victoria area of London.

BELOW: An annotated reconnaissance photograph reveals the points to be attacked in a raid on the power station outside the German town of Quadrath.

close to a bomber, the radar operator in the fighter took over and directed his pilot in for the 'kill', which took place once the pilot had acquired the target visually. Radar countermeasures were at last worked out by the British, but the best solution was the insertion of British night-fighters into the bomber stream. These were able to use their superior radar to search out and destroy the German night-fighters.

Compared with what it was shortly to become, however, the combined Allied bomber offensive was still in its infancy. The weapons had been produced, but it was up to the Allied leaders to discover how they should best be used.

speed and defensive firepower of their bombers would allow them to roam at will over northern Europe by day, the interlocking fields of fire from great 'boxes' of bombers being sufficient to keep the German fighters at bay. With their ability to operate by day, the Americans thought the bombers' main targets should be small but vital centres of communication and war production, which could be hit from high altitude with the aid of the Norden bomb sight. Thus, while the British destroyed German cities by night, the Americans would knock out small but vital targets by day in a gradually increasing round-the-clock bombing offensive.

The Americans made their debut over Rouen on 17 August 1942. Attacks were at first confined to targets over northern France and the Low Countries, and the Americans' confidence in themselves and their aircraft seemed to

be justified. With the arrival of the first Republic P-47 Thunderbolt escort fighters in the UK, during January 1943, the bombers were allowed to start attacking targets in Germany, but the advance in this direction was slowed by the difficulty in getting the P-47s fully operational. It was only in the early summer that the Americans were at last ready to attack objectives such as Bremen and Kiel. As yet they had made no daylight missions deep into occupied Europe, and these was to be their real test.

British losses had meanwhile been rising, largely as the result of the improved German night-fighter defences. Based on a line of radar stations around the north coast of Europe, these stations controlled large numbers of Ju 88 and Messerschmitt Bf 110 radar-equipped fighters. Once the radar station had steered the fighter

FORTUNA I AND II
QUADRATH

CHAPTER THREE
THE FLOOD OF THE JAPANESE TIDE

The US Pacific Fleet, seen here in 1940, was the primary offensive and defensive weapon available to the USA in the Pacific theatre. It was therefore one of the primary targets selected by the Japanese for neutralization in the first minutes of its war of aggression into the Pacific and South-East Asia.

PEARL HARBOR

On 26 July 1941 the government of the USA froze all Japanese assets in the country, a measure that was soon also implemented by the British government and the Dutch government in exile. This triple blow to Japan's position as a trading nation resulted from the Japanese empire's continued expansion on the mainland of Asia: ever since the beginning of the 2nd Sino-Japanese War in 1937 the USA and UK had become increasingly concerned about the growth of Japanese military domination in eastern Asia. Various measures analogous to the freezing of Japanese assets had previously been tried, but Japan had taken little notice until this new move, inspired by the Japanese occupation of French Indo-China, starting on 22 September 1940. The threat implicit in the US move of 26 July was reinforced on 17 August when President Franklin D. Roosevelt warned the government of Japan that any further Japanese efforts to secure a paramount position in eastern Asia would serve to elicit US retaliation to safeguard its policies and financial interests. While these overt moves were setting the scene for what was to follow, it should be noted that American-Japanese negotiations on the means of reducing tension between the two countries were being held in Washington, DC.

The reason why the USA, in particular, was taking these steps against Japan was basically a conflict of interest. Since the Spanish-American War of 1898–99, the Americans had been well placed in the Philippines and other Pacific island groups, inherited from the Spanish, to play a dominant role in Chinese economic affairs. This, combined with the emergence of China from its ancient monarchism into the type of democracy acceptable to the US people, meant that in the USA China had a powerful friend. Japan, too, had only latterly emerged from its self-imposed medievalism. But unlike China, Japan had kept its ancient institutions, while at the same time managing to develop itself rapidly into a modern industrial nation with distinct military leanings. These military ambitions had been exercised at the expense of China in 1894–95, Imperial Russia in 1904–05, and Imperial Germany in 1914. Japan's major problem, however, lay in the fact that although it had turned itself into a major manufacturing nation with great energy, the Japanese empire had neither sufficient raw materials to feed its industries, nor the markets to support them. Raw materials could be obtained from all over eastern Asia, and there was a huge market in China. Hence Japan's interest in securing a political and economic hegemony over the major economic bases in this area, such as

Manchuria, China, South-East Asia, and the British and Dutch East Indies. Its swift advance into the first of these areas inevitably brought Japan into conflict with the western democracies, which also had considerable economic interests in these countries.

By the 1930s, therefore, different political and economic interests had already set Japan and the western powers apart. These differences, crystallized as Japan took over Manchuria, started a war with China, with Japan then turning its attention south to Indo-China and the Dutch East Indies. The USA's feelings in the matter were already plain in its supply of arms to China, via the Burma Road from Lashio, in northern Burma, to Chunking in China, and Roosevelt's two moves, mentioned above, finally made the US position entirely clear. But Japan could not survive without raw materials and a market, and it also needed the oil that was so plentiful in the Indies. Thus the freezing of Japanese assets by the western powers did nothing to resolve the underlying problem: Japan's teeming population needed to live, and western interests were getting in the way.

Poor as the situation was during September 1941, it became immeasurably worse on 17 October 1941 when Lieutenant-General Hideki Tojo became Japanese prime minister with the support of the nation's all-powerful military establishment. While not discounting absolutely the negotiations going on in Washington, on 5 November Tojo revealed to his inner circle the plans for the war he felt was becoming increasingly certain.

By the end of November it had become clear that there could be no basis of understanding between Japan and the USA and, although negotiations continued, Japan now made the decision for war. Drawn up by staffs under the supervision of Field-Marshal Hajime Sugiyama, army chief-of-staff, and Admiral Osami Nagoya, navy chief-of-staff, the basic Japanese plan comprised three sections, based on Japan's inability to wage a protracted war against industrial nations. Firstly, the Imperial Japanese navy was to neutralize the US Pacific Fleet, the western powers' major striking force in the area, while the Imperial Japanese army and other elements of the navy seized the 'Southern Resources Area' and adjacent territories necessary to defend it. Secondly, an impregnable defence perimeter was to be set up. Thirdly, any attempts to break through this perimeter were to be repulsed so decisively that the western powers would sue for peace on the basis of a *status quo*. The whole Japanese plan was based on the two-fold premise that its forces could so maul the western powers in the first stage of the war that Japan would have the time to complete her defensive perimeter; and that the Japanese defence, based on the proven abilities of its forces, and operating on interior lines of communication, could not be breached by the westerners, operating of necessity over scanty lines of communication from main bases in the USA and Australia.

With the decision for war all but taken, steps to secure success in the first stage were set in hand. Here the aircraft-carriers of the Imperial Japanese navy were to play a decisive role in crippling the US Pacific Fleet at its base, Pearl Harbor, in the Hawaiian Islands group. Comprising six aircraft carriers and supported by battleships, cruisers, submarines and oilers, Vice-Admiral Chuichi Nagumo's 1st Air Fleet, otherwise known as the Striking Force, left the Kurile Islands on 26 November, heading by a circuitous and little used route, and in total radio silence, toward a position north of the Hawaiian Islands. The Americans, who had broken the

LEFT: As well as the ships and aircraft of the US Pacific fleet, the Japanese attack on the Hawaiian Islands targeted the aircraft of the US Army Air Forces, such as this Curtiss P-40 fighter, lying badly damaged on the ground.

BELOW: The newspaper headlines tell it all: as part of their grand offensive in December 1941, the Japanese launched a series of carefully planned land offensives under the cover of potent air power.

THE FLOOD OF THE JAPANESE TIDE

The scene of devastation on 7 December 1941 on Ford Island, the US naval air station and repair facility in the middle of Pearl Harbor. The two major failings of the Japanese attack were the escape of the US Pacific Fleet's three aircraft carriers, which were temporarily absent from Pearl Harbor, and the decision not to make another attack for the destruction of Pearl Harbor's repair facilities and fuel farms.

Japanese naval code, knew that Japan was finally preparing for war, but expected that the first blow would fall on the Philippines or Malaya; decoded radio messages indicated that Japanese forces were massing in the vicinity of both of these major objectives. Several pre-war exercises had taken an attack on Pearl Harbor into consideration, but all was peaceful there early on the morning of Sunday, 7 December 1941.

Trainee radar operators on an inefficient set north of Pearl Harbor reported that many aircraft were heading toward the islands, but the base commander dismissed the report, thinking they were the Boeing B-17 Flying Fortress bombers expected at the time, and ordered the radar crews to stand down. What the radar operators had in fact seen was Nagumo's first strike of 190 aircraft, which was soon followed

by another wave of 171. Surprise was complete, and the Japanese pilots found their targets neatly arranged in rows. The warplanes had a field day, allowing the Japanese to rack up a considerable score. This included eight battleships, of which three were sunk, one was capsized, and the remaining four seriously damaged; three cruisers and three destroyers sunk, as was a miscellany of smaller vessels; while on shore, 65 of the US Army's 231 aircraft were destroyed, as were 196 belonging to the US Navy, and 250 machines of the US Marine Corps. Apart from these material losses, the Americans lost some 3,220 men dead and 1,272 wounded, as opposed to the Japanese losses which were slight.

The blow to American strength and pride was enormous. The claim often made that Japan did not declare war before the attack on Pearl Harbor is true

but not completely so. Japan did try to declare war, but its embassy staff in Washington were so slow in decoding the relevant message that the attack had begun before the formal declaration could be made. US intelligence, however, had decoded the message in good time, but the news was not sent out quickly enough to allow the US defences to be brought onto a war footing. Nevertheless, Japan had now entered the war, turning what had previously been a European conflict into a global one.

The only solace the US Navy could find, on assessing the damage after Pearl Harbor, was the fact that the Pacific Fleet's three aircraft carriers, the *Enterprise*, *Lexington* and *Saratoga*, were absent and had therefore escaped damage, it being these ships that would take the war to Japan in the next few months. Despite the intense disappointment of the Imperial Japanese navy's airmen, that they had not been able to come to grips with their opposite numbers, the victory at Pearl Harbor was adjudged a great one, fulfilling the needs of the first stage of the Japanese war plan.

Japan's other objective in this first stage of the conflict was the securing of the Southern Resources Area. Moves to this end were being made at the time of the Pearl Harbor attack, as were mopping-up operations against US bases in the Pacific. Despite the fact that they had repulsed the first Japanese attack, with heavy losses on 11 December, the gallant defenders of Wake Island were overwhelmed in a massive second attack on 23 December, while at the foot of the Marianas Islands group, the tiny garrison of Guam had been swept aside on 10 December.

These tiny US islands, however, were very small fry compared with the Japanese objectives on the Asian mainland and the major island groups off its coast. On 8 December (to the west of the International Date Line, this day in Asia was the same as 7 December in

WORLD WAR II

LEFT: US troops man improvised field defences on Oahu Island, in the Hawaiian group, for a more capable defence in the event of the Japanese launching another attack in the first days of the USA's involvement in World War II.

BELOW: The 'Brooklyn'-class cruiser Phoenix escaped damage in the Japanese attack on Pearl Harbor. It is seen here steaming out of the anchorage, past clouds of heavy smoke from less fortunate US Navy vessels and installations. The ship survived World War II and was sold to Argentina in 1951. Aircraft carriers and cruisers constituted the US Navy's most important Pacific assets during the first half of 1942.

areas to the east of the line, such as Hawaii) the Japanese 38th Division smashed through the mainland defences of the British colony at Hong Kong, forcing Major-General C.M. Maltby's forces to fall back to the island. After a call for surrender had been refused, the Japanese assaulted the island on 18 December, and by 25 December the small British garrison had been overrun.

Farther south, the three divisions of Lieutenant-General Tomoyuki Yamashita's 25th Army had landed at Khota Bharu in northern Malaya and at Singora and Patani just over the border in Thailand on 8 December. The British command in Malaya was in turmoil, and the troops at the front were poorly trained; thus, after the small RAF strength in the area had been overwhelmed by superior Japanese air power, Yamashita's 100,000 men were able to move smoothly inland toward the ultimate object of any invasion of

Malaya, the great island fortress of Singapore. The Japanese split into two main lines of advance, one on each side of the Malayan peninsula, and moved swiftly south. The British commander, Lieutenant-General A.E. Percival, had some 100,000 men under his command, in three divisions, but had expected the Japanese landings to be made farther south. He now tried desperately to regroup his forces to meet the actual threat, but failed to do more than slow the Japanese marginally. Right from the beginning of the campaign, the Japanese had displayed the considerable offensive tactical skill that was to make them so feared in the first two years of the war: operating on light scales of equipment, and without masses of motorized transport, their forward elements were able to slip around through the jungle flanks of British defensive positions and establish roadblocks in their rear. Cut off, the British forces did not have the tactical skills to escape through the jungle, and so had to surrender. Thus the Japanese moved swiftly south, leapfrogging the British defensive positions to keep up the momentum of their offensive. As 1941 ended, the British found themselves being driven steadily to the south.

Soon after the shock of the first landings, the British had been further discomforted by the loss of their only two capital ships in the area. On hearing of the Japanese landings, Admiral Sir Tom Phillips had raced north from Singapore with the battleship *Prince of Wales* and the battle-cruiser *Repulse*, to engage the Japanese forces supporting the landings.

ABOVE: The battleship Arizona *was destroyed in the Japanese attack of 7 December 1941.*

RIGHT: Other victims of the attack on Pearl Harbor were the battleships Oklahoma, Maryland *and* West Virginia. *The* West Virginia *was hit by seven torpedoes, the seventh tearing away her rudder; the* Oklahoma *was hit by four torpedoes, the last two above her belt armour, capsizing her; and the* Maryland *was hit by two 16-in (406-mm) naval shells converted into armour-piercing bombs, neither of which caused serious damage.*

The RAF could not provide air support, and on 10 December, unable to find the Japanese, Phillips turned south. Japanese air strikes found him, and after a furious battle the two British capital ships succumbed to large numbers of bomb and torpedo hits.

Meanwhile the Japanese had also landed in the Philippines, the 50,000 men of Lieutenant-General Masaharu Homma's 14th Army starting to come ashore on Luzon during 10 December. The defence of this client nation of the USA rested on the 130,000 men of General Douglas MacArthur's US and Filipino forces, of which only 22,400 were fully trained. Most of the US Asiatic Fleet was withdrawn to Java, but the air forces in the Philippines, under the command of Major-General Lewis H. Brereton, were expected to administer a rude shock to the Japanese. Quite the contrary took place: an attack on 8 December caught the US air forces lined up neatly on their airfields. Eighteen of the 35 B-17 bombers and 56 fighters were destroyed, as well as a number of other machines. This was particularly shaming for the Americans, since they had received ample warning of Japan's entry into the war. With the destruction of these aircraft, the USA lost their only adequate striking force.

MacArthur's defence plans were based on the likelihood of the Japanese landing at Lingayen Gulf and driving on

to Manila, so he had disposed his forces in two main groupings to the north and south of the capital. But between 10 and 20 December, Homma landed his forces to the north and south of Luzon, where they were able to consolidate and build airfields unmolested by the Americans.

ABOVE: Admiral Isoroku Yamamoto, the architect of the Japanese attack on Pearl Harbor.

LEFT: The battleship Pennsylvania, *largely undamaged, is seen behind the sunken destroyers* Downes *and* Cassin.

THE FLOOD OF THE JAPANESE TIDE

The Japanese were not great advocates of armoured warfare, for they lacked the industrial power and materials for the mass-production of tanks, and most of the terrain over which their armies fought their campaigns was little suited to armoured warfare. This is a Type 89B medium tank, armed with one 2.24-in (57-mm) main gun and two machine guns.

Then between 20 December and the end of the year, further landings were made to secure the islands of Mindanao and Jolo, where more airfields were built. Finally, the force for the main Japanese landings on Luzon arrived in Lingayen Gulf on 22 December. The Japanese came ashore without opposition and soon moved south, the bulk of the Filipino army having been saved only by the resolution of the US forces and the Philippine Scouts.

Another landing was made south of Manila in Limon Bay on 24 December and MacArthur, with his forces caught between the arms of an effective pincer, had to abandon his plan for a counterattack and withdraw toward the last-ditch defensive position in the Bataan peninsula north-west of Manila. Here, he expected to hold out until

reinforcements were brought in by the Pacific Fleet. Although MacArthur was often criticized for allowing his forces to be bottled up in this way, his withdrawal was in fact the right move. The Japanese, who had allocated only 50 days for the conquest of the Philippines, expected MacArthur to defend Manila, where the better Japanese troops could have made mincemeat of the US and Filipino forces. But MacArthur's retreat to Bataan frustrated this expectation, considerably delaying the Japanese plans to take the Southern Resources Area.

Back in Malaya, the start of 1942 found the British in poor shape. Pushed steadily back, their final defence line on the mainland was breached on 15 January, and by the end of the month only the island fortress of Singapore was left. The fortress had been designed

solely against attack from the sea, whereas the Japanese were now attacking from the landward side, where there were no fixed defences or heavy artillery. On 8 February the Japanese landed on the island, and after desperate fighting captured the water reservoirs. This sealed the fate of the population and garrison, which surrendered unconditionally on 15 February, with some 70,000 British troops being taken prisoner. The disaster was total, being the result mainly of poor planning and parsimony before the war. In the short term, it put the Japanese in a fine position for their planned invasion of the rich Dutch East Indies.

The new year also brought further success to the Japanese in the Philippines, albeit at great cost and delay to the overall plan. Two major assaults, in the middle and end of January, were beaten off by MacArthur's forces, but overcrowding and disease were rapidly eroding the Americans' ability to survive. Ordered to escape to Australia, MacArthur handed over command to Lieutenant-General Jonathan Wainwright on 11 March, during a period when the Japanese were waging a war of attrition. On 3 April Homma, his forces now reinforced and rested, was able to launch the decisive offensive, and as the defence forces began to crumble the Americans surrendered Bataan on 9 April. At about the same time, Japanese forces were mopping up on the other islands, on which the defence had dissolved to form nuclei of guerrilla forces; now only the fortress island of Corregidor in Manila Bay remained to deny the Japanese the use of Manila harbour. After an intense bombardment, the Japanese landed on 5 May, and after savage fighting secured this final American position in the Philippines on the following day.

The skill of Japan's fighting forces is borne out by the relative losses in these campaigns: in Malaya 138,700 British against 9,820 Japanese, and in the

The British plan for the defence of Burma had been bedevilled by lack of resources, optimism that it would not be attacked, and divided command. Thus, Lieutenant-General Thomas Hutton had only two under-strength divisions, with totally inadequate reserves and logistical backing with which to oppose the advance of the two strong divisions of Lieutenant-General Shojiro Iida's 15th Army. These heavily supported and reinforced divisions attacked from Thailand toward Moulmein and Tavoy, in the long, thin 'tail' of Burma, on 12 January 1942. Hutton's forces were soon in difficulty, and had to start withdrawing behind the Salween river line by the end of January. Pressing on quickly, the 15th Army outflanked the British by crossing the Salween upstream, forcing Hutton's tired troops to pull back once again, this time toward the Sittang river. Once again the Japanese had outflanked the British by crossing the Sittang first, and part of the 17th Indian Division was lost when the only bridge over the Sittang was blown up on 23 February. Realizing

LEFT: Japanese infantry in the Philippines. Fast, tough, resilient and able to prosper on modest quantities of indifferent food, the Japanese soldier soon disproved the western myth that he was a poor fighting man.

BELOW: Manila, the capital of the Philippine Islands, was protected by US forts in and around Manila Bay. The Japanese took Manila from the landward side, and the exposed guns of the forts, such as this 12-in (305-mm) weapon on Corregidor, proved vulnerable to air attack and largely irrelevant to the campaign.

Philippines 140,000 US and Filipino against some 12,000 Japanese. Most of the Allied losses, however, were made up of prisoners or deserters from the Filipino army.

were secured by the quiet occupation of Thailand, this also providing an overland line of communication with the forces in Malaya.

THE JAPANESE PRESS ON

By the end of 1941 the Japanese were effectively masters of the Malay peninsula and the Philippines, the remaining Allied forces in the areas being bottled up and incapable of taking any initiative. Yet Malaya and the Philippines were only half of the Southern Resources Area, the other two being the Indies, both Dutch and British, and Burma. The Indies offered rich pickings in oil, rubber and other raw materials, while Burma had oil, tungsten and rubber. In addition, the Japanese saw that the seizure of Burma would cut the Burma Road to China, and thus sever their longest-standing adversary's sole remaining lifeline to the rest of the world. Both Malaya and the Philippines offered excellent jumping-off points for the East Indies campaign, and similar advantages for the Burma operation

THE FLOOD OF THE JAPANESE TIDE

hold Rangoon. The British forces therefore prepared to retreat up the Irrawaddy and Sittang rivers, with Alexander only just escaping capture as the Japanese took Rangoon on 7 March, two days after he had taken command.

Although the situation looked hopeless, as Rangoon had been the only major means of surface communication with India, things looked up momentarily with the arrival of the first Chinese troops in the area. These had been offered by Chiang Kai-shek, the Chinese generalissimo, when he realized that his lifeline to the western world was being threatened. The Chinese 5th and 6th Armies, each the equivalent of a strong British division, were under the command of Lieutenant-General Joseph 'Vinegar Joe' W. Stilwell, Chiang's US chief-of-staff. During 13–20 March a defence line was established between Prome on the Irrawaddy and Toungoo on the Sittang, the British holding the former and the Chinese the latter. During this period, Major-General William Slim arrived to assume command of the British 'Burcorps'. By the end of the month, however, the Japanese had driven back the Chinese, forcing the British to retreat to avoid being outflanked. The same thing happened again at Yenangyaung, the location of Burma's main oilfields, during 10–19 April, although this time it was the British who were forced to fall back in the face of Japanese pressure.

As this battle continued, the Japanese also launched an offensive against the Chinese 6th Army in the area

ABOVE: Japanese troops move through the railway yards at Johor Bahru.

BELOW: A Japanese mortar battery in China.

RIGHT: Japanese 12th Army men cross a river in China on an improvised ferry.

that matters were becoming desperate, the British appointed Lieutenant-General Sir Harold Alexander to command, with orders to hold Rangoon. Reinforcements brought British strength back up to some two very under-strength divisions, which Alexander appreciated could not hope to

ABOVE LEFT: The US and Filipino forces' last major bastion area in the Philippines was the Bataan peninsula. Here a US soldier catches a brief moment of rest.

ABOVE: Japanese troops on the move in Thailand, which was an ally of Japan in World War II and in effect under Japanese control.

LEFT: The US survivors after the surrender of Bataan on 9 April 1942 were then subjected to the brutal 'Bataan death march' to their prisoner-of-war camps.

The Allies now split up in order to make their final escape. The British managed to fight their way north-west to Kalewa and thence over appalling mountains to the Manipur plain and India, while the remnants of Stilwell's Chinese forces continued north, some branching off toward Yunnan in China, the rest going with Stilwell north-east to safety at Ledo in northern Assam.

The Japanese were the masters of Burma by the end of May 1942, and China's supply route from the west had been severed. Some 30,000 of the 42,000 British troops involved in the campaign had been lost, together with large numbers of the 95,000 Chinese involved, compared with Japanese casualties of a mere 7,000 men. As the Japanese consolidated, Stilwell set about

retraining his Chinese, while the British attempted to set their house in order to resist any Japanese invasion of India and to prepare the forces for a reconquest of Burma. Deprived of their land communications with China, the Americans had recourse to the expensive and difficult means of flying supplies over the Himalayas from India as engineers set about building a new road to China from Ledo.

Meanwhile, the Japanese had been building on their successes in the southern area. Supported by the carriers of Vice-Admiral Chuichi Nagumo's 1st Air Fleet, three Japanese amphibious forces invaded the East Indies. After landings to secure bases in Borneo and Celebes in early January, the main operations gained momentum. The

ABOVE: Although difficult to assess, as thousands of captives were able to escape from their guards along the way, about 54,000 of the 72,000 prisoners on the Bataan death march reached their destination, with approximately 5,000–10,000 Filipino and 600–650 US prisoners-of-war dying on their journey to Camp O'Donnell.

RIGHT: US troops surrender on Corregidor on 6 May 1942. Of the 13,000 US and Filipino troops on the island, some 11,000 were taken prisoner by a Japanese force, which suffered 900 men killed and 1,200 wounded.

between the Sittang and Salween rivers in the Loikaw and Taunggyi area, and by 23 April the Chinese army had disintegrated, causing the remaining Chinese and the British to fall back, again to prevent being outflanked. But the Japanese 56th Division rushed north, filling the vacuum left by the Chinese 6th Army to seize Lashio on the Burma Road. The Japanese, now three divisions strong, were thus well placed to cut the Allied line of retreat, and headed south-west toward Mandalay to do just this. However, the Allies managed to fall back through this city just before the Japanese arrived on 1 May.

Eastern Force moved via Sulawesi, the Moluccas and Timor toward Bali and Java; the Centre Force advanced via the Macassar Strait and the east coast of Borneo toward Java; and the Western Force moved via the South China Sea and northern Borneo toward Sumatra. Each of these forces had powerful cruiser escorts for the troopships carrying the men of the Japanese 16th Army, and support from land-based aircraft as well as Nagumo's carriers. Under the command of General Sir Archibald Wavell's American British Dutch Australian Command (ABDACOM), the mixed Allied forces could offer no real resistance, and the Japanese moved swiftly south. ABDACOM was dissolved on 25 February, and the forces in the islands were left to fight on under Dutch command. With a few notable exceptions, Allied naval forces in the area came off worse in encounters with the Japanese naval task forces, and the fate of the

Between 29 February and 9 March, when the Dutch East Indies finally capitulated, they made swift progress. At the same time, other Japanese forces had secured bases along the northern coast of New Guinea and in the Bismarck archipelago. On 13 March they also landed on Bougainville, northernmost of the major islands in the Solomon chain.

The US carrier forces were not idle during this period, however. Attacks had been launched on the Gilbert and the Marshall Islands groups on 1 February, on Rabaul on 20 February, Wake Island four days later, Marcus Island on 4

March and on Lae and Salamaua on 10 March. Finally, on 18 April, 16 USAAF North American B-25 Mitchell twin-engined bombers were flown off the carrier *Hornet* to make a nuisance raid on Tokyo. This had an important effect on the Japanese morale, and also, despite the Allied setbacks, in Australia, where General Douglas MacArthur was readying land forces for the counter-offensive. At Pearl Harbor, moreover, the US Navy was preparing plans for an offensive across the Pacific.

In the Indian Ocean, the Imperial Japanese navy had also been making

ABOVE: Japanese troops search a British prisoner.

RIGHT: The deference paid to the emperor in Japan was total, confirmed here as the roadside crowd bows before the motorcade of the Emperor Hirohito.

Dutch East Indies was sealed with the decisive defeat of the Dutch Rear-Admiral Karel Doorman's force of five cruisers and ten destroyers by Rear-Admiral Takeo Takagi's four cruisers and 13 destroyers in the Battle of the Java Sea on 27 February, the allies losing two cruisers and five destroyers. The obsolete aircraft deployed by the Allies in the theatre had already been knocked out, and with the losses of the Java Sea battle were soon augmented as the Allied warships were picked off, leaving the Japanese in control.

new, secure bases from which to plan the destruction of the Japanese.

The war theatre was vast, stretching from New Zealand to the Aleutian Islands Group, but by April 1942 General Douglas MacArthur had taken over as Supreme Allied Commander, South-West Pacific, and his naval opposite number, Admiral Chester Nimitz, as Commander-in-Chief, Pacific. The Japanese, of course, did not wait for the Allied forces to regain their balance, and on 20 April a Japanese invasion force left Truk in the Caroline Islands for the Solomon Islands and New Guinea. The Japanese would then find it easy to attack Australia, the cornerstone of Allied power in the south-west Pacific, from bases to be captured there.

Nimitz was alerted to the Japanese intentions by the same team of cryptanalysts whose warning of the Pearl Harbor attack had been ignored.

LEFT: A victory parade in Tokyo. In the first nine months of the war, the Japanese armies were able to sweep all before them.

BELOW: The fleet carrier Lexington, *seen on fire before sinking in the Battle of the Coral Sea. The battle was a slight Japanese victory at the tactical level, but in strategic terms was a US success as the Japanese were forced to call off their effort to make an amphibious assault on Port Moresby in southern Papua.*

itself felt with the arrival of Nagumo's 1st Air Fleet, its five carriers supported by four battleships. During 2–8 April, Nagumo's warplanes struck at Trincomalee and Colombo in Ceylon, and also sank one aircraft carrier, two cruisers and one destroyer of the British Eastern Fleet before retiring back into the Pacific. Worried by the threat of further Japanese ambitions in the Indian Ocean and even Africa, the British seized the Vichy French island of Madagascar between May and November 1942. In fact, the tide of the Japanese expansion had by now reached full flood.

THE TIDE TURNS: THE BATTLES OF THE CORAL SEA AND MIDWAY

Many disasters followed in the train of Pearl Harbor: the fall of Malaya, the East Indies, and the destruction of Allied naval strength in the Battle of the Java Sea. The precarious Allied command structure, set up in December 1941, was in ruins, and the first requirement for the Allies was to find

THE FLOOD OF THE JAPANESE TIDE

One of the warplanes that helped to check the tide of Japanese success was the Douglas SBD Dauntless two-seat dive-bomber. Small and sturdy, the Dauntless could deliver its weapon with great accuracy. Here, the aircraft are waiting to take off from the fleet carrier Yorktown, *early in 1942.*

He wasted no time in sending two aircraft carriers, the *Yorktown* and *Lexington*, under Rear-Admiral Frank Jack Fletcher, to the new extemporized base at Espiritu Santo. Against these the Japanese mustered two fleet carriers, the *Shokaku* and *Zuikaku*, the light carrier *Shoho* and the seaplane carrier *Kamikawa Maru*. Battle was joined on 3 May when the Japanese landed on Tulagi in the Solomons. The Americans soon launched attacks on the invasion force, and these inflicted considerable damage. Both carrier task forces manoeuvred for two days without making contact, but at first light on 7 May reconnaissance aircraft sent back their sighting reports and an air attack was launched by each side. The first US attack on the *Shoho* did no damage, but the *Yorktown*'s aircraft were able to inflict heavy damage shortly after this.

Within 10 minutes of the first torpedo hit, the *Shoho* was sinking.

The Japanese had no such success, for their aircraft erroneously sank a fleet oiler and a destroyer under the impression they were a carrier and a light cruiser. A later attack, looking for the *Yorktown*, was mauled by the US carrier's combat air patrol and lost nine aircraft. When a group of Japanese aircraft mistook the *Yorktown* for a friendly ship, gunfire accounted for a further 11 aircraft, making a loss of 17 per cent of the Japanese carriers' strength without a proper attack having been launched against either the *Lexington* or *Yorktown*.

On the following day, the US carrierborne warplanes attacked again, managing to damage the *Shokaku* with two bomb hits, but further attacks were not successful. This time the Japanese

pilots were able to strike back, catching the *Lexington* and *Yorktown* together at about an hour before noon. The nimble *Yorktown* was hit by only one bomb and managed to contain the fire which broke out, but the older *Lexington* was hit by two torpedoes and two bombs. The fire was much more serious and about an hour later the ship suffered a severe internal fuel explosion. The vessel continued to blaze and was finally abandoned four hours later, sinking three hours after that.

The US Navy was bitterly disappointed by the outcome of this, the Battle of the Coral Sea, but the Americans' tactical defeat was small consolation for the Japanese, in that they were forced to cancel the amphibious landing planned for Port Moresby, in favour of an overwhelmingly difficult overland advance. As important in the long run was the damage to *Shokaku* and the depletion of the two surviving carrier air groups, which meant that both were unable to take part in the decisive Battle of Midway. The Battle of the Coral Sea had robbed the Japanese of an objective for the first time, and ultimately made certain an eventual Allied victory in the south-west Pacific.

The Japanese were troubled by their failure to secure New Guinea, which did not stop them from pursuing their other objectives in the north and central Pacific. The grand strategic aim had always been to force the Americans into a main fleet action, and although Pearl Harbor had eliminated virtually all of the US Pacific Fleet's battleships, its aircraft carriers were still at large. Realizing that Nimitz was far too wily to fritter away his strength attacking the Japanese homeland, the commander-in-chief of the 1st Fleet, Admiral Isoroku Yamamoto, decided to lay a more subtle trap. If he occupied Midway Island, at the extreme north-western end of the Hawaiian Islands group, Yamamoto knew that the Americans would have to fight him, this island being far too

Grumman TBF-1 Avenger. The Japanese made no changes to their aircraft, which comprised the Mitsubishi A6M5 Reisen 'Zero' fighter, Aichi D3A 'Val' dive-bomber and Nakajima B5N 'Kate' torpedo-bomber, apart from embarking a pair of Yokosuka D4Y1 'Judy' fast reconnaissance aircraft in the carrier *Soryu* to improve the chances of sighting the US fleet. Against the US *Enterprise*, *Hornet* and *Yorktown*, the Japanese could muster the carriers *Akagi*, *Kaga*, *Hiryu*, *Soryu* and *Hosho*, and two seaplane carriers. They had nine battleships, in addition, including the giant *Yamato* and 11 cruisers.

Forewarned of the true Japanese objectives, Fletcher, commanding at sea under Nimitz's overall supervision, was able to ignore the thrust toward the Aleutians. On 2 June Rear Admiral Raymond A. Spruance's Task Force 16 (*Enterprise* and *Hornet* with six cruisers and nine destroyers) and Fletcher's TF 17 (*Yorktown* with two cruisers and five destroyers) were in position some 350 miles (560km) north of Midway. The invasion force was sighted on the following day, but Fletcher let shore-based aircraft from Midway attack it,

LEFT: The Japanese fleet carrier Shokaku under air attack in the Battle of the Coral Sea. This was the world's first naval battle in which the surface combatants did not come within sight of each other.

BELOW: The Japanese navy's most significant ship loss in the Battle of the Coral Sea was the light carrier Shoho, which was hit by 11 bombs and at least seven torpedoes before succumbing.

valuable as an outpost of the US defensive perimeter to be allowed to fall into Japanese hands.

Yamamoto's plan called for an ambitious assault on Midway, backed by a powerful surface fleet including four fleet carriers, while another force would simultaneously occupy the Aleutians, 1,500 miles (2400km) to the north. On paper, this was more than enough to crush the Americans, but had one major advantage in the fact that, once again, cryptanalysis had in good time revealed the broad outlines of the enemy deployment and Nimitz was able to plan his counterstroke in advance. Nevertheless, the Americans had so few ships that the margin between defeat and victory remained very narrow. Only two carriers were available, and they had to be brought from the south-west Pacific. The *Yorktown* had been damaged in the Battle of the Coral Sea, but repairs had been made in an unbelievably short space of three days at Pearl Harbor. Although *Yorktown* had lost much of its air group, this was offset by survivors from the *Lexington*, and as a result the carrier could boast the most battle-hardened aircrew of all the US carriers.

The Battle of the Coral Sea had shown that more fighters were needed, so 50 per cent more Grumman F4F-4 Wildcat warplanes were embarked. The Douglas TBD Devastator torpedo-bomber had already proved most unsatisfactory, being too slow and with an ineffective torpedo, but there was no time to replace it with the new

attack from the US carriers. The aircraft were sent down to the hangars for re-arming with bombs, just 14 minutes before Fletcher's task force was sighted. The report had omitted any mention of a carrier, so Nagumo's calculations still seemed to make sense. The Japanese admiral had been caught off balance, even if he did not fully realize the fact. A series of unsuccessful attacks on his carriers by shore-based aircraft prevented Nagumo from recovering those machines which had been bombing Midway, with the result that many ran out of fuel. Nearly a third of the aircraft which had taken off were lost, but two hours after the first sighting report, Nagumo's carriers were finally ready to face TF 16 and TF 17.

The first attack by the *Hornet* and *Enterprise* was not co-ordinated with that launched by the *Yorktown*, and sustained heavy losses. But there were still 50 aircraft left from the *Enterprise*

ABOVE: The US fleet carrier, Yorktown, *was severely damaged in the Battle of the Coral Sea, but was then repaired with almost incredible speed to play a major role in the Battle of Midway, in which the ship suffered more major damage. Taken in tow, the aircraft carrier was finally torpedoed and sunk by a Japanese submarine.*

RIGHT: Armourers load bombs onto the underwing racks of a Consolidated PBY Catalina on Midway Island, an outpost to the north-west of the main part of the Hawaiian Islands and one of the primary targets for the Japanese in their complex Midway operation.

still having no idea where Vice-Admiral Chuichi Nagumo's main carrier force might be found. By nightfall on 3 June both carrier groups were approaching Midway, 460 miles (740km) apart and completely ignorant of each other's whereabouts. Midway, meanwhile, was under attack from Japanese bombers but held its own, leaving Fletcher and Spruance to concentrate on their main objective, the location and destruction of the Japanese carriers.

By next morning, Nagumo's carriers were only 200 miles (320km) north-west of Midway, which was where the island's dawn patrol spotted them. Five minutes later TF 16 received orders to launch an attack, and soon 97 torpedo-bombers and dive-bombers were airborne. Meanwhile, some 50 shore-based bombers had made an attack on Nagumo's carriers, without success, with a loss of 17 aircraft. Stung by this attack, Nagumo decided to reinforce the assault on Midway by throwing in the 93 aircraft he had retained in case of an

and *Yorktown*'s air groups, and these finally succeeded in crippling the *Akagi*, Nagumo's flagship, then in destroying the *Kaga* and *Soryu*. All three Japanese carriers succumbed quickly to devastating fires which swept through their hangars. The fourth carrier, the *Hiryu*, immediately launched a counter-strike, her aircraft flying straight to the *Yorktown* to hit her with three bombs. The US carrier proved better able to cope with the fire, which inevitably followed, but was badly damaged and unable to recover its own fighters. Yet by heroic exertions the crew managed to get the ship under way again and even launched eight fighters to cope with a second attack from the *Hiryu*. This time, however, *Yorktown* was unable to dodge two torpedoes.

The last fight of the *Yorktown* had a decisive effect on the outcome of the battle. The Japanese had assumed they were opposed by only two carriers, not knowing that the Pearl Harbor dockyard workers had achieved the impossible by repairing the *Yorktown*'s damage in only three days. Having hit one carrier badly, earlier in the day, the Japanese found it unbelievable that the same carrier could be operational again in so short a time. Therefore the carrier which had just been sunk must have been the second carrier, making it safe to assume that both US carriers had been knocked out. In fact there were still two undamaged ships. The *Enterprise* and *Hornet* had very few aircraft left, and only 40 bombers took off for a last desperate blow against the *Hiryu*. Their target was carrying about half the aircraft with which it had started, and although the Zero fighters were able to punish the attackers, they could not prevent the second wave from scoring four bomb hits. The ship started to burn, the fires slowly getting out of control. Incredibly, the other three carriers were still ablaze: the *Kaga* and *Soryu* did not sink until evening, and the *Akagi* lasted until dawn the

following day. The *Hiryu* finally sank at 09.00 the next morning.

Yamamoto and his main body had been too far away to help, but he did realize that the plan had gone badly wrong. By ordering the three smaller carriers, *Zuiho*, *Ryujo* and *Junyo*, south from the Aleutians he had hoped to concentrate a fresh force to trap the Americans in a night action. But Spruance, in command after the disabling of Fletcher's *Yorktown*, wisely took TF 16 well clear to the east as soon as he had recovered the last aircraft. In theory, Yamamoto's four small carriers had mustered enough aircraft to defeat Spruance, but in practice the vast distances made it impossible to bring the ships together soon enough to score decisive hits. Yamamoto decided to bow to the inevitable, ordering his invasion force to withdraw early on the morning of 5 June.

This was the decisive moment of the Battle of Midway. The battle lasted for another two days, during which time other ships were sunk and a submarine put two more torpedoes into *Yorktown* to seal its fate. But these events were only a postscript. Midway marked the high tide of Japanese expansion in the Pacific, and although it did not appear obvious at the time, Japan had lost the strategic initiative. Japanese aircrew casualties were much heavier than those of the USA. Much worse, the Japanese found it almost impossible to replace their highly-trained and combat-hardened veteran aircrews with men of anything like the same calibre. Nor could the shipyards turn out more carriers to replace the four sunk, whereas US shipyards were already turning out fleet carriers in large numbers. Another nail in the Japanese coffin was the fact that, while they could replace the aircraft they had lost, they could do so only with improved versions of the same types, which were approaching obsolescence; the Americans, on the other hand, were mass-producing vast numbers of a new

generation of more advanced warplanes, to be flown by men progressing through a very thorough training programme that involved instruction and guidance by veterans of the early battles. But the most important result of Midway was that the Japanese had failed in their attempt to dislodge the Americans from their defensive perimeter. For Nimitz it was only a matter of waiting until the new ships were ready, before launching his drive across the central Pacific toward Japan.

THE ALLIES TAKE THE OFFENSIVE: NEW GUINEA AND GUADALCANAL

In May and June 1942, the Japanese decided to expand the defensive perimeter they were establishing to shield their newly-won possessions. This expansion was to take place primarily in the south-east, where Papua, the Bismarck and the Solomon Islands were to be taken by the forces of Lieutenant-General Hitoshi Imamura's 8th Area Army. The keys to the territory, the Japanese decided, were Port Moresby on the southern coast of Papua, and the island of Guadalcanal in the Solomons. Major airfields in these two places

The Battle of Midway was a catastrophe of huge proportions for the Japanese, in that they lost four fleet carriers and most of their skilled aircrews, and in the process had the strategic initiative in the Pacific wrested from them by the Americans. This is the Hiryu, *one of the four Japanese carriers to go down in flames before being scuttled. The other three were the* Soryu, Kaga *and* Akagi, *all four of which were veterans of the Pearl Harbor attack.*

Supported by an M5 light tank, men of the US Marine Corps land on Guadalcanal on 7 August 1942.

would allow the Japanese to detect and destroy any Allied force attempting to break through the perimeter. Despite a first rebuff in the Battle of the Coral Sea, Imamura pressed ahead with the plan, but now decided that the only way to take Port Moresby was by means of an overland advance from the north coast across the formidable Owen Stanley range, and from the east after a landing at Milne Bay. His first steps were therefore to land troops at Gona, on the northern coast of Papua, on 11 July 1942, with another landing at nearby Buna shortly after this, then on Guadalcanal on 6 July. The troops on Guadalcanal immediately set about building an airfield, while others in Papua began preparations for the advance toward Port Moresby.

The Americans were also trying to decide what they should do next. General Douglas MacArthur, commanding the South-West Pacific Area, favoured a direct thrust by the army on Rabaul, the town on New Britain where the Japanese

had their theatre headquarters, and Admiral Ernest J. King, the US chief of naval operations, favoured naval action in the Bismarck Islands and New Guinea area to disrupt the Japanese attack against the supply line across the Pacific to Australia, combined with an island-hopping campaign toward Rabaul. The Joint Chiefs-of-Staff mediated between the commander of the South-West Pacific Area and the head of the US Navy, and opted for a three-phase operation: the seizure of the southern Solomons by the forces of Vice-Admiral Robert L. Ghormley's South Pacific Area; the seizure of the rest of the Solomons by MacArthur's forces; and finally the seizure of the north coast of New Guinea, New Britain and New Ireland, also by MacArthur's forces supported by the navy. Ghormley's forces were able to move quickly to their task, but MacArthur's first move was forestalled by the Japanese advance toward Port Moresby.

On 21 July the men of Major-General Tomitaro Horii's South Sea Detachment left their beach-head between Gona and Buna and moved off to the south-west. Local Australian forces could not halt the advancing Japanese, and pulled back before them into the Owen Stanley mountains, fighting desperate rearguard actions but failing to stop the skilful and determined Japanese advance along the Kokoda Trail. By 12 August the Japanese were over the crest of the mountains, and the exhausted Australians, starving and short of all essential supplies, were still falling back. As they approached Port Moresby, the Japanese too began to suffer from the effects of their nightmare crossing of the mountains, and were gradually being slowed by strengthening Australian and US resistance under the command of an Australian officer, Lieutenant-General Edmund Herring. By 26 September the Japanese were halted at Ioribaiwa, only 30 miles (50km) from Port Moresby. Three days earlier, the Australian 7th Division had started a

counter-offensive, soon joined by the US 32nd Division. Ordered by Imamura to fall back, Horii started his retreat at the end of the month, harried unmercifully by the Australian and US forces. This time it was the Japanese who suffered the most terrible privations, especially shortages of food, and many died after trying to eat grass and earth. By 19 November the Japanese were back where they had started in Buna and Gona.

Meanwhile, the other prong of the Japanese assault on Port Moresby had been defeated. On 25 August a regiment had landed at Milne Bay, but after serious fighting with the local forces had been wiped out. Port Moresby was now safe from overland assault.

Despite their losses and hardships, the Japanese were determined to hold Buna and Gona. Already the victims of the speed and aggression of Japanese offensive tactics, the Allies were now to be taught a desperate lesson in Japanese determination and skill in defence, especially from prepared positions. The Allied assault started on 20 November, but at first made no progress whatsoever. Disease had decimated the Allied formations and morale was low. Matters were improved by the arrival of a new commander, Lieutenant-General Robert L. Eichelberger, on 1 December, but it was not until 7 December that the Australians were able to batter their way into Gona against the shattered opposition. Buna still held out, the Australians and Americans finally taking it against fanatical resistance on 22 January 1943. The Japanese had lost more than 7,000 dead and 350 prisoners taken, all wounded very badly. The Allies had lost 5,700 Australian and 2,783 American dead, with a further large number incapacitated by disease.

For the first time, the Japanese had been beaten on land, but they had shown how costly it would be for the Allies to win back all that they had lost. The Australians and Americans, on the other hand, had learned the hard way about survival in the jungle, and especially how to play the Japanese at their own game. The experience of the campaign was digested by the various planning staffs, and the lessons passed on to the other formations which would be taking on the Japanese all over the southern Pacific.

Realizing the Japanese had landed on Guadalcanal, in July and August the Americans accelerated their plans to retake the island. Commanded by Rear-Admiral Frank Jack Fletcher, whose three aircraft carriers were to provide tactical air support and long-range protection, an expedition was prepared. The commander of the landing forces was Rear-Admiral Richmond K. Turner, and the formation to be landed was Major-General Alexander A. Vandegrift's 1st Marine Division, reinforced to 19,000 men.

Moving forward from Noumea, in New Caledonia, the 1st Marine Division landed on 7 August, the main force coming ashore on Guadalcanal and subsidiary forces on Tulagi and Gavutu, just off the Florida Islands. On these two latter islands, where a seaplane base

had been prepared, some 1,500 Japanese were able to put up a spirited defence before being overwhelmed. On Guadalcanal, however, where the marines had landed on the north coast on each side of Lunga Point, opposite the Florida Islands, the 2,200 Japanese quickly dispersed into the jungle, the Americans occupying the airfield area, renamed Henderson Field. As the Japanese pondered their reply and gathered their forces, the Americans set about expanding and strengthening their defensive perimeter around Henderson Field.

Meanwhile the invasion fleet, lying between Guadalcanal and the Florida Islands, was coming under intense Japanese air attack from the bases in New Britain. Then, on the following day, the Japanese sprang a major surprise on the Allies in the naval Battle of Savo Island, just off Cape Esperance, up the coast from Lunga Point. Vice-Admiral Shigeyoshi Inouye, commanding the 4th Fleet from Rabaul, sent Vice-Admiral Junichi Mikawa with seven cruisers and a destroyer to attack the Allied naval forces covering the landings. Arriving off

Savo Island on the night of 8–9 August, Mikawa encountered a force of one Australian and four US heavy cruisers, commanded by the British Rear-Admiral V.A.C. Crutchley. In a confused night action lasting only 32 minutes, Mikawa's cruisers sank all but one of the Allied cruisers, the last crippled without loss to themselves. Mikawa then retired, although he should have gone on to destroy the Allied transport fleet. He did not know, however, that Fletcher had pulled his carriers out of the area because of the air threat. One Japanese cruiser, the *Kako*, was sunk by a US submarine on its way back to New Britain. Shocked by his losses, Turner pulled out with all his naval forces, leaving the marines without support. Left much to themselves, apart from air raids, for the next week, the marines continued to consolidate and prepare for the inevitable Japanese attack. On 18 August a regiment, commanded by Colonel Kiyonao Ichiki, landed east of the marine base. Moving overland, Ichiki's force attacked Henderson Field on 21 August. The day before, the marines had received their first aircraft, and these played an important part in repulsing this and later attacks. For two

ABOVE: Australian infantrymen on the move in conditions typical of the fighting along the Kokoda Trail in Papua during the autumn of 1942. Here the conditions and endemic diseases were as dangerous to them as the enemy.

LEFT: Hit by bombs from a North American B-25 Mitchell twin-engined medium bomber of the US 5th Army Air Force, a Japanese transport ship sinks.

Australian soldiers put on a martial show for the propaganda camera at Port Moresby.

days, Ichiki launched a series of determined assaults, all of which were beaten off by the marines. Surprised in the rear by the 1st Marine Division's reserve regiment, Ichiki's force was driven into the sea and was annihilated.

The next day, the US Navy salvaged some of its pride in the Battle of the Eastern Solomons. A force under Rear-Admiral Raizo Tanaka was trying to run some 1,500 reinforcements through to the Japanese defenders of the island, covered by three aircraft carriers under Vice-Admiral Chuichi Nagumo. The light carrier *Ryujo* was sunk, but the Americans suffered damage to the *Enterprise*, and Tanaka's transport group

got through to deliver its troops and bombard the Henderson Field area on the return journey.

On the night of 7–8 September a marine raiding party attacked the Japanese base at Taivu, capturing the plans for the next Japanese attack on Henderson Field. This materialized on 12 September in the form of a series of punches by Major-General Kiyotaki Kawaguchi's 35th Brigade. The fighting raged for two days before the marines finally repulsed the 35th Brigade, which suffered some 1,200 dead. The action is now remembered as the Battle of Bloody Ridge. Each side was now reinforced: Vandegrift received the 7th Marine and

164th Infantry Regiments, bringing his strength to 23,000, and the Japanese landed the headquarters of the 17th Army and two divisions, being some 20,000 men under Lieutenant-General Harukichi Hyakutake. This reinforcement period lasted until 22 October and was marked on Guadalcanal by intensive skirmishing and patrol activity. It also led to the naval Battle off Cape Esperance during 11–13 October, when a cruiser squadron, commanded by Rear-Admiral Norman Scott, escorting US transports, caught Rear-Admiral Aritomo Goto's cruiser force, also escorting troop transports. Scott's force sank a cruiser and a destroyer and crippled the other two cruisers, but the Japanese landed their troops despite losing two destroyers to land-based bomber attacks afterwards. Between 13 and 15 October two Japanese battleships bombarded Henderson Field, clearly indicating that naval superiority was back in the hands of the Japanese.

During 23–26 October, and under the personal command of Lieutenant-General Masao Maruyama, the Japanese then launched a series of furious assaults on Henderson Field, losing some 2,000 men in the process. None of the attacks came near to succeeding. As the Japanese licked their wounds, Vandegrift expanded his perimeter considerably. Had the 1st Marine Division been capable of taking the offensive, there is little doubt that the Japanese would have lost heavily, but the marines were exhausted, and a land stalemate ensued as elements of the 2nd Marine Division began to arrive in the period up to 8 December. Activity at sea continued, however, with the Battle of Santa Cruz on 26–27 October. Vice-Admiral William L. Halsey had replaced Ghormley, with Rear-Admiral Thomas Kinkaid replacing Fletcher. Kinkaid now met a Japanese carrier force in an action which resulted in damage to two Japanese carriers and one American, and also led to the loss of the US carrier *Hornet*. Although the Japanese had won,

command of the sea. In a series of confused battles, the Japanese lost the battleships *Hiei* and *Kirishima*, and the Americans the cruisers *Juneau* and *Northampton*.

Finally, all was ready for the elimination of the Japanese from Guadalcanal. Patch's offensive started on 10 January 1943, and in the next two weeks the Japanese were driven back from their positions in the jungle west of Henderson Field. By the end of the month, the Japanese 17th Army was penned up in Cape Esperance. From here the destroyers of Tanaka's 'Tokyo Express', as usual brilliantly handled, evacuated some 11,000 survivors during 1–7 February, leaving the Americans in sole possession of Guadalcanal. The battle had been costly, but the psychological boost to the Allies, following this major victory over the Japanese, was huge.

LEFT: One of the US warships which supported the landing on Guadalcanal in August 1942 was the heavy cruiser Quincy. *This was one of three 'New Orleans'-class cruisers lost on 9 September 1942 in the Battle of Savo Island.*

BELOW LEFT: Ground crew prepare to load bombs onto a Grumman TBF Avenger attack warplane on Henderson Field, the prize for which the Japanese and Americans fought the Battle of Guadalcanal.

BELOW: A US Navy destroyer bombards a shore target on 23 January 1943, during the closing stages of the Guadalcanal campaign. This was the time when the last Japanese forces were falling back to Cape Tenaru and their evacuation by the ships of the Tokyo Express.

it was again only through a great sacrifice of experienced aircrew, a fact that was later to be of great importance.

On Guadalcanal, the exhausted Vandegrift and 1st Marine Division had at last been withdrawn on 9 December, their places having been taken by Major-General Alexander M. Patch and the XIV Corps. While Japanese strength

hovered at around 20,000, by 9 January 1943 the Americans had 58,000 men of the 2nd Marine, 25th and Americal Divisions, the last so-named because it had been created from US troops based on New Caledonia.

During the three-phase naval Battle of Guadalcanal during 12–15 November, the Americans once again regained

CHAPTER FOUR
THE ALLIED VICTORY IN EUROPE

Protected by the thick armour of a tank from German air attack, Soviet officers plan their next move on the Eastern Front in 1943. By this time the Soviet forces were very nearly the equal of the German armies in essential weapons and fighting skills.

THE BATTLE OF KURSK

The destruction of the 6th Army in Stalingrad proved that the Germans were not invincible and that the Soviets had an effective army, while the Battle of Kursk five months later showed that Germany could not hope to win the war with the USSR. This great armoured clash was the last time that Germany was able to take the initiative on the Eastern Front. Fighting on ground of their own choosing, and at a time they considered best for their tactics, the German armies were first halted and then thrown back by the size and skill of the constantly improving Soviet forces.

With the spring thaw in March 1943, operations on the Eastern Front came to a temporary halt, and the Germans at last had the time to plan their next move, although the planning staffs in Germany were severely taxed as to what this move might be. The Oberkommando der Wehrmacht (OKW, or armed forces high command), which ran the German war effort in every theatre but the USSR, was of the opinion that the German armies there should go over to the strategic defensive, and so free forces for the western theatres, in which the great Allied invasion was expected shortly. The Oberkommando des Heeres (OKH, or army high command), which ran the war against the USSR under Hitler's overall supervision, agreed with OKW to a certain extent, but thought it essential that there be a limited German offensive in the USSR during the summer to spoil any Soviet intentions for offensive action. Hitler agreed with the OKH, principally because he felt that a striking victory was needed to bolster the flagging spirits of his European allies.

Once they had decided that a limited offensive was needed, the OKH planners decided that the best place to strike such a blow was the great salient jutting into the German lines west of Kursk. The trouble was that this was an obvious choice for such an offensive, so speed of planning and execution was vital if tactical surprise was to be achieved. The German plan was in essence simple, and was based on the familiar pincer theory. Field-Marshal Walther Model's 9th Army of Army Group Centre, commanded by Field-Marshal Günther von Kluge, was to advance on Kursk from the northern half of the salient, while Colonel-General Hermann Hoth's 4th Panzerarmee and General Wilhelm Kempf's Armeeabteilung Kempf, both supplied by Field-Marshal Erich von Manstein's Army Group South, were to advance on Kursk from the south. The Central and Voronezh Fronts would be trapped in the salient and then destroyed, after which German forces would be freed for service in the west.

The OKH wished the offensive, codenamed Zitadelle (citadel), to take place as early in April as possible after the spring mud had dried out enough to allow armoured vehicles to function. But no sooner had the basic plan been formulated than reasons for delay began to pour in: troops could not be moved up in time, and Model decided that his forces were not sufficient for the task in

and make its own plans accordingly. Just about the only thing the Soviets did not know was the time appointed for the actual attack, but they were to be told of this too by a deserter before the offensive began. Although they did not know it, the German armies were to attack without any element of strategic surprise, and in only a few places did the first attacking formations achieve any measure of tactical surprise.

With the exception of the immediate German start lines, the Kursk salient is excellent terrain for armoured warfare, with low rolling hills of firm sandy soil and relatively few towns, the whole dotted with sunflower fields and orchards. Accordingly, the Germans massed most of their mobile forces to the north and south of the salient. Model's 9th Army totalled some six Panzer, one Panzergrenadier and 14 infantry divisions, although only eight of the infantry divisions were to be used in Zitadelle. Supported by some 730 aircraft of Luftflotte 6's 1st Fliegerdivision, the 9th Army was able to field about 900

LEFT: German armour on the move near Kharkov in the summer of 1943. Lying in a German salient, and biting into the underside of the Soviet salient around Kursk, this was at the heart of the fighting that followed Germany's strategic defeat in the Battle of Kursk in July 1943.

BELOW: Soviet infantry move into the ruined outskirts of Belgorod, to the north of Kharkov, as the Soviets sweep over to the counter-offensive after their triumph in the Battle of Kursk.

hand. The April date passed, as did one in May, and at this stage several senior commanders began to have second thoughts about the whole operation: of these the two most important were General Alfred Jodl, chief of the OKW operations staff, and Colonel-General Heinz Guderian, recently recalled to service as inspector-general of armoured forces following his dismissal after the battle for Moscow Both these men considered the offensive to be very dangerous in concept and that it should be abandoned. Guderian also felt that the new Panther battle tanks and Elefant tank-destroyers would be wasted, the divisions which were to use them having not yet been able to train properly. Hitler himself began to have doubts, as did von Manstein, but Field-Marshal Wilhelm Keitel, head of the OKW, and Colonel-General Kurt Zeitzler, the OKH chief-of-staff, managed to overcome Hitler's misgivings. The offensive was finally scheduled for July, by which time ample supplies of ammunition, troops and new tanks would be available, it was believed. Utmost secrecy was to be observed as the preparations for the attack were made.

Despite the German precautions in the matter of secrecy, the Soviets were kept fully informed of all that was happening by their in-country intelligence system and Swiss-based 'Lucy' ring, whose main asset was probably a person working in the high-level communications or coding department in Berlin. By such means, the Soviet Stavka (high command) was able to keep a close watch on the progress of German preparations

tanks, although most of these were obsolescent PzKpfw II, PzKpfw III and early PzKpfw IV types. In the south, von Manstein had more numerous and better-equipped forces: nine Panzer, two Panzergrenadier and 11 infantry divisions, although only seven of the infantry divisions were to be used in the planned offensive. More significantly, von Manstein's forces had some 1,000 tanks and 150 assault guns, these armoured fighting vehicles including about 200 of the new PzKpfw V Panther battle tanks and 94 of the new and even more powerful PzKpfw Tiger I heavy tanks. Air support was provided by the 1,100 aircraft of Luftflotte 4's VIII Fliegerkorps. Artillery support comprised some 6,000 guns and mortars in the north, and 4,000 weapons in the south.

This was a formidable offensive force but one with distinct limitations. The most important of these were the fact that many formations had only recently been reorganized after the debacle at

Stalingrad and Germany's subsequent defeat in the south. They had not achieved their true potential as fighting units as yet, trained reserves and replacements were in short supply, and although Hitler and the staff generals had high expectations of the new armoured vehicles, Guderian and the front-line commanders were all too aware that these had been rushed into premature action, and were still very prone to teething troubles. The Panther, Tiger and Elefant were all somewhat unreliable mechanically, the Elefant suffering from the distinct tactical disadvantage of having no defensive machine gun with which to ward off close-range infantry attack.

Even so, the Soviets were leaving nothing to chance, and were massing truly enormous forces in the Kursk salient for the forthcoming battle. The overall plan was devised by Georgi Zhukov, promoted to Marshal of the Soviet Union in January 1943. Zhukov

sources put the figure as high as 5,000. The Battle of Kursk was therefore to see the deployment of at least 5,600 armoured fighting vehicles – perhaps even 7,000 such machines.

The Soviets knew what the Germans were planning. The Germans, however, had no comparable source within the Soviet high command, and their reconnaissance aircraft had failed to reveal the extent and thoroughness of the Soviet preparations. Having carried all before them in the air for the first two years of the Soviet war, the warplanes of the Luftwaffe had at last been matched by Soviet aircraft. Superior Soviet numbers and an increasing level of skill were to prevail in the long run. The

LEFT: At Kursk the northern half of the planned German pincer operation was the responsibility of Colonel-General Walther Model, seen here, whose 9th Army failed to make any but the most limited inroads into the Soviet defences.

BELOW: German troops prepare for the start of the Battle of Kursk, on whose outcome would depend the future course of the war on the Eastern Front.

was not content with merely stopping the Germans' attempt to eliminate the Kursk salient. Once the German forces were firmly embedded in the Soviet defences of the salient proper, massive offensives were to be launched into the German counter-salients north and south of Kursk in the regions of Orel and Kharkov. The whole Soviet front was then to grind forward remorselessly. In the Kursk salient proper, the Soviets had had four months in which to prepare their defences, based on a series of very strong field fortifications. The first line consisted of five lines of trenches some 3 miles (5km) deep, reinforced with numerous anti-tank strongpoints. In this area, anti-tank and anti-personnel mines were laid at a density of 2,400 and 2,700 mines per mile of front. Some 7 miles (11km) behind the first line lay a similar second line, with a strong third line 20 miles (32km) behind the second. Behind this third line were the front reserves, dug into formidable defences of their own. Finally there were the theatre reserves, the Reserve or Steppe Front, commanded by the redoubtable Colonel-General I.S. Konev, holding the neck of the salient. Here could be formed a final line of defence should the Germans break through that far; at the same time, the salient could

not be cut off and there was the capability of reinforcing either of the two first-line fronts.

In the salient were General K.K. Rokossovsky's Central Front, facing Model, and General N.F. Vatutin's Voronezh Front, facing von Manstein. It was Rokossovsky who had astutely suggested the location of the Steppe Front at the neck of the salient. Even allowing for differences in designation (a Soviet army being equivalent to a strengthened western corps, and a Soviet corps to a reinforced western division), it is clear that the three fronts were very strong. The Central Front had one tank and five infantry armies, as well as two tank corps; the Voronezh Front had one tank and five infantry armies, together with one infantry and two tank corps; and the Steppe Front had one tank and four infantry armies, with the support of a further one tank, one mechanized and three cavalry corps. The numbers of Soviet troops were therefore considerable, and so too were the matériel resources available to them: 13,000 guns, 6,000 anti-tank guns and 1,000 rocket-launchers for the two forward fronts, some 2,500 aircraft deployed by the 2nd and 16th Air Armies, and at least 3,600 armoured fighting vehicles, although some Soviet

Soviets demonstrated at Kursk that heavy tactical air support of ground forces, with masses of aircraft such as the excellent Ilyushin Il-2 Shturmovik, would prove decisive.

All was finally ready on 5 July, after a delay occasioned by Soviet artillery bombardment of the German forming-up areas. There was an intense two-hour bombardment of the Soviet positions, and then the 9th Army attacked. The bombardment failed to crush the Soviet defences, and the one infantry and three Panzer corps immediately encountered stiff resistance. By 11 July Model had fed into the battle all the forces available to him, but the maximum penetration along the 30-mile (50-km) offensive front was a mere 15 miles (25km in the region of Ponyri and Olkhovatka. Near these two villages the Soviet 2nd Tank Army put up a magnificent defence, and furious armoured battles raged at very close quarters. Although the latest German tanks had good armour and armament, making them formidable opponents at long range, the Soviets used the superior mobility and speed of their tanks to keep at close range, where their inferior armament was just as good as the Germans' long-barrelled 2.95- and 3.465-in (75- and 88-mm) guns. In one small area were engaged some 2,000 tanks and self-propelled guns, the losses on both sides being extremely heavy. The 9th Army was now exhausted, the German advance slowed and finally stopped just short of the ridge, after which it was downhill all the way to Kursk. Rokossovsky's forces had broken the northern arm of the pincer intended to eliminate the Kursk salient, causing Model to lose 25,000 dead, more than 200 of his tanks, and more than 200 of Luftflotte 6's aircraft.

In the south, von Manstein attacked earlier, and at first enjoyed better results, largely as a result of his tactics. With a high infantry/armour ratio, Model had decided to use conventional tactics, with infantry, engineers and artillery opening

the way for the tanks to move up. Von Manstein, on the other hand, did not have the infantry for such tactics, and decided instead to use his armour to open the way for the supporting forces. The tactic evolved to meet von Manstein's need was the Panzerkeil (armour wedge), with a Panther or Tiger at the head of the wedge, and PzKpfw III and PzKpfw IV tanks fanning out behind it along the sides of the wedge. During the battle, von Manstein realized this formation was wrong, since the Soviet tanks were closing in to a range where the new tanks' superior guns could not be used to full advantage. He changed the composition of the wedge so that the older tanks were leading to flush the Soviet tanks and anti-tank guns, while the Panther or Tiger followed behind to engage the flushed target at long range.

The 4th Panzerarmee, which was to strike for Kursk by way of Oboyan, made good progress through the Soviet 6th Guards Army, but then ran into the 1st Tank Army and was slowed. At the same time, Armeeabteilung Kempf struck north-east from just south of Belgorod to protect the 4th Panzerarmee's right flank from Soviet reinforcements coming in from the east. By 6 July both the 4th Panzerarmee and Armeeabteilung Kempf had driven deep into the Soviet defences, but the Soviet reserves were beginning to arrive in considerable numbers, the most important of these being the 5th Guards Tank Army, an elite and powerful armoured force. Determined resistance was gradually overcome, and by 11 July, Hoth's left wing, with the XLVIII Panzer Corps as its main striking element, had pushed forward some 15 miles (25km) against the 40th, 6th Guards and 1st Tank Armies. On Hoth's right wing, the II SS Panzer Corps, under the command of General Paul Hausser, was making even better progress, and had pushed forward as far as Prokhorovka after an advance of 30 miles (50km). The Armeeabteilung Kempf was also moving forward well and had reached Rzhavets

on the upper Donets, with a line of Soviet forces keeping it separated from the II SS Panzer Corps. On 12 July the head of the 5th Guards Tank Army reached Prokhorovka, engaging the tanks of the SS Panzer corps, and the largest tank battle in history was about to start.

Hausser's tanks and their crews were by now in fairly poor shape, but the Soviets were able to stop their advance on only the first engagement. With more Soviet tanks on the way, Hausser's position was just becoming precarious when the III Panzer Corps, the spearhead of the Armeeabteilung Kempf, arrived from the upper Donets to take the 5th Guards Tank Army in flank. The battle was confused and desperate, but late on 13 July the Germans seemed to be gaining the upper hand. On this day, however, von Manstein and von Kluge had been summoned to a meeting with Hitler, who told them that Zitadelle was to be called off, for the Allies had landed in Sicily three days before and more troops were needed in the west. A day earlier, moreover, the Central, West and Bryansk Fronts had launched a great offensive against von Kluge's Army Group Centre. Model's small gains were wiped out almost immediately, and by 18 August the German salient around Orel had been eliminated, so von Kluge was only too pleased to hear of the cancellation of Zitadelle. But von Manstein was not happy with the decision. Although he had been against the operation from the start, he now felt he was in a position to destroy a major portion of the Soviet armoured strength in the battle around Prokhorovka. Hitler reluctantly agreed, and von Manstein urged Hausser to complete the destruction of the 5th Guards Tank Army as swiftly as possible. Just as victory was in sight, however, on 17 July Hitler ordered the attack to be broken off, and the SS Panzer corps sent to Italy. The Battle of Kursk was over: it had failed in its major objective, and had in the end also failed in the ad hoc objective of destroying the Soviet armour, just as the distinct possibility of victory had come into sight.

On 3 August the Voronezh, Steppe, and South-West Fronts went over to the general offensive, and by 23 August the Kharkov salient had fallen once again to the Soviets. A general offensive had now started right along the Soviet line from west of Moscow south to the Black Sea, and in a series of co-ordinated attacks, which ended only on 23 December, the Soviets drove Army Groups Centre, South and A to the line of the Dniepr river. The 17th Army was cut off in Crimea, and the Soviets also secured huge bridgeheads across the Dniepr from north of Gomel to south of Kiev (these fell on 6 November) and between Kremenchug and Zaporozhye.

The most significant event of the year had been the German failure to eliminate the Kursk salient. This was the last time the Germans were to hold the initiative on the Eastern Front, and from this time on all they could do was to attempt to maintain their hold. Hitler steadfastly refused to sanction retreat, but the weight and size of the Soviet forces gradually drove the Germans back, despite the latter's great skill and determination in defensive fighting. Stalingrad had signalled the high point of the German advance, but Kursk signalled the beginning of the decline.

THE ALLIED INVASION OF ITALY

As the last battles were being fought in Tunisia, the Allied staffs were already planning the invasion of Italy. Although a heavy toll had been taken of them on land and in the air, the Axis forces were still able to offer strong resistance and it was believed, especially by General Sir Bernard Montgomery, that the Italians would fight hard in defence of their own soil. Allied air forces were waging a war of attrition against the Luftwaffe and Regia Aeronautica, but Axis warplanes could still be a menace to the ships of an amphibious operation, so it was

necessary to advance step-by-step within range of land-based fighter cover. The intention was to capture Sicily, with its airfields, and then, as the opportunity arose, cross over to the toe and heel of the mainland. However, the next main thrust would again be made by sea to a point south of Naples, but still within range of effective air cover.

The expedition was to be a combined US and British undertaking supervised by a supreme commander based in Africa (at first the US General Dwight D. Eisenhower, and then the British General Sir Maitland Wilson). General Sir Harold Alexander's 15th Army Group was to command the two field armies, Lieutenant-General George S. Patton's US 7th, and Montgomery's British 8th Armies. In terms of numbers, the assault on Sicily was to be the biggest amphibious operation so far attempted. On the right, the 8th Army, preceded by a brigade of gliderborne troops, was to land on the east coast with four divisions, turn right and advance north, making for the Strait of Messina and so cut off all the Axis troops on the island. On the left, the 7th Army was to land three divisions, with an armoured division close behind, on a 50-mile (80- km) front on the south coast. It was to be preceded by four battalions of parachute troops, whose task was to seize airfields and other vital points inland. Patton's role was to protect the flank and rear of the 8th Army from interference by the six Axis divisions in the island, two of them Panzer or Panzergrenadier formations of the highest quality.

This was a perfectly good plan, but it was plain to the Americans that Alexander had selected the British 8th Army for the decisive role, and resented the fact. Some US divisions had in fact not performed well in their first actions in Tunisia, but they were now blooded and anxious to show their form. No one, however, resented the slur more than Patton, a brilliant, highly temperamental and intensely patriotic officer who, to

make matters worse, strongly disliked the able, but arrogant and tactless General Montgomery.

From 1943, the tremendous power of the Allies, especially in the air, made the chances of failure remote, but they were still inexperienced. Amphibious landings are always hazardous and the opening phase of this operation was almost a disaster. On the day that Operation Husky was launched on 10 July, Montgomery's troops disembarked efficiently, consolidated, and moved off to capture their first objective, the naval base of Syracuse. But the entire airborne operation was a fiasco. The US Troop

A German motorcycle despatch rider and Italian soldiers. Relationships between the German and Italian forces were often not as amicable as is suggested in such photographs.

Carrier Command was really a logistic force: its pilots were unaccustomed to flying in the combat zone and incapable of the pinpoint navigation required for airborne operations at night. Confused by bad weather and enemy fire, the pilots landed 12 gliders on target and no less than 47 of the 144 in the sea. On the US front, 3,400 of the paratroops reached the mainland, some being as much as 25 miles (40 km) off target and mostly in scattered parties.

The weather was rough, and although Patton's infantry got ashore successfully, there was delay in landing tanks and artillery. At that moment, with one foot in the sea and the other on land, they were violently counter-attacked at Gela, in the centre of the intended beach-head. Here the Americans, especially their regular 1st Division and parties of paratroops, literally 'marching to the sound of the guns', showed superb fighting spirit, stopping the Hermann Göring Division, with its 100-odd tanks, just short of the beach, aided by some astonishingly accurate fire from the guns of the US Navy cruisers covering the landings. This dispelled any notion that the Americans could not fight, or were no match for German armoured forces.

After a good start, the 8th Army then met with stiff resistance. Sicily, with its narrow roads, terraces, and sharp ridges was ideal for defence and gave a foretaste of what the Allies were to face for the next two years as they slogged north along the mainland of Italy. Montgomery was slowed down and almost halted, and Patton viewed this delay with intense impatience, eventually persuading Alexander to let his army go over to a full offensive. Once off the leash, he turned away to his left, made a remarkable dash for Palermo, captured it, and started to race Montgomery for Messina along the northern coast. He won by a short head, but the Germans, in a masterly withdrawal behind a series of defence lines, got clean away across the strait, without their equipment, but

with most of the principal asset, their men, intact.

The 8th Army then hopped unopposed over the strait on 3 September, and its 5th Division began to work its way along the coast from Calabria toward Salerno, where the next act was to be performed. Operation Avalanche, at Salerno, proved to be a desperate affair. It had been preceded by the dramatic fall of Mussolini and the surrender of Italy, and the Allies vainly hoped that the Italian army might even change sides. The Germans had foreseen the danger, however, and brutally disarmed their late ally to prevent this from happening. What many soldiers thought would be a walkover therefore turned into a bloody battle.

Lieutenant-General Mark W. Clark's US 5th Army, with two British and one US division leading, landed smoothly enough on 9 September, but the Germans were ready for them. Salerno is ringed with mountains, affording splendid observation, and between artillery fire and counter-attack the invaders were pinned near the beaches; indeed, the British and Americans could not join up, and for a time no further landings could be made in the British sector. The British 56th (London) Division was driven back, and when the Panzers broke through the front of the US 36th Division, they were stopped only just short of the beaches by US divisional artillery fire at close range. The whole of the shallow beach-head and the beaches themselves were under observed artillery fire, as was the fleet lying in Salerno bay under air attack from the new German guided glide-bombs. There was talk of re-embarkation, but this was sternly quashed by Alexander, who was at the beach-head. Reinforcements were landed, and two British 15-in (381-mm) gun battleships arrived to give added fire support, US heavy bombers were called in and the British 5th Division pressed up north from the toe of Italy, distracting the defence.

The German opposition began to wilt under the massive firepower which met every one of their attacks. The British and Americans began to take the offensive, pushing out the perimeter and making room for the British 7th Armoured Division to start punching along the road to Naples.

Commanding on the Italian front, Field-Marshal Albert Kesselring saw that he had to choose between being destroyed where he stood or breaking clear to fight a rearguard action, protected by an immense belt of demolitions prepared by his engineers. He opted for the latter; not a bridge was left standing and every road was mined. He abandoned Naples and fell back slowly to his main defensive position, the 'Gustav' Line. This ran from coast to coast from the mouth of the Garigliano river in the west to Ortona in the east. The Allied armies, the 5th on the left and the 8th on the right, began to advance toward this, driving in the German rearguards and outposts., a preliminary that was in itself a major task. The Germans proved masters of defensive fighting in Italy, and it was not until the 5th Army had fought one battle to cross the Volturno river and another to capture Monte Camino, that its patrols could even examine the formidable Gustav Line defences immediately behind the Garigliano and Rapido rivers. The rivers were, in effect, the moat of this excellent defensive line, the mountains the bastions, and Monte Cassino the guard tower of the gateway through which the road led to Rome.

The fighting continued until late in December, during which period the 8th Army took Bari and Foggia, fought a three-day battle for Termoli, and crossed the Trigno and Sangro rivers against strong resistance. They took Orsogna after three attempts and Ortona after 12 days, both occasions being notable for some savage street fighting between Canadian infantry and German paratroops. All this hard fighting on the Adriatic coast wore the Germans down

but was strategically useless, for behind each ridge and river was another just as doggedly held. The solution, the Allies felt, was to use their sea-power for yet another landing to outflank the Gustav Line positions and open the road to Rome. The site chosen for this 'Shingle' undertaking was Anzio. If the 5th Army could break through the western end of the Gustav Line and the force landed at Anzio could cut inland, the right wing of the German 10th Army might well be trapped and destroyed. The problem was how to break through the line. An attempt early in January 1944 to cross the Garigliano and Rapido rivers failed dismally. It was then decided that the correct strategy was to force a passage through the Cassino gap along Highway 6 to Rome, but that this would not be possible until Monte Cassino itself had been taken. Accordingly, on 22 January, Major-General John P. Lucas, commanding the US VI Corps, landed single British and US divisions on the beaches at Anzio, and on 24 January Major-General Geoffrey Keyes launched his US II Corps at the Cassino defences.

Lucas has been blamed for not immediately advancing after his successful landing, so creating confusion in the rear of the Gustav Line, but military historians now agree that this would have been folly. The Germans are rightly celebrated for the speed and aggression of their reactions to the unexpected, and if Kesselring had been able to cut in behind to sever its line of communications, the VI Corps would have been helpless for lack of supplies. Lucas wisely paused to secure his beach-head and base, but in doing so was to be besieged for four months. Kesselring had been fully prepared for such a landing. His first move was to send batteries of 3.465-in (88-mm) dual-purpose guns,

ABOVE LEFT: British infantrymen were forced to learn the art of urban warfare in parts of the fighting for Sicily in July 1943.

ABOVE: The Germans handled their armoured resources well in the Italian campaign, but Allied artillery and air power exacted a heavy toll wherever and whenever they could catch German tanks and self-propelled guns.

LEFT: German anti-tank gunners wait for a target to present itself. This is a 2.95-in (75-mm) Pak 40 towed gun, which was one of the most formidable weapons Allied tanks had to face, its shot having the power to penetrate 4.5-in (115-mm) armour at 545 yards (500m).

ABOVE: Salerno, September 1943. German prisoners are marched off toward waiting ships as the Allies secure their first major toehold on mainland Italy.

ABOVE RIGHT: The armistice, which the Italians had secretly signed with the Allies on 3 September, came into effect on 9 September, just as the Allies had begun to land at Salerno.

RIGHT: German soldiers surrender to US infantrymen.

from the air defence of Rome, to form a screen of anti-tank guns around Anzio, the simultaneous issuing of a single codeword launching pre-warned elements of the German reserves, racing down Italy, to form a perimeter defence. These were followed by a division from France and another from Yugoslavia, three regiments from Germany itself, and two heavy tank battalions. Thus, by the time the Royal Navy and the US Navy had, with exemplary speed, unloaded Lucas's formations and he was ready to attack with four divisions, Kesselring had assembled eight divisions to block him. The result was that far from being able to break out and help the 5th Army, Lucas was subjected to powerful counter-offensives which threatened to destroy his position. With his 14th Army containing the beach-head, and the 10th comfortably holding off both the 8th and the 5th Armies, Kesselring was well placed. The VI Corps, however, stood firm, and never looked like being beaten. Lucas himself was vindicated by events, and was very unfairly dismissed when the crisis was over. In the meantime, Alexander felt it essential to help Lucas by making a full-scale attack, and on 24 January the US II Corps began the first of the four battles for Cassino.

Monte Cassino is the name of a spur, crowned by the ancient monastery over-looking Highway 6, its intricate defensive system, garrisoned by three battalions of paratroops, embracing a whole group of peaks. Any attacking force had first to fight its way over the Rapido river, past the town, and then climb 1,500ft (460m) under fire, first to locate and then to assault the cunningly sited German positions in the crags and gullies behind the crest, from which came streams of interlocking machine-gun fire. It was not possible for the Americans to deploy their massive fire support or their tanks in this situation, so the issue had to be decided by close combat. The US 34th Division and the Moroccans and Algerians of the French Expeditionary Corps reached the crest-line and battled there for 18 days, reaching a point within 1,100 yards (1000m) of the great Benedictine monastery; but a kilometre is a very long way in mountain warfare. This first attempt ended only after the US battalions had lost three-quarters of their fighting strength, which were replaced by the New Zealand 2nd and Indian 4th Divisions.

After much discussion, it was decided to attack the monastery directly, and the highly controversial decision was taken to use heavy bombers to blast open the German defences. Major-General F.I.S. Tuker, an experienced Indian Army officer, urged a widely circling attack in the higher ground, in which his skilled mountain troops would bypass the monastery defences, but this was disregarded. Bombing had no effect, for the buildings themselves were not occupied, and after two days the New Zealand commander, Lieutenant-General Sir Bernard Freyberg, stopped the attacks.

On 15 March he started them again, this time asking for Cassino town to be bombed, but this also had little effect except to create a miniature Stalingrad, where Panzergrenadiers and New Zealanders fought at close quarters in the ruins. No attempt was made to co-ordinate bombardments with attacks, the defenders repeating their fathers' tactics of the Western Front, by going to ground in the impregnable rock and concrete shelters, to pop out and man

their weapons when the bombing stopped and the assaulting troops appeared. Every scrap of food, can of water, and box of ammunition for the attackers, had to be carried up by hand, and when not fighting, the attackers were obliged to defend their gains under continuous artillery fire, causing a steady loss of men.

As Tuker had foreseen, it had been useless to attack the Germans at their strongest point. The Indian engineers brought off the extraordinary feat of building a secret track up the mountain. It was fit for tanks, and a squadron drove up it, but to no avail.

Freyberg persisted for three weeks, by which time he had lost 4,000 men. The offensive was finally halted on 23 March, the forward troops were pulled back, and the ground won consolidated. Both sides now paused to rest and recover. Each soldier was mentally and physically exhausted by the cold, the wet, the ceaseless bombardments and the strain of months of bitter fighting. Alexander, advised by his chief-of-staff, Lieutenant-General Alan F.J. Harding, decided to rest and regroup his troops until the spring, when the advent of better weather and dry ground would allow him to use his two primary assets: armour and warplanes. Alexander would then launch a properly co-ordinated

offensive, at the same time using all his resources to break through the Gustav Line with a single concentrated punch, at the same time advancing with maximum possible force from the beach-head at Anzio. This, he felt sure, would break the deadlock. It would be better still if he could destroy the bulk of the 10th Army, where they stood facing him in southern Italy, thus opening up the whole peninsula to a rapid Allied advance to the north. This great operation, since it was to set the crown on a year of hard fighting, was to be called Diadem.

LEFT: Italian civilians read a US proclamation. Most Italians, especially in the south, welcomed what they saw as an Allied liberation of Italy.

BELOW: Numerically and tactically, the most important tank fielded by the Allies in the Italian campaign was the M4 Sherman medium tank. Such a tank is seen here, negotiating a Sicilian sand dune after coming ashore from a tank landing craft.

RIGHT: Throughout the latter part of World War II, the Germans revealed themselves to be masters of defensive warfare. Here German troops rip up a railway line as they pull back on the Eastern Front.

BELOW: The Germans made excellent use of captured equipment of all types. The Marder self-propelled anti-tank gun, for example, was the Germans' own 2.95-in (75-mm) Pak 40 anti-tank gun on a limited-traverse mounting on the hull of the Czechoslovak LT-38 tank, which had been used as a gun tank earlier in the war with the designation PzKpfw 38(t).

THE GERMANS ARE EXPELLED FROM THE USSR

The rapid pace and wide geographical extent of their efforts in 1943 cost the Soviet forces very dearly. Many hundreds of thousands of men were lost, and tanks, guns, aircraft and other war matériel had been expended at a prodigious rate. But as a result of the efforts of its growing armaments industry, in the area east of the Urals, the USSR was able not only to resupply its armies, but also to equip, on a relatively lavish scale, the new formations that were also being brought into existence in large numbers. Hitler had gambled on a quick war, so that the USSR's resources in industry and manpower should not be used to their full extent, and had lost. No matter how great the casualties inflicted on the Soviet forces, the Germans could not destroy enough to force the USSR out of the war. The Soviets fought in a tactical manner which was relatively unsophisticated, exploiting the availability of their supplies of the right

types of weapon, such as the excellent T-34 tank, and the commanders were prepared to expend the lives of large numbers of men. Germany, on the other hand, could not do this: its armies fought a tactically advanced type of warfare, using the latest weapons, but it could not keep up with the losses inflicted by the Soviets, and although in 1943–44 its armies were still of a superior quality to those of the Soviets, this was more than counterbalanced by the enormously superior quantity of the Soviet forces. Supplied by the Americans

and British with considerable war matériel, including large numbers of trucks, the Soviets were gradually developing a characteristic pattern of hard-hitting, fast mobile warfare, admirably suited to their armies and the terrain of the western USSR. With supply outstripping demand, the Soviets were able to keep up an almost non-stop offensive, with fresh troops always ready to take over from exhausted formations.

In 1941 Hitler had ordered Field-Marshal Wilhelm von Leeb's Army Group North not to take Leningrad by direct assault, but rather to invest the city and destroy it by starvation and bombardment. The investment had been completed when von Leeb's forces reached the southern shore of Lake Ladoga, joining the ring of Axis forces around the birthplace of the USSR with the Finnish hold on the region to the north. Leningrad's trials in the following months were appalling, with thousands dying of starvation every day, and disease and cold taking their toll. It is estimated that the people of Leningrad were dying at the rate of 20,000 every day by the end of 1943. Nevertheless, the city continued to hold off the German forces.

Supplies were brought in over the frozen surface of Lake Ladoga, during the winter of 1941–42, but this, of course, ended with the thaw in March 1942, when conditions deteriorated rapidly. In August 1942, the Leningrad and Volkhov Fronts launched a joint offensive, with the aim of cutting the corridor from Tosno north to Lake Ladoga, held by the German 18th Army, but this failed and Leningrad remained under siege. An attempt to link up with the forces locked up at Oranienbaum, farther to the west along the Gulf of Finland, also failed at the same time. In January 1943, however, hope of eventual relief appeared when the Leningrad and Volkhov Fronts finally managed to cut their way through to just south of Lake Ladoga and link up near Sinyavino. Although this 'Corridor of Death' was under constant threat by German artillery, a trickle of supplies reached Leningrad, and German efforts to cut the Soviet land bridge failed. The limits of this supply route precluded the total relief of the city, which lost perhaps 1 million people during the siege, but it did prevent conditions from worsening.

Almost exactly a year after the link to Leningrad had been opened, the Soviets at last managed to free the city from the constant threat of German conquest. At the same time, they drove

the forces of Army Group North, commanded by Field-Marshal Georg von Küchler, back to Lake Peipus in Estonia. On 15 January 1944 the forces of the Leningrad and Volkhov Fronts, commanded by Generals L.A. Govorov and K.A. Meretskov respectively, swept forward, catching the Germans completely off their guard. The Leningrad Front crossed the frozen Gulf of Finland, falling on the left of the German 18th Army, commanded by General Georg Lindemann, while the Volkhov Front crossed the frozen lakes and marshes further to the south to attack the 18th Army's right. By the end of the year, the Soviets had advanced to the line of the Luga river and had taken the historic capital of the area, Novgorod. Lindemann pulled his army back and just evaded encirclement. The 2nd Baltic Front, under General M.M. Popov, had made limited attacks still farther to the south, but in February began a major offensive to advance the Soviet front line to the line running along the Velikaya river south from Pskov, at the southern end of Lake Peipus. When the thaw began at the beginning of March, bringing hostilities to a temporary halt, Field-Marshal Walther Model, who had replaced von Küchler on 29 January, had only just managed to begin to check the Soviets. The German threat to Leningrad had at last been removed after the greatest siege of modern times.

Meanwhile, in the south, the Soviets had been continuing their offensive against the Germans in Ukraine. Supported on its right by Colonel-General P.A. Kurochkin's 2nd Belorussian Front, on 24 December 1943 the 1st Ukrainian Front, under General N.F. Vatutin, struck west in a great offensive from its bridgehead around Kiev. General I.S. Konev's 2nd Ukrainian Front also moved onto the offensive farther to the south, between Kanev and Kirovograd, on 5 January 1944, with General R.Y. Malinovsky's

3rd Ukrainian Front and General F.I. Tolbukhin's 4th Ukrainian Front, on each side of Zaporozhye at the head of the Dniepr bend, joining the offensive on 10 and 11 January respectively. There was nothing the Germans could do but try to extricate themselves as best they could. Field-Marshal Erich von Manstein's Army Group South and Field-Marshal Ewald von Kleist's Army Group A tried to stem the Soviet winter advance, but lacked the strength to halt the vast Soviet fronts. On 29 January, two corps were trapped at Korsun-Shevchenkovsky, and although von Manstein immediately set about putting together a relief force, a major part of the two corps had been lost, together with all the divisions' heavy equipment,

The dead of a Waffen-SS unit, lying in the snow of a typically harsh Russian winter.

THE ALLIED VICTORY IN EUROPE

by the time the relief force and the cut-off garrison met on 17 February. Von Manstein's efforts had been greatly hampered by atrocious winter conditions and the overall exhaustion of his men.

The Soviets continued to grind forward right into April, despite the brilliance of many counter-attacks mounted by the indefatigable von Manstein, who yet again demonstrated his remarkable tactical genius. In the confusion of such operations, it was hardly surprising that another German

army was now cut off. This was the 1st Panzerarmee, commanded by General Hans Hube. Isolated to the east of Kamenets Podolskiy on 10 March, Hube prevented his forces from being pinned down by the superior Soviet armies opposing him. Keeping constantly on the move, and supplied from the air, the 1st Panzerarmee fought a brilliant battle against the Soviet lines of communication, as ordered by von Manstein, who kept a close personal supervision over the whole operation by radio. Unable to pin down this highly mobile force, the Soviets were at a loss to know what to do, slowing their advance in the area. Finally Hube turned west, and in conjunction with an attack south from Tarnopol, by the 4th Panzerarmee, now commanded by Colonel-General Erhard Raus, broke out through the Soviet front line, keeping his forces almost intact.

Yet the Soviets were still moving steadily forward. Commanded by more than competent generals, and supervised from Moscow by Marshal Georgi Zhukov and Iosef Stalin, who kept a personal link open to all senior commanders, the Soviets seemed invincible. Despite the tactical genius of their commanders and their own skill and determination, the German soldiers were outnumbered and driven back. History shows that von Kleist conducted an exemplary retreat, and von Manstein a brilliant one, but Hitler dismissed both of these commanders on 30 March. Colonel-General Ferdinand Schörner, a hard-line Nazi but adequate general, took command of von Kleist's Army Group South Ukraine (ex-Army Group A) and Field-Marshal Walther Model became commander of von Manstein's Army Group North Ukraine (ex-Army Group South).

Vatutin was killed in March and was succeeded on 1 April by Zhukov, and the Soviets pressed forward. The German 6th and 8th Armies in the south were badly mauled, and the great Black Sea port of

Odessa fell on 10 April. By the middle of the month, the Soviets had cleared the Axis forces out of the whole of the USSR to the south of the Pripyet marshes. The Soviet forces had crossed the Bug, Dniestr and Prut rivers, and the Ukrainian fronts were now deep into southern Poland and northern Romania. Trapped in Crimea, the German 17th Army was faced with the impossible task of holding off the 2nd Guards and 51st Armies of Tolbukhin's 4th Ukrainian Front, which attacked south along the Perekop isthmus on 8 April, and General A.I. Eremenko's Independent Coastal Army, which crossed from the Taman peninsula into the Kerch peninsula on 11 April. The 17th Army was driven back towards Sevastopol, from which only a few men could be evacuated. Hitler had insisted that Crimea be held as a jumping-off point for the reconquest of the southern USSR, and his increasing refusal to see the realities of the situation cost Germany the fine 17th Army when the last parts of Sevastopol fell on 12 May.

The winter and spring campaigns had cleared the southern USSR, and Stalin now planned to use the summer offensive to clear the central USSR and Belorussia, just to the north of the Pripyet marshes. The offensive was entrusted, from south to north, to Marshal K.K. Rokossovsky's 1st Belorussian, Colonel-General M.V. Zakharov's 2nd Belorussian, Colonel-General I.D. Chernyakovsky's 3rd Belorussian and Colonel-General I.K. Bagramyan's 1st Baltic Fronts. These four had as their primary task the destruction of Field-Marshal Ernst Busch's Army Group Centre. The offensive was to be launched from the area just to the west of Smolensk and Gomel, the axis being west toward East Prussia. As usual, immediate overall command of the whole operation was entrusted to Zhukov, by now deputy supreme commander of the Soviet armed forces under Stalin. Mustering some 400 guns per mile (250 guns per kilometre), the four Soviet fronts began

which had been completed by 4 July, was a catastrophe of incalculable proportions for the Germans, yet the size of the forces deployed by the Soviets cannot detract from Zhukov's genius in planning and controlling such a successful and speedy campaign. Busch was almost inevitably dismissed by Hitler, who entrusted command of the shattered Army Group Centre to Model, who also kept command of Army Group North Ukraine.

This was only the first stage of the Soviet summer offensive. The Belorussian fronts continued westward, taking Vilnyus on 13 July, Brest-Litovsk on 28 July, and reaching the outskirts of Warsaw by the end of August. Colonel-General Georg-Hans Reinhardt, previously commander of the 3rd Panzerarmee, badly mauled near Vitebsk, succeeded Model as head of Army Group Centre on 16 August when Model left for France, where the situation was worsening after the Allied break-out from their Normandy lodgement. Model's position as commander of Army Group North

LEFT: Soviet 'tankers' rest by their vehicles as the high command plans their next move.

BELOW: Like those of the Japanese, the infantrymen of the Soviet army acquired a first-class reputation for courage and endurance, and performed very capably in offence and defence when well-led.

their offensive against the hapless Army Group Centre after a devastating barrage on 23 June. Disorganized at the front by the Soviet artillery and in its rear areas by the ever-increasing activities of Soviet partisans, now a formidable force, Army Group Centre could not even retreat before the armoured offensive. The Soviets smashed a 250-mile (400-km) gap through the German front, and through this poured massed armour and infantry. The Soviet air forces had total command of the air, and the armour drove forward as swiftly as possible, leaving the infantry to mop up and follow on as best it could. As usual, Hitler expressly forbade retreat, ordering cut-off formations to stand and fight until relieved, even though there were no relief forces to be had. The Soviets retook Vitebsk on 25 June, Bobruysk on 27 June and Minsk on 3 July. For the first time in the war, an entire German army group had been destroyed: 25 of Busch's 33 divisions had been cut off and destroyed, and the Soviets claimed to have killed 400,000 Germans, captured 158,000, and destroyed or taken 2,000 armoured vehicles, 10,000 guns and 57,000 vehicles.

The loss of Belorussia and the destruction of Army Group Centre,

joined still farther to the south on 5 August by General I.E. Petrov's 4th Ukrainian Front, only recently formed. By the end of August, the Ukrainian and Belorussian fronts had reached a north and south line running from Jaslo in southern Poland, past the east of Warsaw, around East Prussia and thence into Lithuania. The advance since the end of July had been small, for the Soviets had advanced some 450 miles (725km) and their lines of communications could no longer sustain further advance.

Yet just as the Soviets began to slow at the beginning of August, there occurred one of the most remarkable and heroic actions of the war. In Warsaw the

ABOVE: Part of the price of defeat: German prisoners-of-war are marched through Moscow to captivity.

RIGHT: Soviet soldiers re-erect a border marking after the Germans have been driven back.

BELOW: Soviet infantry of an elite guards unit attack in the summer of 1943.

Ukraine passed to Colonel-General Josef Harpe, although he was only confirmed in this post after the army group had become Army Group A during September.

No amount of reordering of already shattered commands and forces could halt the Soviets, however. On 13 July Konev's 1st Ukrainian Front, just to the south of the 1st Belorussian Front, had gone over to the offensive, and was

Polish Home Army had for long been secretly planning a rising against the German garrison, once the Soviets were within reach of the city. Despite their anti-Communist feelings, the men of the Home Army, under the command of General Tadeusz Bor-Komorowski, rose against the Germans on 1 August. The 1st Belorussian Front had recently halted, just over the Vistula river from Warsaw, possibly to ensure that this non-Communist Polish armed force would be defeated, and after a hopeless but heroic defence the Home Army was crushed in bitter fighting by the end of September. What was left of Warsaw after the German campaign of 1939, and the reduction of the Jewish ghetto after this, was almost totally destroyed in the vicious two-month campaign by the SS.

On 4 July General A.I. Eremenko's 2nd Baltic Front, General I.I. Maslennikov's 3rd Baltic Front, and General L.A. Govorov's Leningrad Front extended the Soviet general offensive to the north. Together with the 1st Baltic and 3rd Belorussian Fronts, they swept into the Baltic states, occupied by the USSR in 1940, and lost to the Germans in 1941. Army Group North, commanded by Colonel-General Georg Lindemann, was unable to stem the Soviet advance and fell back toward the Baltic. Although this army group was threatened by the distinct possibility of being cut off by the Belorussian fronts' advance toward East Prussia, Hitler again would not even consider the possibility of retreat. Forced back from the line of the Narva and Velikaya rivers, Army Group North eventually found itself in western Latvia, where it was cut off in the peninsula north of a line between Tukums, on the Bay of Riga, and Liepaja on the Baltic Sea, when the forces of the 1st Baltic Front reached the sea on 10 October. Narva had fallen on 26 July, Daugavpils (Dvinsk) on 27 July, Kaunas on 1 August and the bastion of Riga was to fall on 15 October. Colonel-General Heinz Guderian, who had

replaced Colonel-General Kurt Zeitzler as OKH chief-of-staff, was appalled by Hitler's decision to allow this important and powerful force to be locked up by the Soviets, where it would be paralyzed to further Germany's war aims. The men of Army Group North remained trapped and useless in the Kurland peninsula right up to the end of the war, although some units were evacuated by ships of the German navy.

With the threat to Leningrad now removed, the Soviets were able to turn their attention in this region to Finland. In the middle of June, five Soviet armies attacked north-west along the Karelian isthmus and around each end of Lake Onega, and after at first being halted by a skilful Finnish defence, began to make ground. The Mannerheim Line was finally breached, and on 20 June the Soviet forces took Viipuri. Seeing the hopelessness of their position, the Finns sued for and were granted an armistice on 4 September, under the terms of which the Finns had to clear their former co-belligerents, the Germans, out of the country; there was some sharp fighting before this was accomplished. In the far north, on the shores of the Arctic, the German 20th Army was driven back out of the USSR by Meretskov's Karelian Front in October, and the Soviets eventually pushed on into Norway, although the little ports of Petsamo and Kirkenes were able to hold out.

The Soviet advances in northern Ukraine and Belorussia had by now placed Army Group South Ukraine, now commanded by Colonel-General Johannes Friessner, in a difficult position. Any Soviet advance into southern Poland and Hungary would threaten it with being cut off, together with Army Groups E and F in Greece and Yugoslavia respectively, especially if Hitler refused permission to pull back, which seemed likely. The Soviets saw this as clearly as the Germans, and launched an attack into Romania on 20 August with the 2nd and 3rd Ukrainian Fronts. The German

6th and Romanian 3rd Armies were quickly trapped, the Soviets pressing on to the Danube river by 29 August. Romania, long disaffected with the Axis cause by lack of success, capitulated on 23 August, declaring war on Germany two days later. The Romanian 3rd and 4th Armies quickly joined with the Soviets to press the campaign against their former allies. Reaching the Romanian capital on 31 August, the Soviets wheeled west and then north-west to drive into southern Hungary. By 24 September Romania had been entirely overrun.

The 37th and 57th Armies of the 3rd Ukrainian Front continued south-west, however, plunging into Bulgaria, which surrendered on 4 September, and joining the USSR four days later. Beset by partisans and the Bulgarian 1st Army, Army Group E succeeded in pulling back from Greece to link with Army Group F in Yugoslavia. Greatly weakened by the loss of much of the 6th and 8th Armies, Army Group South Ukraine nonetheless attempted to hold southern Hungary, with Army Groups E and F to its right in Yugoslavia. It was an impossible task, and the Soviets moved with ease into Hungary and eastern Yugoslavia where, with the aid of the now-considerable partisan forces of Marshal Tito, they took Belgrade on 19 October. By the end of 1944, the Soviets were firmly ensconced in the Balkans, ready to drive forward into Austria and Czechoslovakia.

The USSR had been cleared. Finland, Romania and Bulgaria had dropped out of the war, the latter two then rejoining it on the other side. The Soviet armies were poised to sweep into the territories bordering Germany and thence into Germany proper. Stalin had every reason to be pleased with the performance of his forces. All Germany could do, given a leadership which refused even the notion of asking for terms, was to fight on desperately in the hope of slowing the Soviets, who were still to have a hard time of it in 1945.

ABOVE: The German defence of southern Italy, especially at Cassino, was synonymous with the great tenacity and fighting skills of the elite German parachute divisions. Here are paratroopers in Rome, before the Italian capital was declared an open city and abandoned to the Allies in June 1944.

RIGHT: British Churchill infantry tanks on the move in open country.

China, the US leadership favoured an offensive strategy and felt that the British were dragging their feet, while the British saw no merit in becoming entangled in the mountains and jungles of upper Burma to help China, which was an ally of only doubtful capability, when they were free to strike farther to the south and east by sea. By contrast, the British felt that, in Italy, they already had a foothold in Europe and wished to exploit it without risking all on the hazardous cross-Channel crossing desired by the Americans. Prime Minister Winston Churchill, always a great exponent of the 'indirect approach', envisaged a wide movement into Austria and central Europe and so into southern Germany. The Americans were, as always, against this on the grounds that it was not the direct approach to the main enemy as mandated by their military philosophy: Operation Overlord against Normandy and the direct approach was their choice,

BREAKING THE GUSTAV LINE
There is a fascinating reversal of thinking to be found in American and British attitudes to the way in which the war would be fought in South-East Asia and Italy. With regard to Burma and

followed by another landing, Operation Dragoon, in the south of France. In addition, General Sir Harold Alexander in Italy was to transfer seven divisions immediately for Overlord, and another six later in 1944 for Dragoon. His role was limited to keeping as many German divisions as possible occupied in Italy.

Alexander supported Churchill's strategy but commanded a multi-national army group: his second-in-command was a US officer, one of his armies was American, and one corps was French. Moreover, the French wanted desperately to fight to liberate France herself, not any other country. Alexander decided, therefore, that the most effective way to carry out his mission was to fix his eyes on the Po valley, the Julian Alps and the Ljubljana gap in Yugoslavia leading to central Europe, driving there as hard as he could with all his force. Although he was comparatively weak in divisions, he had command of the air, overwhelming

resources in weapons, and all the advantages in support services including, most importantly of all, engineers to build bridges. A remorseless drive to the north would keep his opponent as busy as any other more cautious and limited offensives. Such was the background of the Italian campaign in 1944, which saw the commitment of more troops (some 40 divisions on the two sides) than in any theatre, other than that of the Eastern Front.

Alexander felt that his first task was to reorganize his armies and then to launch Diadem for the solution of the Cassino-Anzio stalemate. The plan was to let operations die down on the Adriatic coast and shift the British 8th Army to the centre. Some military experts believe that the secret of mountain warfare is to avoid it, as it offers endless opportunities for delaying action. The new effort was to be made along the Rapido valley below Cassino, to burst through into the Liri valley. The British XIII Corps, under Lieutenant-General Sidney C. Kirkman, in Montgomery's opinion the best artillery officer in the British army, had the leading role with one armoured division, three infantry divisions and 1,000 guns, followed by the Canadian I Corps of one armoured and one infantry division, its task being to bridge the Rapido river and break into the valley defences under cover of a dense and prolonged smokescreen. This lasted from 12–18 May and used 813 tons of smoke munitions and 135,000 artillery smoke shells alone. Altogether, something approaching 1 million shells of all kinds were fired. The German batteries received a barrage of seven tons of heavy shells in a few minutes, and when the Canadians attacked the rear edge of the Gustav Line, known as the 'Hitler' Line, their preliminary bombardment was at the rate of 1,000 shells an hour.

This vast mass of artillery was to switch to the Cassino heights as necessary, to support two Polish

divisions, who were to clear the heights once and for all. On the left of the Liri valley the French Expeditionary Corps, with single Algerian and Moroccan colonial divisions, all experienced mountaineers, was to clear the heights on the left with startling success, while the US II Corps was to attack near the coast. Then, at the appropriate moment, one US armoured, three US infantry and two British divisions were to mount an offensive from the Anzio beach-head and make for Valmonte. As before, their task was to cut Highway 6 and trap the German divisions as they were being driven back from the Gustav Line. The RAF and USAAF were to concentrate on attacking the German reserves as they were moved up, and also on giving close air support to the advancing troops, using new and highly-developed methods of communication from ground to air.

Altogether 41 divisions were involved in this great battle: eight German encircling Anzio; ten in the crucial area of the Gustav Line; six Allied in the Anzio beach-head; and 17 between Cassino and the sea. Diadem was thus a great battle, and one which could have been decisive. Although it was a resounding success, it was excluded from the news and public notice by the launching of Overlord, on 6 June, just after the Gustav Line defences had collapsed, before just failing to achieve complete victory. This was due in part to the courage and tenacity of the Germans, who refused to admit defeat: they extricated their savaged battle groups, formed rearguards, and in spite of the unceasing attacks of the Allied air forces, retreated in order up through Italy to their next main position in the Apennines, namely the Gothic Line. The other cause was a decision by Clark to vary his orders. Resulting from national pride, personal vanity, or a belief that it was politically and strategically important to capture Rome, Clark's decision has long been the subject of

British armour approaches the German Gothic Line defences in northern Italy.

controversy. Leaving only one division to follow the thrust line laid down by Alexander, he swung four US divisions away to the left. He was held up along an intermediate Caesar Line, and it can be argued that had this been allowed to solidify there would have been a long delay if Clark had not broken through it; but there can be no doubt that he had departed from his orders, and the delicacy of Alexander's position was that Clark was allowed to get away with it. As a result the 10th Army escaped.

One of the surprises of the battle was the success of General Alphonse Juin's French-African troops. These were sent into the rugged and roadless mountain sector between the Americans and the British XIII Corps, more or less to keep the Germans in that sector occupied. Juin first infiltrated his infantry, capturing a vital peak which controlled the Liri valley on the south side, as Cassino did on the north. Then,

The Allied armies, by the closing stages of the Italian campaign, had great matériel superiority over the Germans, especially in artillery and, in general, the ammunition needed for it. Here, British artillery is engaged in the fighting for the Gothic Line.

using his *goumiers* (irregular Moroccan mounted infantry), Juin cut through the Gustav Line, came out behind it and caused the defences of the German left flank to collapse, while the British and Canadian armoured divisions, choked with their abundant transport, were still stuck in traffic jams in the Liri valley. Had this been foreseen, or exploited when it happened, the battle might have turned out very differently.

On the other side of the valley, it cost the Poles 4,000 casualties to capture the Cassino heights. Thus the defence of the position, by Major-General Richard Heidrich and his paratroops, cost the Allies altogether some 12,000 casualties, the battle remaining one of the epics of defensive warfare. It was fitting that the Germans should be overcome by their deadliest enemies: on 18 May the 12th Podolski Lancers, fighting as infantry,

raised the Polish flag over the ruins of the monastery.

If Alexander had achieved nothing else he had fulfilled his mission of drawing in reserves. By 6 June, D-Day for Overlord, four divisions had been sent to Kesselring to prevent a total collapse of the German position in Italy and later he was to be given three more. The result was that when the battle to pierce the Gothic Line began, Alexander's numerical superiority had changed to an adverse balance of 20 to 22. However, in air power, weapons and supplies he still had a great advantage. He began his campaign against Kesselring's rearguards as soon as the confusion of the breakthrough and the 5th Army's change of course could be cleared up.

The advancing Allies found that every bridge had been blown, every

verge and detour mined, and everything attractive booby-trapped. For the troops who had fought through the Gustav Line there was none of the excitement of a triumphant advance. All through the hot, dusty Italian summer the long columns of tanks and lorries rumbled forward, hit the enemy, stopped, patrolled, positioned the artillery, and attacked uphill through the terraced fields and orchards, only to find the Germans gone. They then had to form up again, advance to the next ridge, and start all over again. In August, eventually, they began to close up onto the Gothic Line.

North of Florence the Apennines lie diagonally across Italy, offering a natural line of defence from Spezia to Pesaro, and this had been enormously strengthened by the German engineers. The route through the centre was via two mountain passes. Going around the Adriatic flank meant crossing seven river valleys with 12 more rivers barring the way in the wide valley of the Po. It was a battle demanding vast resources as well as good tactics. Good military plans are usually very simple. All they require is first-class staff work and a combination of good troops, reserves and weather. The first was assured, although some of the best divisions were very tired, the second was non-existent, and the third was not going to last for more than a few weeks. Kesselring's veterans were equally tired and depleted, but they had been reinforced with fresh troops and their defences were ready. As things stood there was no question of a quick Allied breakthrough and there was little chance of exploitation should one be achieved, but Alexander and his army commanders decided to try.

The plan, suggested by Lieutenant-General Sir Oliver Leese, who had taken Montgomery's place, was for the 8th Army to be moved back to the Adriatic for a concentrated punch effort up the coast with the Polish and Canadian corps. The main thrust would come from the British V Corps, with four divisions, some 10 miles (16km) inland through the foothills, with the aim of setting the armour loose in the Po valley behind Kesselring's eastern flank. This was to commence on 25 August. Hoping that after two weeks most of Kesselring's reserves would have been attracted to the east, the 5th Army was to attack the Futa and Il Giogo passes, north of Florence, early in September. A great deal of care was taken to conceal the 8th Army's concentration, around its point of main effort, by the elaborate pretence of a build-up in the centre. The first attacks, by Major-General Sir John Hawkesworth, commanding the 46th Division, made in silence and without any preliminary air bombardment or covering fire, were a rapid success. To begin with, his division, with the Indian 4th Division on its left, crossed the Metauro river and attacked outposts manned by the German 71st Division, which were driven back in panic. By the end of August the whole of the 8th Army was hard up against the main German position, its patrols looking at hillsides converted to bare slopes, houses knocked down, trees and vines cleared to provide fields of fire, fields of anti-personnel and anti-tank mines, and the villages turned into machine-gun strongpoints. What looked to be impregnable was pierced, not simply by the weight of fire but by infantry fighting.

On 10 September it was the turn of the 5th Army to attack the fortified passes through the Apennines. Monte Altuzzo, commanding the Giglio pass and very heavily defended, was taken by the 1st Battalion, 338th Infantry Regiment, which lost 250 out of 400 men. All the heroism availed nought, for Alexander ran out of infantry reserves. The hope of a tank breakthrough on the east flank was vain. The British 1st Armoured Division was thrown repeatedly into action against their old foe, the German 3.465-in (88-mm) anti-tank guns: at Ceriano the Bays of the

2nd Armoured Brigade were shot to pieces in a few minutes, the division eventually having to be disbanded. The 8th Army lost 14,000 men killed, wounded and missing. It had advanced 30 miles (48km), losing 200 tanks on the way and now it was stuck. Moreover, it had begun to rain.

At one moment it looked as if the 5th Army, having cleared the passes, might almost have cracked the position open in the centre: there were only another 15 miles (24km) to go and from the forward positions Bologna could just be seen in the plain far below. At that desperate moment even Kesselring himself thought he had lost, but rain, mud, bad flying weather and the defence, stopped the 5th Army's infantry in the mountains just as it had stopped the 8th Army's armour in the plain.

RETURN TO FRANCE: OPERATION OVERLORD

The Allied invasion of north-west France, across the English Channel, was the most critical and the most dangerous operation of World War II. It was critical because it opened the only route by which the military strength of the USA could be brought to bear on Germany to end the war quickly. It was dangerous, because in an amphibious operation failure is complete. This Operation Overlord was the core of Allied strategy and all possible resources were concentrated for it. So far the Allies three assault landings in the western theatre, in Sicily, at Salerno and at Anzio, against relatively weak opposition and on an unfortified coast, had been close-run things. In France, by contrast, a complete German army group, commanded by Field-Marshal Erwin Rommel, awaited the invasion with 32 divisions ready to intervene, three more in the Netherlands, and another 13 divisions of another army group in the south of France. The vulnerable parts of the French coast were defended by the Atlantic Wall, a formidable belt of obstacles and minefields covered by

batteries of guns in concrete emplacements. The disastrous Dieppe raid of August 1942, in which the Canadian 2nd Division had been very severely mauled, had shown just how different breaching the Atlantic Wall would be from landing on an Italian beach or a Pacific atoll.

For logistical reasons the largest force landed by the Allies in the first wave was five divisions, with six more to follow when there was room for them to deploy. All possible scientific and military ingenuity, therefore, had to be devoted to solving three very difficult problems: firstly, to put the assault troops safely ashore in the face of intense fire; secondly, to get tanks and artillery over the ditches and tank-traps barring the way inland; and thirdly, to supply the two armies which would pour into the beach-head, and bring in over the beaches the vast amounts of fuel, ammunition and food needed. New methods and new weapons had to be invented for the battle of the beach-head.

It was planned to saturate the entire defence system with bombing and naval bombardment, but experience taught that, however heavy a bombardment may be, enough men and weapons would survive to decimate the attackers, so close support for the actual run-in to the beach had to be provided. This was achieved by putting armoured self-propelled artillery and also multiple-rocket launchers in the landing craft. The guns then rolled ashore to give normal support until the rest of the ordinary artillery was landed. Large numbers of battle tanks were fitted with 'DD' flotation gear, a British invention which enabled them to swim ashore to fight with the first wave. No less important was the part played by the tanks adapted for special jobs in the physical breaching of the defences and operated by assault engineers. These carried super-heavy mortars for blowing up concrete bunkers, flail equipment to explode minefields, and rolls of matting, fascines,

All this was essential, not in order to win the Battle of Normandy, which was another huge problem looming ahead, but to ensure that Field-Marshals Gerd von Rundstedt (commanding in the western theatre) and Rommel did not win the 'Battle of the Beach-head'. For both battles the Allies had two great assets. The first of these were Air Chief-Marshal Sir Arthur Tedder and General Carl Spaatz, whose RAD and USAAF had won complete command of the air and were thus in the position to help blast the armies forward, block the movement of reserves, and massacre the defeated German columns in retreat. The second was Adolf Hitler, for as a supreme commander he had now revealed himself to be an incompetent; this was for the simple reason that he regarded war as a giant game of chess, which he played on a map sitting in his various headquarters, giving futile orders no one dared to disobey. A single one of these was to lose the Germans the war in France.

The assault was led by three airborne divisions, followed by five seaborne assault divisions with tanks landing on the beaches, followed by six more divisions, with 21 more waiting in England. They were carried by 4,262 aircraft and 4,266 ships of all kinds, supported by 2,300 combat aircraft, which flew 14,600 sorties on D-Day alone. In the weeks before D-Day the heavy coast artillery batteries, which were the main threat to the landings, were bombed out of existence and all the railways and rolling stock, which might have moved von Rundstedt's strategic reserve to the threatened point, were wrecked. Some 80,000 tons of bombs were dropped. At sea two fleets guarded the flanks of the assault force, standing by to give covering fire to the landings, while 29 flotillas of mine-sweepers cleared the Channel coast.

The targeting of the bombing campaign was carefully arranged to avoid giving away the landing site, and an elaborate deception plan was mounted to make the Germans believe that the invasion would be launched in the Pas de Calais. In fact, after a very thorough study the Allied planners had

ABOVE: Germany's Atlantic Wall defences included sizeable numbers of large-calibre guns emplaced in huge concrete casemates, making them proof against heavy bombs.

RIGHT: Men of a US gliderborne infantry regiment await their arrival in France during the early hours of 6 June 1944.

ramps and bridges to make roads inland from the beaches. Even so, the battle would be very hard, and there would be no hope of the rapid capture of a port, or ports in working order, the defenders being certain to have rendered them unusable. Instead, it was decided to build two harbours off the invasion beaches. A fleet of old ships was steamed across and sunk in groups to provide breakwaters, and two 'Mulberry' artificial harbours, made up of floating concrete cylinders, were towed across the Channel. Oil was brought ashore by pipe-line, into which tankers discharged directly.

in the whole enterprise was that of the special parties needing to land just ahead of the assault waves, at exactly the right point of the tide to blow up the underwater obstacles on the beaches.

Timing was, of course, critical, for only certain infrequent days produced the optimum conditions of moon, tide and sunrise. As the perfect combinations only occurred at intervals, and a postponement was fraught with great difficulties, the decision faced by General Dwight D. Eisenhower, the supreme Allied commander, on 3–4 June was appalling: the weather forecast indicated gales and rough seas, with a faint improvement possible. Faced with the alternatives of postponement and the assault divisions being cut off by storm and surf when at their most vulnerable, Eisenhower courageously opted for D-Day on 6 June. The storms had not altogether abated and the bad weather hampered the landings, but it had also led the defenders to relax their vigilance.

Early that morning the airborne troops landed, and at half tide the assault divisions landed under cover of a barrage along the beaches. The naval

LEFT: The complete air superiority of the Allies made daylight movement of German armour in Normandy a perilous undertaking, even when the armour was PzKpfw VI Tiger heavy tanks such as these.

BELOW LEFT: A Sherman medium tank of a Polish armoured regiment in the ruins of the Norman city of Caen.

BELOW: D-Day placed great emphasis on the capabilities of specialized British armour, such as this Churchill AVRE (Armoured Vehicle Royal Engineers), an infantry tank conversion designed to undertake a host of battlefield engineering tasks.

chosen the Normandy coast in the Seine Bay, a long way to the west, as the landing place. The reasoning behind this was long and complex, but the most obvious and important consideration was, in the first wave, room to put ashore a force strong enough to resist any initial counter-attack. In overall command was General Montgomery, his detailed plan involving several components. First was the paradropping or gliderborne delivery of the British 6th Airborne Division to take and hold the

vital bridges over the Orne river to protect the left flank of the proposed beach-head, and of the US 82nd and 101st Airborne Divisions on the extreme right for a basically similar task. The seaborne forces to be landed between the mouths of the Orne and Vire, from left to right, were the British 3rd, Canadian 3rd and British 50th Divisions, leading the assault of the British 2nd Army, and the US 1st and 4th Divisions of Lieutenant-General Omar Bradley's US 1st Army. One of the most crucial roles

ABOVE: 'Omaha' Beach, the most difficult of the Allied assault areas on 6 June 1944, is where the men of the US 1st Infantry Division had a difficult and bloody time landing and then breaking though the German coastal defences.

BELOW: 'Utah' Beach was on the extreme right of the Allied assault on D-Day, and is where the US 4th Infantry Division landed, then drove inland to link up with the previously landed men of the US 82nd and 101st Airborne Divisions.

forces stood in to pound the coastal artillery casemates and radars one last time, and 2,000 aircraft attacked the German defences in depth. The Allies were ashore and from then on never looked like being driven off. The only major problem occurred at the front of the US V Corps, where all but two of the DD tanks foundered in the rough sea and the infantry, checked by heavy fire, lay down on the beach, their morale entirely lost, until late afternoon. Then leadership began to assert itself, and the 1st Division was inland by nightfall.

By 12 June Montgomery had 326,000 men ashore and the series of battles necessary to put the second half of the plan into action had fairly begun. There was much misunderstanding of this plan, which was Montgomery's own, at the time, and some ill-informed criticism of alleged failure on the part of his troops. In fact, both Montgomery's army group of British, Poles and Canadians and Lieutenant-General Omar N. Bradley's Americans fought with great tenacity against the best professional soldiers of modern times, and broke them. In brief, the questioned strategy was for Montgomery's group to attack on the left, around Caen, where a break-out would spell the greatest danger to the Germans and where they would be expected to mass their reserves. This would ease Bradley's task in the west, where he was battering away at the defence perimeter hemming him in, in order to make a gap for his armoured divisions under Patton to burst out into the open country and the enemy rear. In fact, this is what happened, and Montgomery reached the Seine 11 days earlier than he had predicted in his plan.

Once the first phase of seizing and expanding the foothold in Normandy was over Montgomery, with overall operational control, commanded his own 21st Army Group (Canadian 1st and British 2nd Armies) and Bradley's 12th Army Group (US 1st and 3rd Armies). The last of these, under Lieutenant-General George S. Patton, had been formed in the field during the fighting. Bradley was promoted to 12th Army Group commander from the 1st Army, whose command was taken over by Lieutenant-General Courtney H. Hodges.

On 7 July Montgomery reduced Caen to rubble with heavy bombers, a fact which served only to block the line of advance of his own tanks, and then on 18 July, in Operation Goodwood, tried to drive three armoured divisions down an avenue 4,000 yards (3660m) wide, blasted open by more than 5,000 tons of bombs.

Most of this tonnage hit nothing but the soil of France, for conforming to their usual tactics, the Germans' main defence line was several miles in the rear and this mighty hammer blow fell only on their outposts. The three armoured divisions found themselves facing an unshaken defence. They lost rather more than half their tanks, mainly to the guns, but the 1st Panzer Division claimed 80 destroyed in counter-attacks using their new Panther battle tanks. This was rough going, but the British and Canadians had by 29 June attracted four Panzer divisions to their sector. After a pause imposed by storms, which turned the whole Normandy battlefield into mud, Montgomery maintained the pressure on the left by repeated sledgehammer blows against the yielding, but still unbroken, fence of guns and tanks facing the 21st Army Group.

Then, on 25 July, Bradley struck the decisive blow of the second phase, from St. Lô to the west, to capture Coutances in Operation Cobra. It was on the same pattern as Goodwood, with massive air support, but was larger and on a wider front. The air bombardment included 1,500 heavy and 400 medium bombers, but the main effort was made by infantry supported by tanks, with hundreds of fighter-bombers acting as close-support flying artillery. These were linked to the forward battalions by radio, using the new techniques for air–ground co-operation, and as soon as the tanks or infantry ran into opposition the aircraft were in action within a few minutes.

On 1 August Patton's 3rd Army was able to break through south of Coutances to begin the third phase of open warfare. He was able to clear enough of Brittany to remove any threat from the remaining German garrisons, then, on Bradley's orders on 4 August, his axis swung from south-west to due east toward Paris. This was, perhaps, a strategic error, as it led to the failure of all attempts to trap the German 7th Army in the 'Falaise pocket'.

At this point, fortunately for the Allies, Hitler took charge. On 29 July, when von Rundstedt advised him that the Battle of the Beach-head was lost and that the moment had arrived to retreat and establish a new defence line, running north and south along the Seine, Hitler dismissed the veteran but highly capable field-marshal. Rommel had been wounded, and the new commander was Field-Marshal Günther-Hans von Kluge, a good professional like all the German generals, but lacking the nerve necessary to stand up to Hitler.

Hitler saw a peculiar picture on his situation map. From the eastern end of the semi-circular bulge, marking the Allied perimeter, there appeared a long shoot moving first to the south and then veering to the east as it lengthened. This was the US 3rd Army, and Hitler ordered von Kluge to advance into the loop and cut the tentacle off at its root at Avranches. Von Kluge dutifully

assembled six divisions, including 250 tanks, all clearly visible to Allied air reconnaissance, and launched them, fatally, so that the head of the force was jammed between the expanding bridgehead and Patton's army. At this moment Montgomery ordered the Canadians to attack southward to Falaise and Patton to swing one of his corps north to meet it, so that the German counter-offensive was now threatened in its rear. Von Kluge requested but was denied permission to withdraw, and was ordered to advance to Avranches. The German 7th Army was now crammed into a narrow corridor 40 miles (65km) long, its tanks and vehicles blocking the roads three abreast to present a target for the air forces, which massacred them. Meanwhile, the Canadians and Poles were fighting their way toward Falaise and Patton's XV Corps had captured Argentan, 15 miles (24km) away.

LEFT: The Allied landings had the benefit of very heavy naval fire support from a host of warships, small and large, the latter here represented by the British battleship Rodney, *which carried nine 16-in (406-mm) guns.*

BELOW LEFT: A French civilian couple and their friends hear the news of their liberation in company with their American liberators.

BELOW: US troops on board a landing craft. The ships which transported the assault divisions, and those which provided protection and fire support, probably constituted the greatest concentration of ships the world has ever seen.

Fighting as German soldiers always did, the 2nd Panzer Division, against heavy odds and bombarded from the air, threw back the Canadians and held the gap open just long enough to enable some thousands of men to escape the trap, but the bulk of 15 divisions and 2,000 tanks and vehicles were destroyed.

THE INVASION OF SOUTHERN FRANCE: OPERATION DRAGOON

The second French front was to be opened on the coast of the country in Operation Dragoon. At the strategic level the concept was valid: by mid-August, which was the earliest time the operation could be launched, the German last-ditch garrisons still held the Atlantic ports in western France and the Allies' two northern army groups were still being maintained across the

Normandy beaches, so that the Allies' logistical situation would be eased if Toulon and Marseille could be taken intact, and divisions waiting in the USA could be ferried over to join in the fight; the quickest way to end the war was to destroy the armies defending Germany's western frontier, so this was the point at which the maximum force would be concentrated. Ideally, Dragoon should have been launched at the same time as Overlord, but there were not enough landing and other craft. It was not until 15 August that three divisions of Lieutenant-General Alexander M. Patch's US 7th Army assaulted the stretch of coast extending from the east of Toulon to St. Raphaël. On the next day, the leading divisions of the French 1st Army, commanded by General Jean Marie Gabriel de Lattre de Tassigny,

ABOVE: US and British paratroopers get together in the latter part of the Normandy campaign.

RIGHT: Even as the Allies began to move away to the south and east, the beaches of Normandy were still essential for the arrival of landing craft, delivering the supplies on which the advancing Allied armies were dependent.

landed near St. Tropez, their mission being to capture and clear the two ports. De Lattre's initial status was as a corps commander under Patch, but, once his mission had been achieved, he would separate to lead his army as its full complement came ashore, his French 1st and the US 7th Armies forming the 6th Army Group under Lieutenant-General Jacob L. Devers. The 6th Army Group's axis was to be north toward Grenoble and Belfort, and then east to arrive on the right of Lieutenant-General Bradley's 12th Army Group.

The opposition faced by Dragoon was numerically formidable, consisting as it did of Colonel-General Johannes von Blaskowitz's Army Group G with 11 divisions. These divisions, however, were of poor quality and, being mainly occupied in operations against the French Forces of the Interior (FFI, or 'resistance'), were able to provide only a cordon defence of possible invasion beaches, which were therefore penetrated with ease. The Oberkommando der Wehrmacht (OKW, or armed forces high command) sensibly opted to cut its losses and pull back. Von Blaskowitz

was ordered to leave strong garrisons in Marseille and Toulon, in order to deny them to the Allies for as long as possible, and to withdraw his main strength up the valley of the Rhône river to the north, thus concentrating the remaining German forces for the defence of the Reich.

Dragoon was a text-book success. Some 400 aircraft dropped a composite US-British airborne division to control the road network by which any counter-attack forces might reach the beach-head. This was to be established by the US 3rd, 45th and 1st Divisions, supported by the 36th Division and the 1st Combat Command of the French 1st Armoured Division, all covered by a powerful air force and preceded by a tremendous naval bombardment. Patch immediately launched his VI Corps on two axes to hurry the German rearguards along, the left through Avignon and up the Rhône valley, and the right along the Route Napoléon through Digne and Grenoble.

De Lattre had been ordered to wait until his forces had been fully delivered, on about D+10, and then take Toulon.

This looked like being a costly affair. The port was held by some 25,000 troops, ensconced in a ring of 30 forts of old vintage but proof against all but the heaviest weapons, and more modern defences based on earthworks and pillboxes. A deliberate assault with maximum force was required, but to give a German commander ten days in which to improve his defences still further seemed unwise. The initial landing had gone so smoothly and the turnaround of the ships had been so rapid, however, that the build-up was much faster than expected. De Lattre, therefore, opted not to wait and obtained the permission of

ABOVE LEFT: US airborne infantry of the Allied provisional airborne division prepare for their commitment in Operation Dragoon as they wait to board their Waco CG-4 Hadrian assault glider.

ABOVE: As the Allies landed and moved inland, members of the French resistance came to their aid, as indicated here, at Hyères, on the south coast of France just to the east of Toulon.

ABOVE: German prisoners being escorted to the rear along a road in southern France.

RIGHT: US infantrymen take a closer look at an undamaged part of the anti-tank defences of the German Westwall or 'Seigfried' Line, after the fighting had moved farther to the east.

Patch and Devers to begin his operation on 20 August, five days ahead of schedule. De Lattre had the as yet incomplete 1st Free French Division (Brigadier-General Diégo Charles Joseph Brosset), 3rd Algerian Division (Major-General Joseph Jean Goislard de Monsabert), 9th Colonial Division (Major-General Joseph Abraham Auguste Pierre Édouard Magnan) and 1st Free French Armoured Division (Major-General Jean Louis Alai Touzet du Vigier). The commanders were good and the French colonial infantry was adept at operating in broken country. There is a range of inland hills parallel with the coast, north of Hyères, all the way to Marseille, and this offered the most difficult, the most unlikely, and therefore the most promising approach. Accordingly de Lattre sent Goislard de Monsabert, reinforced by a tabor (squadron) of *goumiers*, in a wide sweeping movement around the north and west of Toulon. The *goumiers* were the lethal, semi-regular Moroccan infantry enlisted by the French, who were allowed to wear their own dress and fight in their own way, specializing in reconnaissance and infiltration. Touzet du Vigier, still lacking one combat

command, was launched on an even wider encircling movement outside Goislard de Monsabert to protect his right flank (no one knew, at this moment, the total extent of the German withdrawal) and to hook in south and west of Marseille. Patch had agreed to release his other combat command as soon as it could be disengaged, while Brosset, reinforced by French commandos, moved directly on the Hyères-Toulon axis. The 9th Division would be attached between the 3rd and the Free French as it disembarked, its units marching into action without pause.

The speed with which de Lattre developed his manoeuvre was astonishing. The German units may have been of doubtful quality, but the Free French had to do some hard fighting for Hyères. Three strong forts, located on commanding heights outside Toulon, were taken only at the cost of severe casualties by the divisional

reconnaissance regiment and the commandos, on 22 August. In one of the forts, 250 German dead were counted. The reconnaissance regiment then slipped through the ring of pillboxes and strongpoints into the city centre. Magnan went forward to see where to introduce his leading troops, returning to spur them on. An intensely confused situation then began to develop inside the city, with the badly shaken Germans holding on while Magnan's men surrounded them. Magnan was given the task of mopping up the port and, on 26 August, the last strongholds surrendered and Toulon was free.

Encouraged by this success and guessing that the two things he must avoid were to check the élan of his troops or to give the Germans time, de Lattre decided to attack Marseille immediately, without waiting to consolidate. He disengaged Brosset, sending him together with the 1st Armoured

Division's Combat 1st Command (Brigadier-General Aimé Sudre) to join de Monsabert, reinforcing him with more *goumiers* as they arrived. He then ordered the commanders to close in on a given line surrounding the city, without commiting themselves except to reconnaissance, until he could assess the situation on 23 August. Marseille was defended by German marines, the 244th Infantry Division and a jumble of units, which had been scattered from the beach-head area by the shock of the US VI Corps landing, and 200 assorted guns. To evict such a German garrison from a city in house-to-house fighting might have taken weeks in the old days, but with the whole population of the city against them and every street or suburban road on the perimeter offering a route for infiltration, and with scores of FFI squads harassing them, the German position was untenable. Nevertheless, de Lattre de Tassigny sensibly paused to regroup. He had, apart from his task of reducing Marseille, to cover the left flank of the US VI Corps and as an army commander had to be thinking even further ahead and preparing his formations for the pursuit north. For this he had to assemble his 1st Armoured Division, less the tanks for the attack on Marseille.

All this was well-planned and the French staff work appears to have been both prompt and accurate. As it turned out, but happily enough, the forward troops did not take the slightest notice. Supported by the FFI, one combat team of Sudre's tanks and motorized infantry, plus a battalion of de Monsabert's Algerians, penetrated into the heart of the city and began to wreak havoc. In a short time they were up against the inner defences of the dock area, the ultimate objective of the whole operation. On the outside, the remainder of the 3rd Division, with two more tabors of *goumiers,* was steadily reducing the concrete defences outside the city.

Fortunately, the fortresses were stronger than the defenders, although the Algerians and the *goumiers*, without the benefit of prolonged or heavy bombardment, suffered severe casualties in clearing them. At the earliest possible moment, de Monsabert established his headquarters in the city. From here, he was able to establish contact with the German garrison commander, and after the French had carried the main defences covering the docks, persuade him to surrender on 27 August. Marseille thus fell one month ahead of schedule.

THE ALLIES PUSH ON TO THE SIEGFRIED LINE

By the first day of September 1944, Germany's defensive system on the 'Western Front' had been destroyed. The men who had survived the catastrophe at Falaise had been scattered, and had lost most of their remaining equipment in a vain attempt to hold the line of the Seine river, which the Allied armies had crossed with great dash. Hitler had dismissed von Kluge, who committed suicide, and had replaced him with his favourite 'fireman', Field-Marshal Walther Model. The new commander-in-chief in the west could only rally what troops he had and seek to create the defence of the frontiers of the Reich. The Westwall, the so-called 'Siegfried' Line, was unmanned, and many of its guns had been removed for use in the east. The western frontier of Germany, in fact, was wide open to any fast-moving assault. Why Eisenhower did not attempt it has since been the subject of debate. Whatever the verdict, the factors include the major stumbling block that the Allies had given no thought to what they should do after breaking out of their Normandy lodgement. There was no overall scheme, and the unexpectedness of their pre-schedule success had taken all the Allied generals by surprise. All the armies swung east or north-east and advanced as best they

could. On 1 September the Canadian 1st Army was driving up the Channel coast, in the process providing relief to the cities and towns of southern England by overrunning the launching sites for V-1 flying bombs; the British 2nd Army was racing for Brussels; the US 1st Army was some 80 miles (130km) past Pans; and the US 3rd Army was as far forward as Verdun. The US 7th Army and the newly-formed French 1st Army had advanced some 200 miles (320km) north from their landing sites on the French Riviera. This General Dwight D. Eisenhower believed to be a satisfactory situation as he assumed full control of all operations and relegated General Sir Bernard Montgomery to the more limited command of his own British/Canadian 21st Army Group. Eisenhower favoured a broad-front advance so that all his divisions could exert their full force, their flanks secure as they spread across France.

The immediate difficulty he faced was that, partly as a result of winning the Battle of Normandy 11 days ahead of schedule, the necessary ports had not

The Allies had built up a good overall picture of the Siegfried Line right from the start of the war, when reconnaissance flights were flown by aircraft such as the Bristol Blenheim Mk IV twin-engined warplane.

yet been captured and cleared. Therefore, the supplies necessary for the vast Allied armies had still to come via the one surviving Mulberry harbour, over the beaches and then up the lines of communication by lorry, for the Allied bombing campaign, which had totally wrecked the French railway system and made it useless to the Germans, had also, of course, denied its use to the Allies. Eisenhower had to feed some 2.25 million troops, and provide fuel for almost 450,000 vehicles, of which some 5,000 were front-line tanks. As the lines of communications lengthened, the supply lorries themselves began to consume supplies at an increasing rate: thus Eisenhower had to decide either to halt units not needed for the immediate pursuit, so that the available supplies could be delivered to small, spearhead

formations, or the whole advance slowed down. If the advance was slowed, the Germans would have time to consolidate the defence of the frontier before the pursuing forces could arrive. The answer was simple, but its implementation was fraught with difficulties.

Montgomery argued vehemently and with considerable reason that the northern route was strategically the most important and that all resources should be concentrated on it for a swift major advance. However, this would have meant halting the US 1st and 3rd Armies, which was impossible for political reasons: Eisenhower could not check his US armies and give a British general the honour of winning the war with Germany. Bradley and Patton saw Montgomery's plan as the means for the British general to keep himself in the limelight. Patton was determined to press on, giving Eisenhower the choice of either halting (or even recalling) him, or of keeping him supplied. Even a supreme commander could not override two such powerful subordinates, and the best he could do was to give the northern front priority.

While the armies were advancing and high command was being distracted by argument and the problem of supply, it completely forgot that the key to a resolution of the supply problem, especially in the northern sector, was the rapid capture of Antwerp as a working port. Montgomery was intent on an expedient to accelerate his advance, namely the use of the airborne formations lying idle in England, to clear the network of river obstacles ahead of him as far as the bridge at Arnhem, in an operation to take place in mid-September. In the meantime the German resistance began to strengthen.

The Allied armies had some enjoyable weeks of motoring through France with an occasional skirmish, but were then brought abruptly to a halt. The Westwall was not a line of fortifications in the same sense as was the Maginot Line. The

Germans were superb exponents of the concept of defence in depth: each position was covered by more behind, and backing these were more parties of troops ready to counter-attack and drive out successful intruders. Into this the Americans had to batter a way, bit by bit, with heavy artillery, while in the Netherlands the 21st Army Group was being hampered by the maze of defended waterways. The Allies had lost the race to the frontiers and the German 'Watch on the Rhine' had been established.

THE BATTLE OF ARNHEM

Despite his rebuff by General Dwight D. Eisenhower, General Sir Bernard Montgomery was confident that the task of his 21st Army Group was the seizure of the Ruhr, Germany's industrial heartland, to which there were two avenues of approach. One extended due east, which would mean a bloody battle of attrition to breach the Westwall, and the other extended to the north-north-east, in the direction of Arnhem. The Westwall defences ended near Cleve, and if Arnhem, with its great road bridge over the Rhine, could be secured, the

defences could be outflanked to the north. This latter approach would not be easier than the former, for the Netherlands was the worst possible terrain for armoured warfare, being flat, low-lying, wet, and divided by a network of dykes and drainage ditches. To reach the lower Rhine at Arnhem it was first necessary to cross three wide navigation canals as well as the Maas and Waal rivers. One option was as unattractive as the other for ground operations, but lying idle in England was the whole of Lieutenant-General Lewis H. Brereton's Allied 1st Airborne Army, inactive since D-Day. No fewer than 17 plans to employ parts of this army had been made and cancelled, generally because the objectives had been overrun by the ground forces, or because the weather had deteriorated and German resistance had stiffened.

Montgomery now revived and revised the original but unrealized 'Comet' plan, for the seizure of Nijmegen and Arnhem by one reinforced division. This was now developed into the parallel 'Market' airborne and 'Garden' land operations. The forward elements of the British 2nd

Army had reached the Meuse-Escaut Canal, 70 miles (110km) from Arnhem, and crossed it south of Borkel. The new plan was to drop a whole airborne corps: the US 101st Airborne Division, under Major-General James A. Gavin, would seize and hold the bridges over the Wilhelmina Canal at Son and the Willemswart at Veghel; the US 82nd Airborne Division, under Major-General Maxwell D. Taylor, the bridges over the Maas at Grave and the Waal at Nijmegen; and the British 1st Airborne Division, under Major-General Roy Urquhart, the bridge at Arnhem in 'Market'. At the same time the British XXX Corps, under Lieutenant General B.G. Horrocks, would drive up the road through Eindhoven, which connected all these points, the Guards Armoured Division leading, and join up, in 'Garden', with the lightly-armed airborne troops as rapidly as possible. This armoured advance was absolutely

OPPOSITE ABOVE: British armour passes through Falaise on the southern side of the Normandy lodgement at the time of the Allied break-out in August 1944.

OPPOSITE BELOW: A Universal (or Bren gun) Carrier of a Canadian airborne unit at Falaise, in August 1944.

LEFT: Men of the US 82nd Airborne Division prepare for their part in the Arnhem operation, namely the capture of the bridge over the Maas river at Grave.

ABOVE: A British paratrooper in action at Arnhem in September 1944, when the forces were surprised to have landed in the area in which two SS Panzer divisions were being refitted.

ABOVE: The success of Operations Market and Garden depended on the progress of the British XXX Corps from the Meuse-Escaut Canal to reach the British 1st Airborne Division before it succumbed to German counter-attacks at Arnhem. There was only a single road, and the XXX Corps could advance at only a snail's pace in the face of German tank and artillery opposition. This is an Archer self-propelled anti-tank gun of the XXX Corps. The Archer was in essence the superb 17-pdr anti-tank gun on the hull of the obsolete Valentine infantry tank.

TOP RIGHT: German troops at Arnhem, where ad hoc battle groups checked the British airborne soldiers for a time just long enough for heavier German units to reach the scene.

ABOVE RIGHT: Captured British airborne soldiers with their Waffen-SS captors in the aftermath of the Arnhem fighting.

essential for success, as the strength of airborne forces lay in the surprise of their sudden descent, their weakness being a lack of heavy weapons, especially for prolonged defence against armour.

There were many who argued that the whole operation was too risky, but it was agreed by all responsible that it must go on. Planning had gone too far, the morale of the troops would be in danger if they were not used, and in any case the conduct of war is nothing but a choice between dangers. Great strategic rewards demand great tactical risks, and the tactical risks at Arnhem were clear enough. Airborne troops, most experts believed, should be dropped in the dark, to obtain the element of surprise, and as close to their objectives as possible, if not on top of them. For various reasons, of which the most telling was the belief of the Royal Air Force that the Arnhem area was strongly defended by anti-aircraft artillery, the assault was made by day, the drop zones for the paratroops and the landing zone for the gliders being 8 miles (13km), or at least a three-hour march, from the vital bridge. Three hours is too much time to give gratuitously to an opponent, rightly

feared for his ability to react rapidly and aggressively. Even so, if Urquhart had been able to implement his plan all might yet have turned out better: Urquhart proposed to put one whole brigade in close defence of the bridge and three more around it in a solid defence perimeter, giving him some 10,900 high-

grade infantry supported by light artillery and 6-pdr anti-tank guns with which to hold off any counter-attack. Unfortunately, the lack of aircraft imposed a three-day build-up over the period 17–19 September, by which time only one battalion of the whole force had been able to reach its objective.

Another factor militating against Allied success was the date. The third week in September was too late, and this was not only on account of the weather. Intelligence showed that the efforts of Field-Marshal Walther Model, of Army Group B, to revitalize shattered German formations and man the Westwall were succeeding, and resistance was stiffening everywhere. The most serious problem was that the II SS Panzer Corps (9th and 10th SS Panzer Divisions), commanded by the able General Willi Bittrich, was in the Arnhem area to rest and re-equip: this fact was known to some Allied intelligence agencies, but for a variety of reasons was ignored.

On the German side there had been much discussion about the next possible move by the Allies, but no firm plans had been made. But it had proved enough for Model to be in overall command in the area, with Colonel-General Kurt Student, himself a paratrooper, in command of the sector, and Bittrich in local command, with their headquarters in the vicinity of the drops. All acted immediately, and the speed of the three commanders was matched by that of the German soldiers, who were schooled to seize their weapons and throw themselves into action at once, without panic or even doubt, under the first leader who rallied them. German officers were expected to behave as the situation demanded without asking permission or waiting for orders. The II SS Panzer Corps was therefore immediately appropriated; Student called up some parachute Kampfgruppen (ad hoc battle groups) from the Köln area, and took control of an infantry division passing by train through his sector to another command. In a very short time the German defences were being mobilized and local counter-attacks were being mounted.

A series of misfortunes was about to fall upon the luckless 1st Airborne Division, which no amount of heroism could overcome, the first of which was a stop line of youths of an SS Panzergrenadier training battalion. Behind this was another battle group from the 9th SS Panzer Division's infantry, with some light armoured vehicles, with another forming and a third hastening to the road bridge. The airborne troops were therefore involved in precisely the kind of operation for which they were not fitted: an attack by light infantry on a strong all-arms force, without the benefit of armoured co-operation and heavy artillery firepower. All the same, Lieutenant-Colonel John Frost managed to fight his way with most of his 2nd Parachute Battalion to the Arnhem road bridge, and there held on.

The second misfortune was the German discovery, on the body of a US officer killed in a glider crash, an operation order outlining the entire plan.

ABOVE: A 25-pdr field gun of the Canadian 5th Field Regiment in action near Nijmegen.

LEFT: The sky fills with parachutes as the British 1st Airborne Division descends toward its drop zones outside, and in fact too far outside, Arnhem.

Survivors by the wreckage of their Waco CG-4 Hadrian glider. It was the task of the US 101st Airborne Division to take and hold the bridges over the Wilhelmina Canal at Zon and the Zuit Willemsvaart Canal at Veghel.

Thus Student and Bittrich knew in a matter of hours every move to make: thus revealed, the LZs near Arnhem were soon ringed by AA guns. The third misfortune was the complete failure of the 1st Airborne Division's radio sets, with the sole exception of the light regiment of the Royal Artillery. Thus everyone from Urquhart's headquarters, down to battalions, was out of touch with one another and the air force. Urquhart himself went forward with one brigadier but was unable even to talk back from his own jeep to his own headquarters, only 2 miles (3.2km) distant, and was himself caught up in the fighting and was unable to get back, while the brigadier was wounded. The command system thus disintegrated at this crucial stage of the battle, and the battle itself into a series of bitter but wholly unco-ordinated small combats. Only Frost's battalion, less one company but with some divisional troops who had rallied to him, hung on grimly to the area commanding the north end of the unblown Arnhem road bridge. The rail bridge had been blown in the face of Frost's C Company, which had been ordered to take it.

Meanwhile things had been going successfully, if behind schedule, on the road from the south. The Americans had had a much easier landing, so their troubles started only later, when Student's counter-attacks began. By 18 September the 101st Division had a firm grip on their objectives and had linked with the tank battalion of the Irish Guards. Eindhoven was clear, while farther to the north, the 82nd Airborne Division had the bridge over the Maas at Grave and was fighting hard in Nijmegen for access to the Waal bridge. The Guards Armoured Division's tanks, supported by the guns of the XXX Corps and air attacks, were rolling, but soon came to a halt. It was impossible to deploy off the roads without bogging down, and to make matters worse the roads ran along high embankments, along which the tanks were perfect targets, silhouetted against the sky, for the 3.465-in (88-mm) anti-tank guns sited on both sides. Making matters worse, the weather worsened, so that both the air resupply of the men at Arnhem and the provision of air support to the troops fighting up the road were interrupted. Thus it was not until 22 September that a great combined effort pushed elements of the British 43rd and US 82nd Divisions across the Waal and secured the Nijmegen bridge. But on the same day the Guards Armoured Division had to send a brigade back to assist the 101st Division at Veghel, where it was being attacked from the east and west simultaneously. Although the fighting along the corridor was severe, it was overshadowed by the tragedy in Arnhem: the 82nd Division lost 1,400 men and the 101st Division more than 2,000; they were to lose another 3,600 between them before the ground taken was finally secured.

In Arnhem close-quarter fighting of savage intensity continued unabated. By 19 September Urquhart appreciated that he was not able to fight his way through to reinforce Frost or take up his planned positions, and decided to form a close defensive perimeter in the small town of Osterbeek on the northern bank of the Rhine, 4 miles (6.5km) downstream of Arnhem. If he and Frost, at the northern end of the Arnhem bridge, could hold out in house-to-house fighting there was still a chance that the XXX Corps might break through in time, but this hope soon faded. The division nonetheless fought on. After tragic delay, the Polish 1st Independent Parachute Brigade Group was dropped opposite Osterbeek, south of the river, but its task was impossible: the brigade suffered heavy casualties on landing, and could neither cross the river to reinforce Urquhart nor turn south to help open the road, for Bittrich had sent a battalion of Panzergrenadiers with a company of Panther tanks to block it.

The situation at the end of the week was that the 9th SS Panzer Division was systematically reducing the Arnhem positions, while the 10th SS Panzer Division was still blocking the last few miles between the XXX Corps and the Arnhem bridge, and both the US airborne divisions were under counter-attack from east and west. It soon became clear that the only course was to use the infantry of the British 43rd Division to close up to the river bank at Osterbeek and evacuate what was left of Urquhart's formation before they were killed or captured. The division achieved its task with courage and skill, actually making an assault crossing to the north bank, while the massed guns of the XXX Corps put a box barrage around Osterbeek, and the engineers in boats brought out most of the unwounded men of the garrison under intense fire. So intense was the whole level of the fighting and so numerous the acts of gallantry that this fine feat was not seen as very remarkable. Some idea of the nature of the fighting is discernible from the casualty figures: the 1st Airborne Division lost 6,400 men, of whom 1,200 were killed, while the 9th SS Panzer Division and its reinforcing units lost 3,500 men.

THE 'BATTLE OF THE BULGE'
On 15 December 1944 three German armies crashed into a weakly-held sector of the Allied front in a hopeless counter-offensive, known to the Germans at the

time as *Wacht am Rhein* (Watch on the Rhine) and later to the world at large as the 'Battle of the Bulge'. By 28 January 1945 the Germans were back on their start lines, leaving behind 19,000 dead as well as 111,000 wounded, missing or taken prisoner, and having lost hundreds of irreplaceable tanks and assault guns. In the matter of timing Hitler's intuition, always better than his strategy, had been perfect. By the end of the year the Allies were mentally balanced between the over-confidence born of their great victories and the unpleasant shock, particularly to the Americans, of what was involved in trying to break into the Westwall. This involved a series of costly battles, reminiscent of the static meatgrinding of World War I. But breaching the Westwall was only a matter of time and resources: the long term assessment was that the German war machine was running down, and that lack of fuel for its armour would prevent anything but a dogged defence for what remained of the war. Some intelligence staffs had noticed some significant troop movements and predicted, correctly, the fact but not the location of an offensive. No notice was

taken, and there was an air of cautious relaxation along all the US and, to a lesser extent, British sectors of the front, except those opposite the Westwall.

Hitler planned to repeat the success of 1940 with a Blitzkrieg offensive through the least likely and therefore most weakly-held part of the Allied front, namely the Ardennes region and its forests, hills, steep ridges and deep ravines. Three armies, under the command of Field-Marshal Walther Model's Army Group B, were to take part: the newly-created 6th Panzerarmee of Colonel-General 'Sepp' Dietrich was to make for Liège and Antwerp; the 5th Panzerarmee, under General Hasso-Eccard von Manteuffel, was to head for the vital communication centre at Bastogne, and from there to Namur and Brussels, and thence Antwerp; and the 7th Army, under General Erich Brandenburger, was to break through and swing left to protect von Manteuffel's left from a counter-attack from the south. The German build-up was undertaken in the utmost secrecy, and it was a week before the Allied commanders discovered the Germans' intentions: at first they imagined it to be

ABOVE: British airborne troops load the trailer of their Jeep from an Airspeed Horsa assault glider outside Arnhem. By comparison with the German formations in the area, the British troops lacked heavy weapons but fought with great courage and determination to hold their positions for considerably longer than had been thought possible.

LEFT: A British 6-pdr anti-tank gun in action at Arnhem. This was the heaviest anti-tank weapon which the Allies could deliver by air.

ABOVE: The bridge over the Nederrijn (lower Rhine) at Arnhem. The British managed to take and hold the northern end until eventually forced to surrender, but the Germans held the southern end throughout the battle.

RIGHT: Paratroopers of the US 101st Airborne Division at Bastogne, where they fought as conventional infantry against the encircling Germans in the Battle of the Bulge. Here they recover parachuted supplies.

merely a spoiling attack to hinder the advance of Lieutenant-General Patton's US 3rd Army toward the Saar.

Fortunately for the Allies, the Germans no longer had the resources for war on this scale, or the men, tanks, aircraft or even fuel. The bulk of the new Volksgrenadier (people's grenadier) infantry comprised under-age boys and old men, who fought with courage and determination but without the battle craft of their predecessors. Even the once-elite paratroops, of whom two divisions were used, were of a low standard. Only the tank crews of the superb PzKpfw V Panther battle and PzKpfw VI Tiger heavy tanks were up to the old standard, and many of the junior officers and sergeants, bred in the old German tradition, were full of the attacking spirit.

The Allied high command was nonetheless taken completely by surprise when there began an offensive by nine Panzer and Panzergrenadier divisions, as well as 12 infantry divisions, totalling some 700 tanks and supported by 2,000 field guns. These forces smashed into and through a thin screen of only nine US infantry regiments, backed by one armoured division spread out over 100 miles (160km) of front in little more than an outpost line with no main line of resistance behind it. The troops themselves were either resting, like the 4th Division, severely handled in recent Westwall fighting, or new to the theatre and only half-trained, like the 106th Division fresh from the USA. The US situation was worsened by very severe weather, low morale, and the fact that much equipment (especially radio sets) were being serviced or repaired. The VII and VIII Corps of Lieutenant-General Courtney H. Hodges's US 1st Army in this sector were totally unprepared, morally and physically, to receive a massive offensive.

Early in the morning of 16 December the US forward posts came under a violent bombardment in the dark and prevailing fog, followed by a major assault. Almost inevitably there was a measure of panic in the American ranks, the front was broken in many places, some troops fled to the rear, artillery were abandoned, and many men surrendered. Most men, however, both seasoned and green, fought hard and well. It is the response to initial defeat, with communications cut and total confusion abroad, which is the acid test of any army, and this the US forces passed with distinction.

Counter-attacking where they could and grimly hanging on where they could not, the US soldiers held points vital in the terrain, such as crossroads, bridges and communication centres, and offering little opportunity for cross-country tank manoeuvre. St. Vith and Houffalize held out for long enough and Bastogne, where six roads meet, did not fall. These and a host of other brave actions checked the Germans, as a result of which the entire schedule for *Wacht am Rhein* was delayed, buying the time for the resources of Lieutenant-General Omar N. Bradley's US 12th Army Group to be redirected and positioned for a massive

counter-stroke. All the same, the picture as seen from the headquarters of numerous Allied formations was enough to cause great dismay. Accurate information was at a premium and not readily available, so no one knew how well the fragments of the 1st Army were still fighting. What seemed ominous was that the front had been shattered, and particularly mortifying was the fact that US soldiers were being actually outfought and, worse, surrendering in droves. The 28th Division was effectively destroyed, and the 106th Division had lost its two forward regiments, which were encircled and corralled inside a thin German cordon. All the rear areas, rich in food, munitions and petrol stocks, seemed wide open to capture.

From the first day of *Wacht am Rhein*, the winter weather had included snow, low cloud and fog, and this had grounded the most devastating Allied weapon, its tactical air power. Command decisions were difficult as the German salient, driven into the Ardennes, separated Hodges and most of his 1st Army from Bradley's 12th Army Group headquarters and Patton's US 3rd Army in the south.

General Dwight D. Eisenhower, the allied supreme commander, saw the

correct solution at once and insisted on it to Bradley and Patton. Eisenhower placed the US armies north of the bulge, the 1st and 9th under the command of Field-Marshal

Montgomery, with instructions to hold the line of the Meuse, to shorten the defence line by withdrawing if it became necessary, to create a reserve, and then to attack from the north. The 3rd Army was to cease its battle of attrition along the Saar, and swing north to make a massive blow against the German southern flank. Nothing was more to Patton's taste, and the feat performed by his staff of picking up the bulk of his army, turning it through a right angle to start it marching north across the cluttered lines of communication was exemplary. The only snag arose from bad Anglo-US relations and a difference in outlook. Bradley, in particular, was incensed that any US troops should be placed under British command, especially when that commander was Montgomery. The US Army, furthermore, did not believe in withdrawal, even for the best tactical

ABOVE: The few US divisions holding the front in the first stage of the Battle of the Bulge were green formations gaining acclimatization, or experienced formations sent to a quiet sector to rest and recuperate after a long time spent in combat.

LEFT: German troops with US prisoners in the Ardennes.

German advance, the Panzer-Lehr and 2nd Panzer Divisions met the US 2nd Armored Division and the British 3rd Royal Tank Regiment, the only British unit to be seriously engaged, near Dinant, while Patton's three corps attacked north-east, astride the Bastogne axis and into the base of the salient due north of Luxembourg. Patton's tactics, based on an unprepared headlong rush, proved very costly against unbroken Panzer units, but success was worth the cost. The turning point in the battle was in fact a change in the weather: the cold increased, with mud and slush turned to hard-frozen ground, the clouds and fog lifting to allow the sun to shine through. This was ideal flying weather, and the US 9th Army Air Force flew 10,305 sorties in the period 23–31 December. Thus the

ABOVE: Men of one of the two German parachute divisions committed to the Ardennes operations.

ABOVE RIGHT: A German Tiger II tank passes a column of US prisoners taken during the Ardennes offensive.

RIGHT: Burning and abandoned, US vehicles partially block a road in the Ardennes.

reasons. Thus Bradley privately ordered Hodges to ignore the orders to withdraw and go over to the attack as soon as possible.

Montgomery's highly professional moves secured the line of the Meuse using his own troops, thus freeing Hodges and Lieutenant-General William H. Simpson to organize the northern counter-offensive with their US 1st and 9th Armies. At the western tip of the

fate of Army Group B was sealed. The cost to the Americans was men and matériel they could replace, but as far as the Germans were concerned, their losses in the offensive were absolute, thus opening the door of the Third Reich to the Allies.

THE BOMBER OFFENSIVE 1943–45

At the Casablanca Conference of January 1943, Prime minister Winston Churchill and President Franklin D. Roosevelt met at Casablanca to decide on the general strategy of the war after the Axis forces had been expelled from Africa. High on the list of matters to be decided was the manner in which the efforts of the Royal Air Force's Bomber Command and the US 8th Army Air Force, both based in the UK, could be co-ordinated to devastate the war-making capability of the Axis powers. Bomber production was still increasing, so in the months to come the force would continue to develop still further as a devastating weapon. Now Churchill and Roosevelt, together with their military advisers, had to select and prioritize the types of target to be

attacked. The result was the 'Pointblank' directive, which laid down the types of target to be attacked. The prioritization of the targets was later changed with considerable frequency, but was initially U-boat construction yards, aircraft manufacturing, transportation systems, oil plants and other targets vital to the German armaments industry. The British were allowed to continue their night raids on centres of civilian population.

While the implications of the directive were assessed and revised target lists created, the bombing effort continued as before. By the middle of the year, however, a new sense of purpose was discernible in the activities of Bomber Command and the 8th AAF, joined from October 1943 onwards by the US 9th AAF, operating from bases in the Foggia area of southern Italy. In the period 20–24 June, Bomber Command undertook its first 'shuttle' mission, in which aircraft setting off from the UK bombed Wilhelmshaven, then flew on to North Africa, the Italian naval base of La Spezia being attacked on the return trip. Nine days earlier the 8th AAF had

attacked the U-boat yards at Wilhelmshaven, but caused only slight damage. The problem currently hampering the 8th AAF was the lack of escort fighters with adequate range to escort the bombers to and from their targets, and it was not until the end of the year that the North American P-51 Mustang arrived, allowing the bombers to make deep penetration raids with proper escort all the way. The Americans devoted July to attacks on the German aircraft industry, principally the part producing fighters. Although the short-term results were good, the concentrated raids finally made the Germans see the wisdom of dispersing their production facilities, and this was now set in hand as

ABOVE: A German painting of the Messerschmitt Bf 110 heavy fighter, shown in action in its most important night-fighter role.

LEFT: Allied air attacks wrought terrible devastation upon all of Germany's internal transport network. This is a German locomotive, destroyed at Munster in an air raid.

Against the backdrop of descending incendiaries, an Avro Lancaster heavy bomber of the Royal Air Force's Bomber Command is silhouetted against the fires already burning in the great port city of Hamburg.

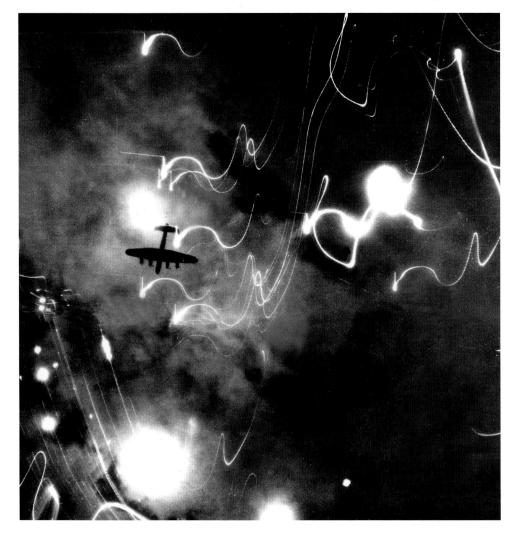

a matter of urgency. At the end of July the British struck the first major blow against a German city, when massive raids destroyed nearly all of Hamburg, the firestorms caused by the incendiaries being responsible for most of the damage. Apart from their dead, the Germans had also been left with about 750,000 homeless, and this seriously impeded the effort to restore the city to a functioning level after the raids. On the night of 17–18 August Bomber Command then struck at the German secret weapon research centre at Peenemünde on Germany's Baltic coast. Although not absolutely certain of the importance of the target, Bomber Command effected a heavy raid, which caused much damage, slowing down the development of the V-2 ballistic missile.

The Americans now learned a hard lesson on the need for escort fighters on deep penetration missions. On 1 August 178 bombers set off from North Africa to bomb the oilfields at Ploesti in Romania. Picked up by German radar in Greece, the bomber force was harried mercilessly by German and Romanian fighters, losing 54 of its number. Damage was caused to the refinery, but did not halt production for long, and as if this were not enough, the Americans next lost 60 out of 376 bombers despatched to strike the ball-bearing factories at Schweinfurt. A similar raid on 14 October was even more costly, with 60 bombers lost out of 291. The machine guns of the bombers were not enough to defeat the cannon-armed fighters, flown by the Germans with great determination and courage. After the Schweinfurt debacle, the Americans suspended deep-penetration daylight missions pending the arrival of P-51 escort fighters. The first of these arrived on 3 December, and the Americans then resumed their daylight offensive.

The culmination of the British bombing year was the beginning of the Battle of Berlin in November. Up to March 1944, some 16 major raids had been targeted against the German capital, causing great damage and giving the Germans a very hard time of it. By this time the British bomber force had been joined by large numbers of the latest bomber, the comparatively small de Havilland Mosquito. Of wooden construction and powered by two engines, the Mosquito was able to carry a very useful bomb load, and was in fact a far more cost-effective aircraft than most heavy bombers. It could deliver its bomb load with great accuracy at all altitudes, although its optimum was low to medium altitude, and its speed made it more than a match for any German fighter. So versatile was the basic design that all sorts of variants of the aircraft were produced: night-fighter, attack-fighter, fighter-bomber, passenger transport, photographic reconnaissance platform and meteorological workhorse. The

German night-fighters were also improving, and the electronic battle became very intense late in 1943 and early in 1944. By this time, the British were also using a number of electronic navigational aids, with good results.

During the first half of 1944, relentless pressure was maintained against Germany. The Americans had now grouped together as the Strategic Air Forces, under Lieutenant-General Carl A. Spaatz, the 8th AAF in England and the 15th AAF in Italy enabling a single command organization to direct very large numbers of bombers onto the chosen targets with great ease. Spaatz also worked closely with Air Chief-Marshal Sir Arthur Harris in co-ordinating the US and British efforts: a target might well be visited by Bomber Command in the night and by the 8th and/or 15th AAFs on the following day, or vice versa.

Most important for the Americans, however, was the 'Big Week' effort during the period 20–26 February 1944, the object of which was to grind down German fighter strength. Although Bomber Command raided the same targets at night, the week was essentially a US effort. While the bombers attacked fighter manufacturing factories to destroy the Germans' source of supply, the escort fighters had a field day with the German fighters sent aloft to attack the bombers. Here the true worth of the superb Mustang was shown to its full extent. Although Spaatz lost 244 bombers and 33 fighters during the Big Week, the Germans lost 692 fighters in the air, plus many more on the ground and in the factories. The factories themselves were also severely damaged. The same basic task of grinding down the Luftwaffe was continued through to May, causing the Germans to lose 2,442 fighters in action and 1,500 more from other causes.

There was now a change in the emphasis of the bombing campaign. The strategic bombers were relieved of conventional targets and were tasked

with the isolation of the forthcoming battlefield in northern France. The object of this campaign of May and June 1944 was the preparation of the area for the Allied landings in Normandy. Both the strategic and tactical air forces were employed to destroy all the means of communication in northern France, the Low Countries and western Germany. Tunnels were caved in, bridges dropped, railway lines cut, marshalling yards destroyed, canals breached, and roads bombed. The idea behind the campaign was that Normandy and Brittany be isolated, so that in June, when the Allies landed, the Germans would be unable to rush up reinforcements with their usual speed. Great care had to be taken, however, that no pattern emerged from the bombing lest the Germans deduced where the landings were to take place. At the same time as this campaign was being waged, the Allied air forces were attacking and ruining nearly every airfield in the area. By the time of the Normandy landings, there were scarcely any German aircraft in northern France, and those which had survived the Allied onslaught had been withdrawn.

ABOVE LEFT: The British 12,000-lb (5443-kg) 'Tallboy' bomb, carried only by specially adapted Avro Lancaster bombers, was designed to penetrate the ground or pass through concrete before detonating.

ABOVE: A German 1.5-in (37-mm) anti-aircraft gun being readied for night operations.

LEFT: One of the two mainstays of the US heavy bomber effort in the European theatre was the Boeing B-17 Flying Fortress, seen here in its ultimate B-17G form, with a chin barbette carrying two 0.5-in (12.7- mm) machine guns to deter head-in attacks by German fighters.

run them. To all intents and purposes, by the end of 1944 Germany had been paralyzed by her lack of fuel and the absence of a transport system.

The strategic bombing campaign continued into 1945, with German resistance slowly dying away. Even though the Germans had the best turbojet-powered fighter of the war, the Messerschmitt Me 262, which could have posed a very real threat to Allied air superiority in 1944, the type had not been placed in full-scale production early enough, and the few examples in operation were unable to stem the tide. With no fuel for training, the German pilots had also deteriorated in quality from the great days of 1940 to 1943.

The area bombing concept reached its conclusion on the night of 13–14

ABOVE: Bearing the weight of the British night-bombing offensive by Germany was the Avro Lancaster heavy bomber and its seven-man crew.

ABOVE RIGHT: The ruins of the German city of Dresden after the combined British and US attacks on it in February 1945.

RIGHT: Water pours through the breach in the Möhne dam, caused by the 'bouncing bomb' attack of the Avro Lancaster bombers of No. 617 Squadron, RAF, on the night of 16–17 May 1943.

Once the Allied landings had secured the intended initial lodgement, the strategic bombers returned to their task of destroying Germany's ability and will to wage war. From July to December the heavy bomber campaign reached its peak. Virtually without a break, British and US bombers concentrated their attacks on the Germany transport system, oil industry, and other sources of power. By the end of 1944, Germany's ability to fight a war had at last been seriously affected. There was little fuel left for vehicles and aircraft, and even though the production of matériel was still rising, the Germans had no way of delivering such guns, tanks and aircraft to the fighting troops. And even if the troops had received them, they could not

work with a great raid on the day after the RAF's night attack.

The last remnants of the Luftwaffe were eliminated in the period 21–24 March, when the Allies' air forces flew more than 40,000 missions to seek out these last survivors of the German air force. Thereafter, the strategic bomber force was used in direct support of the ground forces for the rest of the war.

LEFT: The port of St. Nazaire is attacked by US bombers in 1943.

BELOW LEFT: There being no defence against the V-2 ballistic missiles in flight, the Allies sought to destroy them during their manufacture.

BELOW: Made homeless by an Allied air attack, German civilians pick their way through the rubble of their city.

February, when the baroque city of Dresden was utterly destroyed. Although the city had little military significance, and was full of refugees fleeing from the Soviets, a great Bomber Command raid

was launched. The incendiaries took an immediate hold in the old city, and uncontrollable firestorms of horrific intensity swept all before them. The 8th AAF completed Bomber Command's

TOP: US troops, with a quadruple 0.5-in (12.7-mm) machine-gun mounting, cover the approach to the Remagen bridge over the Rhine.

ABOVE: As Soviet forces entered their country, the Bulgarians changed sides. Here a Bulgarian and a Soviet soldier fight side-by-side.

THE END OF THE ROAD FOR NAZI GERMANY

In 1944 the Soviet forces on the Eastern Front had launched three major offensives, all of which succeeded: the spring offensive had pushed the Germans back out of the Ukraine and away from Leningrad; the summer offensive had concentrated in the central sector of the front, and had driven the Axis forces out of Belorussia, back into Poland and the Baltic states, and had halted with its spearheads just outside Warsaw; the autumn offensive had once again been a two-part drive, the Ukrainian fronts having been pushed back in the south and the Axis forces back into the Balkans, before being forced to retreat into Hungary and Czechoslovakia after the defections of Bulgaria and Romania; in the north, the Baltic fronts had moved forward once again, driving through to the Baltic and trapping Army Group North in the Kurland peninsula.

The Soviets were now poised near to the borders of Germany, the curtain for the final act rising on 12 January 1945 when the armies of Marshal K.K. Rokossovsky's 2nd Belorussian Front swept over the Narew river just north of Warsaw and fell on the German 2nd Army. At the same time, the Soviet 47th Army set about taking Warsaw, which fell on 17 January. Rokossovsky's troops drove all before them, advancing north-west up the right bank of the Vistula river toward the Baltic, and cutting off Colonel-General Georg-Hans Reinhardt's Army Group Centre near the sea between Elbing and Danzig.

While its right was being threatened by Rokossovsky's front, Army Group Centre also found its left to be in no better position: General I.D. Chernyakovsky's 3rd Belorussian Front had also driven forward, in conjunction with General I. K. Bagramyan's 1st Baltic Front, to reach the sea north of Memel. Reinhardt had begged to be allowed to disperse his forces in order to meet this threat, but Hitler had refused, and now the whole army group had been cut off and was in desperate straits. By 8 February 500,000 Germans had been pinned against the coast in a few isolated pockets. Hitler at last saw that he had been wrong and gave permission for the survivors to be taken off. This the German navy did, in an extraordinary evacuation quite the equal of Dunkirk,

leaving the last German beach-heads to hold out as best they could for the rest of the war, the last surrendering only on 9 May. Some of the troops in Kurland were pulled out at the same time, as were some 1.5 million civilians. But the cost was appalling, as the Germans had no air cover to fight off the Soviet attack warplanes: by the end of the evacuation the German navy comprised only one heavy and one light cruiser.

Having fallen, East Prussia was the first part of the Third Reich to be taken by the USSR in World War II.

While these northern forces were taking East Prussia, the armies of Marshal Georgi Zhukov's 1st Belorussian Front and Marshal I.S. Konev's 1st Ukrainian Front had been surging forward under devastating artillery support across the Vistula river to the south of Warsaw. Only the 9th, 4th Panzer and 17th Armies of Colonel-General Johannes Harpe's Army Group A were there to make the vain effort to stop the Soviets. The German task was impossible, and by 17 January the Soviets had advanced almost to the German-Polish border near Katowice and Czestochowa. Confident of their vastly superior manpower and matériel strength, Zhukov and Konev pressed on as far and as fast as their logistics organizations could support them. These organizations had a difficult task: more than 1.5 million Soviet soldiers were pressing steadily forward, supported by 28,000 guns, nearly 3,500 tanks and self-propelled guns and some 10,000 aircraft. The Germans, on the other hand, could not find even a fraction of the supplies needed by their 600,000 men, 8,250 guns, 700 tanks and 1,300 aircraft, despite the fact that they were working on interior lines of communication.

Zhukov, in particular, appeared to be moving forward irresistibly, and by 31 January the 1st Belorussian Front reached the Oder river, only some 40 miles (65km) east of Berlin. In Zhukov's rear, however, as in everyone else's, there

WORLD WAR II

Pomerania and Konev's in Silesia, to straighten their lines. Konev's advance took him to the line of the Neisse river, so that by the end of the month the two fronts were lined up only 40 miles (65km) from Berlin along 100 miles (160km) of the Oder and Neisse rivers. By the end of March, the 1st Belorussian Front had reached the sea at Kolberg and was opposite the great port of Stettin on the left bank of the Oder. In the south, meanwhile, the 1st and 4th Ukrainian Fronts had again pushed well forward into Czechoslovakia, defended by Field-Marshal Ferdinand Schörner's Army Group Centre. Further south still, in Hungary, Budapest had fallen to Marshal R.Y. Malinovsky's 2nd Ukrainian Front on 14 February, and the 2nd and 3rd Ukrainian Fronts had then pushed on to the general line, Nagyatad/Lake Balaton/Lake Velencei/Esztergom/Banska Stiavnica by 6 March. From here it was an easy push into the rest of Hungary and thence into Austria in the direction of Vienna.

But Hitler's desperate preoccupation with oil once again came into play: Colonel-General 'Sepp' Dietrich's 6th SS

LEFT: A British mechanized column moves deeper into Germany as the defending forces begin to crumble.

BELOW: Soviet 'tank-rider' infantry move forward on a T-34/85 medium tank.

were large numbers of German pockets, bypassed and contained in the furious advance, but now ready to be mopped up. Most of the smaller pockets were eliminated in short order, but some held out for long periods in dogged displays of defensive fighting. As ever insistent on the need to hold ground, Hitler had demanded that key cities, such as Deutsche Krone, Poznan, Glogau, Breslau and Oppeln be held, and held they were for some time, in some cases right up to the end of the war.

Zhukov's great central drive had also had the effect of splitting Army Groups A and Vistula, the latter surprisingly commanded by Reichsführer-SS Heinrich Himmler, who had apparently decided he was as capable as the next man of leading an army group, without any military training. Admittedly his force was nothing but a motley of troops, but this was all the more reason to have had an experienced commander. After a short time Himmler retired from his command in favour of Colonel-General Gotthard Heinrici, who was able to pull the command together to a certain extent.

In the middle of February both Soviet fronts attacked again, Zhukov's in

195

Panzerarmee, resting in the area after its mauling in the Battle of the Bulge, was to strike south-east between Lakes Balaton and Velencei to retake the Balaton oilfields. Other formations were to join in to the south to expand the offensive and administer a sharp check to the Soviets' general drive. Dietrich's offensive was launched on 6 March, and at first good progress was made; but the weather was very bad, the ground thick with mud, and the Soviet defence steadfast. As the German armour was gradually slowed by the terrain and lack of fuel, the Soviets counter-attacked, driving the Germans back. General Otto Wöhler's Army Group South could find no reply, and soon the 2nd and 3rd Ukrainian Fronts were over the border into Austria. Vienna fell on 14 April, and a day later the Soviets were well beyond the city.

Between December 1944 and April 1945, therefore, the several Soviet fronts had pressed on from the line Kaunas/Bialystok/Warsaw/eastern Czechoslovakia/Budapest/Belgrade to a line from Stettin in the north to Vienna in the south, with a large German salient in eastern Czechoslovakia. Only in two places could the Germans make a defence in what was left of Germany, between the Western army groups advancing from France and the Soviets advancing from Poland and Czechoslovakia. By previous agreement at the Yalta Conference of February 1945, the western Allies were to halt on the Elbe river, west of Berlin, leaving the rest of Germany to the Soviets, with Berlin as the chief prize.

Under the overall supervision of Zhukov, the plans for the Berlin campaign were carefully laid. While the 2nd Belorussian Front drove across northern Germany from the Oder to the Elbe, the 1st Belorussian and 1st Ukrainian Fronts would close in on Berlin from the north and south, cut it off, and then fight their way in to final victory. Zhukov and Konev had no illusions about how bloody this fight

would be. The figures of men and matériel are available for this climactic battle of the war against Germany. In Berlin itself, for example, were 2 million civilians and a garrison of 30,000. But holding the outer defences were about 1 million German troops. To take on this formidable array, Zhukov and Konev could between them muster some 2.5 million men. Although the German troops were on the whole mediocre, with little in the way of munitions, the Soviets knew they would put up an excellent defence. The defences themselves were mainly to the south of the city, for here there was no natural defence line such as the Havel river to the north. Of course, these were last-ditch defences, and nothing like as strong as the German positions 40 miles (65km) away on the west bank of the Oder and Neisse rivers, which was the only place where there was a possible chance of beating the Soviets back.

The Soviet offensive started on 16 April, preceded by one of the most intense artillery bombardments ever seen: along Zhukov and Konev's fronts there was one gun every 13ft (4m). After enormously thorough artillery preparation the Soviets stormed across the rivers, only to be met by heavy fire. By 18 April the two Soviet fronts had each secured only two small bridgeheads, some 3 to 7 miles (5 to 11km) deep. Two days later, however, the Germans were crushed in scenes of terrible carnage. Zhukov and Konev pressed on as quickly as they could, and linked up west of Berlin on 25 April. The only part of the German river defence force to remain reasonably intact was the 9th Army, soon joined by part of the 4th Panzerarmee, in a pocket near Markisch Buchholz, some 30 miles (50km) south-east of Berlin.

The 2nd Belorussian Front attacked on 20 April and soon drove through the defences of Colonel-General Kurt Student's Army Group Vistula. Army Group Centre, well to the south of

Berlin, had been split from the rest of the German defences by Konev's wedge-shaped advance. On 25 April US and Soviet forces met at Torgau on the Elbe, where the shattered remnants of the river defence forces were desperately trying to break through to the west before the Soviets' rear areas were consolidated.

Finally, it was Berlin against the 1st Belorussian and 1st Ukrainian Fronts as the Soviet attack was launched on 26 April. By 28 April Zhukov's 2nd Guards Tank Army had reached the Spree river in the northern outskirts, but further to the south Konev's 8th Guards and 1st Guards Tank Armies had nearly reached the Tiergarten in the centre of the city. If the two Soviet forces could only link up, Berlin would be cut into western and eastern halves. Hitler, by now totally demented, spent all of the time he had left calling on the 9th Army to break through and relieve the capital, which could by now barely hold its own. Although the two Soviet fronts were only 1 mile (1.5km) apart on 28 April, it was to take them another four days of murderous close fighting to link up across the Reichstag and Chancellery, where Hitler's bunker was situated. On 30 April, however, Hitler committed suicide, after appointing Grand-Admiral Karl Dönitz as his successor.

The fall of Berlin, in what was one of the bloodiest battles fought in the 20th century, left only one other major pocket of German resistance, namely Schörner's last-ditch defences in Czechoslovakia. A diehard Nazi, Schörner had been given this command by Hitler because of his political loyalty. Although the war was lost, Schörner was determined to fulfil his orders to hold this important industrial area to the north-east of Prague, his methods of securing the co-operation of his men being that anyone refusing an order or showing any signs of sloth was shot. To the north was the 1st Ukrainian Front, to the east the 4th Ukrainian Front, to the south-east and south the 2nd Ukrainian Front, to the south-west

the US 3rd Army, and to the west the US 1st Army. Only to the south was there any hope of escape, and here the 3rd Army and 3rd Ukrainian Front were hourly closing the gap. Schörner had some 1 million men, but without fuel and ammunition they were unable to halt the Allies. By 6 April the 2nd and 4th Ukrainian Fronts had overrun Slovakia in the east. A month later and they were well into the prosperous region of Moravia, but at this moment the Czech partisans arose in the Germans' rear, severely affecting their communications. Two days later, on 8 May, the Soviets to the north, east and south launched a massive onslaught, in which Prague was taken on 9 May. Schörner finally surrendered with his last German forces still fighting on 11 May.

The Soviets estimated that German losses in the last three months of the war on the Eastern Front were 1 million civilians dead as well as 800,000 fighting men, with 12,000 armoured vehicles, 23,000 guns and 6,000 aircraft captured.

While the Soviets were overcoming German resistance in the east, the western Allies were advancing. After the fighting in the Ardennes had died down, it would have been clear to anyone except Hitler that the only hope for Germany was an end to the war. This was not to be, and as long as the German army held together and could use the remnants of the Westwall, the floods in the Low Countries, and the barrier of the Rhine as a defensive system, it was plain that the task of defeating it would be long and bitter. It was for this reason that General Eisenhower insisted on the maximum concentration of force in France. The British were once more pressing for a main effort in the north, with Lieutenant General Patton clamouring for more action with as many divisions as possible in the 3rd Army sector, while General Jean de Lattre de Tassigny was demanding a greater share of the action for his French 1st army and for France. Eisenhower only considered these

LEFT: With a Soviet tank in the foreground, this is the end for Germany as Soviet warplanes fly over the ruined Reichstag.

BELOW LEFT: The Battle of Berlin was very hard-fought, the Soviets using huge numbers of men as well as their full panoply of air power, artillery and armour to batter the German defence into defeat. This is an ISU heavy self-propelled gun, which was based on the chassis of the KV-1 heavy tank, revised for a barbette mounting of either a 4.8- or 6-in (122- or 152-mm) gun, the latter being the one shown here.

ABOVE: Dead Waffen-SS men lie alongside their destroyed armoured personnel carrier.

BELOW: One of Berlin's landmarks to remain only slightly damaged was the Brandenburg Gate.

possible, 'bouncing' a crossing where he could and making a formal assault with maximum artillery and air support where the defences were strong, then advancing from these bridgeheads into the heart of Germany. The next move was to encircle the Ruhr industrial area on which the German economy depended, even though already wrecked by the bomber offensive, and mop it up, while the Allied armies drove forward to the Elbe to meet the Soviet forces.

The first move was by Lieutenant-General Jacob L. Devers's 6th Army Group in the south. A local counter-offensive, aimed at the recapture of Strasbourg, was beaten off in January and then the French 1st Army, its colonial troops much reduced in numbers after sacrificial fighting and suffering from cold and frostbite, were initially checked in an attempt to liquidate the 'Colmar pocket', which was badly dented but still holding. Devers then reinforced the French with the US XXI Corps and the attack was resumed. De Lattre deployed Major-General Leclerc's 2nd Armoured Division, the Free French and his US corps on the north of the salient, covering the nose which protruded into the Vosges with the French 10th Division, while his I Corps (2nd and 4th Moroccan Divisions and 9th Colonial Division) attacked from the south. The US 109th Infantry Regiment drove the Germans from Colmar on 1 February, chivalrously allowing the French troops to enter the city first. By 5 February the attacks from north and south had met, and by 9 February the last Germans not already killed or captured were over the Rhine.

On 8 February, away in the north, Field-Marshal Montgomery launched the Canadian 1st Army, under General Sir Henry Crerar, into Operation Veritable, whose aim was to advance from the Nijmegen salient, break through the Westwall, clearing the Germans out of the Reichswald forest, Cleve, Goch and Xanten. The attacks were planned with extreme care, with great reliance placed

on powerful and highly skilled artillery. A fire plan of great complexity was prepared, first to suppress the German artillery and then to soften up the German positions, with special attention given to precise fire on concrete bunkers. Once the attack had started a barrage was to be put down on the forward enemy localities, to stand there for 70 minutes until the assaulting divisions closed up to the German positions; it would then begin to roll forward at the rate of 300 yards (275m) every 12 minutes, with six regiments on each divisional front providing four belts of fire altogether 500 yards (455m) deep. The total number of guns and howitzers employed was 1,050, supplemented by light anti-aircraft guns, anti-tank guns, machine guns, the guns of tanks, heavy mortars and a regiment of rocket-launchers. The Reichswald was cleared by 13 February, Goch by 21 February and Xanten on 26 February. This was the most severe fighting seen on the left bank of the Rhine, the 21st Army Group's casualties numbering 16,000 and the Germans losing 23,000 prisoners and an unknown number of killed and wounded.

On 23 February Lieutenant-General William H. Simpson's US 9th Army, under command of the 21st Army Group, crossed the flooded valley of the Roer in assault boats (Operation Grenade), making sufficient progress to deploy armour by 1 March. Simpson cleaned up his objectives with a loss of 7,300 men, but captured another 30,000 prisoners. These two battles went a long way to crack the still unbroken will of the German army.

In the meantime, the US 1st Army of Lieutenant-General Courtney H. Hodges was grinding its way forward in the sector from Köln to Koblenz when the battles of attrition were enlivened by a flashing *coup de main* undertaking. The defenders were withdrawing in some confusion, and without a continuous front, when some US tanks and armoured infantry drove between them to capture

time, by a huge concentration of anti-aircraft artillery. But between the air attacks and a continual bombardment by heavy artillery the bridge collapsed. This was too late, for by that time the US engineers had thrown sufficient bridges across the river to ensure that the forward troops could be maintained.

Lieutenant-General Patton, of the US 3rd Army, was not to be outdone. He had a stiff task which needed to be undertaken methodically by stages, which did not suit his temperament, but which he nevertheless carried out with precision. He first broke through the Westwall in the Saar and then crossed the Mosel, which meant an advance through broken and hilly country until he could uncover the Rhine from Koblenz to Mainz. He had his eyes fixed on the river, for he was determined to cross before Montgomery's projected date, 24 March, and the day before managed to put six battalions across at Oppenheim at the cost of 28 casualties.

LEFT: One of the last photographs of Adolf Hitler, taken during an inspection of boy soldiers, before he committed suicide on 30 April 1945.

BELOW: At Reims, on 7 May 1945, Colonel-General Alfred Jodl, the chief-of-staff of the Oberkommando der Wehrmacht (armed forces high command), signs Germany's document of unconditional surrender on behalf of Grand-Admiral Karl Dönitz, Hitler's successor as head of state. On Jodl's left is General-Admiral Hans-Georg von Friedeburg, commander-in-chief of the German navy.

Remagen, where they discovered that the Ludendorff Bridge across the Rhine was unblown and only lightly guarded as it was being used to allow the units still west of the Rhine to cross. This was reported and the local commander, Brigadier-General William M. Hoge, ordered it to be seized. There was a blunder on the German side; the demolition charges were ready laid but when they were triggered only one exploded, causing a crater at the western end. The Americans rushed the bridge on foot under small arms fire, cutting the wires to the explosive charges as they went. Soon they had fought their way across, digging in on the far side. Curiously enough, Hoge's initiative was not followed up, the officers in the command chain referring ever upward until Lieutenant General Omar N. Bradley, at 12th Army Group headquarters, was reached. Bradley ordered Hodges to push across every formation he had in hand and by 12 March a bridgehead 14 miles (23km) wide was securely held by three divisions supported by tanks. In this way, the formidable obstacle was cheaply crossed and the way to the heart of Germany lay open. Counter-attacks were beaten off, as were suicidal Luftwaffe missions, for a

ABOVE: Field-Marshal Sir Bernard Montgomery presides over the surrender, by General-Admiral Hans-Georg von Friedeburg and General Hans Kinzel, of all the German forces in northern Germany, at Lüneberg Heath, south of Hamburg, on 4 May 1945.

RIGHT: The room in which Adolf Hitler committed suicide on 30 April 1945.

The planning for Plunder was based on the technique for landing on a coast rather than on a simple river crossing and, like Dragoon, embodied every possible refinement to ensure the crossing was successful and that there were minimal casualties. The main assault was to be carried out by the British 1st Commando Brigade, directed on Wesel, the British 15th Division in the centre of the British sector, and the US 30th and 79th Divisions of Simpson's 9th Army south of the Lippe canal. H-hour was 02.00 on 24 March. At 10.00 two airborne formations, the British 6th and the US 17th Airborne Divisions, were to parachute in or be landed close enough to the river to be within supporting range of the artillery on the left bank.

In the British sector the difficulty of putting enough artillery across in the early stages made it necessary to deploy it in full view of the Germans on the right bank, and therefore a permanent smokescreen was generated to cover the whole front, while to aid manoeuvres at night banks of searchlights, sited near the

river, provided 'artificial moonlight'. The artillery fire plan was once more large and elaborate. Some 200 heavy bombers blasted a path for the commandos as they approached Wesel, with more than 660 tanks poised to follow. Some of the Scots companies were in tracked amphibians (LVTs or Buffaloes) with orders not to disembark on the farther bank but to motor on, providing their own covering fire for objectives deep in the proposed bridgehead. The Scottish troops met with very strong resistance near the east bank, but were eventually able to clean it up.

By daylight, Eisenhower went to view the fly-in of 400 aircraft, carrying paratroops, followed by 1,300 more towing gliders, a total of 14,000 troops of the British 6th and US 17th Airborne Divisions arriving in an endless procession which filled the sky. This required the most careful co-ordination with the field artillery fire, as shell trajectories were high enough to intersect the aircraft flight paths and meant that, at times, fire on the German anti-aircraft artillery and other fire-

On 31 March, anxious lest the Americans should cross the Rhine first, Jean de Lattre de Tassigny secured a bridgehead at Speyer.

On 24 March Montgomery launched his grand spectacular: Operations Plunder, the Rhine crossing, followed by Varsity, the airborne descent on the far side. This has been represented as an example of over-caution, but the same considerations also applied to Veritable. The German high command, which was apprehensive about the northern thrust, had also made a fair appreciation of its scope and direction and one of the last of its good formations, the 1st Parachute Army, barred Montgomery's way. The river at his intended crossing point, between Emmerich and Homberg, is 1,000 yards (915m) wide and fast-flowing, and it was Montgomery's intention not to have a fight for the bridgehead but to drive through to a great depth in order that the subsequent advance could continue without check.

support had to be denied. All went well, however, and by the end of the first day's fighting the British and Americans had joined up and were 6 miles (10km) beyond the river.

To the south Eisenhower's other two army groups were advancing from their bridgeheads, with no substantial resistance. It was estimated that only some 6,000 disorganized troops were opposing Devers. The orders for the December and January counter-offensives, followed by Hitler's desperate command to hold ground without yielding, had in fact left the surviving German formations in position for destruction. Some divisions were by now just headquarters and a few scratch troops, like the Volkssturm, and some were only combat teams (Kampfgruppen). Facing west, there was altogether only the equivalent of some 26 full-strength divisions, representing the last scrapings of German manpower. Nevertheless there would be much sharp fighting ahead, first on all fronts and then in pockets, as small groups of SS troops or paratroops decided to hold out to the bitter end.

The scheme of manoeuvre for the Ruhr battle was for the 9th Army to encircle the Ruhr from the north and the 1st Army from the south, linking at Lippstadt and trapping the German forces, who had intended using its cities to fight a long, delaying battle. This was complete by 6 April. Three corps were given the task of entering the sack so formed, carving it up and reducing it sector by sector. Within was the headquarters of Army Group B, under Field-Marshal Walther Model, who refused a futile order from OKW to break out, but at the same time felt unable to surrender formally. He told his troops to fight on or just go home as they chose, then committed suicide. Some 317,000 prisoners, including two dozen generals, representing some 19 divisions and various army and corps headquarters, plus 100,000 air defence troops, were captured.

While this last great battle of the war in the west was going on, the remaining US armies were surging forward to the Elbe with ever-increasing momentum, while farther north the Canadians and British advanced against more dogged resistance from formed bodies of troops. Eisenhower then made a major alteration to his final plan. He had originally intended to make Berlin his final objective, but a number of considerations supervened. Allied intelligence believed the Germans might take to guerrilla warfare and that there was a plan to establish a 'national redoubt' in the mountains of Bavaria, so he ordered the US 3rd and 7th Armies to swing south. To go on to Berlin, Eisenhower estimated, might be too costly to be worthwhile so late in the war. With the main German armies facing him destroyed, Berlin had ceased to be a purely military objective, apart from which the Soviets were closer to it than he was himself. He feared that a head-on contact between the Soviets and Allied troops might lead to awkward confrontations, and sought some clear natural feature on which they could meet in orderly fashion, for which he regarded the Elbe as ideal. He also felt that there was little point in capturing territory only to hand it back to the Soviets according to political agreements already entered into by the Allies. He therefore resisted the British demands to be allowed to go on to Berlin and also Simpson's similar request when he had secured a bridgehead over the Elbe. On 24 April officers of the US V Corps met Soviet representatives at Torgau on the Elbe and the forward movement ceased.

With Hitler's death on 30 April, what central authority there was disappeared, and the Reich began to surrender piecemeal. The representatives of the Germans in the north surrendered to Montgomery, with effect from 08.00 on 5 May. At the same time, large German forces, east of the Elbe, surrendered to Simpson, many civilians attempting to cross to the west bank to escape the

Soviets. For a formal surrender the Allies insisted on complete capitulation on both fronts, and this took place at the Allied supreme headquarters in Reims in France at 02.00 on 7 May.

THE ITALIAN CAMPAIGN COMES TO AN END

During the spring of 1945 the same opponents faced each other in Italy: the Allied 5th and 8th Armies, and the German 10th and 14th Armies. Only some of the principal actors had changed roles. Field-Marshals Albert Kesselring and Sir Harold Alexander had become theatre commanders, the latter of all the Allied forces in the Mediterranean. Army Group C was now led by the excellent Colonel-General Heinrich von Vietinghoff, and the ambitious Lieutenant-General Mark W. Clark had succeeded Alexander in command of the 15th Army Group. Major-General Lucian K. Truscott, who had commanded the US VI Corps at Anzio, in succession to Lieutenant-General John P. Lucas, now led the US 5th Army, and Lieutenant-General Sir Oliver Leese, transferred to Burma, was succeeded by Lieutenant-General Sir Richard McCreery.

Alexander's orders from the Combined Chiefs-of-Staff Committee for 1945 had been to continue with the pressure on Army Group C, hard enough to prevent the withdrawal of any German divisions from Italy, and if von Vietinghoff withdrew to a new defence line in the foothills of the Alps, to follow him. This was an invitation to limit operations to a few cautious, small-scale attacks. Two more good divisions of Canadians had been taken away to strengthen the Canadian army on the Western Front, and although Clark had received a Brazilian division and a specialist US mountain division fresh from the USA, and McCreery two Polish brigades and a Jewish Palestinian brigade, the numerical odds against the 15th Army Group were still 17 to 23 against in terms of divisions.

Two troopers of the Special Air Service and an Italian partisan near Castino, in northern Italy, during April 1945. SAS operations behind the German lines made German communications almost impossible.

The war was nearly over. Eisenhower's armies had crossed the Rhine in three places in March, the Soviet vanguards were at the frontier of Austria, Army Group C was well-equipped and up to strength and in an extremely strong position, and there was no point in incurring many more casualties. Moreover, a German emissary was secretly in touch with Alexander's headquarters concerning the possibility of a negotiated surrender in Italy. Another costly offensive, it could be argued, that made little sense. Alexander and his commanders were of a different opinion. Their deficiency in manpower was more than offset by their superiority in armour, artillery and air power, so they continued to argue that the only way to carry out their mission effectively was to mount a full-scale offensive. They felt they had fought too hard and for too long to relax now without the victory they believed to be rightly theirs and, strangely enough, so also did the soldiers.

The Italian front was divided by geography into two distinct sectors, both ideally suited for defence. Opposite the US 5th Army the road north was barred by 10 miles (16km) of crags and precipices, fortified and garrisoned by the best of the German infantry. The British 8th Army's front line was along the flood banks of the Senio river, and four more defended river lines lay beyond. On the right the way was barred by the waters of Lake Comacchio and floods created by the breaching of the dykes along the rivers. Across the whole 50 miles (80km) of front there was only one dry gap, where the road north to Argenta ran between the lake and the floods, offering a way round the whole river network. McCreery fixed his sights on this.

Clark's plan was for the 8th Army to attack early in April, using all the air power available, and that when McCreery had attracted the German reserves to the east, the 5th Army would in its turn take it over for a thrust in the centre. The 8th Army's last offensive was a triumphant

combination of tactics and technology. A large number of DD amphibious tanks and tracked amphibious infantry carriers had reached the theatre, and these converted the expanse of water facing the 8th Army's right from a barrier to an avenue reaching the heart of the 10th Army's defences. As a first move British commandos and Royal Marines secured a safe start line on the south and east of Lake Comacchio, and then two brigades of the 56th Division in assault boats attacked the eastern shore and secured the wedge of dry land leading to Argenta. This was the doorway through which McCreery intended to pass his armour. If the bridge over the Reno river at Bastia could be secured he would have the side door to the whole of the 10th Army's defence system, for then, after crossing the Senio, his right-hand divisions could link with the 56th Division and fan out toward the Po.

On 9 April the 10th Army's artillery areas received thousands of tons of fragmentation bombs from heavy bombers, then by medium bombers, followed by fighter-bombers in close support of the attacking infantry. A series of barrages were fired from 1,000 guns. The far bank was doused with burning fuel from flame-throwing tanks,

and the assault began. The infantry crossed, followed by tanks and the welter of specialist armoured vehicles. By 16 April the 10th Army was still fighting doggedly, but the veteran 6th Armoured, 78th and 56th Divisions had fanned out north of Argenta in the Po valley and were inching forward. Von Vietinghoff's line was near breaking point.

Truscott began his attack in clear skies on 14 April. It was a sign of the times, perhaps, when a German division in defence actually disintegrated and ran. The US 10th Mountain Division was enthusiastic and fresh, and it had been specifically trained in mountain warfare, unlike the normal US troops. Now, in the same manner as the Moroccan *goumiers* in the Gustav Line, the American mountain troops led the way through the remaining northern foothills of the Apennines. The remnants of the 14th Army had to come down from the peaks or be cut off. Truscott's main thrust was directed east of Bologna, because one of the peculiarities of von Vietinghoff's position was that its final stop-line was the Reno river, which curled all around his centre and left, but could be outflanked in the west by Truscott where it rose in the Apennines, or at the Argenta gap. The Americans and British

LEFT: Italian partisans and civilians at the time of the German surrender.

BELOW: Mussolini and his mistress hang by their feet in Milan the day after they had been executed by a partisan firing squad on 28 April 1945.

was won, crossed the Po and raced for the Alpine passes. The ceasefire was ordered for 1800 hours on 2 May. It had been 21 months and 13 days since the touchdown on the Sicilian beaches, and the long, bitter and forgotten war was finally over.

were now moving with great impetus, while throughout the back areas of Army Group C the RAF and the USAAF were ready to pounce on any movement of German troops.

It was Clark's desire to catch the whole German force south of the Po, and to destroy it there with the river at its back: this he achieved. Any remote possibility that it could have escaped had been denied by Hitler himself. Before the Allied offensive had started von Vietinghoff had asked for Hitler's permission to fight a mobile battle of withdrawal and so keep his army intact, but was accused of 'wavering' and of revealing 'defeatist attitudes', and ordered to hold. When von Vietinghoff finally ordered a withdrawal his front had already collapsed. As he had foreseen, the

only hope would have been to have ducked the hammer blows of Allied air power and artillery and to have slipped back across the wide and flooded Po.

On 22 April the South African 6th Division, leading the 5th Army's advance, and the British 6th Armoured Division travelling west, met each other behind the retreating Germans at a village appropriately called Finale. The Germans were trapped and in complete disorder, except on the Mediterranean coast, where a mountain corps remained in good order until the end. Even the paratroops began to surrender. Most of the German heavy equipment was left on the south bank, the units which had got away having been harried by the Italian partisans, while the Allied divisions, hardly able to realize that their battle

CHAPTER FIVE

THE DEFEAT OF JAPAN

A 6.1-in (155-mm)) howitzer of the US Marine Corps in action on one of the Solomon Islands group. Throughout the war with Japan, the US forces possessed significantly greater numbers of heavy artillery.

ASCENDING THE LADDER OF THE SOLOMON ISLANDS

Their defeats of 1942 and early 1943 in Papua and Guadalcanal worried the Japanese high command severely, for in this area now lay the greatest danger of an Allied breakthrough into the Southern Resources Area so vital for Japan's continued ability to wage the war and prosper economically once it was over. The decision was therefore taken to reinforce the area strongly. The key to the region's defences was Rabaul, on New Britain, and it was to this that men and matériel were sent to replace those lost in the Papua and Guadalcanal battles. From

Rabaul these additional resources were to be allocated as the local commanders saw fit, mostly to the garrisons in the Huon Gulf in north-eastern New Guinea and in the Solomon Islands chain as far to the south-east as New Georgia Island. The Japanese had no joint command structure, and it thus depended on the good sense of commanders whether or not the army and navy acted in co-operation. In this area, however, it was good: overall command was exercised by Vice-Admiral Jinichi Kosaka, commanding the 8th Area Army of Lieutenant-General Hitoshi Imamura. The 8th Area Army controlled two

formations, Lieutenant-General Hotaze Adachi's 18th Army in New Guinea, and Lieutenant-General Iwao Matsuda's 17th Army in the Solomon Islands. Given that this threatened area was the key to the naval-controlled defence perimeter on which Japan's fate hung, Admiral Isoroku Yamamoto, the commander-in-chief of the Combined Fleet, kept a watchful eye on the situation from his headquarters in Truk, far to the north in the Caroline Islands.

The general Allied strategy for the area had been fixed in July 1942, and following the defeat of the Japanese attempts on Port Moresby and Guadalcanal, the forces of General Douglas MacArthur's South-West Pacific Area were ready to begin the drive on Rabaul. The South Pacific Area was dissolved, Vice-Admiral William F. Halsey's naval forces in the area becoming the 3rd Fleet, which was allocated to MacArthur's overall command. The drive on Rabaul was to have two axes. Supported by the aircraft of Lieutenant-General George Kenney's US 5th Army Air Force, Lieutenant-General Walter Krueger's US 6th Army was to advance up the coast of New Guinea and then invade the western end of New Britain before making the final assault on Rabaul. At the same time, Halsey's forces were to 'island-hop' through the Solomon Islands toward the north-west and thus in the direction of Rabaul. The one major problem that had to be overcome was a command and related logistical one: although under MacArthur's strategic command, Halsey was still dependent on Admiral Chester Nimitz's Pacific Ocean Areas for men and matériel. MacArthur and Halsey

The Japanese were considerably shaken on 4 September 1943 when the Australian 9th Division of the New Guinea Force, now commanded by General Sir Thomas Blarney, landed east of the main base of Lae in the Huon Gulf. A day later the US 503rd Parachute Regiment dropped at Nazdab, inland of Lae, thus completing the isolation of the garrison. The airborne 'air-head' was swiftly reinforced by the Australian 7th Division, which was airlifted from Port Moresby. The Allied forces at Salamaua and Lae now attacked simultaneously, Salamaua falling on 12 September and Lae on 16 September. While the Australian 9th Division advanced around the coast, the Australian 20th Brigade was shipped around to Katika, where it landed on 22 September, cutting off the garrison of Finschhafen, which fell on 2 October.

After its capture of Lae, the Australian 7th Division had moved up the Markham river valley, inland of the Saruwaged and Finisterre ranges of

LEFT: A tank landing ship of the US Navy disgorges supplies for the men of the US Marine Corps somewhere in the Solomon Islands group.

BELOW: The wreckage of a Mitsubishi G4M 'Betty' twin-engined bomber, again somewhere in the Solomon Islands group. Japanese warplanes were notable for their very long range, but this capability was bought only by the sacrifice of protective features, such as armour for the crew and vital systems, and protection for the fuel tanks.

worked very smoothly as a team, however, which overcame many of the problems that might have defeated two less tolerant commanders.

The advance through New Guinea was finally made possible by the capture of Buna on 22 January 1943. Some preparatory movements had already been carried out, the most important of these being the airlift to Wau, about 30 miles (50km) south-west and inland of the major Japanese coastal garrison of Salamaua, of an Australian brigade from Lieutenant-General Edmund F. Herring's New Guinea Force. The brigade established a forward base and threatened the Japanese as MacArthur put the finishing touches to the main assault plans and readied his forces. To make the Japanese think that his drive would be straight along the coast, a battalion of the US 32nd Division was landed at Nassau Bay on 30 June, just to the south of Salamaua, and this battalion, together with the Australian 17th Brigade from Wau, now threatened Salamaua from the west and south. At the same time the US 158th Infantry Regiment took Trobriand Island, and the US 112th Cavalry Regiment took Woodlark Island, both of

these lying north-east of the south-eastern tip of Papua. This completed the clearance of Japanese garrisons in Papua between Buna and Milne Bay undertaken in October and November 1942.

THE DEFEAT OF JAPAN

US infantryman and a Sherman medium tank combine to flush out Japanese defenders on the island of Bougainville late in 1943.

As an initial move, the island of Rendova, just off New Georgia, was taken as an artillery base on 30 June. The main landings went in near Munda on 2 July, the assault forces being the 37th and 43rd Divisions with US Marine support. Overall control of the ground force was exercised by Major-General John P. Hester, later to be replaced by Major-General Oscar W. Griswold. The Japanese were commanded by Lieutenant-General Noboru Sasaki, who led his men ably, so the fighting was extremely bitter, and at first it was the raw US troops who came off the worse in desperate struggles in the jungle. The 25th Division had to be committed on 25 July, and after regrouping and resting his forces, Griswold finally took Munda airfield on 5 August. The back of the Japanese resistance had been broken, and all organized opposition ended on 25 August. There had been heavy casualties on each side.

On 15 August, meanwhile, a US regimental combat team (about the equivalent of a British brigade) had leapfrogged past Kolombangara, which had an important airfield, to land on Vella Lavella. After building an airfield the Americans were withdrawn and replaced by the New Zealand 3rd Division, which was able to crush the last Japanese resistance by the middle of September. The Japanese on Kolombangara, realizing their impossible situation, evacuated the island, and the central rung of the Solomon Islands was in Allied hands by 7 October.

The last major rung before New Britain was the large island of Bougainville, which had several airfields. To distract the Japanese, the 3rd Marine Parachute Battalion landed on nearby Choiseul Island on 27 October. The battalion was evacuated a week later, having accomplished its task. Also on 27 October, the New Zealand 8th Brigade Group landed on Treasury Island, which was quickly secured as an advanced base for the Bougainville

mountains, and then crossed into the Ramu river valley as it made for Madang, which fell to the Australian 11th Division on 24 April 1944. Overland advances and landings from the sea completed the isolation and destruction of other Japanese garrisons on the Huon peninsula during the same period. Of the 10,000 Japanese troops in the area, half had been killed, the other half dispersed into the cruel jungle of the region.

While the Australians were mopping up on the Huon peninsula, the US 6th Army had secured a toehold on the western end of New Britain. The 112th Cavalry Regiment made a diversionary landing at Arawe, on the south coast of New Britain on 15 December 1943, and 11 days later the 1st Marine Division came ashore at Cape Gloucester at the western tip of the island. The division quickly secured a beach-head with two

airfields, after 1,000 Japanese had been killed in a hard, four-day battle.

Halsey's forces had also been active during this period as they began to move up the 'ladder' of the Solomon Islands group. After a brief pause to rest and reorganize after their defeat of the Japanese on Guadalcanal, the Americans resumed with the capture of the Russell Islands, just to the north-west of Guadalcanal, by the 43rd Division on 21 February, but this was only a preliminary move. The basic US plan was now to bypass the main Japanese garrisons, concentrating instead on a series of outflanking movements to secure key air bases and so isolate the Japanese garrisons. This would avoid heavy losses and, it was hoped, neutralize the Japanese bases.

The first major step up the ladder was New Georgia Island, where Japan's main air bases in the Solomons were located.

operation. Moving forward from here, the 3rd Marine Division landed at Empress Augusta Bay on Bougainville on 1 November. At first, Japanese resistance was light, and a naval base and airfields were soon operational within a beachhead 10 miles (16km) wide and 5 miles (8km) deep. Japanese opposition then grew, and by the end of the year the perimeter had hardly been advanced. The only real chance the Japanese had had of evicting the Americans from Bougainville had been in the Battle of Empress Augusta Bay on 2 November, but the radar-equipped ships of the US task force proved too powerful for the Japanese force, which lost a cruiser and a destroyer, and had most of its other vessels damaged. To complete the ascent up the Solomon Islands ladder, on 15 February 1944 the New Zealand 3rd Division took Green Island, to be used as the location of a forward airfield for attacks on Rabaul.

Realizing that the actual conquest of New Ireland and eastern New Britain would be extremely costly, the Allies had by now decided merely to cut them off, leaving them to 'wither on the vine' in their isolation. So it was necessary,

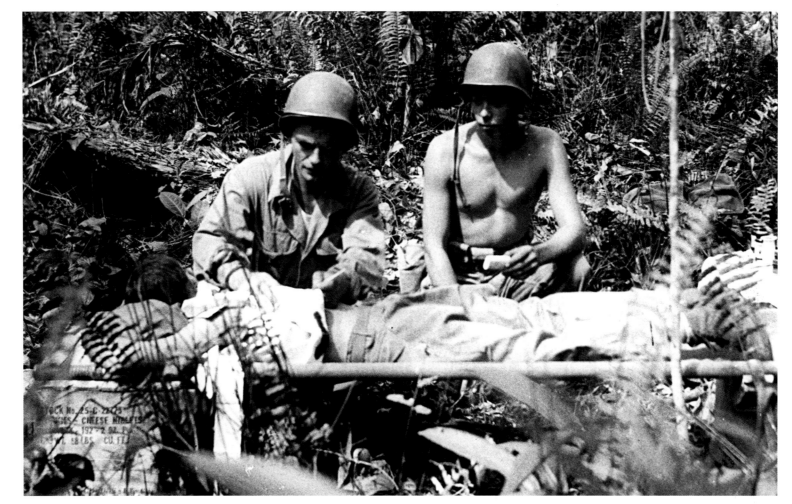

finally, to take the islands north of New Britain and New Ireland to complete the encirclement. Accordingly, MacArthur's

forces moved on the Admiralty Islands and Halsey's on the St. Matthias Islands. A reconnaissance of Los Negros in the Admiralties on 29 February met little opposition and the 1st Cavalry Division quickly moved in to secure the island by 23 March. A landing was also made on Manus on 15 March. Halsey's 4th Marine Division landed unopposed on Emirau in the St. Matthias Islands group, moving swiftly forward to Mussau. New Britain and New Ireland, with their great bases at Rabaul and Kavieng, were now cut off. On New Britain, the 1st Marine and 40th Divisions had been moving steadily east, and on 6 March the 1st Marine Division had made a forward landing at Talasea on the Willaumez peninsula. It was now decided to halt the US forces where they were and henceforward to contain the Japanese. Gradually, Australian forces assumed the task of keeping a watch on the Japanese for the rest of the war, freeing

ABOVE: US front-line medical personnel train under tropical and jungle conditions typical of the Solomon Islands group. The location is Arundel Island off New Georgia.

LEFT: Landing craft, carrying men of the 3rd Marine Division, approach the coast of Bougainville for a largely unopposed landing around Cape Torokina on 1 November 1943.

ABOVE: Men of the US Marine Corps on New Georgia, which was assaulted by forces of the US Army and USMC from 30 June 1943.

RIGHT: Wounded US soldiers on a beach in New Georgia wait for transport out to a hospital ship or a warship equipped with major medical facilities.

covered by Kenney's aircraft, freeing Mitscher for other tasks.

While the Australians were pressing into Madang, far to the rear, MacArthur's two landings were committed on 22 April. The 24th and 41st Divisions landed on each side of Hollandia, which fell on 27 April; in two days a pair of reinforced regiments secured Aitape. In both places the fighting had been very heavy, and although the US forces lost only 550 killed, Japanese dead totalled more than 14,000, the other Japanese in the area having been dispersed into the jungle. MacArthur's forces now advanced in bounds along the coast, taking Sansapor island, at the western end of New Guinea, on 30 July, and bringing the New Guinea campaign to an end. Blarney's Australian forces, meanwhile, had been fighting to a halt a last-breath offensive by the 18th Army in the area of Wewak and Aitape. This was finally crushed on 5 August.

Now that Japan's defensive perimeter had been breached, MacArthur was able to turn his attention to the Philippines group.

MacArthur's US divisions for further operations. The successful neutralization of Japanese strength in the area also allowed the 3rd Fleet to be returned to Nimitz's control in June.

The Japanese perimeter had been horribly dented, but the authorities in Tokyo decided that the western end of New Guinea could still be held by Lieutenant-General Jo Iimura's 2nd Area Army, based in Hollandia, just over the border in occupied Dutch New Guinea. Here a great complex of airfields and supply dumps had been built, but there were few troops in the area. Most of the 18th Army's surviving men, some 65,000 strong, were based in the areas of Wewak and Madang.

In an action of some genius and great risk, MacArthur decided to bypass the 18th Army and go for Hollandia itself, even though this was beyond the range of Kenney's aircraft. Although Nimitz had lent him Vice-Admiral Marc A. Mitscher's Fast Carrier Task Force to provide air cover, MacArthur decided to land forces at Aitape, at the same time

as the Hollandia landings, to secure the airfields there. The Aitape landing could be covered by aircraft based at Saidor, and once Aitape's airfields were in US hands, the Hollandia landings could be

THE ISLAND-HOPPING CAMPAIGN IN THE PACIFIC

The forces of Vice-Admiral William F. Halsey's US 3rd Fleet had made the first island-hopping operations in the course of their advance up the Solomons' ladder, but the technique could not be used there to full effect. In the Central Pacific, however, there was more than ample scope for such tactics, for in the vastnesses of this ocean, with Japan's bases scattered over a multitude of little islands and atolls separated from each area by hundreds of miles of open sea, the steadily growing strength of the US Navy could be used to transport and support the formations of the US Army and US Marine Corps to overwhelm the lesser Japanese garrisons with local superiority of forces. Having fewer ships, the Japanese could not match the US forces' level of strategic mobility, and the US leadership believed that this should make it possible for its forces to close gradually on Japan without encountering the need to tackle major bases until the later stages of the campaign.

While General Douglas MacArthur was firmly in favour of a methodical approach to Japan via New Guinea and the Philippine Islands group, Admiral Ernest J. King, the chief of naval operations, and Admiral Chester W. Nimitz, commanding the Pacific Ocean Areas, favoured a more indirect approach across the Central Pacific to take Formosa or part of the Japanese-held mainland of China. In the thinking of the US Navy, the Imperial Japanese empire would then be cut in two, separating Japan's industry and population from the raw materials and food which they obtained from the south. This, the US Navy believed, would greatly weaken Japan and so facilitate the final assault on the Japanese home islands should this prove necessary. The grand strategic question of which plan was better did not have to be answered until 1944, so until then there was room for both the US Army and the US Navy to advance in their own areas, MacArthur in the South-West Pacific and Nimitz across the Central Pacific. The

US armaments factories were by now delivering matériel in quantities so vast that there was ample for MacArthur and Nimitz, even though the war against Japan in general possessed a lower priority than the theatres in which the Germans were being fought.

To a great extent Nimitz was helped by MacArthur's efforts: feeling that the South-West Pacific constituted their greatest threat, the Japanese had responded by sending to this theatre the best of their air units from the separate army and navy air forces, with the result that the Central Pacific garrisons were left with mere handfuls of aircraft and indifferent crews. Even the good aircrews were being killed in large numbers, and their replacements, moreover, were decidedly inferior. The Japanese suffered yet another blow with the death of Admiral Isoroku Yamamoto, commander-in-chief of the Combined Fleet, on 18 April 1943, when his aircraft was shot down by Lockheed P-38 Lightning long-range fighters operating

ABOVE: Long-range air power projection in the Pacific theatre rested primarily with the Consolidated B-24 four-engined bombers of the US Army Air Forces. This aircraft is seen in 1944, during a raid on Koror, one of the main islands of the Palau Islands group.

LEFT: US troops survey Japanese gun emplacements after they had captured the tiny island of Tarawa, in the Gilbert Islands group, in an immensely costly battle between 20 and 23 November 1943.

THE DEFEAT OF JAPAN

ABOVE: After taking Tarawa and other islands of the Gilbert Islands group late in 1943, the US forces moved north-west to tackle the primary Japanese garrisons in the Marshall Islands from 30 January 1944. Here the US flag flies from a shattered coconut palm after the island of Kwajalein had been taken on 1–4 February 1944.

RIGHT: US infantrymen during the fight for Guam, the most southerly of the larger islands in the Mariana Islands group, taken between 21 July and 10 August 1944.

was built around the large numbers of fast fleet and light aircraft carriers emerging from US yards at a remarkable pace, supported by modern and modernized battleships as well as large numbers of cruisers, both heavy and light, and exceptionally capable fleet destroyers. When commanded by Halsey, this force was known as the 3rd Fleet, which became the 5th fleet when commanded by Vice-Admiral Raymond A. Spruance. The main offensive element of this was the Fast Carrier Task Force, led by Vice-Admiral Marc A. Mitscher. Other air support came from the US Army's 7th Air Force, commanded by Major-General Willis H. Hale, operating from the Ellice Islands group. For landing operations, Nimitz had some 100,000 men, plus all their transports and the supply facilities necessary for far-flung operations.

The first objectives for the Central Pacific drive were the Gilbert and the Marshall Islands groups, whose capture would provide real estate for the airfields required for the air forces which would provide support for the next step forward. These two large groups of tiny atolls were

from Henderson Field on Guadalcanal. This was yet again a direct result of US cryptanalysis, in this instance of the itinerary of Yamamoto's tour of inspection. Yamamoto was succeeded by Admiral Mineichi Koga, who lacked the strategic genius and popularity of his predecessor.

Throughout the first nine months of 1943, Nimitz built up his forces and planned his campaign. With the return of Vice-Admiral Halsey's 3rd Fleet from the Solomon Islands in June, Nimitz was able to assemble the greatest naval force ever created, which constantly grew until the end of the war. The main striking force

to be taken in two phases: November 1943 for the southern part (Makin, Tarawa and Apamama in the Gilberts), and late in January and early in February 1944 for the northern part (Eniwetok, Kwajalein and Majuro in the Marshalls). The landing forces had little idea what they were up against, for every major islet fringing each atoll had been heavily fortified, and was defended by first-class troops.

Makin and Tarawa were to be assaulted on 20 November, and for a week before had been saturated with bombs and naval gun fire which, unknown to the attackers, made almost no impression at all. Deep within their coral, concrete and coconut-log bunkers, the Japanese were safe from anything but a direct hit, but waited for the inevitable assault. Makin fell to the 165th Regiment of the 27th Division on 23 December, but its 600 defenders had held up the Americans for far too long to suit Major-General H.M. 'Howling Mad' Smith, commander of the V Amphibious Corps. All of the 250 combat troops were killed, and the 100 prisoners were all Korean labourers.

craft that could crawl over reefs and onto the shore. These emerged as LVTs (landing vehicles tracked), which were armoured and tracked amphibious personnel carriers and tanks. The southernmost of the Gilbert Islands, Apamama, fell quickly on 21 November.

The Japanese Combined Fleet had no aircraft and could only lie impotently at anchor in the Truk lagoon.

Kwajalein was defended by some 8,000 men under Rear-Admiral Monzo Akiyama. The 7th Division landed and overran the island during 1–4 February. The 4th Marine Division took other islands in the group. The lessons of Tarawa had been well-understood, and the Americans suffered only 372 dead and about 1,000 wounded out of some 41,000 men landed. All but 230 of the Japanese defenders were killed. Majuro

LEFT: A Japanese tank is knocked out by the 77th Infantry Division at Yigo, Guam.

BELOW: Japanese prisoners-of-war on Guam. It was only in the fighting for the Mariana Islands that the US forces began to take more than the smallest handfuls of Japanese prisoners.

By comparison with Tarawa, however, Makin was a simple task. Rear-Admiral Keiji Shibasaki had some 4,700 seasoned troops, and formidable defences including 8-in (203-mm) guns and 400 pillboxes and bunkers. Reconnaissance had not revealed the presence of an inner reef, on which most of the landing craft had been grounded, forcing the men of the 2nd Marine Division to wade hundreds of yards through a curtain of fire. Their losses were appalling. The marines were then trapped on the beaches, and 1,500 of the 5,000 men landed had become casualties by nightfall. Reinforcements in the next two days suffered comparable losses, but gradually the marines forced the defenders back. The last pocket of Japanese resistance was overwhelmed on 23 November, by which time the Americans had lost 985 men killed and 2,193 wounded. The Japanese lost all but about 100 taken prisoner, of whom only 17 were combat soldiers. In the long run, however, the Central Pacific forces benefited from their experience on Tarawa, having learned the tactics necessary and seen the need for landing

RIGHT: A US flamethrower in action on Kwajalein atolls in the first days of February 1944.

BELOW: Truk, in the Caroline Islands group, was a vital centre for the protection of the Japanese defence perimeter in the central Pacific, and the Combined Fleet was often based in its great lagoon. Truk was therefore a primary objective of attacks by US warplanes. On 17–18 February 1944 Vice-Admiral Marc A. Mitscher's Task Force 58 (five fleets and three light carriers with battleship and cruiser support) attacked Truk, where the lagoon accommodated some 50 merchantmen, protected by three light cruisers and eight destroyers as well as 350 land-based aircraft.

had been occupied on 30 January, but the islets of the Eniwetok atoll were to prove another tough nut to crack. On 17 February two battalions of the 22nd Marine Regiment came ashore on Engebi, at the north of the atoll, and met little resistance; but on 19 February two battalions of the 106th Regiment met very determined and fierce resistance when they landed on Eniwetok atoll itself. Only after two days of heavy fighting was this little area of coral declared secure. Two battalions of the 22nd Marine Regiment encountered similar opposition on Parry Island, when they landed on 22 February, and it took a day's hard fighting to crush the Japanese. This sterling defence had been mounted by Major-General Yoshima Nishida's 1st Amphibious Brigade, an experienced unit some 2,200 strong. The

Americans suffered some 339 dead, but all the Japanese were killed. Flamethrowers proved particularly effective in assaulting bunkers.

Mitscher's carriers had meanwhile struck at Truk on 17–18 February. Although Koga managed to escape with the Combined Fleet, the US carrierborne aircraft sank 200,000 tons of merchant shipping and destroyed 275 aircraft on the ground. Koga retired from Truk as a permanent base in favour of anchorages in the Philippine Islands group. On 1 April Koga was killed in an accident, and was succeeded as commander-in-chief of the Combined Fleet by Admiral Soemu Toyoda.

Late in May 1942, as part of their deception plan for the Midway operation, the Japanese had sent a force north against the Aleutian Islands group off the coast of Alaska. The task of Vice-Admiral Boshiro Hosogaya's Northern Area Force of two light aircraft carriers, seven cruisers and 12 destroyers was to establish bases in the Aleutians, in the islands toward the western end of the chain. Once again as a result of cryptanalysis, the USA

one light cruiser and four destroyers. The Battle of the Komandorski Islands was a long-range gun duel in which the US cruiser *Salt Lake City* was crippled and the Japanese cruiser *Nachi* were very seriously damaged. As the Japanese closed in for the kill, however, three of the US destroyers also closed in for a torpedo attack, forcing Hosogaya to turn away for home.

Rear-Admiral Thomas Kinkaid, commanding in the North Pacific, ordered Rear-Admiral Francis Rockwell to land the 7th Division on Attu to clear out the Japanese. This landing went in on 11 May, and after 18 days of fighting in appalling terrain and bitter weather Attu was declared secure. Only 29 of the 2,500 Japanese defenders were captured, and the Americans lost 561 dead and 1,136 wounded. On 15 August a joint Canadian and American force landed to fulfil a

LEFT: US marines in the fighting for Garapan on the western side of Saipan Island, in the Marianas group, during mid-June 1944.

BELOW: Men of the US Marine Corps land on Saipan on 15 June 1944. The vehicle (left) in an amphibious tractor (amtrak), the type of armoured and tracked landing craft and assault vehicle which proved so successful in the Pacific campaign's later operations, especially when fitted with a tank turret carrying a short-barrel howitzer for close-support fire.

was able to lay its plan in adequate time, and Nimitz detached about one-third of his forces to protect the Aleutians. Hosogaya managed to outmanoeuvre Rear-Admiral Robert Theobald's force, however, and twice shelled Dutch Harbour, much to the embarrassment of the Americans, before retiring westward to establish bases on Kiska and Attu on 6 and 7 June respectively. Air support for the garrisons of Kiska and Attu was provided by land-based aircraft operating out of Paramushiro, the most northerly of the Japanese-owned Kurile Islands, that lay to the south of the tip of Kamchatka.

There was no compelling military need for Nimitz to eject the Japanese from his Northern Pacific Area other than injured US pride, caused by Japanese occupation of American soil. Nevertheless, the decision to do this was taken in 1943. On 26 March, Hosogaya was convoying reinforcements to the islands with two heavy and two light cruisers, as well as four destroyers, when he fell in with Rear-Admiral Charles McMorris's force of one heavy cruiser,

THE DEFEAT OF JAPAN

A British infantryman of the 14th Army on patrol in Burma during 1944.

similar function on Kiska, but found that the Japanese had gone. The 4,500 defenders had in fact been lifted off a fortnight earlier, when the Japanese high command realized that the sacrifice of the garrison would serve no purpose.

THE SECOND ROUND OF THE WAR IN BURMA

In 1943 the Allies strongly desired to take the war back to the Japanese, but lacked the means to do so in a major way, despite the fact that the Japanese position, at least in theory, was weak. The 'Greater East Asia Co-Prosperity Sphere' had expanded with great speed and to a very large extent, and was, in

theory, ripe to be pricked and deflated. The Japanese armed forces were fully committed to one major land campaign in China and another in the Pacific, so only a small fraction of the Japanese army faced the British-Indian forces to the west in Burma, Lieutenant-General Joseph W. Stilwell's Chinese Army in India to the north, and the many Chinese armies to the east.

Unfortunately for the Allies, the best Indian divisions had already been despatched to the Middle East, and those available in India were low in morale and required training for jungle warfare. The majority of the Chinese armies were useless, and only the Chinese Army in India (CAI) was in any position to fight in any effective manner. Stilwell was determined to get to grips with the Japanese as soon as possible, but the British generals were equally determined to resist taking the offensive until they had trained their men to fight the Japanese effectively. In this respect the dismal defeat of the first offensive in the Arakan coastal region of Burma had strengthened this resolve. In January 1943 three brigades of the Indian 14th Division were advancing with great difficulty along the Arakan coast toward the port of Akyab. The Japanese resistance was light, but it was the terrain which provided the greatest difficulty: mountains, roadless jungles, mangrove swamps and tidal creeks made movement immensely slow and difficult, and the men and animals were more than decimated by the region's diseases.

There was also the oddness of engaging in combat with the Japanese, who at times would attack with phenomenal courage and great tactical skill, but at others preferred to dig themselves into bunkers, impervious to all but the heaviest artillery shells, holding the bunkers until the very last individual Japanese had been killed. Even a reversion to the methods of a previous century and digging in a 3.7- in (94-mm) howitzer to blast the bunker at close

range over open sights failed, although it did pave the way to the bunker-busting techniques, using tanks and guns, that were perfected at a later date.

For six weeks the Indian 14th Division, reinforced with brigade after brigade, tried unsuccessfully to break through. Then, when the men of the attackers were exhausted, the Japanese counter-attacked, the Allied resistance broke, and the whole force, badly shaken, returned to India.

Another threat to the Japanese appeared 600 miles (965km) away to the extreme north of Burma. The CAI had been created by Stilwell from the remnants of the Chinese divisions he had led on foot out of Burma in 1942, together with new units flown from China. These had been collected at Ramgarh, in Bihar, and trained on US lines under Stilwell's direction. The training was undertaken on a 'conveyor-belt' system, in which squads of hundreds of men learned to aim and fire their weapons on a strict schedule with a minimum of frills. These squads were then grouped in companies and battalions for training under their own Chinese officers. The battalions were all-Chinese, and Stilwell commanded them via advisers and liaison officers at the regimental and divisional levels. Stilwell's greatest problem was the Chinese system of dual command, ordered by Generalissimo Chiang Kai-shek, who interfered constantly by signal, always on the side of urging caution and obstructing Stilwell's orders for offensive action. Stilwell's task was to drive the Japanese south and so clear the way for a new road through northern Burma for the movement of munitions and supplies to the Chinese, now cut off by land and sea and being expensively supplied by air. With the newly-organized 38th Division leading, the CAI started south on 28 February 1943.

The Japanese were content at this time to remain on the defensive in Burma, but this was a defence of the

active type. In northern Burma Lieutenant-General Shinichi Tanaka's 18th Division was deployed in a 100 mile (160km) long series of outposts from a point to the south of Ledo to Fort Hertz, but Tanaka nonetheless made local attacks and administered some sharp jolts to the intruders. Such was the prestige of the Japanese and their aggression that the British-Indian outpost garrisons were soon retreating north and the Chinese 38th Division of General Sun Li-jen was halted. Primarily the military adviser and chief-of-staff to Chiang Kai-shek, Stilwell felt he had to take command of the CAI in the field, and after a great deal of persuasion managed to get it creeping forward in December: even when compared with the rest of Burma, the Patkai hills and the Hukawng valley were appallingly difficult areas in which to live, let alone stage an offensive.

Tanaka was deterred from exploiting his easy successes in the north by the unexpected intrusion of the Indian 77th Brigade of British and Gurkha troops into northern Burma from 8 February 1943. This had infiltrated, largely undetected, across the Chindwin river, which was then the line of contact between the British in Assam and the Japanese in what was no ordinary raid.

Brigadier Orde Wingate had been ordered to study the possibilities of warfare behind the enemy lines by Field-Marshal Sir Archibald Wavell, the commander-in-chief in India. On the basis of the guerrilla methods he had already tested in Ethiopia, Wingate had already evolved the concept of 'long-range penetration' using scattered company-strong columns controlled by radio and supplied from the air. These columns could move through the jungle, using it as a covered approach for attacking vulnerable Japanese rear areas.

Operation Longcloth had been intended as part of a combined British and Chinese offensive, but when this was cancelled Wingate persuaded Wavell to let him go ahead alone, in order that his new strategy and novel methods of training troops on guerrilla lines could be fairly tested in battle. By no purely objective military criterion could this first Chindit experiment be judged a success, for all the courage and self-sacrifice shown by the troops, who accepted that no sick or wounded could hope to be evacuated. All went fairly well at first: some successful skirmishes were fought against the Japanese and the railway to the north was cut. Wingate, whose intentions were never clear, even in his own mind, then rashly moved into an

area where his force was in grave danger of being trapped. He extricated part of it by the expedient of abandoning all his heavy weapons and animals, and dividing his men into small parties. However, part of his force did not receive the order to withdraw and failed to return: the survivors suffered terrible hardships from fatigue, starvation and disease. Of the original 3,000 men, some 800 failed to return and of the survivors only 600 were fit for further active operations. But when the public learned that for three months a commando-type force had been at large and on the rampage behind the lines of the apparently invincible Japanese, there was an enormous uplift in morale.

Wingate's message was simple and its effects were far-reaching. For the British it was that the Japanese could be defeated, and for the Japanese that the jungle could be penetrated and the Chindwin front was now vulnerable. The Japanese now began to think less about the defence of Burma and more about attack, and began the planning that was to lead them to Imphal and Kohima.

LEFT: By a time early in 1944, the British, Indian, Gurkha and commonwealth soldiers, fighting the Japanese in Burma, had lost their fear of the Japanese jungle fighters, and had learned to stand and fight even if their lines of communication had been cut or severed.

BELOW: Even when cut off, as happened during the Battle of Imphal, the British and commonwealth troops could be assured of the air delivery of sufficient food, ammunition and other essentials.

THE DEFEAT OF JAPAN

The battle for Peleliu, in the Palau Islands group, lasted from 15 September to 25 November 1944, and cost the US forces 2,336 men killed and 8,450 wounded, while the Japanese lost 10,695 men killed and 202 taken prisoner. This is the wreckage of a Japanese tank, it turret ripped off by an internal explosion.

CENTRAL PACIFIC SUCCESS

With the Gilbert and Marshall Islands groups taken, and the Aleutian problem being solved, Admiral Chester W. Nimitz, commander-in-chief of the Pacific Ocean Areas and of the Pacific Fleet, focussed on his next Central Pacific objective, the Mariana Islands group, in the spring of 1943. These are of rock rather than coral, and offered a different set of problems for the assaulting land forces. The three main islands to be taken were Saipan, Guam and Tinian, and it was decided to attack them in that order. The primary strategic objective of the undertaking was the capture of land areas large enough for the creation of the bases from which the long-range bombing of Japan could be effected, using the new Boeing B-29 Superfortress four-engined heavy bomber. Working on the basis of pre-war maps and aerial reconnaissance photographs, US Army Air Force engineers calculated that they could build an enormous complex of airfields on the islands, sufficient to allow the war to be taken to Japan in a major way.

The targets in the Marianas were softened on 11–12 June by a visit from Vice-Admiral Marc A. Mitscher's Fast Carrier Task Force, and some 200 Japanese aircraft and many merchant ships were caught and destroyed in this initial sweep. Vice-Admiral Richmond K. Turner's V Amphibious Force of 530 ships, and the 127,000 men of the III and V Amphibious Corps, commanded by Major-Generals H.M. Smith and Roy S. Geiger respectively, arrived off the islands on 15 June, after steaming from the rendezvous point of Eniwetok.

Commanding in the Marianas was Vice-Admiral Chuichi Nagumo, commanding the Central Pacific Area Fleet, which had no ships. Nominally in command of the land forces, constituted by the 31st Army, was Lieutenant-General Hideyoshi Obata. At the time of the American invasions Obata was away in the Palau Islands group, so command of the ground forces was undertaken by the senior commander on each island.

After a feint attack on Mutcho Point, on the centre of Saipan's west coast, by reserve regiments of the V Amphibious Corps, the real attack was delivered on each side of Afetna Point, farther to the south, by Major-General Thomas E. Watson's 2nd Marine Division and Major-General Harry Schmidt's 4th Marine Division to the north and south respectively. Both landings were strongly contested by the forces of Lieutenant-General Yoshitsugo Saito. Although American intelligence had estimated that there were 20,000 Japanese on Saipan, Saito had 25,469 army troops and 6,160 naval personnel. By 18 June the Americans had reached the eastern coast of the island before turning north and south to crush the halves of the Japanese defence into the ends of the island. The 27th Division, commanded by Major-General Ralph C. Smith, had been committed on 17 June, which did little to speed up the pace of the US advance.

The Japanese southern pocket at Nafutan Point was soon contained by a single battalion of the 27th Division and was destroyed on 28 June, the rest of the division having been ordered to line up between the two marine divisions for the northward advance, scheduled for 23 June. Fighting to a different set of tactical precepts, the army division soon fell behind the more probing marine divisions, and Howling Mad Smith precipitated a major inter-service argument, by replacing Ralph Smith with Major-General George W. Griner. The problem was not Ralph Smith, but

assumed command of what was left of the defence.

The two marine formations landed north and south of the Orote peninsula, on the western side of the island, during 21 July, with the 77th Division following the 1st Provisional Marine Brigade later in the day. Fighting was again severe, but not as hard as it had been on Tinian. The halves of the corps linked up in a good beach-head on 22 July and then turned north to the capital of Agana and on to the tip of the island at Ritidian and Pati Points. As on Saipan, the Japanese defended with great courage, launching counter-attacks when they were able, but were slowly driven back. The end of the organized resistance came on 10 August on Mount Machanao, at the north-west tip of the island. US casualties totalled 1,919 dead and 7,122 wounded, but the Japanese total was as usual far higher at 17,300 dead and 485 taken prisoner.

This left only Tinian to be secured, the invasion of which was scheduled for 24 July. The assault was undertaken by

LEFT: Mail call for men of the US Marine Corps on Tinian Island in the Marianas group on 30 July 1944, just two days before the end of organized Japanese resistance on the island.

BELOW: A Japanese tank, destroyed by men of the US Army's 77th Infantry Division near Yigo on Guam Island in the Marianas group.

rather the differences in tactical doctrine that existed between the US Army and US Marine Corps. After heavy fighting, by the end of the month the three divisions had reached a line running roughly across the island from Garapan on the west coast. The 2nd Marine Division was pulled out of the line as the advance continued to move into a narrower part of the island. By 7 July the Japanese position was desperate, and Saito issued orders for a last suicidal counter-attack from Makunsha. Beaten back with great loss by the 27th Division, this marked the end of the road for the Japanese. Although US progress had been slowed by the absence of tactical air support, as a result of Mitscher's departure for the Battle of the Philippine Sea with his Task Force 58, the Japanese were finally crushed by 9 July. Rather than surrender, hundreds of civilians killed themselves by jumping off the cliffs at Marpi Point. The Japanese troops suffered some 27,000 dead, but 2,000 were taken prisoner, while the US forces suffered some 3,126 dead and 13,160

wounded, most of them marines. Both Saito and Nagumo committed ritual *seppuku* to avoid capture.

Guam was next on the objective list, and was to be taken by the 3rd Marine and 77th Divisions, commanded by Major-Generals Allen H. Turnage and Andrew D. Bruce respectively, as well as the 1st Provisional Marine Brigade, led by Brigadier-General Lemuel C. Shepherd, of Geiger's III Amphibious Corps. Command of the Japanese forces on this largest of the Marianas had been entrusted to Lieutenant-General Takeshi Takeshima, the commander of the 29th Division, although only one regiment of the division was present on the island. In all, Takeshima had some 13,000 soldiers, and some 5,500 naval personnel were commanded by Captain Yutaka Sugimoto. It should be noted that Obata had hurried back from the Palau Islands on learning of the US landings on Saipan, but had been able to proceed no farther than Guam. He left the command arrangements as they were, but when Takeshima was killed on 28 July,

the 2nd and 4th Marine Divisions, commanded by Watson and Major-General Clifton B. Cates respectively, of the V Amphibious Corps, now commanded by Major-General Harry Schmidt since the elevation of H.M. Smith to the post of Commanding General, Fleet Marine Force, Pacific. The 27th Division was in reserve after its hard time on Saipan. Although the senior commander on the island was Vice-Admiral Kakuji Kakuda, commander of the 1st Air Fleet, tactical command was exercised by Colonel Kaishi Ogata of the 50th Infantry Regiment. Ogata had some 4,700 army personnel, with Captain Goichi Oya leading the 4,110 personnel of the 56th Naval Guard Force.

While the 2nd Marine Division launched a feint towards Tinian town in the south-west of the island, the 4th Marine Division landed on two tiny beaches on the north-west tip of Tinian, early on 24 July, meeting only relatively light resistance. The 2nd Division then arrived from its feint, landing across the same beaches. The two divisions fought off an ineffectual night counter-attack, and on the following day moved off to the south, the 2nd Division on the left and the 4th Division on the right. Progress was steady, and by 28 July the two divisions had taken half the island. The Japanese were gradually penned up in the south-east of the island, and the final assault went in on 31 July, with all organized resistance ending on 1 August. As usual, Japanese losses had been very heavy (6,050 men killed and 235 taken prisoner) compared with the marines' loss of 290 dead and 1,515 wounded.

With the three islands secured, the engineers arrived with their equipment to start work on the great airfield complexes needed for the air side of a three-pronged strategic offensive against Japan: air attacks on industry from bases in China and the Marianas; submarine attacks on shipping, especially tankers to starve Japan of raw materials and oil; and the combined land and sea offensive to

retake Japan's conquests and invade the home islands if necessary. B-29 operations from the Marianas started on 28 October with a raid on Truk, but soon great numbers of these strategic heavy bombers were winging their way to Japan from the Marianas.

With his Central Pacific offensive complete, Nimitz could turn his attention once more to the debate on the best route by which to approach the Japanese home islands. Both he and MacArthur, the main protagonists of the two different schools of thought, attended the conference in Hawaii during July, at which President Franklin D. Roosevelt made his decision. The fall of the Marianas and their defeat in the Battle of the Philippine Sea had the result, in Japan, of bringing about the fall of Lieutenant-General Hideki Tojo's government on 18 July, to be replaced by a slightly more realistic one under General Kumaki Koiso.

THE BATTLE OF THE PHILIPPINE SEA OR THE 'GREAT MARIANAS TURKEY SHOOT'

In March 1944 the Americans set in motion their operation to capture the Marianas so that airfields could be built for the Boeing B-29 Superfortress heavy bombers which were to attack and cripple industry and transportation in the Japanese home islands. But the Marianas were also a useful staging post for Japanese ships and aircraft in transit between the home islands and the south-west Pacific, and therefore featured strongly in Japanese strategic thinking. The Japanese naval forces were commanded by Admiral Soemu Toyoda, with the 1st Mobile Fleet led by Vice-Admiral Jisaburo Ozawa and comprising five battleships, nine carriers and 13 cruisers. Toyoda was certain that the next American thrust would be to the south, so he and Ozawa planned to use a decoy force to lure the Americans from the Marshall Islands group toward Ulithi in the Caroline Islands group or

alternatively to the Palau Islands, from which they could be attacked by aircraft. But somehow the Japanese ships had to be kept out of reach of the US carrierborne warplanes. The Americans had a fast carrier force of seven fleets and eight light carriers, carrying 700 fighters and nearly 200 bombers. In addition, the US invasion forces would be covered by escort carrier groups, carrying more than 300 fighters and bombers. The Japanese could muster more than 600 aircraft in the Marianas and western Carolines and, furthermore, were able to reinforce them by flying in fresh aircraft from the home islands via Iwo Jima.

To preserve their carriers the Japanese therefore planned to stay out of the reach of US carrierborne aircraft but within the range over which their own carrierborne warplanes could attack: they would hit the US carriers which, according to the plan, would already have been damaged by Japanese land-based aircraft, land on Guam to refuel and rearm, and attack the US carriers for a second time on their way back to their carriers. But the Japanese aircraft were basically inferior to those of the Americans at the technical level, and were flown, moreover, by completely indifferent crews, whereas the American air groups were composed of experienced and confident aircrews, with hundreds of replacements on the way.

On 6 June 1944 Vice-Admiral Mitscher's Task Force 58 left the lagoon of the Majuro atoll in the Marshall Islands, and five days later its warplanes made the first sweeps over Guam, Saipan and Tinian. The Americans reported enormous successes, but their intelligence had underestimated the numbers of shore-based aircraft, making them mistaken in their belief that they had wiped out the Japanese defenders. A heavy bombardment of Saipan started on 13 June, followed by the landing of 20,000 men two days later. As soon as the Japanese were certain that the attack was not a diversion, Ozawa was given

would be able to draw the greater weight of the US attack, so leaving his five carriers intact for a decisive blow against Spruance.

Thereafter matters began to go awry for the Japanese. During the evening of 18 June Ozawa imprudently broadcast an appeal to the shore-based air forces for a maximum effort on the following day: US high-frequency direction-finding stations picked it up, passing a fairly accurate estimate of Ozawa's position to the 5th Fleet during the same evening. Spruance reacted with his customary caution and refused to close at once, but he did order TF 58 to strike against the Guam air forces to make certain that Ozawa would get no support from that quarter.

On the following morning Ozawa's carriers began the first strikes against the 5th Fleet, but just after the Japanese flagship *Taiho* had flown off aircraft for the second wave she was torpedoed by the submarine *Albacore*. The brand-new 30,000-ton carrier was in no danger of sinking from a single hit but the blast

LEFT: The M1 carbine was developed as an intermediate-power weapon for the use of second-line troops and those needing to carry other equipment, but its light weight, small size and adequate short-range stopping power soon made it attractive to men fighting at close quarters with the Japanese. These are men of the 22nd Marine Regiment, three of whose battalions took Parry Island in the Kwajalein atoll complex on 22–23 February 1944.

BELOW: The US Army's 77th Infantry Division fought on Guam Island in the Marianas group. This photograph was taken on 26 July 1944 as the division advanced across to and then north along the eastern side of the island.

the order to sail. On 13 June he left Tawitawi in the Sulu Islands archipelago, with the giant battleships *Yamato* and *Musashi* among other ships. Unfortunately for him, a lurking US submarine reported the departure of the fleet, while another spotted it emerging from the San Bernadino Strait into the Philippine Sea on the evening of 15 June.

Admiral Raymond A. Spruance, commanding the US 5th Fleet, was kept informed of the expected attack, and wisely postponed the landing on Guam to allow the transports to be kept well clear of the battle area. Leaving only a force strong enough to cover the Saipan invasion, Spruance concentrated his ships about 180 miles (290km) to the west of Tinian, for he was determined not to be lured away until he knew the whereabouts of the main Japanese fleet. Ozawa, for his part, was confident that his plan was going well, for he had kept out of range of the US carrierborne warplanes, and his own aircraft had reported the position of the US force. On the night of 18–19 June Ozawa divided his force into an advance guard under Vice-Admiral Takeo Kurita, with four battleships and

three medium-sized carriers, keeping the main force of six carriers under his own command. He hoped that Kurita's force, some 100 miles (160km) ahead of him,

had ruptured her aviation fuel lines, the ventilation system allowing lethal fumes to permeate the entire ship. All that was needed was a spark to send a series of explosions ripping through the ship; to make matters worse, an improperly refined grade of oil was being carried as furnace fuel, which also produced inflammable vapour. When it exploded it blew the bottom out of the engine room, and most of the 1,700 men aboard *Taiho* died with her in the holocaust.

Ozawa suffered another disaster about three hours later when the submarine *Cavalla* put three torpedoes into another of his carriers, the *Shokaku*, which soon sank to leave Ozawa with only four carriers. Meanwhile, the air attacks on the 5th Fleet were not going as well as hoped. Most of the bombers and torpedo-bombers had been detected on radar and intercepted before they got within range of their targets. But the later strikes gave the Americans a close shave. The battleship *South Dakota* was hit by a 551-lb (250-kg) bomb and a damaged torpedo-bomber crashed into the side of her sister, *Alabama*; two carriers were damaged by bombs and several more escaped damage by good luck and frantic manoeuvring. More than 50 Japanese aircraft had got through the screen, and would have produced impressive results in the hands of more experienced pilots.

The Mobile Fleet launched four strikes, totalling nearly 400 aircraft with the shadowing reconnaissance aircraft. Losses ran to 243 aircraft, a further 30 or more returning with serious damage. By the following day the surviving seven Japanese carriers had only 68 fighters and 32 bombers still operational. The aircraft based on Guam had been wiped out, with 52 destroyed on the ground, 58 shot down and many more seriously damaged. In contrast, the US Navy had lost only 30 aircraft, six of them by accident rather than in action. But the most grievous loss of all was in aircrew. Over 400 Japanese died, whereas the Americans were able to save 17 out of the 44 aircrew shot down.

The Americans found that the scale of attacks had swamped their fighter-direction capability, and it became hard to distinguish between friendly and hostile radar contacts. Under the stress of protracted combat the US pilots tended to forget the need for radio discipline, and the controllers had difficulty in getting through top-priority messages concerning enemy attacks.

Early in the afternoon of 19 June Ozawa turned north-west to refuel his ships, but Spruance contented himself with recovering his aircraft and continued on a westerly course. Spruance had no accurate idea of Ozawa's movements, but did not order the night search which might have produced some information. Next morning, at first light, reconnaissance revealed nothing, and a special long-range search was sent too far north of Ozawa's position to achieve anything of importance. Nothing was known until mid-afternoon, by which time the Mobile Fleet was 300 miles (480km) away. This meant that any attack would require the returning aircraft to land in darkness, and few of the US pilots had been trained in this difficult technique. But Mitscher did not hesitate to order an attack, and by 16.30 85 Grumman F6F Hellcat fighters, 77 Curtiss SB2C Helldiver dive-bombers and 54 Grumman TBF Avenger torpedo-bombers were airborne.

The US warplanes reached the Mobile Fleet in fading light, and between 18.40 and 19.00 committed themselves in a series of co-ordinated attacks. The defending fighters, about 40 Mitsubishi QA6M Reisen Zero machines, fought with skill and determination: they managed to hold off the Hellcats and broke into the large US formations. In spite of being outnumbered the Zeros succeeded in shooting down six fighters and 14 bombers, but were so heavily outnumbered that they lost 25 of their own number. The carrier *Hiyo* was hit by aircraft from the *Belleau Wood* and sank. Ozawa's flagship, the veteran *Zuikaku*,

was set on fire by several bomb hits, and the *Junyo* was hit by a single bomb from one of the *Lexington*'s aircraft. The smaller carriers, *Chiyoda* and *Ryuho*, were also damaged, as were the battleship *Haruna* and the heavy cruiser *Maya*, but Ozawa was able to extricate his force and return to Okinawa without further loss.

The Americans paid a heavy price for making their attack at such a distance. The desperately weary pilots and observers, many of whom had been in combat throughout the day, had to fly back as night fell. As their fuel gauges approached the 'empty' mark, pilots looked for a friendly warship near to which they could ditch. For those who managed to land on their carriers there were still the hazards of a night-landing, and many crashes resulted. Mitscher ignored the risk of giving his position away to any lurking Japanese submarines by switching on the deck landing lights in order to give his aircrew a chance of survival. Some 80 aircraft were lost through lack of fuel or landing accidents, but the escorting destroyers were fortunately able to rescue 160 out of the 200 aircrew forced to ditch in the sea.

The 5th Fleet was angry and frustrated by its failure to destroy Ozawa's entire Mobile Fleet, and many felt that Spruance's caution had robbed them of a decisive victory. The disaster of the *Taiho* went unnoticed, and if the US Navy had known that three and not two fleet carriers had been sunk, feelings might not have run so high. On the Japanese side there was no such doubt about the decisiveness of the victory, and Ozawa offered his resignation. Another large part of Japanese air power had been wiped out with virtually nothing to show for the sacrifice.

The Philippine Sea and the Mariana Islands were now under US control, a prerequisite for the invasion of the Philippine Islands group, and the Japanese defensive perimeter had been badly breached. The performance of the US Navy's submarines had been remarkable, not only in the combat role when sinking two carriers, but in the less glamorous job of reporting the passage of the Mobile Fleet at two vital moments. In retrospect the only doubt about the Battle of the Philippine Sea can be over Spruance's failure to locate Ozawa on the night of 19 June. Had that happened it would have been possible to have struck earlier on the following day.

THE BATTLE OF LEYTE GULF

As with the US landings in the Marianas, the Japanese planned a bold response to any US invasion of the Philippine Islands group, which in the event was a descent on Leyte on 20 October 1944. But this time there was a difference, for the Japanese leadership had finally begun to admit the possibility of defeat, and was planning a final gamble in a desperate attempt to retrieve Japan's fortunes.

The plan had been carefully constructed by the staff of Admiral

Soemu Toyoda, commander-in-chief of the Combined Fleet, and involved almost all of the surface fleet as well as the surviving carriers, with a decoy force to lure away a sizeable part of the US fleet and three other surface forces to smash their way through to the invasion beaches to destroy the invasion fleet with gunfire. The Japanese forces were therefore divided into four parts. The Main Body or Northern Force, under Vice-Admiral Jisaburo Ozawa, comprised the fleet carrier *Zuikaku*, the three small carriers *Chitose*, *Chiyoda* and *Zuiho*, two battleships converted into hybrid battleship carriers but without aircraft, three cruisers, and eight destroyers. Force A or Centre Force, under Vice-Admiral Takeo Kurita, comprised the super-battleships *Yamato* and *Musashi*, the battleships *Nagato*, *Kongo* and *Haruna*, 12 cruisers and 15 destroyers. Force C or the Southern Force was divided into a Van Force under Vice-Admiral Shoji

Nishimura and a 2nd Striking Force under Vice-Admiral Kiyohide Shima, and comprised the old battleships *Yamashiro* and *Fuso*, four cruisers, and eight destroyers.

ABOVE: Ground crew and brother pilots salute a pilot about to take off for a kamikaze mission in his obsolescent Mitsubishi A6M Reisen Zero fighter, carrying heavier-than-standard bombs.

LEFT: The cruiser Birmingham *eases up to the light carrier* Princeton, *which was hit by a kamikaze warplane off Leyte, in the Philippine Islands group, sinking on 24 October 1944.*

ABOVE: US aircraft carriers come under Japanese air attack during the Battle of Leyte Gulf.

RIGHT: Left essentially naked of aircraft and aircrews as a result of the Combined Fleet's earlier losses, the fleet carrier Zuikaku *was part of the Japanese decoy force in the Battle of Cape Engano, within the Battle of Leyte Gulf, and was sunk on 25 October 1944. The other three carriers, which the Japanese lost in the same battle, were the light carriers* Chitose, Chiyoda *and* Zuiho.

Although the Southern Force had the same objectives, its two admirals were responsible to different superiors, a division of command which was to prove disastrous. The Northern Force had the task of steaming south from Japan toward the Philippines, with the sole object of luring Admiral William F. Halsey's Fast Carrier Task Force away from the invasion area in Leyte Gulf: Ozawa's task was thus to accept casualties in order to make certain that the other three groups could have a free hand in sinking the invasion fleet. Kurita's Centre Force was to steam from Borneo through the San Bernardino Strait to Leyte Gulf, where it would link with the two halves of the Southern Force which had fought their way through the Surigao Strait between Leyte and Mindanao. This massive concentration of ships would then fall on the huge fleet of transports lying helpless off the invasion beaches.

For once the US Navy's submarines did not detect the Japanese movements,

and Ozawa's departure from the Inland Sea on 20 October went unnoticed, with the result that he was not yet functioning properly as a decoy. But submarines did

spot Kurita's force passing Palawan three days later, and the *Darter* succeeded in sinking his flagship, the heavy cruiser *Atago*, and damaging her sister the *Takao*. The *Dace* sank a third heavy cruiser, the *Maya*, giving the Japanese plan a poor start. Part of Shima's force was also sighted and that night Kurita's force was seen in the Mindoro Strait. However, the watching submarines still failed to report the whereabouts of Ozawa's decoy force. The US Navy acted on the assumption that such major Japanese forces must be on their way to Leyte Gulf through the Surigao Strait, with Halsey disposing his forces accordingly. Vice-Admiral Marc A. Mitscher's Task Force 38 was divided into four groups, and three of these were stationed 125 miles (200km) apart in the area to the east of the Philippine Islands. Task Group 38.3, under Rear-Admiral Forrest C. Sherman, was the most northerly, located off central Luzon, with four carriers, two battleships and four light cruisers. Task Group 38.2, under Rear-Admiral G.F. Bogan, had three carriers, two battleships and three light cruisers, and

or north-east. The result was that the Central and Southern Forces were sighted by noon, making for the San Bernardino and Surigao Straits, but the Northern Force was still undetected. Halsey prudently ordered his three task groups to concentrate, taking the precaution of ordering the fourth group, Task Group 38.1, under Vice-Admiral J.S. McCain, back from its refuelling position 500 miles (800km) to the east. In the meantime, however, TG 38.3 was attacked by shore-based aircraft, which succeeded in damaging the light carrier *Princeton*. While other ships were trying to help the blazing carrier, Ozawa launched his aircraft against them, but the raw pilots had great difficulty finding their targets. Although Ozawa had only about 30 aircraft left after his fruitless attack on TG 38.3, this hardly affected the plan, his purpose being to attract attention to himself. At last Halsey ordered a search to the north, the direction from which the attack had come, but of course Sherman's task

LEFT: The light carrier Belleau Wood *was hit by a kamikaze aircraft but survived.*

BELOW: A Japanese destroyer explodes after a bomb from an attacking US warplane had penetrated into its forward magazine and detonated the stored ammunition.

was off the San Bernardino Strait. To the south, off Samar island, was Task Group 38.4 under Rear-Admiral R.E. Davison, with two fleet carriers, two light carriers, one heavy cruiser and one light cruiser. Halsey's flagship, the battleship *New Jersey*, was with Bogan's Task Group 38.2 to the north. This was

the most powerful fleet assembled during the entire war, but it could still be caught off balance if the intentions of the Japanese were misunderstood.

At dawn on 24 October Halsey ordered air searches from Lingayen, on the west side of Luzon, down to the north of Mindanao, but not to the north group was under heavy air attack and could not comply until about 14.00. It was 16.40 before the American reconnaissance aircraft found the Northern Force, by which time it was 190 miles (305km) away to the north-north-east, too far away for an attack.

Kurita's Centre Force was all the while under heavy attack from US carrierborne aircraft. After incessant attacks the 64,000-ton *Musashi* was hit by some 20 torpedoes and slowly became unmanageable. The heavy cruiser *Myoko* was also badly damaged, but Kurita's force had not otherwise been hit. Nevertheless, he decided to reverse course for a while to escape further attacks and to wait until he received confirmation that the Americans had swallowed the bait. Halsey obliged by concluding that the Centre Force had been so severely mauled as to be no longer a threat to the 7th Fleet, which was covering the invasion in Leyte Gulf. Acting on that assumption he declared that Ozawa's force was the main Japanese force, ordering all his battleships and carriers to make pursuit. The trap had been sprung. The US staff organization now compounded the error. At 15.12 on 24 October Halsey sent a message to his forces indicating his intentions of forming a new task force of battleships and carriers to stop Kurita's Centre Force off the San Bernardino Strait. This was only an intention, but it was read by Vice-Admiral Thomas C. Kinkaid of the 7th Fleet and others to mean that the force had already been formed, leading them to assume that the exit was guarded. In fact no ships at all were guarding the strait, and there was nothing standing between Kurita and the invasion fleet.

To the south, Nishimura's force was heading steadily toward the Surigao Strait, where the 7th Fleet had been alerted to the danger. The old battleships under Rear-Admiral Jesse B. Oldendorf, which had been detailed for shore bombardment in association with the landings, were warned at 12.00 to prepare for a night engagement. Unfortunately, the battleships had only a small proportion of armour-piercing ammunition, and had already used half their high-explosive projectiles against the Japanese beach defences. The cruisers and destroyers were also low on ammunition. But Oldendorf's captains remained confident they could hold their own in a night action as a result of their efficient radar and fire-control systems.

Just after 22.36 on 24 October the Van Force of the Southern Force was detected by a Mindanao PT-boat patrol, followed by the Rear Force at a distance of about 30 miles (50km). The PT-boats attacked as the two Japanese forces steamed up the strait, firing 34 torpedoes, but only one hit was obtained on a light cruiser. By 02.00 Shima and Nishimura were still progressing well, but came under destroyer attack about an hour later. This attack damaged the *Fuso* and *Yamashiro*, each of which was struck by a single torpedo. Neither ship suffered major damage, but three of the four Japanese destroyers were sunk or badly damaged. A second destroyer attack was then committed, its torpedoes hitting the *Yamashiro* for a second time and sinking a destroyer. At 03.49 the battleship *Fuso* blew up after a succession of torpedo hits, breaking in two and drifting off to the south. The flagship *Yamashiro* seemed indestructible, for she took another two torpedoes at about 04.11 without stopping. The US were using classic destroyer tactics, in which they completely shattered the Japanese formation, leaving only the *Yamashiro*, the cruiser *Mogami* and a single destroyer to face Oldendorf's six battleships. In fact the destroyer attacks were still in progress as the head of the Japanese line came into range of the US battleships and cruisers, which were crossing the 'T' of the Japanese advance and could therefore all pour a withering fire onto the *Yamashiro*. The Japanese battleship was soon ablaze from stem to stern. The *Mogami* escaped by a miracle, but the *Yamashiro* capsized at 04.19, taking most of the crew down with her. Seeing the destruction that had overtaken the other ships, Shima turned about in an attempt to avoid the same fate, losing only one destroyer in the process, but when daylight came his ships were subjected to heavy air attacks, which at last accounted for the *Mogami*.

While Nishimura was being annihilated in the Surigao Strait battle, Kurita seemed to be in sight of victory. Not until 04.12 on 25 October was any check made as to whether or not the San Bernardino Strait was guarded, and even then an answer from Halsey was not available until 06.45. Then the escort carriers learned the news that they were practically within gun range, for at 06.55 the *Yamato* opened fire on them with her 18.1-in (460-mm) guns at a range of 29,965 yards (27400m). Despite the fact that these small carriers were almost defenceless, with their aircraft carrying only light bombs and their hulls lacking all armour protection, they fought heroically and ultimately successfully against Kurita's ships. The screening destroyers sacrificed themselves to save the carriers, and only the *Gambier Bay* was sunk, at a cost of three US destroyers. Baffled, the Japanese withdrew to the north, just as it seemed to the Americans that they were going to brush through the limited opposition they could put up, and so get to the invasion fleet. Kurita's change of plan was probably caused by the strain of incessant attack, coupled with his lack of adequate intelligence. He was aware that Nishimura's forces had been wiped out, and was also worried about his fuel supply. But whatever the cause, it was a golden opportunity thrown away, having been the finest Japanese chance since Pearl Harbor to inflict a major defeat on the US Navy. After more aimless manoeuvres, Kurita withdrew at midday.

Kurita was harried by US carrierborne aircraft, but it was Ozawa who was the target of Halsey's full wrath. The aircraft of the US carriers sank the carriers *Zuikaku*, *Zuiho* and *Chiyoda*. This was later called the Battle of Cape Engano, and marks the end of the series of titanic battles which, collectively, are known as the Battle of Leyte Gulf. In terms of tonnage and numbers of ships involved it was the greatest sea battle in history, and achieved the virtual extinction of the Imperial Japanese navy. The Japanese had come close to victory, although more as a result of US mistakes than their own skill. Had the US commanders made use of the intelligence at their disposal, the Centre Force would have been stopped sooner and the Northern Force would have been dealt with as well.

THE US FORCES INVADE LEYTE

In July 1944 the USA had the difficult problem to face of what to do next in the Pacific. General Douglas MacArthur favoured an assault on the Philippine Islands group and thence Japan, while Admiral Nimitz considered that the US

forces should now move toward an invasion of Formosa or of a Japanese-held part of China before the final assault on the Japanese home islands. President Franklin D. Roosevelt had to

decide between the two options, whose protagonists argued their cases at a conference held at Pearl Harbor in July. Roosevelt finally came down on the side of MacArthur, and Nimitz, despite having lost the argument, committed his planning staffs wholeheartedly to the task of co-ordinating army and navy plans for the Philippines operation: MacArthur's forces would take Mindanao, the southernmost large island of the Philippines group, while Nimitz's forces took Yap Island in the Caroline Islands group as an advanced base. The two forces would then combine for the assault on Leyte, and finally as MacArthur went on to take Luzon, the main island of the Philippines, Nimitz would take Iwo Jima and Okinawa, farther to the north, as the bases for the final landings on Japan itself.

First of all the two commanders set about securing themselves adequate forward bases. On 15 September men of the US Amy landed on Morotai Island, in the northern part of the Halmahera Islands group in the Moluccas, secured the island against scant Japanese opposition and set about building an

ABOVE: Rocket-firing landing craft saturate the Japanese beach defences with high explosive just before men of the US 6th Army start to land during 20 October 1944 on the eastern side of Leyte Island, the first of the Philippine Islands group to be liberated from the Japanese.

LEFT: Supported by a mass of warships, US landing craft and amtraks are lined up ready for the run into the assault beaches on Leyte Island on 20 October 1944.

opposition, and soon became the US 3rd Fleet's main base.

To support the Morotai and Peleliu operations by diverting the attention of the Japanese, the aircraft carriers of Admiral Halsey's 3rd Fleet had struck at targets in the Palaus, Ulithi and Yap on 6 September, but had met with little opposition. Halsey then moved north against targets in the Philippines during 9–13 September. Yet again there was minimal opposition, so Halsey informed Nimitz that the landings planned for Yap and Mindanao were unnecessary, and that the target date for Leyte should be brought forward. The Joint Chiefs-of-Staff Committee agreed, and with Nimitz's offer of the loan of the III Amphibious and XXIV Corps, MacArthur was able to bring forward the Leyte operation from 20 December to 20 October.

The landings on Leyte were preceded by the usual naval operations to suppress Japanese air power. During 7–16 October Halsey's warplanes had

ABOVE: Men of the US 6th Army land on Leyte Island.

RIGHT: General Douglas MacArthur and staff land at Palo beach on Leyte Island during 20 October 1944. As he had promised in 1942, he and his men had returned to liberate the Philippine Islands.

airfield. On the same day US Marines of Major-General Roy S. Geiger's III Amphibious Corps landed on Peleliu, where they encountered resistance as determined as any met by the US forces in World War II. The defence of Peleliu, under the capable leadership of Colonel Kunio Nakagawa, meant that the island was secured by the Americans only on 13 October, after each side had suffered heavy losses. The last vestiges of the fighting finally ended on 25 November, by which time the army's 85th Division had been brought in to reinforce Major-General W.H. Rupertus's 1st Marine Division. Meanwhile, army troops of Geiger's immediate superior, Vice-Admiral Theodore Wilkinson, of the III Amphibious Corps, had taken Angaur, at the extreme southern tip of the Palau Islands group, during 17–20 September, and the vast atoll of Ulithi, some 100 miles (160km) to the west of Yap. The last was taken without

WORLD WAR II

struck at Okinawa's airfields before turning to do the same at Formosa. Here, however, two of his cruisers were damaged, and Halsey took the considerable gamble of using them as a decoy for the Japanese air forces, which rose to the bait and were decimated by Halsey's aircraft. These fast carrier sweeps cost Japan some 650 aircraft and their irreplaceable aircrew. Just as significantly, most of the warplanes had been the replacements for those lost in the Battle of the Philippine Sea, sent to Formosa from Japan by Admiral Soemu Toyoda, commander-in-chief of the Combined Fleet. Japan's carriers were now almost naked of aircraft. Halsey's success off Formosa was complemented by the success of three formations of the US Army Air Forces, namely the 5th AAF from New Guinea, the 7th AAF from the Marianas and the XX Bomber Command from China, all of which launched major raids at Japanese targets within their ranges.

All was now ready for the Leyte invasion by Lieutenant-General Walter Krueger's 6th Army. During 14–19 October, the 700 ships of Vice-Admiral Thomas C. Kinkaid's 7th Fleet moved Krueger's 200,000 men from their advanced bases toward Leyte. The two attack forces, the VII Amphibious Force under Rear-Admiral Daniel E. Barbey, and the III Amphibious Force under Vice-Admiral Theodore S. Wilkinson, were supported by the six battleships of Rear-Admiral Jesse B. Oldendorf, which were able to lay down a formidable volume of heavy gunfire to aid the land forces, and by the aircraft operating from the 16 escort carriers of Rear-Admiral Thomas L. Sprague's Task Group 77.4. Providing long-range support and protection were the eight fleet carriers, eight light carriers and six battleships of Halsey's 3rd Fleet. As usual, all of these naval forces were provided with ample cruiser and destroyer support. The one blemish in the otherwise excellent organization for the Leyte operation was

a measure of divided command, MacArthur controlling the 6th Army and 7th Fleet, and Halsey the 3rd Fleet. Still smarting from their failure to sink all the Japanese carriers involved in the Battle of the Philippine Sea, the men of the 3rd Fleet had the primary function of seeking out and destroying the Japanese fleet should the occasion arise, the secondary function being the covering of the Leyte operation. This was to have nearly disastrous consequences in the Battle of Leyte Gulf.

To defend the Philippine Islands group, General Tomoyuki Yamashita had the 14th Area Army of 350,000 men. But to cover the possible landing areas and to keep the active Filipino guerrilla movement in check meant that these troops had to be spread over a wide area.

On Leyte there was only the 16th Division, commanded by Lieutenant-General Shiro Makino, totalling only 16,000 men. This was part of Lieutenant-General Sosaku Suzuki's 35th Army, entrusted with the defence of the southern Philippines.

The landings took place on 20 October against minimal opposition. The 1st Cavalry and 24th Divisions of Major-General Franklin C. Sibert's X Corps landed in the area just to the south of Tacloban on the eastern side of the island, and the 96th and 7th Divisions of Major-General John Hodge's XXIV Corps slightly farther south, in the area of Dulag. By midnight on the first day, 132,500 men and nearly 200,000 tons of supplies had been landed. The Americans quickly pressed on inland

US solders display captured Japanese flags.

A man of the British 14th Army reports the results of a reconnaissance effort in Burma during 1944.

before the Japanese could strengthen their defences. Part of the 16th Division had established a beach-head on each side of the Juanico Strait, between Samar and Leyte, by 24 October. By 30 October, the US forces occupied most of the north-eastern corner of the island, as far west as Carigara on the north coast, and in the west as far as the lower slopes of the central mountain chain as far south as Burauen, although the front line was only lightly held. MacArthur, and President Sergio Osmena of the Philippines, came ashore on 22 October.

By 30 November the Americans had pushed further forward, but Suzuki had moved into Leyte. As the 16th Division fought stubbornly to delay the US forces, Suzuki would ship in another 45,000 men and 10,000 tons of supplies before 11 December, when all Japanese ship movements to Leyte were halted. Progress into the mountains was virtually halted, and heavy rain made movement extraordinarily difficult. The X Corps edged slowly toward Limon and Pinamopoan, on the north coast, by means of land and amphibious advances,

and by 7 November the XXIV Corps tried unsuccessfully to take the mountains overlooking the main Japanese base of Ormoc, on the west coast, against superb defence by the 16th and 26th Divisions. The Japanese defence was finally outflanked on 7 December when the US 77th Division was landed just south of Ormoc. Limon and Ormoc both fell on 10 December, and forces from north and south met at Libungao on 20 December. The Japanese were now cut off from their one remaining port, Palompon, to which a few sailing vessels were still operating. Organized Japanese resistance ended on 25 December, but mopping-up operations against the starving Japanese continued for some time. A beach-head on Samar had already been secured, and on 15 December a US brigade landed on the island of Mindoro to start building an airfield for the forthcoming Luzon operations. By the beginning of 1945 the Americans had secured Leyte, the southern tip of Samar, and enclaves on the south and west coasts of Mindoro. Japanese losses up to this time exceeded 70,000, those of the Americans being 15,584.

THE BATTLES OF KOHIMA AND IMPHAL

Lieutenant-General Renya Mutaguchi's Japanese 15th Army crossed the Chindwin river early in March 1944, with every man carrying enough ammunition and food for three weeks, a supply train of 3,000 horses and 5,000 oxen, and 17 mountain guns carried on 10 elephants. The Japanese objective was Imphal, the great logistical base the British were creating for the liberation of Burma. With enemies on three sides building, the Japanese leadership in Burma now believed that a passive posture was too dangerous. The best course, and one suited to the Japanese temperament, was to knock out the nearest opponents. It was a huge gamble, because there were no roads or bridges between Burma and Assam, and victory had to be won while

the supplies lasted. The Japanese, however, had spotted the weakness in the widely dispersed British positions. Although Mutaguchi had only three divisions, he was able to choose the points to strike. In February a limited offensive in the Arakan had drawn the reserves of Lieutenant-General William J. Slim's 14th Army to that area. Mutaguchi believed it would be a month at least before the 14th Army could be reinforced in Assam. He was to be proved wrong: the British flew in reinforcements and supplies in days, but Mutaguchi's utter defeat resulted not only from the Allies' superior air power, armour and artillery, but also from the capacity of the British, Indian and Gurkha infantry, over a period of four months, to take on and defeat the Japanese in close combat, which had hitherto been a particular speciality of the Japanese.

The Battle of Imphal is, of course, simply a label for a whole series of battles fought from 15 March to 22 June. Hitherto the Japanese had seemed invincible, but the retraining of the British and Indian troops had not merely improved tactics and weapon skills, but had also unleashed courage and devotion fully equal to coping with the Japanese. The medical services had also greatly reduced losses from tropical diseases.

When the battle began the British had drawn back from 20 to 50 miles (32–80km) from the Chindwin river, watching the barrier with army patrols and an observation corps of tribesmen (called V Force), organized by British officers. The closest point of the railway from India to Jorhat in the far north-east was Dimapur, and from here the only supply route was the road through Kohima, a small settlement on a ridge providing a natural defensive position, to Imphal, a valley about 15 miles (24km) wide, overlooked by mountains rising to 6,900ft (2100m). Here the roads from Kohima, Sangshak, Tamu and Tiddim met, as well as a smaller road from Bishenpur to Silchar which also gave

the defence with such details as could be gleaned from reinforcement camps and logistic units. The initial dispositions of the IV Corps were, in any case, for an advance, not a defence. They were very vulnerable to an aggressive foe, such as the Japanese, who had the initiative and could strike wherever they chose. When the excellent British intelligence system began in February and March to receive evidence that the Japanese were about to launch a full-scale offensive, plans had to be made to form a solid defensive ring round Imphal. This meant pulling in the outlying units, but not too fast: they had to delay the Japanese in order

LEFT: The wreckage of the district commissioner's bungalow, scene of some of the most savage fighting in the Battle of Kohima, itself one of the bitterest fights of World War II.

BELOW: A Gurkha soldier moves up toward a Japanese position. Throughout World War II, the Gurkhas showed themselves to be magnificent fighting men, especially in close combat.

access to Imphal. Road in the context of this area is a purely nominal term, for these surfaces were unmetalled and only just motorable until the military engineers improved them. Troops moving by road could be blocked or ambushed, while movement through the jungle up and down the dense forest on the mountain slopes was painfully slow.

Imphal was therefore a strategic centre of communications. Three airfields, two of them capable of all-weather operations, had been constructed, and the area included dumps of supplies and ammunition of all kinds, the headquarters of the IV Corps, commanded by Lieutenant-General G.A.P. Scoones, and a garrison for the Indian 23rd Division. Two other

formations were also in the area, the Indian 17th Division around Tiddim and the Indian 20th Division around Tamu. The 2nd Division, which reinforced Kohima, was British. Because of the width of the front and the nature of the country, the three Indian divisions were each spread over some 40–50 miles (65–80km). Imphal is 130 miles (210km) from Dimapur and 90 miles (145km) from Kohima, and the 17th Division was 160 miles (255km) south and the 20th Division 80 miles (130km) to the south-east. There was nothing except V Force and a battalion of the Assam Rifles between Homalin, where the right-flank division of the Japanese was to cross the Chindwin, and Kohima, where Colonel H.V. Richards had been sent to organize

THE DEFEAT OF JAPAN

British troops in the wreckage of Kohima after the Japanese had been driven back.

to allow the mass of civilian labour, working on the roads and in the depots, to be removed to safety, but they were not to tangle with the Japanese too closely and become pinned down.

The real danger was in the north, or the British left. The great weakness of the IV Corps' position was that its supply lines did not come from rear to front but along the front from left to right. If the Japanese were to take or bypass Kohima, cutting the railway at Dimapur, not only the IV Corps but also Lieutenant-General Joseph W. Stilwell's Chinese divisions would be starved to death. British intelligence suggested that the biggest force that could come by this roadless northern route was a regiment. In fact a nasty shock was in store: the whole of the Japanese 31st Division arrived at Kohima, cutting the road between there and Dimapur.

The Japanese tactics, which so far had proved successful against the British, were simple and effective: they would encircle the opposition, establishing road blocks of bunkers behind, the brigades thus trapped being either caught between two fires, or being forced to leave the road in panic, seeking to escape through the jungle, abandoning all their guns, equipment and vehicles in the process. The Japanese now discovered, however, that this was no longer the pattern of events. The 14th Army had a new spirit. If cut off, its units and formations stood to fight until they had prevailed or were relieved, and if they could not be supplied by road they were nourished from the air. All the logistics units had been taught to do the same. This the Japanese had yet to find out, although they could have taken warning from the beating they had taken in Arakan in February.

The Japanese, accordingly, spread their effort: their 33rd Division against the 17th Division, 15th Division against the 23rd Division, two separate columns from the 33rd and 15th Divisions reaching for the 20th Division, and the 31st Division against Kohima.

At first the situation as seen by Slim looked very dangerous. Elements of all three of his divisions were cut off and had to fight their way out with some loss, while a Japanese force appeared in the heart of the Imphal base and seized the commanding height of Nunshigum. The Kohima garrison was cut off, and the Japanese then blocked the road behind the relieving brigade. Once again it seemed that the Japanese would succeed in routing their opponents. Stilwell, who had a very low opinion of 'limeys' and their fighting ability, was very alarmed: halting his own operation, he offered Slim a Chinese division to protect Dimapur and the railway, on which he and his large engineer force, building the road, entirely depended. Slim, however, and his chiefs, General Sir Henry Giffard and Admiral Lord Louis Mountbatten, were steadfast. Stilwell's offer was politely refused and he was told to get on with his own operation. To the surprise of the Japanese the Indian 5th Division, which had been drawn into the Arakan fighting as they had planned and should have been a month's journey away, was flown in complete with its artillery to Imphal. The 5th Division won the Battle of Nunshigum. The Indian 50th Parachute Brigade, sent hastily to Sangshak, was cut off but stood and fought until ordered to break out, thus giving Scoones invaluable days to rearrange his defences. The British 2nd Division was sent to break through to Kohima and open the road to Imphal. The Japanese here made the fatal mistake of fighting tooth and nail for the Kohima ridge: had they bypassed it and made a dash for Dimapur, things might have turned out badly for the British, for a long delay might have starved out the Imphal garrison.

The course of events seemed very slow, as always in jungle warfare, but Scoones was tightening his defences and fought battle after battle, slowly going over to the offensive. On 4 June Mutaguchi ordered Lieutenant-General Kotoku Sato to pull his 31st Division back from Kohima, and shortly after this his 15th Army collapsed, only fragments of it managing to stagger back across the Chindwin, weakened by starvation and disease, and leaving behind 30,000 dead.

THE US ARMY CLEARS THE PHILIPPINES

The clearance of the last Japanese resistance on Leyte by the end of 1944 opened the way for the assault on Luzon, the main island of the Philippines group, where General Tomoyuki Yamashita and the majority of the men of his 14th Area Army were located. Yamashita had some 260,000 troops under his command, and these he divided into three main groupings to defend the key areas of the island. Yamashita himself and 152,000 men formed the 'Shobo' Group in the north of the island; Lieutenant-General Rikichi Tsukada and 30,000 men formed the 'Kembu' Group in the Bataan peninsula area; and Lieutenant-General Shizuo Yokoyama and 80,000 men were

the 'Shimbu Group', entrusted with the task of holding the rest of the island, including Manila, the capital. Yamashita appreciated that once the Americans had landed he could expect no reinforcements and therefore decided on a slow defensive campaign, the intention being to tie down as many US troops as possible for as long as possible. With only 150 operational aircraft he could not hope to contest mastery of the air, even at the outset of the campaign, therefore *kamikaze* suicide aircraft were to be used against the US invasion fleet approaching the landing areas, thus giving the pilots as many targets as possible. The US forces would be allowed to land without opposition, as Yamashita thought it unwise to risk his forces in the presence of overwhelming US air and naval gunfire support, and the Japanese would pull back slowly to the inaccessible mountains, where strong defensive positions had been prepared so that the Japanese soldiers could sell their lives as expensively as possible. The Japanese commander had no intention of being drawn into a costly street battle for Manila, and on the whole his plans were sound.

The US plan was also simple. Lieutenant General Walter C. Krueger's 6th Army had some 200,000 men, and

ABOVE: Men of the US Army's 40th Infantry Division in action on Panay Island in the Philippines group. Only part of the division was used, this landing on the south coast at Iloilo on 18 March 1945.

was to be convoyed from Leyte to Lingayen Gulf, 100 miles (160km) north of Manila, on the west coast, by the 850 vessels of Vice-Admiral Kinkaid's 7th Fleet. As at Leyte, Vice-Admiral Oldendorf's battleship force was to provide heavy gunfire support, while long-range cover and air support would come from the aircraft carriers of Admiral Halsey's 3rd Fleet and from the airfields on Leyte, now occupied by the aircraft of General George C. Kenney's Far East Air Forces. After landing, the 6th Army would advance south across the central plain of Luzon to Manila and its magnificent harbour. Other forces would spread out to engage the Japanese wherever they could be found.

The invasion fleet left Leyte Gulf on 2 January 1945 for Lingayen Gulf, where the landings were to take place on 9 January. Although the *kamikaze* aircraft did not achieve the results for which the Japanese had hoped, many warships were severely damaged and the escort

LEFT: Men of the US 6th Army start to land at Lingayen Gulf on Luzon, the main island of the Philippines group, on 9 January 1945. At first the Americans met only limited resistance as the Japanese commander, General Tomoyuki Yamashita, wished to preserve as much as possible of his 14th Army for a protracted defence.

THE DEFEAT OF JAPAN

General Tomoyuki Yamashita surrenders the remnants of his 14th Army on 2 September 1945, after the end of World War II. The surrender was taken by two ex-prisoners-of-war, Lieutenant-General Jonathan Wainwright, who had surrendered the last US forces in the Philippines on 6 May 1942, and Lieutenant-General A.E. Percival, who had surrendered the British and commonwealth forces in Singapore on 15 February 1942.

carrier *Ommaney Bay* was so badly damaged that she had to be abandoned. On 7 January, however, the Americans launched a series of major raids against Japanese airfields on Luzon, and the Japanese aircraft which escaped destruction were flown to Formosa. It was a sad tactical error on the part of the Japanese, the main damage by the *kamikaze* aircraft having been done to warships rather than the more vulnerable and important troop transports.

On 9 January the 6th Army started to pour ashore at Lingayen: on the left was Major-General Innis P. Swift's I Corps of the 6th and 43rd Divisions, and on the right Major-General Oscar W. Griswold's XIV Corps of the 37th and 40th Divisions. By nightfall, the 68,000 men of

the two corps were well placed in a beach-head 17 miles (27km) wide and 4 miles (6.5km) deep. The XIV Corps was to advance to Manila, while the I Corps on the left flank dealt with any Japanese interference from the Shobo Group. Swift's corps found the Japanese prepared positions very tough, and Griswold was unwilling to advance very far until the I Corps had cleared his left flank. But by 23 January, the XIV Corps was in the area of Clark Field, where it was involved in a week of heavy fighting before it could move on yet again.

Lieutenant-General Robert L. Eichelberger's 8th Army had assumed responsibility for the southern islands of the Philippine archipelago when the 6th Army sailed north for the Luzon

campaign, but it was now decided to use this to help Krueger's formation. On 30 January, therefore, Major-General Charles P. Hall's XI Corps landed in the Subic Bay area, seizing Olongapo before moving off east to Danilupihan, which fell on 5 February, completing the isolation of the Kembu Group in the Bataan peninsula. Yamashita had foreseen this possibility, however, and refused to have major forces locked up in the peninsula as had been the case with the Americans in 1942. So before the pincers of XIV and XI Corps closed at Danilupihan most of the Kembu Group had reached temporary safety to the north-east. Even so, the XI Corps had two weeks of costly fighting before it, clearing the remnants of the Japanese group from Bataan on 21 February.

The other 8th Army formation used on Luzon was the 11th Airborne Division, commanded by Major-General Joseph M. Swing. On 31 January, two regiments of the division were landed at Nasugbu, south of Manila, moving quickly inland. The third regiment was dropped on Tagaytay Ridge farther inland, on 3 February, encountering only small-scale resistance before linking with the rest of the division, which then moved north toward Manila, which was reached on the following day.

Although ordered by Yamashita not to defend the city, Rear-Admiral Mitsuji Iwafuchi and 18,000 fanatical naval troops decided to make a last stand. The 37th Division drove down from the north into the city, while the 1st Cavalry Division moved around the east of Manila to link up with the 11th Airborne Division. Casualties on both sides were appalling, and by 22 February the Japanese had been driven back into the old walled town, where they made their last stand. Manila was almost totally destroyed in the fighting, the Japanese having fired great sections of streets as a defensive measure. By the end of the battle on 4 March, some 100,000 Filipino civilians, at least 16,665 Japanese, and

1,000 Americans had been killed, with another 5,500 Americans wounded. Manila was only half the prize, however, for the harbour in Manila Bay could not be used until the Japanese garrisons on Corregidor and Fort Drum had been eliminated. An amphibious assault and airborne landing on Corregidor, on 16 February, were followed by severe hand-to-hand fighting before the island was declared secure on 27 February. Some 4,417 Japanese dead were found, and only 19 prisoners were taken. US losses were 209 killed and 725 wounded. Fort Drum fell quickly on 13 April, after fuel oil and petrol had been poured into its ventilators and set on fire, incinerating the entire Japanese garrison. A landing was made on Caballo Island during the same day, but did not fall for two weeks, whereas Carabao Island fell without a fight.

By the middle of May the southern half of Luzon had been cleared, but Yamashita was still fighting an excellent campaign in the mountains of the north. For the rest of the war the Americans tried in every way they could to flush the Japanese out, but in the end were content to keep them bottled up in the Cordillera Central and Sierra Madre. When he surrendered at the end of the war, Yamashita still had 50,000 disciplined men. Yet the Luzon campaign had cost the Japanese 192,000 dead and just under 10,000 captured in combat, compared with fewer than 8,000 US dead and 33,000 wounded.

As the 6th Army was reducing Luzon, the 8th Army was involved in clearing the southern Philippines, defended by the remaining 100,000 men of Lieutenant-General Sosaku Suzuki's 35th Army. Between February and August the 8th Army was involved in some 50 amphibious landings. Normally the pattern was similar: the US forces landed and the Japanese pulled back into the interior of the island in question, where they were mopped up by local Filipino forces once the US forces had secured their main objectives and pulled out for the next landing. The exception to this rule was Mindanao, where Suzuki had two good divisions. A series of US landings on the north, south and west coasts, with all forces pushing on into the centre of the island, led to the 35th Army being cut off, but it nonetheless held out in two major groups in the east of the island for the rest of the war. The 8th Army's campaign had cost 2,556 US dead and 9,412 wounded but, as usual, Japanese losses were much higher, being some 50,000 in all.

THE IWO JIMA AND OKINAWA CAMPAIGNS

The fall of the Philippines sealed the fate of Japan, largely as Japanese shipping could no longer move between the home islands and the rich Southern Resources Area for raw materials and oil. The Americans, however, were still to face serious problems in their final approach to the Japanese home islands, principally from fanatical Japanese defence on the islands of Iwo Jima and Okinawa. The capture of these was to be one of the three final preparatory phases to the invasion of Japan proper, the other two being the destruction of what was left of Japan's merchant fleet by the US submarine force, and the destruction of Japan's industrial potential by Boeing B-29 Superfortress heavy bombers, operating from China and the Marianas.

Iwo Jima is a small volcanic island 4.67 miles (7.5km) long by 2.5 miles (4km) wide, and of considerable

BELOW LEFT: Men of the 5th Marine Division are pinned down on the black volcanic sand of Red Beach, at the southern end of the US landing on Iwo Jima on 19 February 1945.

BELOW: Soldiers of the US Marine Corps and the 'stars and stripes' on top of Mount Suribachi, the highest point of Iwo Jima, on 23 February 1945.

ABOVE: A US marine wastes as little time as possible as he operates in the 'Death Valley' area of Iwo Jima.

RIGHT: The US forces which landed in Okinawa on 1 April 1945 were two corps, one comprising two US Army divisions and the other two US Marine Corps divisions. These are US marines, who were involved in some notably savage combat in the area.

significance despite its miniscule size. Lying at the foot of the Bonin Islands chain, south of the main Japanese island of Honshu, Iwo Jima was a great asset to the side which controlled it: in Japanese hands, aircraft were able to operate from its two airfields to attack Boeing B-29 Superfortress heavy bombers, operating from the Mariana Islands group against Japan, and in US hands the airfields could be used as emergency landing fields for crippled bombers, and also as bases for long-range escort fighters to protect the bombers over Japan itself. At this time the Japanese were also building a third airfield.

Fully conscious of the island's importance, the Japanese were determined to prevent Iwo Jima from falling into US hands. Lieutenant-General Tadamichi Kuribayashi had under his command some 22,000 men from army and navy combat units. For months these men had been honeycombing the northern plateau with strongpoints, gun emplacements and other bomb- and gunfire-proof positions. Kuribayashi realized this type of defence would limit him to static operations, but

saw that there could be no alternative in so small an area and in the face of overwhelming US matériel superiority.

The US assault was preceded by the most intense softening process yet seen in the Pacific war, with more than two months of incessant bombing, followed before the landings by a continuous three-day barrage by six battleships and their supporting forces. Under the overall command of Admiral Nimitz in Hawaii, the assault force was under the local command of Admiral Spruance's 5th Fleet: the 3rd and 5th Fleets were in fact the same ships, the former designation used when Admiral Halsey commanded and the latter when they were led by Spruance. The land force commander was Lieutenant-General Holland M. Smith, the assault force itself being Lieutenant-General Harry Schmidt's V Amphibious Corps of three US Marine divisions.

The landings were made on 19 February 1945, and were met with determined and accurate Japanese fire as the vast pre-landing bombardment had, inevitably, failed to crush the Japanese defences. The landing area was a black volcanic sand beach on the south-eastern side of the island, the landing forces being Major-General Keller E. Rockey's 5th Marine Division on the left and Major-General Clifton B. Cates's 4th Marine Division on the right, with Major-General Graves B. Erskine's 3rd Marine Division remaining at sea as a floating reserve. Despite some 2,420 casualties, the marines made good progress, cutting the island in two by the end of the first day. The next day, part of the 5th Marine Division turned south to assault the dominating heights of Mount Suribachi, at the southern tip of the island. As usual, the Japanese defence was unflinching, and it was not

until the morning of 23 February that the US flag was hoisted on the summit of the volcano.

The 4th Marine Division, meanwhile, was making slow progress toward the north, fighting every inch of the way through the elaborate and well-concealed Japanese defences. Elements of the 3rd Marine Division came ashore to aid the 4th Marine Division on 21 February, with the rest of the division landing two days later. Thereafter, all three divisions of V Amphibious Corps began to creep forward a few hundred yards every day, the 5th Division on the left, the 3rd in the centre and the 4th on the right, supported the whole way by the guns and aircraft of the 5th Fleet. Vastly superior US strength had its effect, and the Japanese were driven steadily north before the marines. By 11 March Kuribayashi's last survivors had been penned up in an area around Kitano Point, Iwo Jima's northernmost extremity. But it was only on 16 March that the island was declared secure, and on 26 March that the last Japanese resistance ceased.

The Marine losses were 6,891 dead and 18,070 wounded; of the Japanese, almost the entire garrison, as a mere 212 prisoners, was taken. Yet the value of the island was proved when 16 crippled B-29s landed safely on the island. By the end of the war, it has been estimated, the lives of 24,761 aircrew had been saved, 2,251 B-29s having been able to land on the island in emergencies.

The final stage of the advance toward Japan was to be the conquest of the Ryukyu group, a tail of islands stretching south from Japan itself. Okinawa is the largest island in the chain, some 60 miles (95km) long and between 2 and 18.5 miles (3 and 30km) wide, with a considerably varied terrain. Virtually unknown outside Japan before the war, Okinawa was a difficult problem for the US planners, about which reconnaissance aircraft had been unable to secure good information. It was estimated that the

garrison numbered about 65,000 men, with the main defensive area likely to be in the southern third of the island, where its four airfields were located. In fact, Okinawa was garrisoned by the 130,000 men of Lieutenant-General Mitsuru Ushijima's 32nd Army, and there were also 450,000 civilians on the island. Ushijima had been ordered to hold the island at all costs: it was expected by the Japanese high command that *kamikaze* attacks on the US fleet during the landing would be decisive, the losses in ships being sufficient to force the Americans to withdraw, enabling the 32nd Army to mop up any forces that had landed. Ushijima elected to fight the same sort of campaign as Yamashita in Luzon: he would attempt to hold the strategically important southern end of the island from a great complex of fortifications built into the hills, thus compelling the US forces to mount a costly series of frontal assaults in order to break through his defences. Despite the hopes of the high command, Ushijima had no illusions of being able to hold the Americans on the beaches should the *kamikaze* attacks fail.

As at Iwo Jima, the responsibility of getting the troops to Okinawa and protecting them once they had landed was allocated to Spruance's 5th Fleet, with the Joint Expeditionary Force led by Vice-Admiral Richmond K. Turner. The land operations were to be the job of Lieutenant-General Simon Bolivar Buckner's 10th Army of 180,000 men, with ample reserves held in New Caledonia and other islands farther to the north of this southern base. The beach area selected for the landings was just to the north of Hagushi Bay, on the western side of the island. Two corps were to land in the first wave: the 6th and 1st Marine Divisions of Major-General Roy S. Geiger's III Amphibious Corps on the left, and the 7th and 96th Divisions of Major-General John B. Hodge's XIV Corps on the right. As the island was beyond the range of US land-based

tactical air support, the 10th Army and the invasion fleet would be wholly reliant on the carrierborne warplanes of Vice-Admiral Marc A. Mitscher's Fast Carrier Task Force (Task Force 58) and the four British carriers of Vice-Admiral Sir Bernard Rawling's Task Force 57. Unfortunately for the Americans, Okinawa lay within range of Japanese aircraft from Formosa and Japan.

Scheduled for 1 April, the main landings would be preceded by the usual intense bombardment and the capture of a number of subsidiary targets in the area as forward bases. On 26 March, the 77th Division, under Major-General Andrew D. Bruce, was landed in the Kerama Islands group, some 20 miles (32km) south-west of the main beaches on Okinawa, to secure them as a fleet anchorage. Little resistance was met, and the capture of a large number of suicide boats was enough to ease the minds of the naval command. On 31 March, the 77th Division moved forward to capture the Keise Islands group, only 10 miles (16km) from the main assault area, as a heavy artillery base for the support of the III and XIV Corps. During the same period, the carrier forces ranged over the area trying to neutralize the Japanese *kamikaze* aircraft, of which some 193 had been dispatched, the US and British destroying 169 of them. Those that got through, however, inflicted heavy losses on the US carriers, which were lacking the armoured flight decks of the British vessels. Nonetheless, the carrier activities had destroyed part of Japan's *kamikaze* potential that might otherwise have been used against the more vulnerable invasion fleet.

The vessels carrying the invasion force, some 300 warships and 1,139 other ships, had meanwhile approached Okinawa, and the four assault divisions went ashore without opposition on 1 April, securing a good beach-head for the 60,000 men who landed on the first day. A feint attack by the 2nd Marine Division against the south-east coast

THE DEFEAT OF JAPAN

Fitted with the turret of the M8 self-propelled gun, with its 2.95-in (75-mm) short-barrel howitzer, and carrying sand bags for additional protection along the tops of their hulls, these LVT(A)4 amtraks are heading for the assault beaches on Okinawa.

helped to distract the attention of the 32nd Army as the main force landed. The next day the two corps set about their allotted tasks. The III Amphibious Corps turned left, where it encountered little resistance in securing the northern two-thirds of the island by 13 April. This was a reversal of Buckner's earlier decision to leave the clearance of the north until after the main Japanese positions in the south had been overrun. The last organized resistance in the north was finally overcome on 20 April on the Motobu peninsula, although many Japanese escaped into the hills to wage a guerrilla campaign against the Americans. While the 6th Marine Division undertook this task, Buckner had also changed his mind regarding another earlier decision, and now ordered the 77th Division to take the island of Ie Shima, where there were 2,000 Japanese troops and a labour force, so that airstrips could be built for tactical support warplanes. The division landed on 16 April, securing the western half by the end of the day. But it was to be a bloody eight days before the rest of the island could be overrun.

Back in the south, the XIV Corps had been having a far rougher experience. After pushing through to the east coast, across from the landing areas on the west coast by 3 April, the corps had turned right as the III Amphibious Corps turned left. As yet little opposition had been met, but the few prisoners taken revealed the reason for this: the 32nd Army was waiting in the south, and the real battle had yet to begin. On 4 April, XIV Corps reached the Machinato Line, the US divisions pressing on slowly against strengthening resistance before being brought to a halt by 12 April.

Ushijima's plan was proceeding as intended, but the Japanese commander then deviated with costly results. The Japanese 24th and 62nd Divisions launched a two-day counter-offensive, which the US forces repelled with heavy losses. A temporary lull settled over the southern battlefield on 14 April as both sides rested and reassessed the situation. His frontal assaults having failed, Buckner now determined to launch a surprise attack by the 27th Division, previously the army's floating reserve. The attack went in on 19 April and was a

failure, as was that of the following day. The Machinato Line was finally pierced on 24 April, but the Americans were again brought to a halt on 28 April, this time in front of the Japanese main defence, the Shuri Line. Buckner paused again to reconsider his approach and rest his weary divisions.

Meanwhile the first *kamikaze* aircraft attacks had been launched on 7 April against the ships lying off the island, and although 383 of the 355 *kamikaze* and 340 conventional attack aircraft had been shot down, damage had been caused to many ships and quite a few smaller vessels had been sunk. At the same time, the biggest *kamikaze* of them all was approaching the island. This was the super-battleship *Yamato*, escorted by one light cruiser and eight destroyers. Carrying just enough fuel to get to Okinawa and loaded with as much ammunition as it could carry, the *Yamato* was to sink as many US ships as possible before sinking in shallow water to serve as a maritime fortress. Encountered by Mitscher's carrierborne warplanes on the afternoon of 7 April, the *Yamato* survived four hours of attack before sinking, together with the cruiser and four destroyers. The aerial *kamikaze* effort was then resumed, with more than 3,000 missions launched on 12–13 April. The US losses were heavy, with 21 ships sunk, 43 very seriously damaged, and 23 badly damaged.

Ushijima launched an offensive by the 24th Division on 3 May, but this had been bloodily repulsed by the next day. Buckner, meanwhile, was reorganizing his forces for the final offensive. For Buckner's attack of 11 May, the III Corps moved into the right of the line with the XIV Corps moving into the left, which pierced the Japanese defences at both ends of the line. Ushijima began to pull back from the Shuri Line on 21 May, and by the end of the month the Americans had broken through toward the south coast. However, there was still plenty of fight left in the 32nd Army,

and the hills of the southern tip of Okinawa suited their tactics admirably. Buckner pressed home his offensive against gallant resistance, and the last organized defence ended on 22 June. Ushijima committed suicide just before the end, with Buckner having died from wounds received from artillery fire four days earlier. The fighting continued sporadically for another few days, and Okinawa was declared secure on 2 July.

The cost to both sides had been very high: the US forces lost 7,373 men killed and 32,056 wounded on land, and 5,000 killed and 4,600 wounded at sea; the Japanese losses were 107,500 dead and 7,400 taken prisoner, with possibly another 20,000 dead in their bunkers as a result of the US tactics of using flame-throwers and burning petrol, and then sealing the bunkers with demolition charges. In matériel terms, the USA had lost 36 ships sunk and 368 damaged, as well as 763 aircraft, and Japan 16 ships sunk and at least 4,000 aircraft expended.

THE STRATEGIC BOMBER WAR AGAINST JAPAN

The Americans and the British placed great faith in strategic bombing during World War II, partly because it offered the chance for costly land operations to be avoided or made less costly by the reduction of the opponent's ability to fight, and was also, at least during the early stages of the war, the only practical means of striking back at Germany and Japan. Once the campaigns had got under way they generated their own momentum and thus became almost impossible to stop, even in the event of the Allied leaders wishing to flout public and military opinion.

In the war against Japan, the bombing campaign was exclusively a US effort, culminating in the use of the Boeing B-29 Superfortress heavy bomber for day and night pinpoint and area attacks on Japan's vulnerable civilian, industrial, transport, fuel and communications systems. The campaign

began in a very small but significant way on 18 April 1942 when, launched from the deck of the aircraft carrier *Hornet*, some 800 miles (1300km) from Tokyo, 25 North American B-25 Mitchell twin-engined medium bombers of the US Army Air Forces struck at Tokyo and then flew on to China. The raid lacked any military importance, but it was a profound shock to the Japanese people, and came as an important boost to Allied morale at a very black time.

There were no more raids in 1942, and 1943 was devoted mostly to the building of Major-General Claire L. Chennault's 14th Army Air Force in China. This had begun life as the American Volunteer Group, flying fighters for Generalissimo Chiang Kai-shek against the Japanese in China, had become the China Air Task Force after

the USA's entry into the war against Japan, and was now in the process of being built up into a powerful offensive and strategic weapon. The efficiency of Chennault's air force is attested by the fact that, in 1944, the Japanese launched a series of very large offensives to deprive him of his airfields. It should be noted, however, that as yet Chennault's bombers had struck only at targets within China, and as far afield as Formosa to the east and Manchuria to the north-east.

In May 1944 the first B-29s arrived in India en route to China, and from the latter's bases these were at last able to strike at targets in southern Japan. The headquarters for this new and rapidly growing strategic force was the XX Bomber Command. The first B-29 raid was made on 5 June, the objective being railway communications in the Bangkok

Major General Curtiss E. LeMay (smoking a cigar), commanding the US Army Air Forces' bomber formations based in the Marianas Islands, discusses a raid with subordinate commanders and senior aircrew.

RIGHT: The heavy bomber type which blasted and burned the heart out of Japan in 1944–45 was the Boeing B-29 Superfortress. This was flown by an 11-man crew in the form of a pilot, co-pilot, flight engineer, bombardier, navigator, radio operator, radar observer, two blister gunners, a dorsal gunner and a tail gunner.

BELOW: Superfortress heavy bombers are seen on one of the five great airbase complexes which US engineers created on the islands of Tinian (three), Saipan (one) and Guam (one) in the Marianas. These are aircraft of the 29th Bombardment Group of the XXI Bomber Command's 314th Bombardment Wing, based on North Field, Tinian.

region of Thailand. Further exploratory missions followed before the B-29s made their first raids on Japan on 15 June. Although based on airfields in the Calcutta area of India, the B-29s staged through Chinese airfields, whose runways had been lengthened by means of Chinese labour, and fuel brought in by the thousands of tons. Striking from this forward base area, the B-29s raided Japanese steel production in Kyushu, the island at the south-west end of the chain of Japanese home islands.

Commanded by Major-General Curtis E. LeMay, the XX Bomber Command went from strength to strength between June and December 1944. The main trouble lay in the fact that there was still no adequate land route to China, which meant the B-29s had to remain based in India, too far from Japan for raids to be directly launched. The bombers still had to stage through China, refuelling from aircraft which arrived with fuel instead of bombs. Even from China, the B-29s were able to range only

as far as Kyushu, where they met with determined Japanese fighter opposition. Armed with 12 0.5-in (12.7-mm) machine guns and one 20-mm cannon, however, the B-29s were able to give a good account of themselves. Well streamlined and fitted with four powerful engines, they were also very fast, giving the Japanese fighters little time to get into the attack, their own speed superiority being marginal.

The main weight of the strategic bombing campaign was not to come from China but rather from the Marianas, the final objective of Admiral Nimitz's Central Pacific offensive. As soon as Saipan, Guam and Tinian had been captured in July and August 1944, Boeing B-17 and Consolidated B-24 bombers of the army air forces moved onto the captured airfields, their objectives being not targets in Japan, but in Iwo Jima and the Bonin Islands farther to the north, in preparation for the landings soon to take place. But while these raids got under way, engineers were hard at work lengthening and strengthening the existing runways, and building a vast complex of bases wherever room could be found. As soon as adequate facilities were ready in

October, the first B-29s of the XXI Bomber Command moved in and set about preparing for the assault on Japan.

At first only exploratory missions were undertaken, the B-29s from the Marianas blooding themselves in a raid on Truk on 28 October. By November all was ready, and the B-29s launched their first sorties against Japan on 24 November, when more than 100 bombers raided an aircraft production facility on the outskirts of Tokyo. For the rest of the year the B-29s continued to raid Japan, building up a store of experience under combat conditions About four times every three weeks the bombers set off, between 100 and 125 strong. They climbed the whole way, so that when they crossed the Japanese coast they were at altitudes above 30,000ft (9145m). As with earlier raids from China, fighter opposition was very strong, the Japanese having deployed their best pilots in the most modern aircraft to meet the threat. The fighters over Japan were tough opposition, but the bombers also had to run the gauntlet of other excellent fighters operating from Iwo Jima. The gauntlet naturally had to be run twice, once on the way in and once on the way out. Many bombers, damaged on the way in, were shot down over Japan, while others damaged over Japan were dispatched by the Iwo Jima-based interceptors on their way back to the Marianas. By the end of 1944, worthwhile results were being achieved, but losses were too high for the campaign to be continued indefinitely. The XXI Bomber Command was losing B-29s at an average of 6 per cent per mission, when losses under 5 per cent were only acceptable in a prolonged campaign such as this.

In January and February 1945, the Joint Chiefs-of-Staff Committee met several times in an effort to solve the problems of the strategic campaign against Japan. The results had been quite good, although not as good as had been hoped and expected, but the losses were

too high, and the weather at high altitude over Japan was very poor, throwing many bombers miles off course and making optical bomb-aiming a chancy business. Radar bombing was, of course, a possibility, but this did not offer the same degree of accuracy, it being small but vital defence facilities that the XXI Bomber Command was trying to hit. And although production had dropped as a result of civilian dislocation during the bombing, Japan had profited from the small scale of the first raids to the extent of appreciating the problem and dispersing her armament industry. The Joint Chiefs-of-Staff finally decided that what was needed was a greater concentration of effort, and that the best way of securing this was the transfer of the XX Bomber Command from India to the Mariana Islands, so that the whole

of General Nathan Twining's 20th Army Air Force could strike together. Until the move could be effected, General Curtis E. LeMay was moved to command the XXI Bomber Command which, it was felt, could profit from his experience.

The arrival of LeMay led to a complete change of tactics, the high-level attacks with HE bombs by day giving way to low-level runs with incendiaries, carried out at night when the Japanese fighter arm was all but impotent. The new tactics were initiated with a fire raid on Tokyo on 25 February 1945, but it was on the night of 9–10 March that LeMay's tactics really proved themselves. Some 334 B-29s raided Tokyo, flying quite low and dropping 1,667 tons of incendiaries The effect was devastating: a vast firestorm was started, gutting the

As the capital of the Japanese empire, Tokyo came under heavy attack, largely from incendiaries, and suffered enormous devastation as well as a huge loss of life.

THE DEFEAT OF JAPAN

The Boeing B-29 Superfortress was too fast and flew too high to be a simple target for Japanese anti-aircraft guns and interceptors in daylight operations. The Japanese lacked adequate radar and night-fighters so, in practical terms, the Superfortress was invisible to them at night.

centre of the city, in which 83,000 were killed and 100,000 more injured. Some 51 per cent of Tokyo was destroyed in this and four other raids during the next 10 days. The bomb tonnage dropped was 9,365, the B-29s carrying three times the normal load when operating at medium to low altitudes. Only 22 aircraft, or some 1.4 per cent of the 1,595 sorties dispatched was lost.

Meanwhile, Iwo Jima had been captured, allowing the B-29s to make emergency landings there. At the same time, the problem of Japanese fighters had been removed and the fighters of the VII Fighter Command installed in their place. Flying Republic P-47 Thunderbolt and North American P-51 Mustang fighters, the VII Fighter Command was now able to escort the bombers right over Japan, further reducing the Japanese fighter arm's ability to tackle them. Daylight raids could now be made once more, and as the Japanese fighters were increasingly being grounded for lack of fuel (the result of the US submarine offensive against Japanese tankers) or shot down by the escort fighters, the B-29s were able to dispense with most of

their defensive armament, the weight thus saved being used for an increase in the bomb load.

The campaign reached its climax between May and August 1945, with the arrival of the XX Bomber Command. The B-29s were able to roam at will over Japan, now that the heart of industrial Japan had been burned out. The largest cities after Tokyo, namely Kobe, Osaka, Nagoya and Yokohama, were all almost entirely destroyed, the superb US target intelligence work enabling virtually every worthwhile target to be wiped out. HE bombs were dropped in industrial areas to break up the concrete foundations on which machine tools sat, and the B-29s also undertook mining operations offshore. By August 1945, the strategic bombing campaign had brought Japan to its knees.

VICTORY IN BURMA
With the end of the campaign for Kohima and Imphal, the Allied high command was able to resume its strategic offensive in Burma, which was characteristically of the threefold type. The Americans had only one objective in

Burma: to open the road to China in order to supply and mobilize the myriad Chinese armies against the Japanese occupying mainland China. The British were motivated by the desire to liberate imperial territory, with one school of thought believing that instead of an endless campaign in jungle and mountain, an air and seaborne invasion to capture Rangoon would be quicker and cheaper. The third view, strategically very orthodox, was held by Lieutenant-General Sir William Slim, commanding the 14th Army. He believed he had the measure of the Japanese, and that if they could only be persuaded to stand and fight in central Burma, the 14th Army could destroy them there. Privately, he resolved to take Rangoon from the landward side, in the belief that this could be done more quickly and reliably than by an amphibious force short of many of the necessary craft and hampered by all the delays imposed by special training and complicated staff planning. This is how the final campaign turned out in Burma in 1945.

The difficulties were formidable. The units of the 14th Army were physically tired, and the 1944 battles and the pursuit through the jungles in the monsoon rain, which had chased the Japanese back across the Chindwin, had resulted in 45,000 casualties, although many of these would recover. The 14th Army would have to advance over the same difficult terrain which had frustrated the Japanese, with a much more modern force making heavy demands on artillery ammunition and petrol. The first calculations of Slim's logistical staff indicated that no more than 4.5 divisions could be brought to bear because of the difficulties of supply. Yet the Japanese in Burma had admittedly widely deployed, and deficient of modern weapons, some 10.67 divisions and as many as 100,000 service troops had been able to function effectively as infantry on demand. This still formidable force was being rebuilt by the newly appointed commander of

the Burma Area Army, Lieutenant-General Hyotaro Kimura.

The 14th Army's logistical difficulties were overcome by enormous feats of engineering and improvisation: hundreds of miles of new roads were built, surfaced with sacking dipped in bitumen; transport ranged from elephants to aircraft; the engineers built rafts, each large enough to float 10 tons of supplies along the rivers, pushed by outboard motors; the greatest Bailey bridge in the world, 1,154ft (351.75m) long, was built across the Chindwin at Shwegyin; and locomotives to restart the Burmese railways, wrecked by bombing, were flown up in pieces for re-assembly, or were brought up whole on tank transporters all the way over the mountains from India. This effort allowed Slim to deploy six infantry divisions and two tank brigades.

The Japanese, numerous and still determined, fought determinedly until the end, but had been hard hit in 1944. Their diversionary attack in the Arakan in February 1944 had been smashed, and the Chinese Army in India had destroyed the 18th Division by August. The 14th Army had been attacked by 115,000 men and had killed (or caused to die of wounds, sickness or starvation) 65,000 more. The plan for 1945 was a compromise. In the north the CAI, now commanded by the US Lieutenant-General Dan Sultan, Stilwell having been relieved, with the all-British 36th Division, was to clear northern Burma up to the Chinese border as far as Lashio, while the British XV Corps was to embark on an amphibious campaign among the islands and creeks of the Arakan to pin the Japanese forces there, the 14th Army advancing up to the line of the Irrawaddy river to take Mandalay.

Slim's own plans went a step further than this. His 14th Army had two major formations in the shape of the XXXIII Corps (2nd, 19th and 20th Divisions with a brigade of tanks) and the IV Corps (7th and 17th Divisions with a brigade of

tanks) plus the 5th Division in reserve. The XXXIII Corps was directed on the Irrawaddy from the north and north-west to cross the river 50 miles (80km) downstream and 100 miles (160km) upstream and close the pincers on Mandalay. This, Slim hoped, would draw the bulk of the Japanese defence to that area. Then, when this was under way, the IV Corps would move with great secrecy down the Gangaw valley, which meant building a completely new first-class road, and with the Royal Air Force holding off every Japanese reconnaissance aeroplane, would thrust for Meiktila. Meiktila and Thazi, on a nodal point of the central road and railway system, comprised the main Japanese supply base, being strategically more important than Mandalay or even Rangoon; if the Japanese armies in central Burma were starved and defeated Rangoon would be indefensible. While the battles of central Burma were at full blast, Slim's staff officers were working on the advance to Rangoon.

All went according to plan, which was implemented, almost alone, by Slim and his 14th Army. However, credit must be given to the contribution of the Chinese 5th and 6th Armies and the 36th Division, which started south as soon as Myitkyina had fallen in August 1944; but their efforts relaxed by mid-March and the Chinese were diverted home just as the main clash in central Burma was at its height. The XV Corps cleaned up the Arakan, but there was no way of developing its further thrust. It was thus the IV and XXXIII Corps of the 14th Army which took on the hard Japanese core and destroyed it.

The final battle for Burma was a complex affair, involving an advance up to and across the Chindwin; the secret move of the IV Corps, so that it arrived to threaten Meiktila from a totally unexpected direction; the crossing of the Irrawaddy, a river 1,750 yards (1600m) wide in places, with shifting sand banks and strong and treacherous currents, in

four places along a distance of 150 miles (240km); a number of operations aimed at provoking the Japanese into a counter-attack before destroying them.

The XXXIII Corps advanced in the north, the Indian 19th Division crossing the Irrawaddy north of Mandalay in January and turning south along the east bank. The Indian 20th Division crossed 40 miles (65km) farther downstream of the city on 12 February and the British 2nd Division on 24 February, on their left. The crossing points were cunningly concealed but were not unopposed. Japanese reaction was prompt, but true to their doctrine they attacked the bridgeheads on a piecemeal basis, which allowed them to be destroyed on the same basis. Then, with all the freedom conferred by air supply and air support, the three divisions fanned out to cut the routes south of Mandalay to Rangoon and east to Maymyo, while inside this envelopment two pincers closed on the city itself. Kimura reacted satisfactorily, by Slim's terms, pulling in his forces for a battle around Mandalay, only to find he had been fooled by an elaborate deception to make him believe that all the weight of the British offensive was in the north. The IV Corps, complete with its armour, had secretly advanced down the Gangaw valley to force a passage across the Irrawaddy some 100 miles (160km) to the south-west of Mandalay and only 50 miles (80km) from the vital depots at Meiktila. Seeing the danger, Kimura switched his forces there, but was too late. By 1 March, Major-General D.T. Cowan's Indian 17th Division, with the 255th Tank Brigade, had surrounded Meiktila, which fell in four days. Almost the whole Japanese garrison, strongly dug in and amply provided with artillery and ammunition from the depots, was killed. The Japanese immediately counter-attacked, and now the armoured/mechanized columns were able to take toll of them in the open, so that a continuous series of battles was fought across the entire front. At the same time,

THE DEFEAT OF JAPAN

RIGHT: Men of the US 475th
Infantry Regiment in northern Burma
during 1944.

BELOW: Men of the Royal Marine
commandos in action in Burma during
1945.

Mandalay fell after much bitter street
fighting. On Mandalay Hill, converted to
a fortress and taken by British and
Gurkhas in hand-to-hand fighting, the
defenders had finally to be burned out by
rolling drums of petrol into their bunkers
and setting fire to them with tracer
bullets. A sign of the times, however, was
that the ancient Fort Dufferin, the keep
of the city and proof against heavy
artillery and bombing, was tamely
evacuated. By the end of March, the
decisive battle of central Burma had been
fought and won, and Slim was anxious to
advance on Rangoon.

At this point there was almost a
serious setback. The sudden withdrawal
of the Chinese and US forces in the north
was tolerable, but what was totally
unexpected was the decision to use the
US Army Air Forces' transport aircraft,
hitherto at the disposal of the 14th Army,
to ferry them out, which severely affected
the whole mobility of the 14th Army.
Fortunately, the Combined Chiefs-of-
Staff Committee in the USA relented
after appeals came from Admiral Lord
Mountbatten, of the South-East Asia
Command, and the British chiefs-of-staff

in London. The diversion of the US air
transport facility was therefore delayed
until 1 June or the fall of Rangoon,
whichever was the earlier. In fact the real

deadline was 15 May, as the monsoon
rains could be expected on that date,
slowing or halting all armour and
interfering with air operations. Thus
Rangoon had to be taken in 40 days;
there were 250 miles (400km) to be
covered, as the crow flies, and Japanese
resistance was strong.

Slim ordered the IV Corps to drive
straight down the road from Meiktila to
Rangoon down the valley of the Sittang
river, with divisions leapfrogging past
each other and armoured battle groups
leading without any regard for their
flanks. They would get to Rangoon first
and then turn back to mop up or
consolidate, should any Japanese
resistance flare up behind them. At the
same time, at Slim's request, the
'Dracula' seaborne operation was
reduced in size so that it could be
expedited and Rangoon attacked from
the sea to coincide with the last stages of
the land advance and thus pin any
reserves. On the other, longer route to
Rangoon down the valley of the

Irrawaddy river through Prome, the XXXIII Corps was to advance from the west. The Japanese forces who attempted to come in from the east were checked by a resistance movement, carefully fostered in advance by the Karens, and by a technique developed in Burma by the Chindits: clandestine ground observers with radio sets calling for RAF attacks. By 22 April Slim's primary advance in the Sittang valley had reached Toungoo. On 1 May, the day before Dracula was to be implemented, a reconnaissance aircraft over Rangoon saw painted on the roof of a jail, which was known to hold many British prisoners-of-war, the words: 'Japs gone. Exdigitate' (RAF wartime slang meaning 'pull your finger out').

The pilot of a de Havilland Mosquito had decided to land on Rangoon airfield, where he damaged his aircraft; he walked to Rangoon, hitched a lift downriver in a sampan, and brought the news that Rangoon was empty. The Japanese had indeed left in panic, and the landings were unopposed.

The Japanese had yet to surrender, however, and the last phase of the war was both cruel and unnecessary. For the field army surrender was impossible; in fact Japanese-speaking liaison officers could not persuade some to do so even after the order to cease fire from the Emperor Hirohito himself had been broadcast from Tokyo: it was believed to be a propaganda trick. The surviving Japanese, without ammunition or supplies, were in the hilly tract of the Pegu Yomas, to the west of the IV Corps' route, and were now cordoned off by a belt of strongpoints down the road. The Japanese were ordered to break out and cross the dangerous Sittang river by raft, or by swimming, and then make for Thailand to continue the struggle. The weather was bad, the river in flood, many were ill and all were starving. The Japanese were shot down in very large numbers by the Indian 17th Division as they crossed the road, or from Bren gun posts along the banks when they were in

the river. Many were drowned and many more killed by the villagers on the east bank. At last, a few survivors gave up.

THE WAR IN CHINA

Japan's interest in China, principally as a market for its growing industries, extended from the later part of the 19th century. From 1931, however, Japan had stepped up its pressure in China, especially in the military sense. Various incidents in the 1930s culminated in the so-called Marco Polo Bridge Incident of 7 July 1937, when Chinese and Japanese troops clashed just outside Peking in an affair carefully engineered by the Japanese. Here, at last, was the excuse for which they had been waiting, and the Japanese wasted no time in launching a full-scale invasion of China.

Although Chiang Kai-shek's Chinese forces numbered some 2 million men, whose quality was poor, as were both leadership and weaponry. Chiang's main interest at this time, and in the years to

come, was the problem of the Communist guerrilla forces of Mao Tse-tung, although the two sides in the civil war had nominally resolved their differences in the face of the foreign threat. The Japanese army, on the other hand, was a comparatively small but nonetheless formidable force, well-equipped and ably led, having great fighting ability and skill. Unlike the Chinese, moreover, the Japanese had excellent army and navy air forces, and these played important strategic and tactical roles until the advent of the American Volunteer Group checked their activities. China's most powerful weapon, it could be argued, was world opinion, or rather US opinion, of the Japanese invasion, whose almost total condemnation led to a gradual increase in the supply of money and modern weapons to Chiang's government.

Initially, the Japanese had it all their own way. Between July and December 1937, forces from Manchuria made large

Admiral Lord Louis Mountbatten, the Allied commander-in-chief in South-East Asia, takes the salute during the victory parade in Rangoon, the capital of liberated Burma, in 1945.

ABOVE: A Japanese machine-gun team in Burma. By this time, though still full of fight, the Japanese in the Burma campaign were short of all necessities, even by their own spartan standards, including food, fuel, ammunition and medicine.

RIGHT: Japanese infantry in China. By 1944, in the Chinese theatre, the primary task of the Japanese armies was to capture food by overrunning areas as soon as the harvest had been gathered, and to take and hold the areas from which the US Army Air Forces could launch Boeing B-29 Superfortress heavy bomber raids on Japan.

gains to the north of the Yellow river. Large areas of Chahar and Suiyuan were taken, but the main effort went into a drive south down the railway toward Hankow, Nanking and Sian. Civil unrest behind them, combined with problems of logistics, served to halt the drive of the Japanese North China Area Army in December, while farther to the south, the Japanese China Expeditionary Army attacked Shanghai on 8 August. The Chinese put up a surprisingly effective resistance, and it was not until 8 November that the Japanese were able to clear the city. By the end of the year further reinforcements had allowed the army to move inland along the line of the Yangtze river to take Nanking, the Chinese capital, by 13 December. By the end of the year, therefore, Japan had taken two large and strategically important areas of China. With Chiang's attention drawn more to this threat than to themselves, the Communists had also profited, securing most of north-west China for themselves. Nevertheless, it should be noted that the Communists' 8th Route Army, under the command of the able Chu Teh, had been helping the

nationalist cause considerably with raids on the Japanese. Indeed, in the only major battle against the Japanese fought by the Communists on 25 September, the 8th Route Army's 115th Division had ambushed and cut to pieces the Japanese 5th Division in the Battle of P'inghsinkuan in northern Shansi.

On 12 December, the Japanese made a grave strategic error in dive-bombing British and US gunboats on the Yangtze river, and sinking the American vessel *Panay*. The attack was quite unprovoked, and caused enormous British and US anger. Although Japan immediately paid a large indemnity, US public opinion was now even more firmly against the Japanese.

Determined to link their two areas of control, the Japanese launched renewed offensives in January 1938. The North

China Area Army struck south again after securing all of Shantung, and although its progress was steady, a nasty surprise lay in wait. During April, some 60,000 Japanese were cut off at Taierchwang by 200,000 Chinese under General Li Tsung-jen. After a desperate struggle, the Japanese hacked their way out to the north again, but only at the cost of 20,000 dead. After a swift regrouping, the North China Area Army renewed its advance in May, taking Kaifeng by 6 June. By the end of the month, the whole of the rail line between Nanking and Peking was in Japanese hands. Then, advancing west from Kaifeng to take the key junction of Chengchow, on the Hankow railway, the Japanese were rebuffed when the Chinese breached the Yellow river dykes, flooding large areas and causing the

Japanese to lose many men and much matériel. The offensive was cancelled in July.

The Japanese then shifted their main line of advance further south, and once again made progress toward Chiang's capital of Hankow. The city finally fell after bloody fighting on 25 October. Chiang again moved his capital, this time to Chungking, farther up the Yangtze river in the province of Szechwan.

On 12 October, meanwhile, the 23rd Army, part of the 6th Area Army, had landed near Hong Kong, moving quickly on Canton, China's most important port after Shanghai. Canton fell on 21 October, but the Japanese then felt it necessary to reconsider their overall strategy. It was now decided that instead of the rapid advances of the previous 18 months, a war of attrition would be waged. With civil unrest and guerrilla

operations rife in the areas they had conquered, the Japanese considered additional conquests futile, and instead decided to concentrate on destroying Chiang's forces wherever they could be found. Only after the Chinese armies had been destroyed, the Japanese felt, could the rest of China be occupied and pacified. In 1939, therefore, the Japanese confined themselves to securing a number of ports previously left untouched between Shanghai and Canton, taking the island of Hainan, and straightening their line in the Hankow and Wuchow regions of central China.

Activities in 1940 were limited to the Communists' so-called '100 Regiments Offensive' between 30 August and 30 November, when guerrillas attacked Japanese posts in Shansi, Chahar, Hopeh and Honan, disrupting the Japanese rear areas very successfully. For their part,

ABOVE: A Chinese artillery observation post, its officer passing instructions to the battery it controls. By 1945 the Chinese were moderately well-equipped with US weapons, but many senior officers were still concerned with preserving their commands, with a view to fighting the Communist forces as soon as World War II was over, rather than taking the war to the Japanese.

LEFT: Chinese infantry in action.

THE DEFEAT OF JAPAN

had led it to a world war, Japan's activities in China slumped considerably.

The year 1942 was also marked by the continued lull in operations, with Japanese attention turned toward the consolidation of her conquests in South-East Asia and in the Pacific. The Japanese, therefore, remained on the defensive in China, and Chiang confined his efforts to supporting the British in Burma. For only here, via Rangoon and the Burma Road, could American matériel aid reach him. Within China, acute command problems were arising between Brigadier-General Claire L. Chennault, commanding the China Air Task Force (lately the American Volunteer Group), and Lieutenant-General Joseph W. Stilwell, Chiang's chief-of-staff and military adviser. With the cutting of the Burma Road and the institution of the airlift of supplies 'over the hump' of the eastern Himalayas, there were not enough supplies to go round. Concerned with the security of China on land, Stilwell wanted the supplies for the Chinese army, while Chennault, on the other hand, who considered that the war could only be taken to the Japanese by his growing air power, requested priority for his own needs. The eventual allocations satisfied neither party, although as Stilwell had believed in a near parity of supplies for each party, he was the better satisfied.

In 1943, China's position was desperate, its isolation from western sources of supply having profound effects on its armed forces. Had the Japanese been interested in major offensives, the Chinese would have found it hard, perhaps even impossible, to check them. But the Japanese were content to launch the first of their series of 'rice offensives'. With many of their combat veterans transferred to active theatres, the Japanese armies in China now had large numbers of raw recruits. The rice offensives, which were local attacks with limited objectives, were an ideal means of blooding them. The idea behind the offensives was for the Japanese to drive into a hitherto untouched area of China after the rice crop had just been harvested. The Japanese would advance swiftly, seize the harvest to feed themselves, and then pull back. In one of these offensives, however, the Japanese suffered a sharp rebuff at the Battle of Changteh, when US air support enabled the Chinese to throw the Japanese back in an action that lasted from 23 November to 9 December. Roosevelt, meanwhile, who had been the arbitrator in the Chennault-Stilwell controversy in favour of the former, was now promoted to major-general and appointed to the command of the new 14th Army Air Force in China. Chennault was thus able to increase the scope of his attacks on the Japanese rear areas. Chiang's efforts in 1943 were restricted mainly to the establishment of a blockade of the Communist-controlled areas of north-west China, despite the truce between the two parties.

In 1944, the Chinese Communists and the Japanese came to an unofficial truce, although it is still not known whether this was negotiated or merely allowed to happen. The result was that the Japanese were able to deploy troops from this area in more important zones, and the Communists were able to consolidate yet further their hold on north-west China. Most of the Japanese forces from the north were shifted south for an offensive against Chennault's airfields. Built by hundreds of thousands of Chinese coolies, these were now numerous and well-placed to make strategically significant raids on Japanese positions as far afield as Formosa and Manchuria. The most important of these bases were Nanning, Liuchow, Kweilin, Lingling, Hengyang and Chihkiang, all but the last being on the old Hanoi to Changsha railway, and at Laohokow and Ankang on the upper Han Chiang river. The Japanese now decided that these must be eliminated, the northern pair by an attack from Kaifeng, and the

Many armed elements in China were less well-equipped with modern US weapons, these men having a miscellany of captured weapons and even, in the foreground, a locally made black-powder weapon.

the Japanese devoted 1940 to Indo-China, which they began to occupy in September. This proved to be the first link in the chain of events that was to take Japan to war with the USA. In 1941, the Japanese launched a series of reprisal raids for the 100 Regiments Offensive. The series continued into 1943, costing the Communists some 100,000 dead. Now, preoccupied with the events that

southern bases by a three-pronged offensive from Indo-China in the south, Canton in the east, and Changsha in the north-east. Throughout the period from January to May 1944, the Japanese planned their offensives carefully and gathered supplies. At the same time, General Yasuji Okamura's China Expeditionary Army undertook a series of attacks intended to clear the railways of north-east China of the guerrillas plaguing them and so ease the problems of the Japanese logistical staffs.

Not foreseeing what was to come, Chiang allowed Stilwell to use the best Chinese formations for an offensive in Burma, starting in May. Four days before this Chinese Yunnan offensive started on 11 May, the Japanese launched their east China offensive. In fierce fighting the Japanese advanced steadily against patchy opposition. Most of Chennault's airfields were lost by the end of November, by which time the Chinese position was desperate. The Yunnan offensive in Burma was called off and the two best divisions flown back to China by US aircraft. Chiang, whose relations with Stilwell had been poor for some time, finally had him replaced by Major-General Albert C. Wedemeyer on 18 October. Wedemeyer reorganized the Chinese defence, and in a counter-offensive east of Kweiyang on 10 December, finally brought the Japanese to a halt.

In January and February 1945, however, the Japanese again went over to the offensive in south-east China, making great conquests on each side of the Hanoi to Hankow railway. In March, the offensive was extended into central China, and the region between the Yangtze and Yellow rivers was seized, together with its major rice crop. For the Americans, the important airbase at Laohokow was a major loss when it fell on 8 April after a sterling defence beginning on 26 March. The Chinese

LEFT: Mao Tse-tung, the leader of the Communist movement in China, was ultimately the victor in the civil war which was resumed after the surrender of Japan.

BELOW LEFT: Chinese Communist soldiers with Japanese Type 97 medium tanks, probably supplied by the Soviets from the stocks they had captured in Manchuria, or possibly seized from the failing Japanese forces in China.

RIGHT: The history of Russian and Soviet rivalry with the Japanese in eastern Asia, extending back into the latter part of the 19th century, saw a Japanese victory in the Russo-Japanese War of 1904–05, which settled into an armed neutrality after a succession of border clashes, some of them sizeable, in 1938–39. These are Japanese troops in action on the disputed border with the USSR in 1939.

RIGHT: The history of Russian and Soviet rivalry with the Japanese in eastern Asia, extending back into the latter part of the 19th century, saw a Japanese victory in the Russo-Japanese War of 1904–05, which settled into an armed neutrality after a succession of border clashes, some of them sizeable, in 1938–39. These are Japanese troops in action on the disputed border with the USSR in 1939.

BELOW: Before entering the war against Japan, the Soviet armies had rested and rebuilt the strength of their Far Eastern forces with armies and other formations that were of very high combat capability after their defeat of the Germans.

counter-attacked on 10 April, halting this central offensive, and later managed to do the same with renewed offensives against Changteh and Chihkiang. With the tide of war now running very strongly against them, the Japanese realized they were overextended in China, particularly at the expense of the Kwantung Army in Manchuria, where the Soviets were now looking distinctly threatening. From May onwards Okamura began to pull in his horns and rationalize his positions. He was not fast enough. Chinese offensives had cut the Japanese links with Indo-China by the end of May. The Chinese offensives continued, and by the beginning of July some 100,000 Japanese troops were cooped up inside a defensive perimeter

at Canton. Ably supported by US air power, the Chinese drove north-east, pushing the Japanese before them toward Kaifeng, the great airfield complex at Kweilin falling back into Allied hands on 27 July. The Chinese drove on into August, when the armistice came, and the Japanese laid down their arms, most of which were gladly seized by Mao's Communists and Chiang's nationalists. With the Japanese threat removed, the Chinese civil war was resumed in full.

THE SOVIET WAR AGAINST JAPAN

The Soviets and Japanese had signed a Non-Aggression Treaty on 13 April 1941, yet just under three-and-a-half years later Soviet forces were to invade Manchukuo (the Japanese puppet state of Manchuria) as well as Inner Mongolia and Korea and even parts of Japan, in the form of the southern half of Sakhalin Island and the Kurile Islands group. The reason was quite simply that the USSR wished to regain the portions of the tsarist empire lost in the Russo-Japanese War of 1904–05. At the Yalta Conference of February 1945, between Churchill, Roosevelt and Stalin,

the two western leaders agreed to the USSR's ambitions in the east if they entered the war against Japan within three months of the conclusion of the war against Germany.

The UK and USA wished for Soviet intervention so that Japan's forces would be yet further weakened before the Allies launched the great invasion of Japan planned for November 1945; and Soviet intervention was almost certainly sure to destroy Japan's Kwantung Army.

A large part of Japan's heavy industry was based in Manchukuo, and it was from here that Japan's invasion of northern China in 1937 had started. At its peak, the Kwantung Army had been a mighty force, but relative peace on this front, coupled with the constant and growing demands from other fronts as the war progressed, meant that the best formations and equipment had been bled off to supply the needs of other Japanese forces. In the middle of 1945 the Kwantung Army was still formidable on paper, but its matériel was obsolete, and its under-strength divisions were mostly manned by reservists.

For his invasion, however, Stalin assembled powerful forces, with the best

LEFT: A Soviet cavalry patrol on the border between Outer Mongolia and Manchuria, the latter being a Japanese puppet kingdom otherwise known as Manchukuo.

BELOW: A Japanese cavalry patrol in an occupied part of Inner Mongolia.

front, the Japanese fell back in good order and dug in on the slopes of the Khingan mountain range. But Malinovsky's armour burst through in the south, outflanking the more northern Japanese positions. Thereafter, the Soviets pressed on swiftly and ruthlessly, crushing or bypassing Japanese centres of resistance to ensure the greatest speed. Changchun had fallen by 20 August, as had Mukden. The 6th Guards Tank Army rolled on to Port Arthur, which fell on 22 August. The lightning advance of these forces had broken the back and the will of the Kwantung Army, in a display of dazzling mobile warfare rarely seen before or since. Great credit must go to

of modern equipment, and men and commanders well versed in the techniques of modern mobile warfare after the war with Germany. Three large fronts, or army groups, were gathered for the offensive, although only two were to play major roles. West of Manchuria was Marshal R.Y. Malinovsky's Trans-Baikal Front of five armies, one of them a tank army. These would strike south toward Peking in China, and south-east toward Tsitsihar, Harbin and Changchun. During their south-east thrust the armies of the Trans-Baikal Front were to link up in Manchuria with the armies of Marshal K.A. Meretskov's 1st Far East Front, striking west with four armies from eastern Siberia. In the north was the 2nd Far East Front, under General M.A. Purkaev, which was to take the great northern bulge of Manchuria, only lightly held by the Japanese. Other formations of the 1st Far East Front, notably the 16th Army, were to invade the Japanese southern half of Sakhalin Island from the north. Finally, a mixed force of marines and infantry was to invade and take the Kurile Islands from Kamchatka, with the aid of the Pacific

Fleet. Overall command was exercised by Marshal A.M. Vasilevsky, and once the Trans-Baikal and 1st Far East Fronts had linked, the Soviets were to drive on Port Arthur, one of the most important objectives of the campaign.

On the whole, the problems the Soviets were due to face were geographical and climatic, especially in the west, where Malinovsky's forces would have to cross large parts of the waterless Gobi Desert. But in the east, on the Ussuri river front, the Japanese had long realized that in a war with the USSR this area would be very vulnerable, and had accordingly built fixed fortifications in great depth. To deal with these, the Soviets deployed forces experienced in dealing with German fixed defences.

Two days after the first atomic bomb was dropped on Hiroshima on 6 August 1945, the USSR declared war on Japan. The powerful air forces, gathered for the Manchurian campaign, struck out at Japanese targets as the armies rolled over the frontiers swiftly and irresistibly, with the exception of some of the 1st Far East Front's formations. On the Mongolian

THE DEFEAT OF JAPAN

After the Soviet victory in the lightning war against the Japanese in eastern Asia, the defeated Japanese were set to work on tasks such as levelling the border defences by filling in anti-tank ditches and the like.

the Soviet air forces, which kept the tanks supplied with fuel and the men with water and food.

Farther to the south, others of Malinovsky's forces had struck down through the Gobi Desert toward Kalgan and Chengteh, the latter falling on 18 August, which allowed the Soviets to press on to the coast. Both Kalgan and Chengteh were taken with the aid of the Chinese Communist 8th People's Army.

In the east, Meretskov's forces initially had considerable trouble with the fixed defences between Lake Khanga and the sea, the Japanese even going so far as to launch counter-attacks which the Soviets found very dangerous. By 14 August, however, the 1st Far East Front had broken through the fortifications and appalling terrain to open country. The advance on Harbin now got under way in earnest. Aided by the Pacific Fleet, operating from Vladivostok, the Soviet land forces were also probing far into Korea, the 2nd Far East Front in the far

north was making steady progress against moderate opposition, and the 16th Army was moving well down into Sakhalin.

On 14 August, the Japanese surrendered unconditionally, but not the slightest notice was taken of it by the Soviets, who were determined to secure all their objectives before halting. The Soviets claim, however, was that in defiance of their government's surrender order, many Japanese units, especially in the Kirin and Harbin areas, continued to offer stiff resistance. On 17 August, the commander of the Kwantung Army got in touch with Vasilevsky and attempted to arrange a ceasefire, but the Soviet commander refused on the grounds that Japanese forces were still fighting after the previous surrender. The reason was probably that Japanese communications had broken down and the relevant formations did not know of the surrender, or if they did, their commanders had ordered them to fight on regardless. The major industrial city

of Harbin was taken by the 1st Far East Front on 18 August, while the Soviet advance continued apace elsewhere. By the time all the Japanese forces in Manchuria had laid down their arms on 27 August, the Soviets had seized all of their objectives.

Any assessment of the campaign must take into account the weakness of the Japanese, but the Soviets' performance was nonetheless a staggering one. Battle-wise and tough, they had clearly learned much from the Germans' manifest ability with armoured and mobile forces. Although these casualty figures are probably too low, it cannot be by too much, with 8,219 dead and 22,264 wounded. The Soviets also claim to have killed 83,737 Japanese, wounded an unknown number, and taken at least 600,000 prisoners. Most of the latter were shipped off to the USSR and, as with many of the USSR's German prisoners, a great number were never seen outside the USSR again.

If the performance of the Soviets was good, that of the Japanese was odd. Even allowing for the fact that it was at the end of the war, and that morale was low, some units had quite uncharacteristically given up without a fight. Other formations, however, continued to fight showing the old Japanese bravura despite the obsolescence of their equipment and the poor physical condition of most of the men.

At minimal cost, the USSR had secured for itself a vast slice of eastern Asia, together with an excellent year-round port.

THE ATOMIC BOMBINGS OF HIROSHIMA AND NAGASAKI
With the conquest of Okinawa completed, the Americans were faced with the appalling prospect of invading Japan. Plans were drawn up for Operation Olympic as a series of 6th Army landings on Kyushu on 1 November 1945 and for Operation Coronet as a series of 1st and 8th Army

not to use the new weapon. The bomb was there, and so was the means to deliver it in the form of the 509th Composite Group, USAAF, which had been training in the deserts of Utah with its Boeing B-29 Superfortress bombers. The debate was heated, but in the end most senior commanders consulted, and Secretary of War Henry L. Stimson, thought that the new weapon should be used. Japan still had enormous military strength, they reasoned, and why should US lives be lost in their hundreds of thousands when a means of preventing this was available? Truman agreed with reluctance. At the Potsdam Conference in July, Truman told Clement Attlee, the British prime minister in succession to Winston Churchill, about the weapon and his decision to use it. In the Potsdam Declaration of 7 July Truman and Attlee called on Japan to surrender, warning that refusal to do so would entail the 'inevitable and complete destruction of the Japanese armed forces and . . . the utter devastation of the Japanese homeland'. When Japan failed to reply, Truman gave his authority for the first atomic bomb to be dropped.

The target selected was Hiroshima, a city of some 300,000 people, which was an important military objective but, as yet, little affected by conventional

LEFT: The mushroom cloud rises over Hiroshima after the US atomic bombing of this port city on 6 August 1945.

BELOW: The 'Fat Man' was the 21-kiloton atomic bomb dropped on Nagasaki on 9 August 1945. This was an implosion-type weapon with a plutonium core, whereas the 13–16-kiloton 'Little Man' bomb dropped on Hiroshima was a gun-type weapon with a uranium core.

landings on Honshu on 1 March 1945. Judging by past performances, the Japanese would put up a powerful and fanatical defence, and American planners estimated that the invasion forces would suffer at least 1 million casualties before the back of the defence was broken. What else could the Americans do? It seemed unlikely that the Japanese would surrender unconditionally, and so the Allies would have to invade the Japanese home islands in order to bring the Pacific war to a successful conclusion.

Unknown to all but a very few high-ranking officers and politicians, another solution was being worked upon. For some time, the possibilities of using radioactive materials for explosive purposes had been suspected, and a large team of Allied scientists had spent a great part of the war trying to develop a weapon based on uranium or plutonium. At last, the scientists were ready for their first practical test at Alamogordo in New Mexico. An atomic device was triggered by remote control on 16 July 1945 and a light 'brighter than a thousand suns' burst over the desert. Seconds later an enormous blast shook the ground and the air. The atomic bomb was feasible.

The problem for Harry S. Truman, who had become president of the USA on the death of Franklin D. Roosevelt on 12 April 1945, was to decide whether or

ABOVE: Seen on returning to its base on the Mariana Islands group after its mission, the B-29, named Enola Gay, *was the bomber which dropped the atomic bomb on Hiroshima.*

BELOW RIGHT: Blasted and irradiated, this is only a part of the ruins which had once been Hiroshima.

attacks. On 6 August a B-29, named *Enola Gay* after the mother of its pilot, Colonel Paul Tibbetts, took off from the Marianas and headed for Japan. The air-raid warning was sounded in Hiroshima, but seeing that there were only a few planes overhead, most people failed to take cover. The bomb was dropped, and exploded at exactly the intended place and height, with a force equal to that

of the detonation of between 13,000 and 16,000 tons of TNT. Exact figures are still not available, but it seems that 78,150 people died almost immediately and another 70,000 were injured. Most of the centre of Hiroshima was completely destroyed.

The impact of the bomb on Japanese politicians and military leaders was profound but at the same time was

viewed with incredulity. The dropping of a second bomb on Nagasaki, on 9 August, altered that and convinced Japan's leaders that the war must end. The Nagasaki explosion, of some 21 kilotons, killed 40,000 and injured 25,000 people out of a population of some 250,000. Luckily for the Japanese, the country on which the city is built is hilly, and this diverted much of the blast.

The Emperor Hirohito at last made a firm decision and insisted on peace. There were inevitably dissenters, and a coup had to be put down in Tokyo. Following discussions by radio, Japan agreed to an unconditional surrender, which in fact had several conditions for the benefit of the Japanese: the emperor was to remain, and Japan also was to remain undivided.

A ceasefire came into effect on 15 August, although many Japanese refused to believe the emperor's broadcast and fought on for a few more days. They imagined it to be an Allied trick, for none of them had ever heard the

WORLD WAR II

emperor's voice before, so great had been his apolitical seclusion. Gradually, however, peace fell over the battlefields of the Pacific and Asia during the next few days. On 28 August General Douglas MacArthur and the first US occupation forces arrived in Japan, and the real impact of defeat began to be felt by the average Japanese. The formal end of the war against Japan came on 2 September, in a ceremony on board the battleship *Missouri* in Tokyo Bay.

Now that about 50 million people had lost their lives, World War II was at last over.

LEFT: The mushroom cloud rises over Nagasaki on 9 August 1945 after the explosion of the world's second atomic bomb.

BELOW LEFT: This wristwatch, recovered from Hiroshima, stopped at the moment of the first atomic bomb's detonation, shortly after 08:15 on 6 August 1945.

BOTTOM LEFT: The devastation in Nagasaki, some 880 yards (805m) from ground zero, the point on the ground 1,540ft (469m) below the bomb's aerial detonation, was exactly halfway between the Mitsubishi steel and arms works in the south and the Mitsubishi-Urakami torpedo factory in the north.

BELOW: The Japanese surrender delegation on board the US Navy's battleship Missouri *in Tokyo Bay on 2 September 1945.*

INDEX